STOLEN
CHILDHOOD

BLACKS IN THE DIASPORA

Darlene Clark Hine, John McCluskey, Jr., and David Barry Gaspar
General Editors

STOLEN CHILDHOOD

SLAVE YOUTH IN
NINETEENTH-CENTURY AMERICA

WILMA KING

INDIANA UNIVERSITY PRESS

Bloomington & Indianapolis

This book is a publication of

Indiana University Press
601 North Morton Street
Bloomington, IN 47404-3797 USA

http://www.indiana.edu/~iupress

Telephone orders 800-842-6796
Fax orders 812-855-7931
Orders by email iuporder@indiana.edu

The paper used in this publication meets the minimum requirements of American
National Standard for Information Sciences Permanence of Paper for Printed
Library Materials, ANSI Z39.48-1984.

Manufactured in the United States of America

Library of Congress Cataloging-in-Publication Data

King, Wilma, date.
    Stolen childhood : slave youth in nineteenth-century America /
Wilma King.
        p.   cm.
    Includes bibliographical references (p.   ) and index.
    ISBN 0-253-32904-3 (cloth : alk. paper)
    1. Slavery—United States—History—19th century—Sources.
2. Afro-American children—History—19th century—Sources.
3. Afro-American families—History—19th century—Sources.
4. Slaves—Emancipation—United States.
5. United States—History—19th century.
I. Title.
E441.K59 1995
306.3'62'083—dc20   94-49163

ISBN 0-253-21186-7 (pbk. : alk. paper)

5 6 7 8 9 02 01 00 99 98

To the memory of my father
and for his children, and their children,
and their children, and . . .

The slave population, as you remark, "has had vast influence on the past, and may affect the future destinies of America, to an extent which human wisdom can neither foresee nor control."

—Timothy Pickering
to the Honorable John Marshall*
January 17, 1826

*Marshall Papers, Earl Gregg Swem Library, The College of William and Mary, Williamsburg, Virginia.

CONTENTS

ACKNOWLEDGMENTS
xi
ABBREVIATIONS
xiii
INTRODUCTION
xvii

1.

"You know I am one man that do love my children"
SLAVE CHILDREN AND YOUTH
IN THE FAMILY AND COMMUNITY
1

2.

"Us ain't never idle"
THE WORLD OF WORK
21

3.

"When day is done"
PLAY AND LEISURE
43

4.

"Knowledge unfits a child to be a slave"
TEMPORAL AND SPIRITUAL EDUCATION
67

5.

"What has Ever become of my Presus little girl"
THE TRAUMAS AND TRAGEDIES OF
SLAVE CHILDREN AND YOUTH
91

6.

"Free at last"
THE QUEST FOR FREEDOM
115

7.

"There's a better day a-coming"
THE TRANSITION FROM SLAVERY TO FREEDOM
141

NOTES
169

APPENDICES
215

BIBLIOGRAPHY
223

INDEX
247

ACKNOWLEDGMENTS

The first opportunity to discuss this work publicly came from the Association for the Study of Afro-American Life and History's 71st annual convention; however, I canceled the October 18, 1986, presentation because of my father's sudden death. It is ironic that his funeral services fell on that same afternoon. Afterwards, Sheila Miller, librarian at East Pike Elementary School, Indiana, Pennsylvania, invited me to discuss my research with the sixth graders at East Pike. I protested saying that I was not writing a book for children, rather it was about children. Sheila insisted that the pupils would understand and appreciate my work. I gave in and was delighted to find the pupils at East Pike and subsequently the Eisenhower Elementary School, also in Indiana, Pennsylvania, truly interested, or truly polite, in knowing about the lives of enslaved children in nineteenth-century America. They posed questions that only those of their ages could. Their questions were helpful.

I owe huge debts of gratitude to colleagues who kept an eye out for materials relevant to my research. A special thanks goes to Darlene Clark Hine and David Barry Gaspar for their comments and encouragement in its early stages. Michael P. Johnson, Linda Reed, and Howard V. N. Young, Jr., provided beneficial comments after reading the entire manuscript. Robert L. Hall generously shared "Prolegomena to a Social History of Slave Whippings in the United States," Jacqueline Goggin provided a chapter from her biography of Carter G. Woodson, and Lee Formwalt brought the Polly Ann Johnson case to my attention. My debts to these historians can never be repaid adequately. Other colleagues and friends including Edward Ayers, Richard Corby, Marcia Darling, Charlotte Fitzgerald, Beverly Guy-Sheftall, William H. Harris, Barbara Hill Hudson, Norrece T. Jones, Jr., Irwin Marcus, Stanley Warren, and Hoda Zaki either shared research or provided pertinent references.

Without assistance from the staffs in the manuscript collections at Duke University, Hampton University, University of Virginia, and the College of William and Mary my work would remain incomplete. Archivists at the Library of Congress, Mississippi Department of Archives and History, National Archives, North Carolina Department of Archives and History, Southern Historical Collection, Virginia State Library, and Wisconsin State Historical Society were equally helpful.

I owe special thanks to librarians at Indiana University of Pennsylvania including Mary Sampson, director of the Interlibrary Loan Office; Richard Chamberlin, reference librarian; and Walter Laude, director of technical services.

ACKNOWLEDGMENTS

Their student assistants also earned my expressed gratitude.

Financial support came from several sources. In the initial stage of research the National Endowment for the Humanities awarded a travel to collections grant which introduced me to the Southern Historical Collection at Chapel Hill, North Carolina. The Virginia Foundation for the Humanities and Public Policy granted a summer residency at Charlottesville, Virginia, in 1987 which allowed me to use the special collection at the University of Virginia library. The 1991 NEH Summer Seminars for College Teachers, "Slavery and Freedom" at the University of California, Irvine, under the direction of Michael P. Johnson, provided the financial support and work environment while I completed the research for the last chapter of this work. Indiana University of Pennsylvania's Department of History, Faculty Senate, and Graduate School were generous with both research support and released time. Michigan State University provided released time during the 1991–1992 academic year for the completion of this book.

Undergraduate assistants Kim Ault, Andrew Conroy, and Kellee Durkin along with graduate assistants Carole Occhuizzo, James Koshan, Gary Link, and Gary Denholm at Indiana University of Pennsylvania willingly and cheerfully helped with many of the details for this manuscript.

Finally, my family as usual provided the kind of help and support that only a family can and will.

The assistance from colleagues, friends, and family helped to bring this work to fruition. I am grateful. Their help was bountiful enough for me to bear alone all criticism regarding the merit of this work.

ABBREVIATIONS

REPOSITORIES

DU	Perkins Library, Duke University, Durham, North Carolina
EGS	Earl Gregg Swem Library, The College of William and Mary, Williamsburg, Virginia
FSSP	Freedmen and Southern Society Project, University of Maryland, College Park, Maryland
GDAH	Georgia Department of Archives and History, Atlanta, Georgia
HNOC	Historic New Orleans Collection, New Orleans, Louisiana
HUA	Hampton University Archives, Hampton, Virginia
LC	Library of Congress, Washington, D.C.
MC	Museum of the Confederacy, Richmond, Virginia
MDAH	Mississippi Department of Archives and History, Jackson, Mississippi
NA	National Archives, Washington, D.C.
NCDAH	North Carolina Department of Archives and History, Raleigh, North Carolina
SC	South Caroliniana Library, University of South Carolina, Columbia, South Carolina
SHC	Southern Historical Collection, University of North Carolina, Chapel Hill, North Carolina
SHSW	State Historical Society of Wisconsin, Madison, Wisconsin
TU	Tulane University, New Orleans, Louisiana
UVA	Alderman Library, University of Virginia, Charlottesville, Virginia
VSL	Virginia State Library, Richmond, Virginia

ABBREVIATIONS

PERIODICALS

AA	*American Archivist*
AANY	*Afro-American in New York Life and History*
AH	*Agricultural History*
AHR	*American Historical Review*
AJDC	*American Journal of Diseases of Children*
AJLH	*American Journal of Legal History*
AJP	*American Journal of Psychiatry*
AJS	*American Journal of Sociology*
AM	*Atlantic Monthly*
AQ	*American Quarterly*
BHM	*Bulletin of the History of Medicine*
BHR	*Business History Review*
BS	*The Black Scholar*
CAN	*Child Abuse & Neglect*
CWH	*Civil War History*
FHQ	*Florida Historical Quarterly*
FS	*Feminist Studies*
GH	*Gender and History*
GHQ	*Georgia Historical Quarterly*
GM	*Geoscience and Man*
JAC	*Journal of American Culture*
JAF	*Journal of American Folklore*
JAH	*Journal of American History*
JBS	*Journal of Black Studies*
JEH	*Journal of Economic History*
JER	*Journal of the Early Republic*
JFH	*Journal of Family History*

ABBREVIATIONS

JFV	*Journal of Family Violence*
JH	*Journalism History*
JIH	*Journal of Interdisciplinary History*
JMF	*Journal of Marriage and Family*
JMH	*Journal of Mississippi History*
JNH	*Journal of Negro History*
JNMD	*Journal of Nervous and Mental Disorders*
JPH	*Journal of Presbyterian History*
JPsy	*Journal of Psychohistory*
JSH	*Journal of Southern History*
JS	*Journal of Sociology*
JSocH	*Journal of Social History*
JSpH	*Journal of Sport History*
JWH	*Journal of Women's History*
LaH	*Louisiana History*
LH	*Labor History*
MHR	*Missouri Historical Review*
MHSB	*Missouri Historical Society Bulletin*
MR	*Massachusetts Review*
MVHR	*Mississippi Valley Historical Review*
NCGSJ	*North Carolina Genealogical Society Journal*
NCHR	*North Carolina Historical Review*
NEQ	*New England Quarterly*
NYH	*New York History*
NYSJM	*New York State Journal of Medicine*
PH	*Pennsylvania History*
PMHB	*Pennsylvania Magazine of History & Biography*
PR	*The Psychohistory Review*

ABBREVIATIONS

PSA   *Plantation Society: Plantation Society in the Americas: An Interdisciplinary Journal of Tropical and Subtropical History and Culture*

RD   *Reader's Digest*

RHR   *Radical History Review*

SA   *Slavery and Abolition: A Journal of Comparative Studies*

SAQ   *South Atlantic Quarterly*

SE   *Southern Exposure*

SFQ   *Southern Folklore Quarterly*

SM   *Scribner's Monthly*

SP   *Southern Planter*

SQ   *Southern Quarterly*

SS   *Southern Studies*

SSH   *Social Science History*

SW   *Southern Workman*

SwHQ   *Southwestern Historical Quarterly*

TH   *Trends in History*

THQ   *Tennessee Historical Quarterly*

VMH   *Virginia Magazine of History*

VSSJ   *Virginia Social Science Journal*

WJBS   *Western Journal of Black Studies*

WMQ   *William and Mary Quarterly*

WS   *Women's Studies*

WTHSP   *West Tennessee Historical Society Papers*

INTRODUCTION

Most slave societies in the New World used massive importation of Africans to maintain their populations. In the United States, by contrast, the population sustained itself through reproductions. Less than one million Africans were imported into the country before the Atlantic slave trade ended in 1808. Although enslaved children fell into an "actuarially perilous category," the population had increased to 3,952,760 by 1860. Of that population 56 percent were under twenty years of age. The ability to reproduce the population is the most distinctive feature of slavery in North America. This factor alone makes a study of enslaved children and youth important because the majority of those in bondage in the United States by the Civil War were born in North America rather than in Africa. They survived the institution of slavery because their teachers relied upon firsthand experiences of bondage and used the deference ritual for their own benefit.[1]

The purpose of this study is modest. Its aim is to extricate enslaved children and youth from the amorphous mass of bond servants. Placing them in the foreground will help to answer questions about enslaved families in nineteenth-century America. Framing questions about youngsters and their place in the slave community will address issues such as those highlighted by historian Willie Lee Rose in 1970. "The disturbing truth," she wrote, "is that we know less than we ought to know about childhood in slavery" despite the "significance psychologists and sociologists attribute to experiences of infancy and youth in development of personality."[2]

The locus of power in antebellum America rested in the hands of whites, many of whom viewed slaves, regardless of their ages, as children. In explaining characteristics of "Sambo," which Stanley M. Elkins attributed to southern lore, he described the interaction between slaveholders and slaves. The relationship, he wrote, "was one of [the slave's] utter dependence and childlike attachment: it was indeed this childlike quality that was the very key to his being." Any hint of Sambo's "manhood" had the potential for scorn, while "the child, 'in his place,' could be both exasperating and lovable." After the Civil War, a small ex-slaveholder remembered that her slaves, including an adult man and two women, "were like so many children to be clothed & nursed & fed & were constantly to be looked after."[3]

The idea that "Negroes are naturally of a childlike character," prevailed into the twentieth century and prompted Melville J. Herskovits to address it as the first of five misconceptions in *The Myth of the Negro Past*. Herskovits asserted that Africans and their descendants were neither childlike nor credulous. Far

INTRODUCTION

from being "childlike" throughout their lives, slaves were forced to confront adult situations of work, terror, injustice, and arbitrary power at early ages.[4]

Surprisingly, the amount of published work on children is quite large because no one methodology dominates, and researchers across disciplines, i.e., women's history, sociology, anthropology, labor history, history of medicine, and literature, reflect an interest in the subject. One of the most ambitious studies about the young, *Children and Youth in America,* appeared in 1970. It is a massive work that includes white, African American, and Native American children, but it is a history of public policy for children rather than a history that deals with the realities of human growth and development. A more recent work edited by N. Ray Hiner and Joseph M. Hawes, *Growing Up in America,* comes nearest to studying children in a comprehensive manner. Other publications about the black family in America include discussions about slavery, but none of the studies emphasize the presence of youthful chattel.[5]

Data on slave children exist in general studies of slavery such as John W. Blassingame's *The Slave Community,* Herbert Gutman's *The Black Family in Slavery and Freedom,* Eugene Genovese's *Roll, Jordan, Roll,* Leslie Owens' *This Species of Property,* and Thomas L. Webber's *Deep Like the Rivers;* however, they do not fully address many questions of interest, such as child-rearing practices of nineteenth-century African Americans, relationships between children, their parents, siblings, peers, and others.[6]

Resources for such a study are vast, but the data must be ferreted out from newspapers, dissertations, theses, scholarly journals, court records, census returns, and published sources along with unpublished diaries, plantation records, and manuscripts of antebellum planters, travelers, and observers of social, economic, and political conditions in America. Furthermore, slave narratives, including those of Solomon Northup, Frederick Douglass, and Harriet Jacobs along with the voluminous collection of interviews from the Federal Writers Project, notwithstanding criticisms by many historians, offer the best sources of primary data from ex-slaves. The majority of those interviewed were children and youth, less than twenty years of age when slavery ended.

Despite this vast array of resources pertinent to a study of enslaved children and youth, "few historians have stressed this aspect of slavery." Children have received little attention because they, more than other enslaved persons, were "silent and invisible." This enormous population did not write or speak for itself and was often ignored by others. The size of the youthful population, the fact that most of them were born in the United States, and that they survived make such a study all the more meaningful. Children's history has come of age, and there is now greater interest in the black child than ever before.[7]

Studies of the young must address the questions: "Do age groups have histories?" "What did concepts of youth and adolescence mean in the nineteenth century?" and "Has childhood changed over time?" Some scholars argue that adolescence is a modern concept and no systematic body of literature existed

INTRODUCTION

with the word "adolescence" until the twentieth century. Aside from the personality traits including the "storm and stress" and uncertainty of adjustment associated with the teens, adolescence is the period between the onset of sexual maturity and full incorporation into the economic sphere.[8]

In the nineteenth century, the time lag between those two intervals functioned differently for white boys and girls, poor or wealthy, and blacks. White middle- and upper-class boys often left home to receive a formal education when they reached their early teens, thereby delaying their entry into the world of work. They enjoyed a distinctive period of youth. Some poor white boys became apprentices and also had an adolescence of sorts. It was a different matter for white girls since no significant social role existed for them outside of marriage; consequently, they experienced no prolonged time set aside for adjustments to responsibilities.[9]

Furthermore, this discourse further complicates the issue since historical records are often unclear in distinguishing between enslaved adults and children. Social customs rather than age alone determined whether one called bond servants "boy" or "girl." Consider the lack of clarity in the matter when a nineteenth-century slaveholder explained:

> I have an unruly negro girl whom I am anxious to dispose of as soon as possible and supply her place. Will you be so good as to look out for me a breeding negro woman under twenty years of age. Also a young active negro man. If you cannot meet with the slaves aforesaid I will be willing to purchase a young or middle aged negro man with his wife and children. I shall be glad to hear from you immediately as the negro of who I wish to dispose is a very dangerous character.

The age of the "girl" in question is unclear. The age difference between the "young active man" and a young negro man with wife and children also lacks specificity.[10]

Age was important in shaping a sense of self, yet those in question did not speak about themselves in age-specific terms. Kept ignorant deliberately, slaves often dated their age by their size or memorable events. Booker T. Washington knew that he was born near Hale's Ford, Virginia, but he did not know "the month or the day." The South Carolinian Calib Craig explained it this way: "Dont none of us know de day or de place us was born. Us have to take dat on faith." Lucy Daniels remained unclear about her date of birth when she said, "I don't know how old I been when de war end. If I been in de world I wasn't old enough to pick up nuthin'." Sylvia Cannon left no doubt when she said, "I just ain' able to say bout my right age."[11]

Richard A. Wright, author of *African Philosophy*, notes that most Yorubas did not know their age but dated their existence by events since age without events made little sense. That was normal for the Yorubas but incompatible for nineteenth-century Americans among whom Africans lived. Douglass lamented that "the larger part of the slaves know as little of their age as horses know of theirs." By contrast, he said, "The white children could tell their ages." Douglass was not alone in feeling the injustice of being "deprived of the same privilege."[12]

Many white children knew their ages, but there was flexibility about who was an adult in nineteenth-century America. Twenty-one years of age was long considered the end of upper adolescence and the beginning of adulthood. Even so, white males were considered adults at eighteen in some cases and at twenty-one in others. Slaveholders often considered bond servants adults when they became full hands at age sixteen years or younger. The onset of menarche was another factor which catapulted the girls into adulthood.[13]

The 1850 Census of the United States divided slaves into groups consisting of those below five years of age under the heading "Infancy," while the second category, "Youth," included those from five to twenty years of age. Gradual abolition laws delineated the ages at which slaves were to receive their freedom. Once freed, minor apprentices remained bound to employers until eighteen and twenty-one years of age for females and males respectively. I have used age-specific data with eighteen and twenty-one as the upper limits for females and males respectively. On occasions when the data are unclear or there are exceptions, I call the reader's attention to this matter to maintain the integrity of the study.[14]

Stolen Childhood argues that enslaved children had virtually no childhood because they entered the work place early and were more readily subjected to arbitrary plantation authority, punishments, and separations. These experiences made them grow old before their time. Furthermore, parents tried to protect their offspring, who learned that mothers and fathers were also vulnerable to cruelties. Childhood and adulthood were closely linked during slavery when children and adults experienced many of the same atrocities which were comparable to those suffered by people living in a nation under siege.

Olaudah Equiano, who was taken from Africa at eleven years of age, experienced the pain of separation from his family and place of birth. When fear of the unknown engulfed Equiano, a shipmate comforted the child. As a freedman, Equiano reflected upon youth in slavery and posited:

> When you make men slaves you deprive them of half their virtue, you set them in your own conduct an example of fraud, rapine, and cruelty, and compel them to live with you in a state of war.

Slaveholders created a situation which equipped their slaves to fight until they became independent of deprivations imposed by others. That state of war existed until slavery ended.[15]

If slavery is analogous to war, a look at the lives of children who experienced war should provide a better understanding of the ordeals of the most vulnerable victims. Children, because of their inability to protect themselves from devastation, suffer intensely from both slavery and war. The twentieth-century diaries of

INTRODUCTION

Anne Frank and Zlata Filipovic give pause to what war does to children. The girls wrote about terror, hunger, and death. Zlata cried out "DESPAIR!!! MISERY!!! FEAR!!! That's my life." Describing herself as an innocent schoolgirl, Zlata said she was "a child without a childhood."[16]

To be sure, enslaved nineteenth-century children and youth did not live continuously amid the actual bombardment of war or fear of going to a concentration camp, but their experiences with separations, terror, misery, and despair reduced them to children without childhoods. Although this state of war atmosphere was pervasive, it was more evident in some facets of the children's lives than in others.

The first chapter of this volume focuses on childbirth, the children's place in the family, child-rearing practices, and children's relationships with parents, siblings, and the larger slave community.

Chapter 2 examines the work of enslaved children and youth in large and small households. Whatever the nature of the work or geographical region, bond servants began working at early ages. Slaveowners benefited from slave labor to the extent that they assured themselves of a productive work force by minimizing a slave's nonproductive years at the beginning and end of the life cycle.

To be sure, slaveowners provided for some leisure activities after completing work assignments. And it is in chapter 3 that play and other leisure activities (i.e., corn shuckings, dances, "courting") are examined. Slaves, regardless of their ages, divided their leisure between utilitarian and nonutilitarian activities.

Chapter 4 examines the education and religion of slave children and youth as separate leisure activities. The education and religion of enslaved people were far more complicated than any other leisure activities. Once slaves gained literacy, slaveholders lost control over what they learned and how they worshiped. On another level, informal education gained through proverbs and animal trickster tales helped them survive the institution of slavery.

Slavery as a system of control did not survive without intimidation. Chapter 5 examines the tragedies and traumas experienced by youthful chattel. "My heart was heavier than it had ever been before," wrote Harriet Jacobs, "when they told me my new-born babe was a girl." Based upon her experiences, the mother believed her child might encounter such abuse. Attempts to protect children from the hardships of slavery were ever-present.[17] Chapter 6 shows the variety of ways that children and youth escaped from slavery (i.e., running away, manumissions, Civil War) along with the costs of being free.

The final chapter repeats the themes discussed in chapters 1 through 5. At the outset, the chapter argues that children were often at the center of the battle to reunite families and gain economic independence as former bond servants and their progeny made the transition from slavery to freedom.

STOLEN CHILDHOOD

"YOU KNOW I AM ONE MAN THAT DO LOVE MY CHILDREN"*

SLAVE CHILDREN AND YOUTH IN THE FAMILY AND COMMUNITY

> Oh, child! thou art a little slave:
> And all of thee that grows,
> Will be another's weight of flesh,—
> But thine the weight of woes
> Thou art a little slave, my child
> And much I grieve and mourn
> That to so dark a destiny
> My lovely babe I've borne.
>
> — "The Slave Mother's Address to
> her Infant Child"**

If childhood was a special time for enslaved children, it was because their parents made it so. They stood between them and slaveholders who sought to control them psychologically and to break their wills to resist. Parents also looked out for their children's physical well-being. Frederick Douglass recalled how his mother came to his rescue after the cook Aunt Katy refused to give him bread. His mother's intercession taught him that he "was not only a child, but somebody's child." He remembered that being upon his mother's knee, at that moment, made him prouder than being a king upon a throne.[1]

Enslaved parents had an unusually heavy responsibility, for they not only had to survive, but they also had to ensure that their children survived under conditions that were tantamount to perpetual war between slaveholders fighting to control their chattel while the bond servants were struggling to free themselves from the control of others. The African heritage was an important factor in how enslaved mothers and fathers guided their children through the strife. This chapter examines the place of children in the slave family and community, the conditions

---

* Henry L. Swint, *Dear Ones at Home: Letters from Contraband Camps* (Nashville: Vanderbilt University Press, 1966), 243; Herbert G. Gutman, *The Black Family in Slavery and Freedom, 1750–1925* (New York: Vintage, 1977), 7.

** "The Slave Mother's Address," in Lunsford Lane, "The Narrative of Lunsford Lane, formerly of Raleigh, N.C." (Boston: Torrey, 1842), in *Five Slave Narratives: A Compendium,* ed. William Loren Katz (New York: Arno Press and *New York Times,* 1968), 4.

surrounding their birth, the attitudes of enslaved children toward their parents and siblings, and the attitudes of slaveowners toward their youthful chattel.[2]

Child-rearing practices among African Americans had roots in their traditional customs; motherhood, however, took on two unique characteristics for enslaved women in the United States. First, because of an accepted pattern of matrilineal or matrifocal families in traditional African societies, many African women reared children without help from the fathers. Moreover, the disproportionate number of men taken by slave traders left many women with dependent children to care for and a greater portion of the work, ordinarily completed by men, to perform. The women managed with the help of other women. Like their sisters in Africa, many American slave women adjusted to parenting without spouses due to circumstances beyond their control such as imbalances in the sex ratio and the propensity of slaveowners to sell men separately. Second, motherhood—an honorable status in African society—was no longer an exclusive matter between a woman and her partner once enslaved in North America. Parents viewed their children as family, while owners often saw them as chattel with profit-making potentials.[3]

Thomas Jefferson's meaning was obvious when he wrote that "a child raised every 2. years is of more profit than the crop of the best laboring man." He considered the "labor of a breeding woman as no object" and instructed his plantation manager to impress upon the overseer that "it is not their labor, but their increase which is the first consideration with us." Jefferson was not alone in this philosophy. In 1858 an unidentified author contributed "'Profits of Farming'—Facts and Figures" to the *Southern Cultivator*, which explains his view about the value of reproduction:

> I own a woman who cost me $400 when a girl, in 1827. Admit she made me nothing—only worth her victuals and clothing. She now has three children, worth over $3000 and have been field hands say three years; in that time making enough to pay their expenses before they were half hands, and then I have the profit of all half hands. She has only three boys and a girl out of a dozen; yet, with all her bad management, she has paid me ten per cent. interest, for her work was to be an average good, and I would not this night touch $700 for her. Her oldest boy is worth $1250 cash, and I can get it.

This kind of attitude made, slave parents, especially mothers, part of a twisted mire of tradition and greed. Their children were part of that quagmire, held fast by punishments, sales, or threats thereof.[4]

Despite the tumultuous nature of chattel slavery, many bond servants formed binding relationships, established families, and developed lives for themselves within the confines of bondage. Many slaveowners acknowledged conjugal relationships, recorded slave births by family units, and insisted upon monogamy. They reasoned that marriage and children fostered "happiness" and usurped restiveness. When Jim and Ellen, slaves belonging to the Sumter

County, South Carolina, planter McDonald Furman, "commenced housekeeping" in 1838, he gave them "a bench table, 2 iron pots, a dutch oven skillet, 2 tin buckets, 4 cups 2 pans, 3 spoons, [and] a bedstead." The gifts indicated his interest in maintaining their household and life together. Most slaveowners did not endow newlyweds in this manner.[5]

William Ethelbert Ervin, a plantation owner in Lowndes County, Mississippi, made provisions in 1847 for slave families to live in their own houses and recognized a division of labor which required the husband to provide wood and look out for his family's well-being. He was to "wait on his wife" and she, in turn, was to "cook & wash for [her] husband and her children and attend to the mending of cloths." Slaveowners sometimes forbade marital discord in the quarters by spelling out rules. At least one slaveholder believed it was "disgraceful for a man to raise his hand in violence against a feeble woman" whom he viewed as a wife, mother, and companion in leisure.[6]

In a half-century of record keeping, the Virginia planter John C. Cohoon listed his slaves in family units with the father's name appearing first, which suggests that he viewed men as the heads of the household. The one exception was the pair Rachel and David. It appears that Rachel had at least one child before Cohoon either acquired David or David became Rachel's spouse. Regardless of the placement of parents' names, slaveholders made provisions for their offspring. "The little negro children," wrote one slaveholder, "must be taken care of." Another plantation record said, "The Children must be particularly attended to," before adding, "for rearing them is not only a duty, but also the most profitable part of plantation business."[7]

By the nineteenth century, companionate marriages were common, and marital fidelity was accepted among many slaves. Moreover, there were some long lasting unions where children grew to maturity in the presence of parents who went to great lengths to remain together. For example, in October 1842 Sukey and Ersey, two enslaved women in St. Louis, suggested having themselves and their young children sold to someone in their vicinity once they learned of a pending separation, a subject of "much pain," from their respective husbands. They could not "bare to go to Texas, with a parcel of strangers." Being "much attached" to their husbands and children, the women who described themselves as in "much distress" begged their owner to consider their request.[8]

The slaveholders' financial status and need for laborers determined the number of slaves they owned. For example, by 1860 approximately one-half of the slaveholders in Maryland owned less than three slaves; therefore, it is unlikely that each adult slave had a spouse in the same household. Whenever it was feasible, slaveowners avoided difficulties, including unauthorized visits and runaway slaves, associated with abroad marriages. Thomas Jefferson encouraged his bond servants to choose spouses at Monticello with "wedding presents." If they complied with his wishes, he gave them a pot and a bed. Despite such incentives, Jefferson's financial status still determined if the couple remained together.

Nevertheless, slaves tried to forge a family life through regular visits, which sometimes interfered with their daily routines.[9]

Children born to men and women owned by different persons became the property of the mother's owner. The father's owner experienced no increase in wealth or workers. John C. Cohoon serves as an example in this matter. He recorded 104 births among the sixteen families he owned. Of the children, thirty were born into six female-headed households where family sizes ranged from two to nine children. Cohoon listed Dick Pettis, John Saunders, and Henry Arthur as the fathers of several of these children. There is no further information about the men. Nevertheless, their progeny added value to Cohoon's coffer.[10]

The status of the children was clear, but little is known about what their mothers thought about increasing the population or what they could do to shape their children's future. In studies related to childbirth, Natalie Shainess argues that an expectant mother's attitude about her femininity, values, and relationship with an unborn child's father determines how the woman views her pregnancy. Unable to control fertility and make decisions about their bodies, enslaved women had little to say outside of their own worlds about these crucial matters. The amount and kind of support they received from the children's fathers and the larger community also determined how they functioned during pregnancy.[11]

Proslavery critics often claimed that abolitionists used stories of sexual exploitation to politicize their cause; nevertheless, slave women often became pregnant through forced cohabitation or rape. In such cases, it was unrealistic for victims of sexual abuse to expect any consideration from the men if pregnancy resulted. Under different circumstances, attentiveness from the fathers depended upon variables including whether the parents belonged to one owner or were partners in abroad marriages.[12]

Prenatal care for enslaved women in the modern sense was not available, but there were publications which discussed pregnancy. For example, the 1834 *Domestic Medicine or Poor Man's Medicine* contains the chapter "Cautions during Pregnancy" with remedies for such maladies as colic, heartburn, cramps, and frequency of elimination. Enlightened slaveowners were likely to have bought and read such books, and they may have disseminated the information to bondwomen. Moreover, the women probably benefited from folk medicine and advice from older women and midwives in the slave community.[13]

Pregnant women were often ignorant of their bodily functions and needs during gestation. They did not own their persons, nor did they have the resources to assure healthy pregnancies and safe deliveries. Their work could interfere with the blood supply to the placenta and jeopardize the health of the fetus. Some slaveholders were aware of the relationship between heavy physical labor and low-birth-weight babies, but they were not aware of the connection to high infant mortality rates.[14]

An unborn child's fate rested with slaveowners, who required physical labor from the pregnant and nonpregnant alike. When Jenny, a weaver owned by the

Virginia iron master David Ross, missed work, he was "suspicious of her real complaint." Afterwards, Jenny suffered a miscarriage. Ross wrote "similar accidents to her's is the natural lot of humanity," but he remained puzzled about the circumstances. He believed "imprudent punishments[,] accidental hurts[,] falling down or violent alarms" were possible causes; even so, Jenny had not experienced any unusual disruptions. Ross then wondered about her work as a weaver. "If it be injurious to pregnant women," he wrote, "I never was informed of it." He appeared concerned when he wrote, "I hope she is doing well." Possibilities for financial loss, reduced productivity, and a tinge of guilt were factors responsible for Ross's new attitude about her condition.[15]

Ross's suspicion about Jenny's absence does not mean he was insensitive. Pregnancy often excused women from heavy labor, and they sometimes made such claims solely to escape work. Owners, Ross included, were cautious about women "playing the lady" at their expense. "Breeding and suckling women" usually received special work assignments. One slaveowner informed his overseer that "such women as may be near being confined must be put only to light work." On other plantations aged slaves, children, and pregnant women worked in "trash gangs," agricultural labor units which performed less strenuous chores.[16]

Until owners and overseers knew the women were pregnant, they continued their work as usual. Two women, Treaty and Louisine, who belonged to the Georgia slaveholder John B. Lamar, suffered miscarriages in 1855. Lamar suspected that his overseer Stancil Barwick was abusive, but Barwick maintained that he did not know that Treaty was pregnant and was not aware of Louisine's "condition" until she aborted the fetus. It is possible that neither he nor the women were aware of their conditions or that their work caused the miscarriages.[17]

The loss of a fetus among enslaved women was not uncommon. "I ain' never been safe in de family way," said Josephine Bacchus, an ex-slave from South Carolina when interviewed by a Work Projects Administration (WPA) interviewer in the 1930s. She attributed her inability to have a "nine month child" to the lack of "good attention" during slavery. In the late 1830s, slave women on a Georgia plantation owned by Pierce Mease Butler told their pitiable stories of aborted fetuses, difficult births, and infant deaths to his wife Frances Anne Kemble and asked her to help modify their work. The women were essentially correct in believing that a link existed between heavy work and the health of an unborn child, but heavy work is probably most detrimental during the earlier stages of gestation.[18]

Regardless of the conditions, childbirth in antebellum America was frightening and dangerous for mothers of any race or class. Possibilities of death, the mother's or child's, sometimes both, accompanied pregnancies. Two significant changes occurred in the nineteenth century to ease such anxieties. As male doctors slowly replaced midwives, some men were simultaneously participating in childbirth. Doctors and husbands often provided safer deliveries and emotional support. White women were the primary beneficiaries of these changes. Midwives, female relatives, or friends ordinarily delivered slave children, but if complications arose beyond the ken of those present, slaveowners sought the help of medical doctors. Abroad marriages, work schedules, and other separations usually precluded the presence of many slave fathers.[19]

There is an extant account of one slave father participating in the births of his children, which occurred under adverse conditions. The mother, a runaway living in a cave, bore three children with the help of only her husband, who "waited on her with each child." Although older girls sometimes assisted their mothers, the woman's children were too young to help.[20]

The legal status of an African American woman determined that of her child. The Virginia Assembly passed a law in 1662 declaring that "all children born in this country shall be held bond or free only according to the condition of the mother." This was contrary to English common law, which based status upon the condition of fathers. Slave women relegated their children to a life of bondage since slavery, in the United States, was an inherited condition. Children belonged to slaveholders for life even if their mothers became free after childbirth.[21]

Unlike its legal status, the size of a slave family varied. Many births were one and one-half to two and one-half years apart. Systematic breastfeeding in conjunction with general poor postnatal health, which interfered with the fertility of enslaved women, may account for the spacing of their children. Other factors, abstinence while breastfeeding and involuntary abstinence because of abroad marriages, also help to explain the intervals between births. Miscarriages, stillborns, or infants dying before receiving a name and having it placed in record books are other factors for consideration.[22]

If enslaved children survived more than a few days, one of the most important activities in the newborn baby's household was the selection of a name. Africans usually waited a week or more before naming their children and marked the occasion with a celebration. American slaves probably did not hold a celebration, but they followed the African tradition of naming children in honor of close relatives, thereby placing the child firmly within the kin network. Female children received their grandmother's name more frequently than their own mother's name. The firstborn male often received his father's given name or that of a grandfather. The ex-slave Isiah Jefferies's anecdote about his name indicates his parents' desire to establish generational connections and his grandfather's respect for that linkage. Jefferies's peers called him "Uncle Zery"; by contrast, his grandfather refused to use the title. "I was named atter him," Jefferies stated, and he believed his grandfather was "too proud of dat fact to call me any nickname."[23]

Five of the families owned by John C. Cohoon were direct descendants of Jacob and Fanny, the parents of eight children. Their son Henry, born October 2, 1811, married Harriet and fathered fifteen children. Two of their children, James Henry and Henry, received their father's name Henry, known as Harry perhaps to avoid confusion. Only one of the children, James Henry, had a middle name. Further family linkages are evident in the names of a son and daughter, Jacob and Fanny, for the paternal grandparents.[24]

Jacob and Fanny's second child Mary became the mother of a daughter on February 27, 1836, and of a son on September 14, 1837. Mary and her husband Bob named the children for their maternal grandparents. Harry and Harriet also named a son and daughter in honor of their paternal grandparents. Harry had avoided confusion with his name and that of his sons on one hand but probably exacerbated it among Mary's children and his own offspring on the other hand. Ultimately, respect for Harry's parents was paramount.

Another of the older couple's children, Rachel, born in 1828, was the mother of six children born between 1850 and 1862. Two of her offspring bore names of Rachel's siblings, but the grandparents' names do not reappear. The same was true of Matilda, Jacob and Fanny's daughter who was born in 1835. Only Margaret, another of Jacob and Fanny's daughters and born in 1831, did not duplicate family names for any of her children.[25]

In the seventeenth and eighteenth centuries it was also customary for slave children to receive African "day names" such as Cudjo, Mingo, and Cuffee. During the nineteenth century there were noticeable changes in naming practices, at least among slaves in the South Carolina low country. The use of day names which actually denoted the day of birth gave way to the practice of using those names as family names. Traditionally, girls born on Friday received the name Phebe or Phoebe, but the use of the name in the nineteenth century bore little relationship to the day of birth. The Cohoon slaves, Harry and Harriet, named their ninth child Easter, although she was born in mid-September. Slaves did not use place names such as London, York, and Troy as frequently as before, but when new states came into the Union names including Missouri and Indiana appeared. As slaves became more familiar with biblical personalities, they selected names of amiable figures and avoided those with less desirable qualities, such as Delilah and Jezebel or Saul and Absalom.[26]

Occasionally slaveholders involved themselves in the naming process and bestowed Greek and Christian names upon newborn slaves. Slaveholders also chose the names of popular heroes. It is unlikely that Maria acted alone when naming her son Polk, born April 29, 1845, especially after learning that his younger brother was named "in honour of General [Zachary] Taylor" by the owner, a western Tennessee businessman, John Houston Bills. When Lucinda gave birth to a baby boy in 1849, Bills wrote, "Call him Jefferson for that Apostle of Liberty." The use of historic names on the Bills plantation shows his influence rather than the women's being au courant with national events or admiring Thomas Jefferson, the "Apostle of Liberty" who emancipated a few slaves during his lifetime.[27]

Slaveowners intervened silently in the naming process with their own surnames, which reflected ownership rather than kinship. It was not uncommon to refer to slaves as John Newton's Sally or Sarah Willingsley's Osborne. Jacob

Stroyer explained that his father, an African, secretly maintained the name Stroyer; however, he used Singleton, his owner's surname while enslaved.[28]

The assessment of slave children ranked higher with slaveholders than the naming of children. Newborns were assets of little worth, but over time their financial value appreciated. The price of slaves varied according to age, sex, and health. The 1819 inventory and appraisal of slaves belonging to Robert Moore Riddick listed twenty-one-year-old Maria as worth $325 and her eighteen-month-old daughter as worth $80. The value of the thirty-year-old Charlotte was $275 and her three-year-old son Charles's was $150, while her daughter Edith, a "child at breast," was worth only $25. Mingo, an old and ill slave, was worthless according to the record. The Louisiana slaveholder James Coles Bruce listed the seventy-year-old slave "Old Daniel" and described him as "old and decriped." The remark "no earthly use" followed the name of One Leg Bob, a fifty-year-old-male. The age and health of these two men rendered them worthless monetarily. Plantation inventories display a callous indifference in listing the value of slaves, yet they were handy references should slaveholders wish to sell or hire out their slaves for pecuniary purposes.[29]

Frances Kemble, an astute observer of conditions on her husband's plantation, noted that some enslaved women had a "distinct and perfect knowledge of their value to their owners as property." She conceded that they were not far off the mark in thinking they added to the number of their owner's "livestock by bringing new slaves into the world." They made claims upon his "consideration and good will" in proportion to the number of children they bore. Kemble based her observation, in part, upon the mothers who proudly informed her of the size of their families. "Look missis," a woman called out, "little niggers for you and massa; plenty little niggers for you."[30]

Not all enslaved parents put a price tag on their children or used them as bargaining chips. Some mothers and fathers were sorely distressed at delivering their offspring into a life of bondage. At the birth of his daughter, Henry Bibb vowed never to father another child while enslaved. Thomas H. Jones's wails were piercing. "I am a father and have had the same feelings of unspeakable anguish as I looked upon my precious babes," he cried, "and have thought of the ignorance, degradation and woe which they must endure as slaves."[31]

By contrast, April Ellison, a Winnsboro, South Carolina, gin maker, exuded indifference toward his daughter, Maria Ann, after he became free in 1816. As a prosperous landowner, Ellison built a new life for himself and purchased Matilda and their daughter Eliza Ann, while Maria Ann—apparently the offspring of Ellison and another woman—remained in bondage. After fourteen years of freedom, Ellison bought Maria Ann, but he never emancipated her. William McCreight, a white man whom Ellison trusted, held title to his daughter, who lived as a free person. Despite this fact, she remained enslaved technically.[32]

Regardless of a parent's attitude, each slave birth increased the assets of owners who did not ignore slave children. The reverberation of the words, "The little negro children must be taken care of," was left open to interpretation. When contemplating the purchase of Susan along with her three- and five-year-old daughters Margaret and Adelaide, Tryphena Fox, wife of a medical doctor in Louisiana, weighed the positives and negatives. "Of course it increased my cares," she wrote, "for having invested much in one purchase." Fox paid $1,400 for the pregnant woman and the two children in late 1857. The slaveholder's awareness of the long-range value of the purchase was obvious when she asserted, "It will be to my interest to see that the children are well taken care of and clothed and fed."[33]

Well-cared-for children grew into strong healthy adults who could render life-long service, and slaveowners were ever cognizant of that potential. The gulf between a slaveowner's desire and reality often hinged upon the health of the children, who, through no fault of their mothers, entered the world with meager chances of survival. The historian John Blassingame declares that they suffered from neglect and a variety of ills. "Treated by densely ignorant mothers or little more enlightened planters," he writes, "they died in droves." The deaths of the children often had little to do with the lack of proper medical treatment. What the mothers and children ate is of greater importance. The majority of them breastfed the children, but their poor prenatal and postnatal diets limited the milk's supply of nutrients necessary to support life and prevent diseases. Many suckling children consumed milk that would not keep them alive or healthy. Furthermore, the mothers had limited time in which to care for children because of the demands for their labor.[34]

Enslaved mothers, sometimes seen by owners as mere conduits through which they received a steady labor supply, could not control physical conditions that fostered high incidence of mortality and morbidity among their children. Even a cursory look at the medical research on slaves shows the limitations they faced when protecting themselves and their children. Richard Steckel, for example, answers questions about the health of slaves with height records acquired from 10,562 manifests kept by American ship captains engaged in coastal and interregional slave trade between 1820 and 1860 along with the mortality data in plantation records, and the growth curves from eighteenth-, nineteenth-, and twentieth-century populations. Steckel concludes that the quality of life for slave children was exceedingly poor. American slaves, in early childhood, were small in stature by comparison with Caribbean slaves and in selected American and European populations in the eighteenth and nineteenth centuries. Enslaved American children were also smaller than children in developing countries today. There is a connection between the low birth weights of children and the general poor health of women before delivery, including prenatal dietary deficiency, infected amniotic fluids, and heavy work.[35]

Infant mortality rates were high, and communicable diseases were color-blind in antebellum America. Slaveowners and slaves alike lived with sickness and death. Planter diaries and overseer records teem with notations of illness and death. One slaveholder complained in 1861 of the "unprecedented mortality" on his plantation. Twenty of his slaves died within fourteen years. Fevers, intestinal worms, measles, and whooping cough took their toll.[36]

Slaves and slaveholders sometimes resorted to home remedies to ward off maladies. For the "summer complaint," the Louisiana slaveholder Franklin Hudson used a homemade remedy in 1832 with "good success." The medicine consisted of two quarts of blackberry juice, boiled for a "short time" with one-half ounce of pulverized nutmeg, clove, cinnamon, and one-quarter ounce of allspice. After cooling, the recipe called for a pint of brandy. The dosages ranged from a "teaspoonful to a wine glass according to the age of the patient." By 1852 Hudson claimed that tea made from the "tops of grass" was an excellent remedy for the summer complaint.[37]

Slaves also dispensed traditional remedies passed down from the older generation. Herbal and pine top teas soothed ailing youngsters. Ada Davis, who was born in 1857, said, "Mammy wuz a fair nuss," but she added, "Dey com to get her from far and near"—suggesting that the woman was better than fair. The girl learned to prepare and dispense medicines to treat "stomach trubble" and to cure coughs. She believed in the healing qualities of herbs and roots. The methods of treatment were not always in keeping with owners' wishes.[38]

The frequency of illness in the general population caused slave infirmities and deaths to receive little sympathy from many owners. Everard Green Baker, a slaveowner in Mississippi, recorded the death of a seven-year-old slave child who held his hand until her last breath. Afterwards, "she was opened & a large wad of worms [were] found in the smaller bowels." Concluding that the worms caused the child's death, Baker finalized his notations with "weather warm very." The South Carolina slaveowner David Gavin showed no greater sentiments when he summarized his business succinctly at the end of 1859, "Celia's child died about four months old[,] died saturday the 12. This is two Negroes and three horses I have lost this year." The deaths, whether animal or human, translated into financial losses for Gavin, whereas the death was an emotional loss for Celia.[39]

Although daily plantation records appear heartless, diaries often show more consideration for the dead and bereaved. In 1848 A. C. Griffin commiserated about the death of a white neighbor's child, "I hope she bears it with fortitude." She added, "It is very seldom, a family as large as hers can be raised." Mothers, white and black, came to live with the reality that some of their children would not live to maturity. The dreaded reality was even more real for slave mothers, whose children died at greater rates than white children. Sickle-cell anemia, an incurable life-threatening disease, also took its toll among the slave population. In a study of deaths among the African American population in seven slaveholding states in 1849 and 1850, Kenneth and Virginia Kiple found that 51 percent of the deaths among the nonwhite population occurred among children nine years of age and under.

Slave children in that age group constituted 31 percent of the sample. These statistics suggest that slave mothers needed an extraordinary amount of fortitude to adjust to the large number of deaths among their children.[40]

The Kiples admit that the slave children nine years of age and under fell into an "actuarially perilous category" because of deaths related to several ailments including tetanus, teething, and lockjaw. The slave's chance of dying from these ailments was four times greater than that of their white contemporaries. If slave children survived their early years and entered the labor force when they were ten years of age or older, their health improved because of increased food allowances. Until that time, slave parents grappled with the illnesses and deaths.[41]

Slaveowners sometimes took an interest in the health of slave children for reasons that had nothing to do with financial matters. When John Bills's slave woman, Lucinda, delivered a stillborn child in 1860, he observed, "The poor woman is much distressed," and showed concern for her. By contrast, when Susan's "fine mulatto boy" died, Tryphena Fox charged her with neglect. The baby had caught a cold and "died from the effect of it" while in the owner's arms. Fox commiserated, "I feel badly about its death for it was a pretty baby." To be sure, her sentiments were far-reaching, and she admitted taking "a fancy" to the infant who was near the age of her own child, who had died several weeks earlier. Rather than offer consolation to another grieving mother, Fox implied that Susan was callous. The deaths of their children did not change the mistress-maid relationship since the women inhabited different spheres, separated by race and class. Common experiences did not bring them together.[42]

When examining the many causes of death among young slaves, smothering or overlaying has received an unusual amount of attention. The inability to explain these deaths led to the assumption that careless, "wearied" mothers were responsible for the deaths. In one slaveholder's mind, the mother was responsible, regardless of the cause. He wrote, "Dolly overlaid her child (Cathrine), about five months old." Victims of "overlaying" or "suffocation" were generally infants between two weeks and one year of age who died without obvious signs of illness during the coldest months of the year. When explaining the death of her child, the former Tunica, Mississippi, slave Tabby Abby told a federal interviewer that she fell asleep while breast-feeding her only child and "rolled over him and smothered him to death." A tone of guilt lingered in her voice. Abby, like many slave mothers, held herself liable and suffered a needless ordeal.[43]

When comparing contemporary infant mortality rates with antebellum records of suffocation, there are similarities. Medical historian Todd Savitt suggests that Sudden Infant Death Syndrome (SIDS) rather than suffocation caused these deaths. The SIDS explanation is plausible since deaths from "suffocation" continued after slavery ended when reasons for resistance were no longer present. Additionally, the high death rates among African American infants continued notwithstanding changes in the working conditions of many mothers. This further suggests that "tired and careless" women did not overlay their children. Current research suggests that numerous children, regardless of race, class, or the season of the year, stop breathing momentarily during sleep. The cause of SIDS remains a mystery.[44]

Poor prenatal care and diets rich in caloric content but inadequate in nutrients, combined with heavy physical work were overriding factors in low birth weights and the resulting high infant mortality rates. Frances Kemble thought that "the number [of children] they bear as compared with the number they rear [is] a fair gauge of the effect of the system on their health and that of their offspring."[45]

The childless Everard Green Baker, a Mississippi planter, agonized over the death of his dog Luck and wrote: "I do not know what feeling a parent has for a child but if our affections for our species are proportionate to those we entertain for the favorite of the brute creation, I never wish to have children if they are to die before me." He eventually became a father and was overwrought when his son fell ill in 1850.[46]

The high incidence of illness and death among their children affected slave and slaveholding parents. Their reactions ran the full gamut. Many consoled themselves with their religion and saw death as the will of a supreme being, a liberator freeing the deceased from a life of drudgery or a grantor of eternal rest and peace. When talking about her child's death, Tabby Abby said, "I like to went crazy for a long time atta dat." Aside from the mental anguish, some slave mothers were visibly shaken. The former South Carolina slave, Fannie Moore, described her mother's reaction when her younger brother died. The girl cared for the child during the day except when their grandmother could get away "from the white folks' kitchen." When the woman returned from the field one night and learned of the child's death, she knelt "by de bed and cry her heart out," Moore recalled. The mother was also at work when the child's uncle carried the body in a pine box to the cemetery. The girl observed the burial from a distance as her mother "just plow and cry as she watch 'em put George in de ground."[47]

Insensitivity to the woman's need to care for her ailing child compounded her anguish, while further heartlessness kept her from the burial, which was a customary observance in the lives of Africans. This was the hardship of a slave woman who left no written records. Although young, Moore shared her mother's grief. Freedom relieved the girl of this potential agony, but the anguish her mother faced made an indelible impression.

The enslaved woman Lydia felt a sense of relief when death liberated her child from bondage. Her husband, an African, prepared the child's body for burial along with "a small bow and several arrows; a little bag of parched meal; a miniature canoe, about a foot long, and a little paddle." Having armed the boy with a sharpened nail attached to a stick and buried him with a piece of white muslin decorated with "several curious and strange figures," the father anticipated his son's return to his "relations and countrymen," who because of this ritual would recognize and receive the child upon his arrival.[48]

FAMILY AND COMMUNITY

Enslaved mothers had a duty to preserve life, yet they received a short reprieve for neonatal care before returning to work. No doubt a spiritual such as "Sometimes I Feel Like a Motherless Child" or "Nobody Knows the Trouble I Have Had" held meaning for parents and children. The demand for labor impeded bonding and childcare. Some owners allowed one month off and assigned light work following childbirth, while others were less considerate. Slavery robbed many youngsters of a safe and nurturing childhood.

Fanny, one of nearly thirty slaves belonging to an Alabama planter, was "lying in" according to the plantation record in early August 1844, and her name reappears on an August 29, 1844, list of working slaves. Another slave, Charity, delivered a child on September 4, 1844, and was back at work one month later. Both women gave birth during the harvest season, when there was a great need for hands. The amount of cotton that they picked did not equal that of the other women, who made up a substantial portion of the labor force, nor what the new mothers had picked previously, because they either left the field regularly to feed their infants or they were not physically able to resume a full work day so soon after parturition.[49]

One of the most unsettling events in the lives of slaves was the early separation of mothers and children when the women returned to work. In small households, individual childcare arrangements were made. Children sometimes accompanied parents to work. Ideally, domestic servants managed well with their children as they cooked, cleaned, or wove fabric, but there were plenty of places where children could have mishaps. Falling down stairs or creeping too near open fireplaces could be equally disastrous. Harriet Jacobs's toddler wandered outside and fell asleep under the house. Fortunately for the child, she did not attract the attention of a large snake which was basking in the coolness nearby.[50]

The children of field hands sometimes accompanied their parents to work. If mothers did not strap the smallest children who could not keep up on their backs, they left them on pallets at the end of rows, near fences, or under trees away from the hot sun. They also made swings in trees or hammocks between trees to keep the babies up off the ground. In the parents' absence, the children could get into mischief or perilous situations.[51]

On plantations with twenty or more slaves, youngsters went to nurseries where their care was in the hands of slaves either too infirm, too old, or too young to work elsewhere. On the White Hill Plantation in Virginia, a woman "with a halt in her step" attended to the children. When the South Carolina slave Friday became unable to work full time, his job was to "notice the yard and the little Negroes." In situations where scores of children needed care, the help was often inadequate and attention wanting. The James Gadsden nursery had nearly seventy children up to fifteen years of age, while a Florida plantation had forty-two youngsters needing care while their parents worked. In the latter situation, only an elderly man and woman worked along with the assistance of youngsters

STOLEN CHILDHOOD

1. Penn School Collection. Courtesy of
the Southern Historical Collection,
University of North Carolina, Chapel
Hill.

to care for the smaller children. The large number of children coupled with the
long hours and limited help made it impossible to provide good care.[52]

General accounts indicate that plantation nurseries were far from adequate.
By contrast, Susan Bradford Eppes remembered pleasant scenes from her family's
plantation when "Aunt Dinah" ran the day nursery "like the kindergarten of
today." Eppes claimed the old woman "told stories, demonstrated how to make
animals from potatoes, orange thorns, a few feathers." The teacher also gave
attention to "practical living" by helping "her pupils 'set table' with mats made
of the green leaves of the jonquils, cups and saucers of acorns, dishes of hickory
hulls and any gay bit of china they could find; and had them bake mud pies in a
broken stove." Needless to say, Aunt Dinah was in the vanguard of the kindergarten movement for enslaved children.[53]

Of more importance than the entertaining narratives and creative crafts were
chances for the children and elderly slaves, serving in loco parentis, to develop
relationships. Children became attached to caregivers and entered into fictive
associations. The extended family, no doubt, existed on financially stable households which did not undergo major transitions upon an owner's death. In the

FAMILY AND COMMUNITY

2. Three boys. Courtesy of the Valentine Museum,
Richmond, Virginia.

absence of relatives, surrogates or fictive families were valuable. Related or not,
older slaves often showed kindness to children. The plethora of "aunts" and
"uncles" indicates that children learned early on to show deference to their
elders in keeping with a traditional African custom.[54]

Just as enslaved parents had little or no control over the care of their children
while they worked, they had little to say about what their children wore.
Slaveholders issued children one or two garments, called a "shirt" if worn by
boys or a "dress" if worn by girls, each year. Booker T. Washington remembered
that the shirt's fabric was "largely refuse," which made it feel like "a dozen or
more chestnut burrs" rubbing upon the skin. It was the "most trying ordeal"
that he was "forced to endure as a slave boy." There was no mention of shoes for
slaves who went barefoot until the coldest months. Slaveholders either bought
cheaply made brogans or manufactured them at home.[55]

Slaveholders were more concerned about the cost of the slaves' clothes and
shoes than about their comfort. To save money, McDonald Furman ordered the
slave children's clothing cut before the annual distribution of material. This
prevented the parents from "wasting or trading off their cloth." On some
plantations, the wives of slaveowners were responsible for making all clothing.

Furman's miserly attitude contrasted sharply with Tryphena Fox's notion about clothing for the enslaved child Adelaide. Fox delighted in making for the five-year-old girl a "dress up" garment, which she "ruffled . . . & took pains to make it fit her very nicely." She also intended to make a "nice white apron" for Adelaide which was more for style than function. This was a clear departure from the usual shift young slaves wore. Of course, differences in the relationships between the slaveholders and their youthful chattel and the sizes of the Fox and Furman holdings were important in shaping their attitudes.[56]

What slaves wore drew attention from casual observers, visitors, and travelers. The slaveholders were aware of their remarks. Comments about the clothing of slaves prompted W. W. Gilmer to address the matter in the April 1852 *Southern Cultivator*. "A lot of ragged little negroes," he wrote, "always gives a bad impression to strangers." Gilmer drew a connection between material well-being and malleability. On another level, ragged, dirty slave children fostered comments about negligent parents. It was virtually impossible to keep creeping and crawling children clean in cabins with dirt floors. Besides, slaves ordinarily worked until nightfall and had little time afterwards to attend to personal needs. Furthermore, the harsh laundry method including the use of lye soap or mud contributed to the deterioration of their meager clothing supply.[57]

Slave children were aware of their clothing, especially when in the proximity of well-cared-for children of slaveowners or others. One owner claimed a little girl walked "five times faster" wearing a "new" dress handed down to her from a white child. Proud and puffed up, the girl's younger brother showed a similar delight as he strutted around in a "new" bonnet. Slave children did not have to see other children to know of their conditions when suffering from the winter cold. Additionally, cost-conscious owners paid little attention to growth patterns and allowed boys to wear shirts well beyond a time when they met ordinary standards of modesty. An officer in the First Pennsylvania Regiment remembered the inadequate clothes of adolescent boys in Virginia as they served dinners. He wrote:

> I am surprised this does not hurt the feelings of the fair Sex to see young boys of about Fourteen and Fifteen years Old to Attend them. Their whole nakedness Expos'd and I can Assure you It would Surprize a person to see these d—d black boys how well they are hung.

This hardly changed over the years. Gilmer believed an adequate supply of clothes elevated their self-esteem and improved their behavior. Frederick Douglass rejected the idea. "The feeding and clothing me well," Douglass said as he pondered about his childhood, "could not atone for taking my liberty from me."[58]

Families could and did augment food supplies by earning personal money through overwork and the sale of produce or any other articles of value, such as handmade baskets. They also cultivated gardens, raised poultry, collected berries, and hunted game in their free time. Ordinarily, women had fewer opportunities for skilled overwork than men; consequently, they had less money to provide additional rations. However, there were resourceful women who used other tactics to supplement the family rations. A former Missouri slave said, "My mamma could hunt good ez any man." Furthermore, she traded the pelts for "calico prints n' trinkets."[59]

There is evidence to suggest that the lives of children living along the South Carolina and Georgia rice coast differed from those of children in other agricultural areas because of the nature of agricultural production in their region. It favored the task system, in which workers received specified assignments to complete by the end of the day or week. They set their own pace and worked without strict supervision, which allowed a degree of autonomy. At the completion of the job, laborers used any time left over for themselves. In their "free time," they pursued interests to make their lives more tolerable, including spending more time with their children. Some took on extra work to earn money for additional food (for example, sugar, coffee, flour), or clothing, for themselves and their children. Of greater importance, chances to buy freedom for themselves or their children existed.[60]

The children in Low Country households benefited materially from the task system when parents owned livestock and poultry which they sold or traded. The sale of goods involved negotiations, which indicates that slaves had some control over the arrangement. Slaves also insisted upon the observance of customary rights which protected their time and property from infringement by owners. Furthermore, the self-esteem of the children rose when their parents, whom they must have admired, could and did supplement their livelihood and made decisions regarding the family's well-being. With encouragement from parents or by their own initiative, some children had possessions of their own. One ex-slave said that he had raised stock "ever since I had sense," while another said that he had poultry "almost as soon as I could walk." It was not unusual for children to "inherit" property from their parents.[61]

In agricultural regions outside of the Low Country, parents had less to say about their children's material comfort; nevertheless, their emotional well-being regardless of their domicile was of great importance. Bondage determined the quantity of time parents could spend with their children; consequently, mothers and fathers had to determine the quality of that time. The former slave John Collins, of South Carolina, said his father "used to play wid mammy just lak she was a child." He recalled seeing him "ketch her under de armpits and jump her up mighty nigh to de rafters." To be sure, there were other pleasant scenes where slave families showed love and affection for each other. The North Carolina slave Allen, a partner in an abroad marriage, generally crossed a river to visit his wife and children, thereby shortening the distance between their abodes and lengthening their time together.[62]

The status of Allen's family was not unlike that of an untold number of other slave families involved in abroad marriages. The children of the South Carolina couple Sampson and Maria felt the sting of separations more keenly than Allen's children. Following an October 1847 visit to his wife and children, Sampson drowned while crossing the river to return to the rice plantation owned by Charles Manigault. Perhaps his children did not fully understand why their parents did not live together, but it is clear that Sampson cared about his wife and children, and he went to great lengths to visit them.[63]

As enslaved children matured, they established significant relationships with their siblings and peers. Narratives by ex-slave women offer detailed descriptions of early childhood and relationships among contemporaries more frequently than those of enslaved men. The lack of relevant questions or the relative newness of the sibling rivalry concept may explain the absence of its mention in the WPA narratives. It is likely that slaves shared experiences rather than competed against each other in any meaningful way. Slavery created a sense of community or solidarity which faltered in a competitive atmosphere designed to benefit others. Slaves frequently assisted one another and when circumstances allowed created tolerable situations for each other. John Washington, for example, showed sensitivity for his younger brother Booker when he offered to "break in" Booker's new shirt. Booker considered John's sensitivity as "one of the most generous acts that I ever heard of one slave relative doing for another."[64]

Relationships with family members and others in the community helped the children and youth adjust to and endure slavery. "You know I am one man that do love my children," wrote an ex-slave. Although he had not seen the children in many years, the words were linked to memories of their time together before the involuntary separation. Perhaps memories of those times also assuaged the children. In many situations, parents played a major role in the lives of enslaved children. They used their influence and protection whenever possible. Lucy Skipwith, a woman owned by the Virginian John Hartwell Cocke, successfully interceded on her daughter's behalf when he threatened to sell the girl in 1859.[65]

Lucy Skipwith succeeded only by capitalizing upon a close working relationship with Cocke which allowed her to ingratiate herself with him at every turn. The slaveowner spent much of his time in Virginia and during his absence from Hopewell, the Alabama plantation where Lucy lived, she kept him informed about intricate details of everyday life through regular correspondence. Lucy assumed power at Hopewell that no ordinary slave woman possessed. Cocke allowed it since she served as his eyes and ears during his absence. Knowing his interest in the children, Lucy touched a vulnerable spot when she argued that her daughter would be better off in the environment he provided at Hopewell than if she were sold to persons less concerned about her development. She turned her plea into a compliment, and Cocke repaid the favor.[66]

The energy needed to work and to rear children under adverse conditions exacted much from slave parents. They were often too burdened by the duties of being laborers to indulge their children, yet many never stopped trying to foster positive relationships with them. Although she was too busy "to give attention to the training of her children during the day," Booker T. Washington's mother "snatched" a few minutes before and after work to care for him and his siblings. Frederick Douglass never saw his mother "by the light of day" because of the distance between her place of work and his home. Her sporadic nocturnal visits were brief because she always came after work and left early the next day. Her timing suggests that she traveled without permission. Both mothers exerted extra effort for the well-being of their children. Douglass remembered his mother and the sacrifice of her acts.[67]

This raises questions about the responsibility parents bore in protecting their children and the extent to which they would go to succeed. How humiliating was it to arrange for one's own sale in order to keep the family together? How much effort did it take to placate former owners to get information about family and friends? Letters of inquiry written by slaves to slaveholders have uniformly humble tones. Lucy Skipwith trod gingerly with Cocke as she maneuvered the situation to her advantage. What were the true feelings of slave parents toward owners? Lester, a slave in Georgia, wrote to his former playmate and owner in 1857 to inquire about the fate of his daughter in North Carolina. The carefully worded "by Enscribing my Self your long loved and well wishing servant until death" ended his letter. It was more important for Lester to create the climate for a response about his daughter than to let the owner know his true sentiments. Older slaves disguised their feelings and taught their children to do the same.[68]

The parents did all within their power to buffer abuses and cushion denials in order to help youngsters adjust until freed of slavery. Many slave narratives speak lovingly of mothers and fathers whose mettle and prayers encouraged them to endure. William Wells Brown's mother was very special to him. His recollection of her provides the powerful testimony to the interlocked lives of slave mothers and their children. "I half forgot the name of slave," he said, "when she was by my side."[69]

2 "US AIN'T NEVER IDLE"*

THE WORLD OF WORK

> From the time that I can remember anything,
> almost every day of my life has been occupied
> in some kind of labor.
>
> —Booker T. Washington**

Slaves' lives followed an identifiable progression of stages; however, slaveowners truncated segments of the cycle to satisfy themselves. One of the greatest disruptions in their lives was the quantum leap from childhood into the world of work. As a youngster Frederick Douglass remembered, "We were worked in all weather. It was never too hot or too cold; it could never rain, blow hail, or snow, too hard for us to work in the field. Work, work, work, was scarcely more the order of the day than of the night." Work can be rightly called the thief who stole the childhood of youthful bond servants.[1]

Slaveowners initially used children to complement workers, but as they both grew older, children became experienced substitutes for aging adult laborers and finally replaced them. "The rigors of a field," remembered Douglass, "less tolerable than the field of battle, awaited me." A child's entry into the labor force made an impact upon the wider community since it meant an additional hand, despite the size, performing jobs. Enslaved youngsters accomplished many jobs that any adult could complete, even if it took two or more children.[2]

This chapter focuses on the roles of children and youth as bond laborers in the nineteenth-century South. Any study of slaves must examine their work since the expropriation of labor from young and old bond servants was an overarching reason for slavery. Many chores were not gender-specific; therefore, boys as well as girls entered the work place at early ages. They were now more readily subjected to punishment from whites and to separations from their parents through sales or hiring out.

---

* Norman R. Yetman, *Life Under the "Peculiar Institution": Selections from the Slave Narrative Collection* (New York: Holt, Rinehart and Winston, 1970), 40.

** Booker T. Washington, *Up from Slavery, An Autobiography* (New York: Bantam, 1967), 4.

STOLEN CHILDHOOD

A South Carolina overseer said light chores made the children "acquire habits of perseverance and industry." Furthermore, it kept them from mischief. An examination of work patterns and conditions answers questions about the nature of interpersonal relationships with other enslaved children and adults, how youngsters' adjustment to authority in the work place and their attitudes about work provide insight about the conditions under which they toiled.[3]

Throughout history children have worked to help support themselves and their parents. Enslaved youngsters differed in that their parents, who did not benefit directly from their efforts, made few, if any, decisions about their own work and that of their offspring. Slaveowners, who benefited from their toil, often preferred young slaves in order to reap the rewards of their labor indefinitely. Arguments against child labor did not assume national dimensions until near the turn of the twentieth century. The initial concern of reformers was to regulate child labor rather than to abolish it. Had these arguments taken place in antebellum America, slaves would not have figured importantly, for they were chattel without legal rights. Besides, the majority of slaves worked in agricultural pursuits, domestic, and personal services which have defied regulations over time.[4]

Entry into the work place entitled enslaved youngsters to additional food commensurate with extra responsibilities. The planter McDonald Furman, for example, specified that "full allowances" should go to "small [children] that work in the field," while children who did not work received the "half allowance." In 1856 Francis Terry Leak, owner of plantations in Mississippi and Arkansas, authorized "store orders" based upon age and work. Children under ten years of age who were not working received a fifty-cent allowance, and the working children under ten years of age received an allowance of one dollar. He wrote, "Allow each negro 16 & upward 3.00." The slaveholder William Sims provided a rooster and several hens for slave couples. When their children were "large enough to go to the field," Sims asked the overseer to increase their "stock" by one hen. Once the children reached fifteen years of age, they could have their own stock.[5]

The ages at which slaves engaged in regular routines varied according to slaveowners and the size of their holdings. Thomas Jefferson ordered that "children till 10. years old to serve as nurses. from 10. to 16. the boys make nails, the girls spin. at age 16. go into the grounds or learn trades." Moreover, the classification of workers as fractional hands means some were either too young, too old, or too infirm to work full time. A Virginia planter's 1849 property inventory included a partially blind fifty-year-old slave who received the same designation, one-quarter hand, as Harriet, a "sickly" eighteen-year-old slave who was of "very little account." The inventory described seventy-year-old Daniel as an "old and decriped" half-hand, while it listed two other half-hands, Little Bob and Julius, twelve-year-old boys valued at $800 each, as "very good" and a "good boy," respectively.[6]

Young slaves, at Monticello and elsewhere, toiled at specific chores, in labor gangs, and under the task system. Individual chores were most common in personal services, domestic work, skilled crafts, and industrial production. Agriculture work, such as the cultivation of cotton, sugar cane, or tobacco required gang labor, while the rice culture along the coasts of Georgia and South Carolina favored the task system. Each pattern had advantages and disadvantages. For example, the task system allowed some "free time" if workers completed assigned tasks in a timely manner. On the obverse side, tasks were sometimes too large to complete in the allotted time and could incur punishment. Furthermore, individual work allowed slaves to distinguish themselves, but it also meant they faced greater scrutiny than those working in groups. Additionally, community support was not immediately at hand for individuals, whereas gang laborers could find solace among those working nearby.

In an unusual arrangement, William Jemison, an Alabama slaveholder, issued a proclamation to his bond servants effective January 1, 1827, whereby they were under the supervision of the overseer Richard Cole; however, they had some latitude, provided they were honest, careful, and industrious. Jemison proposed to give them "two thirds of the corn and cotton made on the plantation as much of the wheat as will reward you for the sowing it." The slaves were to pay their overseer, clothe themselves, pay their taxes, and doctor's fees. Jemison required one-third of the crop and the return of the tools which he loaned. Without equivocation he wrote, "You are to be no expense to me." He admonished them to divide equally whatever clear money they made in proportion to services rendered by each hand. This arrangement provided incentives for ambitious workers who could serve as role models for the youngsters on Jemison's plantation.[7]

Regardless of the labor system, children began to work at young ages. In an interview near Houston, Texas, in the 1930s, the former slave Jacob Branch remembered his childhood. "Us chillen start to work soon's us could toddle. First us gather firewood. Iffen its freezin' or hot us have to go to toughen us up." Things hardly changed as they grew a "li'l bigger," they had to "tend de cattle and feed hosses and hogs." Branch added, "By the time us good sprouts, us pickin' cotton and pullin' corn." Many ex-slaves claimed they began working as soon as they were old enough to perform simple chores and continued throughout their lives with few exceptions. "I weren't nothing but child endurin' slavery, but I had to work the same as any man," recalled Mingo White, an ex-bondsman from Alabama.[8]

The Georgia-born Andrew Moss claimed he worked in the field when he was too young to manage regular-size tools, but "dey had little hoes," obviously designed for the young workers, who "walked many a mile . . . up and down de rows, followin' de grownfolks" chopping weeds. Accounts such as those from White, Branch, and Moss raise questions about the veracity of the slave's memories and accuracy of the WPA narratives. Did they overstate the case or did slaveholders exact labor from such little children?[9]

STOLEN CHILDHOOD

If Tryphena Fox were representative of other small slaveholders, her attitude about young bond servants offers insight into what owners expected from their youthful chattel. Fox decided to take the seven-year-old Adelaide, whom she described as "not very black" with "good features," on January 1, 1859, and "make a house-girl of her." Fox planned to "take a great deal of pains to bring her up to be faithful & smart & cleanly in her habits." Fox wanted a well-trained slave for life.[10]

After owning the child for little more than a year, Fox knew that Adelaide was "bright" and "quick to learn." The "good natured" child possessed additional characteristics suitable for house servants at Hygiene, the Fox home. In 1860 when Maria, a teenaged servant also owned by Fox, fell ill, she divided the girl's chores between "Old Reuben," the manservant, and Adelaide. Fox reasoned that the child could "shell the corn & feed the chickens & little ducks & turkeys very well." The owner wrote, "You have no idea how useful she is." She added, "& I could hardly get along without her."[11]

The testimony of WPA interviewees does not differ in terms of the jobs they performed and what an owner required of a child at a comparable age. Fox's letters about Adelaide's work span the years between 1858 and 1863. The girl was thirteen years of age when the Civil War ended.[12]

Whether children worked in large or small households for persons who owned or hired them, they performed a variety of chores. In the nineteenth century, an estimated 5 to 10 percent of the slave population and nearly one-third of urban slaves, depending upon the area, worked as hired hands. Based upon a study of slave hires in Elizabeth City County, Virginia, between 1782 and 1810, Sarah S. Hughes posited that "before their childhood ended, most blacks spent at least a year working as a hired servant outside their home household."[13]

Slavery forced children to "grow up" fast and perform "adult" jobs including caring for children. Louise Jones, who was nearly ten years old when slavery ended, recalled caring for babies and using meat skin tied to a string around their necks as a pacifier. Not all nurses were so attentive. Sometimes they became weary of the crying, fretting babies, and they ignored them. At other times, play engulfed the nurses, and they forgot their charges. Enslaved mothers occasionally returned to find their babies unattended, in the sun, covered with flies, or even worse covered with mosquito bites. In their naivete, young caregivers sometimes placed themselves and their charges in danger. The string holding the meat could have easily become entangled about the child's neck with disastrous results. Jones used it to retrieve the meat from the child's throat to prevent choking. Nevertheless, there is no way of knowing how many youngsters suffered injuries or death because of negligence or some unwitting act by youthful caregivers.[14]

Aside from attending to babies, young slaves performed any task thought necessary by owners or persons who hired them. The former slave Charles Davenport, interviewed at Natchez, Mississippi, remembered that "all de little darkies helped bring in wood," pulled weeds, and worked to keep yards swept clean with brush brooms. The Missouri-born Mary Bell had a job that was somewhat unusual. "Dey put me on a pony at meal time," she said, "to ride out to de field and call de hands to dinner." William Hutson, who lived in Tulsa, Oklahoma, when interviewed, said he carried a little black bag when his owner went "a-doctering folks." Frederick Douglass had a variety of early work experiences. He kept fowl out of the garden, ran errands, and accompanied his owner on hunting trips to retrieve the dead birds. Charles Manigault, a South Carolina planter, foresaw the need for "some small boy to gather wood" and perform personal services for a Mr. Venters, such as "run with his umbrella and great coat in case he should be caught by rain in the field."[15]

The little workers were in abundance. Between 1820 and 1860 the number of slaves under twenty years of age exceeded the number of those over twenty years old. Joseph H. Ingraham, an Episcopal minister and prolific writer, mentioned their presence in Not "A Fool's Errand," when he wrote:

> The carriage driver must not only have his deputy ostler. . . . The gardener has his aides; the farm-nurse hers and all this army of juveniles are in full training to take the places, by-and-by, of those to whom they are apprended. . . .

He accurately predicted the outcome of on-the-job training for the children.[16]

After ten years of age, children worked at more routinized domestic, agricultural, or industrial jobs. The size and location of a house, farm, or shop determined the amount and kind of work performed. Cash crops such as indigo, rice, cotton, and sugar cane grew in the South, while wheat grew outside the slaveholding states after the nineteenth century. Corn and other subsistence crops thrived throughout the agricultural region. Domestic and personal service work knew no geographical boundaries; besides, it was adaptable to private and public places such as inns, hotels, or taverns. The freedman Frank Bell, living in Texas when interviewed, used housekeeping skills in the saloon where he worked as a child to keep "everything cleaned up after they'd [patrons] have all night drinkin' parties." Slaves performed industrial work including spinning, weaving, milling, and ginning, in private homes and public establishments of the urban and rural South.[17]

Housewifery and domestic work were the two distinct categories of work for house servants. Domestic work involved preparing and preserving food, cleaning and maintaining living quarters, and caring for children, besides laundering and repairing clothes. Domestic work also encompassed personal services. Housewifery required the care of poultry and livestock in addition to the manufacturing of clothes and household items including soap and candles. The size of a household determined whether these categories were clearly defined or blurred. Furthermore, many of these chores were gender-blind; consequently, slave boys and girls cleaned, served meals, attended to the poultry, and assisted in making clothes. Once the ex-slave George Briggs was old enough to work, he cut branches from hickory trees to make broom handles. He also made whips, shoe laces, galluses, and saddle strings from the leather tanned on the property where he lived in South Carolina.[18]

The Arkansan Lucretia Alexander told federal interviewers about her jobs of cleaning house, putting up mosquito bars, and packing water to field hands. As a boy, the Tennessee-born Henry Bibb's duties included cleaning floors and polishing furniture. The boy also catered to his owner, who sometimes sat motionless in a rocking chair while the child pushed it. "She was too lazy to scratch her own head," he complained, "and would often make me scratch and comb it for her." Bibb continued, "She would at times lie on the bed, in warm weather, and make me fan her while she slept, scratch and rub her feet, but after a while she got sick of me and preferred a maiden servant to do such business." His tone does not convey any unhappiness about a girl displacing him. It was more usual for boys to act as personal servants for men rather than for women.[19]

Cornelius Garner, a youngster in antebellum Virginia, unlike Bibb, seemed to enjoy catering to his owner, who liked "his ho'sses looking fine." Garner said, "I made hit my business to keep dem ho'sses looking spic and span," and "Massa, seeing dat I was inrested in his ho'sses . . . kept me sorta close 'round de house." In such a master-slave relationship, both parties received mutual benefits and each was aware of the other's expectations.[20]

The nature of their jobs and the circumstances under which the former slaves related their life experiences differed. Furthermore, Bibb recounted his experiences through a nineteenth-century autobiography, whereas Garner related his recollections to federal workers in the 1930s. Differences in the times of their narratives matter, as well as the ages of the narrators along with the amount of time spent in slavery. It is doubtful if Garner, as a child, understood the magnitude of the relationship with his owner. Even so, he may have objected to disclosing his true feelings to the interviewer.

An examination of testimony from ex-slaves, which ran the full gamut, offers insights about how young slaves viewed their jobs and themselves as workers. The WPA narratives are sometimes ambiguous, but there is no doubt that Dora Franks of Aberdeen, Mississippi, was boasting when she said, "Before I was bigger'n a minute I could do things dat lots o' de old hands couldn't come nigh doin'." She felt good about her accomplishments. It is not clear if West Turner bragged or complained about plowing at fifteen years of age. He could not reach the plow handles comfortably and managed only by putting his "head under de cross bar" and wrapping his "arms roun' de sides while another boy led the mule" up and down the rows of the Virginia farm where he lived.[21]

Although some women plowed, it was considered by many to be a man's job. For an adolescent boy, work as a plow hand signaled his entry into manhood. Furthermore, men wore pants. One advantage here in separating the men from the boys was to remove any embarrassment caused by wearing shirts that did not hide the nakedness of rapidly growing adolescents. Knowing that the kind of clothing received changed as they reached manhood prompted some boys to become plow hands. Perhaps it played a part in West Turner's eagerness.[22]

James Monroe Abbot, interviewed in Missouri long after slavery ended, reported that he began his job as a house servant when only seven years old. His responsibility was to stand continuously at his owner's bedside to keep flies away during a lengthy illness. "But at las' he died," and the freedman remembered the pleasure of a house-bound child who learned that he could go out to play. Abbot recalled running outside and telling each passerby, "By God, he's daid," without the slightest tinge of grief. The child's sister heard his rendition of the news and accused him of "cussing," rather than admonishing him to show respect for the dead. When he gleefully repeated the message to his mother, she turned her back and began shaking with laughter. Despite the insensitive tone of his message, the mother understood his happiness at gaining a modicum of freedom.[23]

Some children found enjoyment in their work. Julia Frazer, a house servant in Virginia, "liked dustin' best." As she cleaned the library, she fingered through books scattered about the room. Her favorite book contained illustrations of "Injuns and kings and queens wid reefs on dey heads." Annie Terry, interviewed in the 1930s, had no complaints about her work since she "did nothing practically besides play with the little daughter and son" of her owner. Furthermore, Terry's brother was the wagoner, and she frequently rode into town with him.[24]

Testimonies from Frazer and Terry reflect similar working conditions, and the length of their time in bondage was more nearly the same than that of Bibb and Garner. Furthermore, the circumstances under which Frazer and Terry gave their interviews were more alike than in the former instance. Numerous WPA narratives like Terry and Frazer's describe pleasant domestic work experiences. An estimated 20 percent of those interviewed were under five years of age when slavery ended. As a result, those children did not experience full entry into the work force.[25]

If one examines the processes involved in the day-to-day operation of a nineteenth-century southern household, it is obvious that domestic work was quite laborious. Skills necessary for cooking and laundering, two of the most arduous jobs, were beyond the ken and capabilities of most children. Meal preparation included carrying water, chopping or hauling wood, and building fires. Serving fresh vegetables meant gathering produce in addition to shelling, peeling, or washing it. Game, poultry, or fish required dressing, plucking, or scaling, while the cook retrieved other meats from the smokehouse. After the preparations, the final chore involved cooking, serving, and cleaning the kitchen before retiring for the evening. The plantation cook's culinary creations and plain fares had to please and satisfy owners. This was a large job even for adults to perform alone. "The cook must have a strapping lad," according to Ingraham, "to chop wood, bring the water, and be at hand." He added, "two or three small fry" were necessary "to catch the poultry, [and] turn the spit" to roast the fowl.[26]

The entire process of washing and ironing clothes was no less complicated; therefore, the laundress had a separate day for washing and another for ironing. One weekly wash and rinse for an average-size family required at least fifty gallons, or four hundred pounds, of water. Hot water was necessary for washing the clothes; therefore, hauling wood and building fires added more work. Heavily soiled clothes required overnight soaking in cold water before scrubbing and boiling in large kettles to further remove stains. Each time the laundress removed wet clothes from one container to another—from the wash to the rinse or from the soaking water to the wash pot for boiling and then into the rinse— she removed the clothes and squeezed the water out. The final process involved lifting and wringing water from ordinary garments before hanging them on clotheslines outside. The "fancy wash"—special clothes and some household linens—might need starch, therefore requiring another process before hanging the laundry out to dry. The total weight lifted in one day was monumental and exhausted the best of laundresses.[27]

Based upon his observations after living in one of the most densely populated slave states, Ingraham claimed that the slave laundress

> must be waited on by a little Negress, to kindle her fires, heat her irons, and do everything that the dignity of the "lady" in question deem it "derogatorium" for her to put her hands to. The chief washer-woman has from two to four ebony maids who do the grosser work while she does the "fancy washing."

No doubt the clergyman cast aspersions at the washerwomen, yet he was again on the mark in noting that slave children most often assisted with the laundry rather than handling it alone.[28]

As a girl, Lucy Delaney, born in Missouri, had no idea about the amount of work involved in washing clothes when her owner's wife, who was a few years older, insisted that Lucy wash the clothes. With water drawn from the Mississippi River and no knowledge of how to clarify it, Lucy's efforts were in vain. The clothes became more and more dingy with each soaking and boiling. In the meantime, the woman called Lucy "a lazy good-for-nothing nigger." Perplexed and afraid of punishment, Lucy protested that she expected "a poor ignorant girl to know more" about laundering clothes than her owner. The girl believed if the woman "had any feelings" she would have someone to teach her how to wash the clothes. When reasoning failed, Lucy sought help from an older enslaved woman.[29]

In good weather, clothes dried with a minimum of difficulty, yet the washerwoman was ever watchful of sudden downpours. During the winter when there was less sunshine, clothes often dried on makeshift lines inside the house. Under these conditions, clothes sometimes soured before drying. In such cases, the laundering process began anew. Washerwomen, not always succeeding, were also careful to guard against mildew, which ruined the appearance of garments.[30]

Ironing required heating metal "flat irons" to remove wrinkles without burning or otherwise ruining fabrics. The skill needed for this feat was beyond that of most children, and to trust the family's laundry to young inexperienced slaves was to invite disaster.

The former slaves' attitude about domestic work varied according to the situation. Much has been written about the better quality of food, clothing, and shelter of domestics compared to that of field hands. Until recently, many believed domestics were indeed better off; however, a closer examination of records shows that domestic work was a bittersweet experience. House servants did not toil in the hot sun under the supervision of a driver or overseer. Domestics were inside but under the gimlet eye of an owner or someone else in charge who could be as demanding as a plantation overseer. The setting of the sun did not signal the end of their day since they remained at the beck and call of owners night and day.[31]

There was no assurance that the treatment of house servants would be kind or fair. The geographical location, size of the household, and economic status of the slaveowner were determining factors in their fate. Their experiences differed. Chock Archie, a former house slave from Alabama, "received absolutely good treatment," and claimed he knew nothing of the horrors of slavery until visiting his mother's cabin in the quarters. By contrast, many house servants complained about sleeping upon pallets, in the rooms with their owners, in attics, or stairwells. Because of the poor standard of living in the antebellum South, it is understandable that Lue Bradford, a Kentucky house girl, struggled to keep warm. "Sometimes in the winter I would catch afire trying to keep warm as the fire [in the fireplace] would get so low," she recalled, "I had to roll so close that my clothes or quilt would catch afire." Physical comfort was as much of a problem as physical safety for some servants. As a youngster, Delia Garlic incurred the wrath of her owner, who believed she was careless with the child in her care. The woman "whirled" on the girl, picked up a hot iron, "ran it all down" her arm and hand, and took "off all de flesh when she done it." Frederick Douglass described a tragedy that befell a member of his wife's family, a teenaged housegirl, who endured a broken nose and breastbone as a result of a severe beating. Her offense was falling asleep and not responding to the crying infant in her care. The owner, Mrs. Hicks, became irate and attacked the girl with an oak stick and "thus ended her life." Accounts of cruelties abound, and the defenselessness of the children in question adds a different dimension to the study of slavery.[32]

Children working in or about their owner's home were not strangers to other housewifery duties. They fed chickens and gathered eggs, milked cows, and churned butter. The slaveholder's wife made soap and candles and often assumed that she alone could dip candles to perfection. Martha Tabb Dyer, wife of a Missouri slaveholder, dipped eighteen dozen candles in a day, more than half the average, thirty dozen candles, that a skilled candlemaker made in a day. After completion, the slaveholder's wife kept candles locked away and "rationed" them within her own household. Slaves lighted their cabins with pine knots. Although they did not enjoy all fruits of their labor, slave children helped make candles by gathering bayberries for the wax and picked up wood chips to heat the wax or tallow.[33]

STOLEN CHILDHOOD

Children played a larger role in spinning thread and weaving cloth. In households where clothes were made for all members of the household, white and black, the woman of the house was responsible for the overall production. Whether working alone or with the help of servants, all members of the family received some wearing apparel. Two suits of clothes, one for winter and the other for summer, were standard. The manufacture of clothes took place in the main house or in a loom house designed for that purpose. The process involved spinning thread, weaving cloth, and dying fabric before fashioning it into garments of cotton, flax, wool, or other fibers. One ex-slave remembered her childhood days when "de man wud shear de sheep and chillums wud pick de burrs out of the wool . . . wash it and spread it on the grass tuh dry." Youngsters also helped to "card it an' den spin de thread and weave de cloth."[34]

Children learned skills through apprenticeships or by working with others in more casual settings such as the quilting "frolics" and "parties." As a youngster, Dora Franks said "Miss Emmaline" taught her to spin and weave, while the Alabamian Mingo White learned a skill by helping his mother when he thought her nightly chore of spinning and carding four cuts of thread (approximately 300 yards) was "too hard for any one person" after a full day of work as a house servant. If she did not finish it, she received fifty lashes. "Many de night me an' her would spin and card," he said, "so she culd get her task de next day." Working at a more relaxed pace in North Carolina, Mary Armstrong combined spinning with taking care of children. "I spins six cuts of thread a week" and had "plenty of time for myself," she recalled. White's observation was correct about the amount of work expected. His mother finished the assignment and avoided punishments because they worked late into the night. White's sensitivity to his mother was in keeping with that of other slaves, who tended to help others avoid punishment. The efforts of slave parents and others in the community along with the participation in "trash gangs," agricultural units made up of children, pregnant women, and older workers, raised the consciousness of youngsters who imitated their elders.[35]

Sensitivity to the needs of others was a desirable characteristic whether working inside the household or outside in the fields. Besides, working in the house did not mean permanency. The size of the household, poor behavior, failure to perform jobs satisfactorily, or the need for additional hands elsewhere prompted changes. Frank, a dining room servant in a Louisiana household in 1857, annoyed the slaveholder's wife, who believed that he was "too slow and stupid" to perform efficiently; therefore, the owner removed him. Large numbers of children worked about the owner's house until they were old enough to work elsewhere. Prince Johnson recalled that an old slave on the Mississippi plantation where he lived routinely took house servants into the fields to acquaint them with the work. Only a selected number remained in the house after entering their teens. Numerous accounts exist of slaves moving from the house to the field, but the reverse pattern was rare.[36]

The change from domestic work to other forms of labor did not perturb youngsters as much as it did older slaves who had clearer understandings of what each occupation entailed and the status gained or lost with job changes. It is open to question as to how slave children and youths viewed their conditions as they experienced them.[37]

Regardless of their ideas about domestic or field work, most slaves in the nineteenth-century South were field hands and never worked in the house. A relationship existed between the occupations of parents and that of their off-spring. There were many field slaves on farms or plantations where cash crops such as tobacco, indigo, rice, cotton, or sugar cane grew along with foodstuff. Field work was not gender-specific; therefore, boys and girls worked along with enslaved men and women. Although the work was seasonal, there were enough jobs related to agricultural production to keep slaves busy throughout the year.[38]

Enslaved youngsters labored in the fields alongside family, friends, or others. Clayton Holbert remembered that his Tennessee owner "always had a man in the field to teach the small boys to work." William S. Pettigrew, a North Carolina slaveholder, sought the expertise of Eli Moore, a free man, to instruct his slaves in the use of the scythe. Pettigrew was willing to pay Moore $1.50 per day for his instructions. The agricultural work of slaves often required more endurance than skill.[39]

Tobacco, a demanding crop, requires careful cultivation. Hands cropped the center stalk from each plant to prevent seed formation. As this work progressed, children were ever mindful of breaking leaves off, which meant certain punishment. Many ex-slaves vividly recalled worming tobacco, a most unpleasant chore. Without chemical pesticides, they removed insects by hand. Youngsters overlooking pests suffered the consequences. Nancy Williams of Norfolk, Virginia, began working in tobacco fields when she was only five or six years old. Another girl, Crissy, who was "workin' on the next row, and kep whisperin'" to Nancy, "Pick em all off." Either Nancy did not hear or did not understand the warning. "Purty soon old massa come long . . . an' see . . . some of the terbaccy worms." He collected them and "stuffed em inter my mouth," Nancy said. Simon Stokes's overseer gave him a choice of punishments when he overlooked the worms. The boy could either receive a whipping or bite all insects he left behind. Stokes reasoned that the whip "wuz pow'full bad, wusser dan bittin' de worms." Besides, he said, "Yo could bite right smart quick, and dat wuz all dar wuz to it, but them lashes done last a pow'full long time."[40]

After harvesting, more laborious work lay ahead, such as curing, grading, and shipping the tobacco to market. The myriad interests of the Georgia slaveholder Farish Carter are seen in his papers, which list "Billy & Geremiah 9, Seaborn 10, Isaiah 12, George & Smith & Joseph 8, Deniel 11, Willburn 8, Alexander 10" as "Children at Tobacco Factory" in Dalton, Georgia. Carter often bought, sold, and hired out his slaves. In all probability, the children were hired out to help with the final processing of the tobacco.[41]

By the nineteenth century, planters used "fire curing" extensively rather than the "air curing" method. Wood gathered from newly cleared land went into fires built upon earthen floors in tobacco houses. Slave children helped cut and haul wood for that purpose as well as for the manufacture of containers to transport the tobacco to market. Perhaps they kept pace by singing:

> A col' frosty mo'nin'
> De niggers mighty good
> Take yo' ax upon yo' shoulder,
> Nigger, TALK to de wood.

Another variation of the woodcutter's song claimed, "De niggers feelin' good."[42]

In many places of the South, gangs of children were among the workers when cotton ripened each year. There were two primary varieties, long staple or Sea Island, which accounted for about 1 percent of the total production, and the remainder was upland or short staple cotton. Cultivation of the two varieties was so different that each had a separate set of requirements; yet the harvesting processes were identical. Children often picked more upland cotton per day than an adult could gather from the Sea Island variety, which had a low average of only twenty-five pounds per day. The South Carolinian, Thomas B. Chaplin, began his 1845 harvest with four hands in August and added more pickers as needed. By September 21, slaves had gathered only 1,989 pounds of cotton. Later in the season he wrote, "Yesterday I made the best picking of cotton I have made this season: 28 hands old & young, little & big, brought in 963 pounds," or slightly more than thirty-four pounds per person.[43]

The yield was quite different with upland cotton. The daily records from an Alabama plantation in 1841 indicate that three girls, Amy, Emaline, and Fanny, of unknown ages, worked in the field with adults. The amount of cotton they picked within a five-day period was far less than that of other female slaves, which suggests that they were not experienced cotton pickers. The smallest amount they collected occurred on the fourth day because of rain. On October 29 and 30, 1841, their names do not appear, but there is a notation, "Too cold for the children to pick," followed by "No boys excused only girls."[44]

Ordinarily, slaveowners and overseers made little or no distinction based upon gender in many facets of field labor. Both men and women picked cotton, but why the girls received special treatment is open to speculation. Adolescent girls and premenopausal women were likely to miss days from work because of menstrual discomforts. Menstruating women, according to folklore, were to avoid chills and dampness. Owners and overseers made allowances for them. It is unlikely that Amy, Emaline, and Fanny had reached menarche or that all three would have had dysmenorrhea simultaneously.

Two years later the three girls were still among the Ruffin slaves. Each girl now picked more than 150 pounds of cotton per day. By late September Emaline picked 205 pounds, and Amy collected 212 pounds, while Fanny lagged behind with 200 pounds of cotton. Their daily total continued in this manner throughout the 1843 season. In 1844 Amy and Fanny did not appear with Emaline, who regularly picked at least 200 pounds of cotton each day with her highest total of 246 pounds that year. Although it is not clear what happened to Amy, possibilities abound. She could have received another job on the Ruffin plantation, been hired out, or sold. Perhaps she ran away. Fanny was "lying in."[45]

This brief record reveals not only the annual increase in the amount of cotton each girl gathered, it also indicates that they worked in tandem, which further suggests that they complied with standards. The amount of cotton picked one day served as the yardstick for what one could do on succeeding days barring unforeseen events. An ex-slave posited, "If you picked one or two hundred pounds one day, you had that amount to pick every day or get punished." The Ruffin daybook did not record punishments. Perhaps, the girls understood that failure to measure up to expectations resulted in chastisement at the evening weigh-ups. The fate of many slaves hung in the balance along with the cotton.[46]

The value of youngsters working in antebellum cotton fields cannot be overestimated. The North Carolinian Alonzo T. Mial recounted his agricultural successes to Ruffin Horton in December 1859 when he wrote, "I made with 14 hands mostly women and small boys and girls two or more of the latter to make a hand 93 bales of cotton averaging 400 lbs." Before the invention of the cotton gin, youngsters also helped remove seeds from lint. Whether completed by hand or machine, the ginning of cotton simply meant the onset of new labor activities.[47]

Aside from the tobacco and cotton culture, the antebellum South produced large amounts of rice and sugar cane. These two crops receive less attention when compared to cotton because of the size of the geographical areas where grown. The bulk of the rice grew on 60,000 to 70,000 acres of land along the coast of South Carolina and Georgia near Charleston and Savannah.[48]

Gabe Lance, who came of age in the rice-growing region of South Carolina remembered, "All dem rice field been nothing but swamp. Slavery people cut kennel [canal] and cut down woods—and dig big through raw woods. All been clear up for plant rice by slavery people." The planting, cultivating, and harvesting of the grain demanded a great amount of work; therefore, a large ratio of workers per acre existed. In 1860 there were twenty-five planters with 300 to 500 slaves each, while eight planters owned 500 to 1,000 bondsmen and women each.[49]

Slave children and youth were among the gangs of slaves who chopped weeds, cleared ditches, and built canals for cultivating rice. Some of them remembered their earliest job of chasing birds away from sprouting plants. They shouted, waved their arms, rang bells, rattled gourds, and threw stones. Once the rice matured, it was cut with sickles, tied into bundles, and hauled to mills for thrashing, grinding, and polishing. If the final milling operations occurred where the rice was grown, this created additional work for the hands. Martha Kelly, also from coastal South Carolina, remembered that slaves planted and harvested rice.

She said, "dey would have one of dem pestle en mortar to beat it wid." That would turn out "de nicest kind of rice." Maggie Black, a contemporary added, "Heap uv people come from plantation aw 'bout en help whip dat rice." The assistance from others emphasizes the existence of a cooperative relationship between planters which benefited them as well as their slaves.[50]

Another major cash crop, sugar cane, in the plantation South required gang labor. The commercial production of the crop began in the United States in the 1790s when it predated indigo. Cane grows best in areas with warm temperatures, long growing seasons, and at least sixty inches of rainfall per year. Twenty-four parishes in the southern part of Louisiana, bordering on rivers and waterways, provided ideal growing conditions. "Life on the sugar plantation was harsh, the labor more difficult and more constant than on cotton plantations," according to agricultural historian Paul Gates. Comments from R. R. Barrow, owner of a sugar plantation in Terrebonne Parish, Louisiana, are in agreement. On November 8, 1857, Barrow noted that the slaves had worked every night "until 10, 11 & 1/2 11 o clock with a view of getting ready for Rooling."[51]

Farmers do not need to replant sugar cane each year, but this hardly minimizes the amount of labor required to weed fields every two weeks or five times before the lay-by. Slaves used the hoe to clear weeds away, and the process was the same each year.

Cane growers placed the entire operations for processing cane in a state of readiness, for once they cut it work proceeded around the clock until completed. Cane ripened in October but remained in the field to benefit from cold weather until threatened by frost. If left uncut, the saccharin content increased and produced a greater yield of sugar. Growers gambled on letting their cane further ripen by leaving it in the fields, but they knew freezing weather could damage the cane and ruin an entire crop. When the cutting began, gangs of workers wielded sharp knives with blades from twelve to fifteen inches in length to fell stalks. This was a job that older youths and adults performed. Women and children stripped blades away from the stalks.[52]

The kidnapped free-born Solomon Northup spent several years enslaved on a sugar plantation and described the cutting and hauling of cane as proceeding in an orderly manner. "To every three hands there is a cart, which follows," he wrote, "and the stalks are thrown into it by the younger slaves" before being "drawn to the sugar-house and ground." Children accompanied the carts and unloaded the cane, placing it on the rollers, which conveyed it into the building for grinding. After grinding, the cane juice flowed into open vats or vacuum pans for the final processing.[53]

Workers processed sugar either in open vats over fires or in steam-operated sugar mills. Either method required large amounts of wood. The latter method required from two and one-half to four cords of wood to produce one hogshead of sugar weighing 1,000 pounds. Planters satisfied the need for wood in two ways. They gathered driftwood washing ashore with the help of children and stockpiled it until the grinding season or cut it from the forest. The need for wood by sugar growers and others was so great that it threatened the southern forests with depletion by 1830. Woodcutting activities at the Barrow plantation offer only one example of the amount of wood needed each year. As preparation for the grinding season, Jerry and forty other slaves cut fifty cords of wood on September 4, 1857. By September 15, there were 1,580 cords. Although the grinding season was still weeks away, the work continued apace. Barrow anticipated cutting 500 to 1,000 additional cords of wood. Strong boys could use axes to fell trees and chop wood while younger children helped gather, stack, and haul it to the sugar houses.[54]

Aside from the growing and processing of sugar cane, slaves built containers for storage and shipping. Cane growers used fifty-gallon barrels to store molasses, while sugar went to buyers in hogsheads. Slaves also built and maintained levees and dikes; therefore, the cutting and hauling of wood continued apace. The long hours of laborious work took physical and mental tolls. Slave children suffered from the absence of their parents and may have suffered from their presence if they were too weary to attend to the youngster's needs. At bottom, the children felt the keen exploitation of slavery and learned the "adult-like" behavior of restraint and understanding at early ages.[55]

Young children were used less in sugar production than in the cultivation of cotton and tobacco because of the intensity of physical labor. Children in sugar-growing areas served the same role as in other agricultural areas; they assisted adult workers until they were old or strong enough to enter the labor force as full hands.[56]

Few planters could easily grow any two cash crops simultaneously since the harvest season for rice, sugar, and cotton overlapped. Besides, methods used in the rice culture did not lend themselves to the production of cotton, or sugar cane. The differences in soils required for rice and the other crops made it impractical to combine them. It was much easier to grow a cash crop along with foodstuff. Many farms were virtually self-sufficient by producing grains, vegetables, meats, and grasses enough to satisfy human and animal needs.

Wheat, a ready source of cash and food, grew primarily outside the cotton-producing states after the nineteenth century. Methods of cultivation were ancient, and slaves used the sickle as frequently as in preindustrial times. When wheat matures, the harvest must begin immediately otherwise it sheds the grain. Once cut, slaves bundled wheat into shocks, thrashed, and milled it. The former slave Frank Bell explained the division of labor where he grew up in Virginia. Men would scythe and cradle wheat, while women raked the grain from the ground and tied it into bundles. "Den us little chillun, boys an' girls, would come along an' stack' it."[57]

Corn, a heartier crop, required less attention than wheat and was a cheaper food for livestock. Planters often cultivated corn, "the poor man's food, the pioneer's subsistence, the slave's usual handout, the feed for hogs, cattle, poultry, and horses," right along with cash crops. The need for laborers was always great on such farms. Charles Grandy, an ex-slave from Virginia, claimed at "five yeahs ole" he began picking grass from "roun de cawn." His memory was most vivid, having cut his foot "hawin' de cawn" and later injured his arm when "cuttin' tops off'n de cawn." John Edwin Fripp, who owned two plantations on St. Helena Island, South Carolina, found a safer job for the slave children. He put "3 or 4 boys & girls to mind the Crows off the Corn" when it began sprouting. Otherwise birds devastated crops. Shooing away crows was much easier than cutting corn and probably more enjoyable.[58]

Certain food crops could be grown along with corn. As a labor-saving measure, farmers allowed legumes to climb the corn stalks, thus eliminating the need for poles. Additional foods grew in gardens and orchards with the help of enslaved children and youth. For example, in 1859 a North Carolina planter worked several slave women and children to produce "3,500 pounds of corn, 100 bushels of peas . . . [and] a good crop of potatoes."[59]

The use of fruits as dietary supplements had not firmly taken hold in the nineteenth century; however, there were planters who kept orchards for fresh fruits, preserves, and libations. One of the earliest commercial fruit producers, John Hebron, moved from Virginia to Mississippi carrying his slaves in 1834. By 1840 he began shifting from the cotton culture to growing fruits. Using seeds carried by his slaves from Virginia, Hebron became a successful fruit grower. Among the thirty-seven slaves in his labor force were twelve boys under fourteen, and "six were girls from ten to seventeen years of age."[60]

Enslaved children helped to produce the beef, poultry, and dairy products which complemented the diets of slaveholders. The rationing of pork was common; bacon was a major item in the slave's diet. At hog-killing time, November or December, men dazed hogs with a heavy blow to the head, slit their throats, hoisted the carcasses up on a tree limb or a scaffold built especially for that purpose, then dipped the animal into scalding waters to soften the bristles before removal. The processing of the meat (the pickling of ears, tails, and feet; the smoking of hams, bacon, and shoulders; and the making of hog-head cheese or cracklings) was under the direction of the slaveholders' wives or other designated persons.[61]

On large plantations such as John Houston Bills's Tennessee and Georgia holdings, it was impossible for slaves to avoid the total operation. Bills slaughtered ninety-six hogs weighing 14,700 pounds in 1858, which provided meat for his family and eighty-four slaves. Two years later he slaughtered eighty-three hogs, which yielded 12,606 pounds of pork. The role that children played in both cases was minimal other than "toting" water and wood. Of greater importance, they watched and learned how to perform the chores because one day the job would be theirs.[62]

After producing large quantities of food, slaves were often hungry and complained about the lack of sustenance or the poor quality of what they received. They sang:

> We raise de wheat,
> Dey gib us de corn;
> We bake de bread,
> Dey giv us de crust;
> We sif' de meal,
> Dey gib us de huss;
> We peel de meat,
> Dey gib us de skin;
> And dat's de way
> Dey take us in;
> We skim de pot,
> Dey gib us de liquor,
> And say dat's good enough for nigger.

Slaves understood the inequities in their treatment, and their sharp wit did not escape their children. Food allowances increased as children progressed from quarter- or half-hands to full hands; consequently, parents could conceivably push their children into the work place early to acquire more food for the family.[63]

The production of foods for subsistence or cash crops required few skills, whereas other jobs in the house and on the farm demanded proficiency. Skills created more options for hiring out, hiring one's own time, living away from an owner, and the possibility of buying extra goods or freedom from "overwork," income producing extra work. Skills were vital to the day-to-day operation of the nation's economy. Although the need for industrial skill was not large in the South, slave and free persons of color helped fill the need. The well-known sociologist W. E. B. Du Bois wrote:

> Negro carpenters, plasterers, bricklayers, blacksmiths, wheelwrights, painters, harness makers, tanners, millers, weavers, barrelmakers, basketmakers, shoemakers, chairmakers, coachmen, spinners, seamstresses, housekeepers, gardeners, cooks, laundresses, embroiderers, maids of all were found in every community, and frequently on a single plantation.

Owning skilled slaves was more profitable than owning unskilled ones; consequently, slaveholders sought to make many of them skillful in the sense that they wanted slaves who could perform a variety of jobs.[64]

At least 5 percent, or 200,000, of the slaves worked in southern industries in the 1850s. Carpenters were essential, for they often combined skills in the performance of jobs. Tobacco growers needed thousands of laths on which to hang cut tobacco for drying; further curing occurred atop wooden scaffolds before pressing into hogsheads. The size of the plantation's output determined the extent of skills needed. The Virginia plantation owned by William Galt, for example, produced only forty to fifty hogsheads of tobacco annually, so the need for staves was relatively small. By contrast, a large sugar producer in Louisiana estimated his need for containers by counting the staves. "It takes 2500 staves all good [to] make 100 hhds" and "200 good staves to make 100 barrels" and "500 pieces of Barrel Heading" to complete the job, he wrote. The men and older boys cut 20,000 staves measuring 1' X 34" in 1854 alone.[65]

Further work of carpenters included the making of shingles, furniture, wagons, and carts in addition to the construction and repair of private homes and public buildings. Shipbuilding was an entity unto itself. If owners did not have enough work for carpenters, they hired them out to work elsewhere.[66]

A blacksmith's skills were as important as the carpenter's. In fact, slaves often combined skills in small households. Blacksmiths made farm tools in addition to other items such as cooking utensils, horseshoes, hinges, and nails. They kept tools and hardware for other items in good repair. Blacksmiths also made weapons used in insurrections and the chains and shackles to restrain rebels. Their work could be functional or decorative. For example, slave labor went into much of the elegantly forged balconies, grills, and lamp brackets in old New Orleans, Charleston, and Savannah.

Enslaved children learned skills from apprenticeships or by working with others in a more casual setting. Newspaper advertisements asked for "likely young Negroes from 15 to 20 Years of Age" for apprentices. As children became more proficient in the trade, their value increased. John Mathews, an artisan, said, "I had to help my pappy in the shop when I was a child," adding, "I learnt how to beat out de iron an' make wagin tires, an' make plows."[67]

Of the number of industrial slaves, an estimated 10,000 plied their trade in foundries such as Virginia's Oxford Ironworks, established in 1776. Slaves at the establishment manufactured farm tools, shot, shells, cooking utensils, and horseshoes, in addition to supplies for the Virginia and North Carolina militias during the Revolutionary War. Blacksmiths, potters, hammermen, woodchoppers, colliers, miners, and teamsters made up the labor force. Additional crews manned boats that carried their products to market and produced food to sustain workers and animals at the ironworks. The total number of slaves at the Oxford foundry reached 220 in 1811.[68]

Although most of the children were descendants of slaves belonging to the owner of the facility, David Ross, he also hired hands. Ross occasionally bought male slaves between sixteen and twenty years of age. By the time children were fourteen, if not caring for babies, they raked leaves, cleaned finished castings, removed impurities from the ore, and attended to the blast furnaces. Edmund, a seventeen-year-old artisan, specialized in making small cooking utensils. The skill made it possible for him to earn money from overwork to purchase his liberty.[69]

The manufacturing of shoes and clothing required a different set of skills. Although slaves went barefoot many months of the year, slaveowners did make some attempts to provide shoes during the coldest months. They either bought cheaply made brogans or manufactured them at home. The Wilson County,

Tennessee, slave George Knox became an apprentice to a shoemaker at an early age. According to Knox, "he would be given a prestige over the other slaves by not having to go to the farm to work." Bill Simms, a former slave, worked as a cobbler when "just a boy and made shoes for the whole family."[70]

Slave girls had fewer opportunities to acquire craft skills than boys who became carpenters, smiths, masons, and wrights. Girls could have learned the techniques, but they did not have the opportunity. One cannot argue that craft work was too strenuous, considering women plowed, felled trees, and split rails. In all probability, childbearing was the key factor that prevented access to trades for female slaves, since it, unlike picking cotton or pulling corn, would interrupt work that could not be completed as easily by a substitute worker. The work of skilled female slaves was associated with domestic or housewifery chores. Furthermore, pregnant or lactating cooks, laundresses, spinners, weavers, and seamstresses continued with their work as usual.[71]

Slaveowners decided if it were more important to have a new addition to their coffers or to have craft work uninterrupted. It was a matter of arranging priorities to determine whether to focus on reproduction or production. "The extent to which the slaveowner consciously emphasized one or the other," Deborah Gray White writes, "ultimately depended on his need." The historian Jacqueline Jones adds that slaveowners did not encourage females to gain craft skills because they viewed the work performed during the winter (for example, spinning, weaving) as "too important to permit protracted absences from their quarters" if, as skilled workers, women were hired out the same as other artisans and mechanics. The decision not to allow women into the crafts suggests that slaveowners did not have interrupted crafts because of childbearing or winter chores because of craft work.[72]

Housewifery skills were adaptable to industry in the wider world beyond the plantation house. The southern textile industry did not rival the New England industry until after the Civil War; however, cotton mills existed in the antebellum South, and it was not unusual to find enslaved women and children working in the industry. The rising costs of slaves explains the paucity of chattel in southern textile mills after 1850. Mill operators found it more cost effective to hire white women and children than to buy slaves. Until that happened slave women and children worked in textile mills.[73]

Rewards as incentives to work were so common that they need only a brief discussion herein. Pride and elevated self-esteem motivated some workers regardless of their ages. Charles Davenport remembered his youth as a plow hand and bragged, "I sure could lay off a pretty cotton row." One could also boast about the amount of cotton picked, corn shucked, or weeds pulled. By contrast, Edmund marked the small cooking utensils with his special stamp. This was an inducement to continue perfecting his craft. It is understandable that artisans exuded pride in their work because it was a visual representation of what they could do. Their work was both artistic and functional for all to see and use.[74]

STOLEN CHILDHOOD

Ross used rewards and punishments to manage his slaves. He developed the system of "corrections by degrees," for he knew that skilled workers could not be forced to perform satisfactorily. Punishments included reassignments to different jobs, withholding clothing allowances, whippings, and threats of sale. Consultations with those he viewed as the "most sensible" regarding changes in practices were also used. He prided himself on feeding and clothing slaves well when financially feasible. Opportunities for overwork made it possible for slaves to supplement their allowances.[75]

Inasmuch as the iron works encouraged family unity, children grew up in a community where they had positive role models, incentives, and opportunities to learn skills without interference from their owner. Children must have known if their parents were among the "most sensible" of the lot and certainly must have taken pride in knowing that they had some input in making the decisions they lived by. It is questionable as to how serious Ross was about their advice and how he identified the "most sensible" of the group.

Regardless of the kind of work performed or rewards received, parents taught their children the value of mutual cooperation. Slaves helped others ward off punishments by assisting with chores, adding cotton to a slow picker's basket, or doing whatever was possible to help others. A former slave remembered hearing his mother sing as she urged workers along with the warning, "Keep yo' eye on de sun, / See how she run, / Don't let her catch you with your work undone." Children hearing the admonition learned the value of collective efforts and the importance of completing their work in a timely manner. The disappearance of the sun signaled the end of the work day when tallies were taken and punishments meted out if laborers fell short of required work. The additional lyrics "I'm a trouble, I'm a trouble / Trouble don' las' always" offered hope if their efforts failed. The message was useful for most occupations throughout the region.[76]

This examination of the variety of jobs performed by enslaved youngsters answers questions about their adjustment to work. Without a doubt many worked out of fear. Nancy Williams, Crissy, and Simon Stokes probably became good at worming tobacco as a result of their unpleasant experiences. They learned to function within the system and were often helped by parents or others who buffeted shocks. As with all things it was easier to some than others. Adelaide, the child in the household of Tryphena Fox, fared well. Tryphena was impressed with her skills and eagerness to please, so she treated the "little pet house maid" well. Fox once promised Adelaide a present if she were good and cleaned the woman's "room nicely & did all her work." Afterwards, Fox found her room and "all the back part of the house in as good order as if some old woman had charge of it." The girl received "the pretty white glass beads . . . bought for her & you ought to have seen her *face & eyes*," Fox wrote. In such a situation it is difficult to tell who was more elated, the girl or her owner.[77]

The life of Jacob Stroyer was a sharp contrast. He had a difficult time adjusting to authority in the work place, which tells much about his relationship with his superiors. Each time Stroyer fell from the horse, the groom beat him unmercifully. When the boy appealed to his parents, he realized that they were also vulnerable. The floggings continued, and the boy became more obstinate as the groom retaliated with more beatings. Stroyer's situation changed only when he came under the supervision of a different trainer.[78]

Even a cursory look at historical data shows that children made large contributions to the nation's economic growth. Their work was static only in the sense that they were destined to toil as soon as they were useful, and it continued until they were useless. Their work in Virginia's tobacco fields, Louisiana's sugar cane district, South Carolina's rice country, or Mississippi's cotton region differed only in the kind and amount of labor performed. Regardless of the geographical locations, they all worked. It must always be remembered that the work herein was for the slaveowner. As Jacob Branch so aptly said, "Us ain't never idle." There were other chores in the cabins, gardens, or yards before any slave, young or old, could say, "Day is done."[79]

3

"WHEN DAY IS DONE"

PLAY AND LEISURE

> Before the holidays there were
> pleasures in prospect; after the
> holidays there were pleasures of
> memory, and they served to keep out
> thoughts and wishes of a more
> dangerous character.
>
> —Frederick Douglass[*]

As a way of entertaining two visitors in 1848, the Virginia-born Launcelot Minor Blackford built a small cart in which to carry them. He then "got all the little children who could well do it and hitched them to the carriage [and] made them run around the yard with Alice or Richard on it." The youngster added, "They seemed to enjoy it very much." As written, it is not clear if Blackford referred to the children who rode in the cart or to those who pulled it.[1]

This chapter examines many of the ways enslaved children and youth spent their spare time and interacted with others such as Launcelot Blackford. It also seeks to answer questions about competitive play, peer pressure, and social relationships among children. This is an important facet of the overall study because play is voluntary, enjoyable, and it embraces freedom. Many play activities of black children were more like those of white children than activities in any other facet of their lives. Their education, work, and treatment were significantly different. Furthermore, the slave narratives do not mention enslaved and white children working together.

Once slaves began working they "couldn't play 'round at chillun's doing" as easily, yet they found time to enjoy themselves after completing assigned duties. Evenings, Sundays, and holidays offered respite from work and chances for amusement and recreation which provided physical and mental rest and recuperation. "At night let the negroes employ themselves as they please till the bell rings," read a Marengo County, Alabama, slaveholder's 1860 instructions. Willis

---

[*] *My Bondage and My Freedom* (New York: Dover, 1969), 254.

P. Bocock urged his overseer to refrain from any interference unless the bond servants broke "some rule of the plantation." Plantation management records often mention released time for hands since slaveowners knew bond servants were more productive if not driven too hard; hence, it was also helpful to owners.[2]

David K. Wiggins's "The Play of Slave Children," based largely upon WPA narratives, maintains that play taught values and morals of the adult world. But as one study of children's recreation argues, "play bears a special relationship to the study of culture because it is so much a part of the reality of life." Play, the antithesis of work, is often based upon real situations; therefore, youngsters observing values and ideals in one situation could transfer and imitate them in another. Play serves as a socializing agent, bringing children into cohesive units to foster camaraderie, develop leadership abilities, and sharpen skills without regard for practical purposes. Courage, responsibility, and loyalty are by-products of group play.[3]

The properties of play make it possible to create, repeat, or eliminate facets of an activity. "Once played," according to one writer, "it endures as a new-found creation of the mind, a treasure to be retained by the memory." The values of play are timeless and when transmitted from one generation to another they foster a tradition.[4]

Leisure provided the time for the creation and recreation of models, representative of society, when youngsters learned to cope with life's many challenges in a nonutilitarian manner. Since unencumbered time serves a useful purpose under normal circumstances, it follows that persons living under unusual conditions like slavery or war would benefit abundantly from leisure activities that differed from their usual routines.

Slaves spent free time attending to personal needs, resting, or engaging in formal and informal social activities. The former included planned activities involving others in the family or slave community, such as religious services, dances, or corn shuckings. The latter were spontaneous events including gatherings in the quarters after work and free play among children. In either case, opportunities abounded for youngsters to develop interpersonal relationships with others. At early ages, black and white children played together, but after ten or twelve years of age, when slaves began working regularly, the paths diverged and never converged again to the same extent as in their play days.[5]

A tension existed between the time for work and the time for play. The conflict was most aggravating when children had work to do but were more interested in playing. Allen Crawford recalled the cook sending children into the forest for kindling, but they "got to playing and stayed in dem woods 'til almost dark." If the desire to play led to chastisement, they often devised ways to escape both work and punishment. Robert Shepherd found a refuge from "Aunt Viney," who was "sure to have us fetchin' in wood or sweepin' de yards if . . . she could find us."[6]

PLAY AND LEISURE

Until asked about leisure activities, Booker T. Washington claimed it never occurred to him that he had no recreation as a child. He filled his days carrying water, cleaning yards, and transporting corn to the mill for grinding. As an adult he believed he could have been "a more useful man" had there been time for sports during his childhood.[7]

Variations in circumstances and differences in definitions of what constitutes leisure make it difficult to determine the extent to which it existed. In the 1930s some WPA informants, like Jacob Branch, maintained they did nothing but work, while some claimed they did nothing other than play. Children who played "all the time" were probably too young to work. Richard Steckel asserted that "poor nutrition restricted exploration and play." If that is the case, poor nutrition would also restrict other activities, including work. Nevertheless, enough evidence exists to show that bond servants enjoyed leisure and engaged in nonutilitarian activities.[8]

Approximately 10 percent of the WPA narratives contain specific references to more than one hundred kinds of leisure activities. During free moments enslaved children and youth in urban and rural areas used their creativity and imagination for entertainment. Limited space in their living quarters restricted their diversions. The planting, cultivating, and harvesting of crops dictated not only the amount of time at their disposal, but the hour of the day and season of the year as well.[9]

Conditions permitting, enslaved youngsters amused themselves with play and playthings. Boys and girls often played together, but some games were more gender-specific than others. Boys engaged in activities associated with male sports and strength. Marbles were overwhelming attractions for them, while girls played with dolls, participated in ring games, and jumped rope. Home or family life often provided the bases for the play of young girls, regardless of their color. They pretended to dress up, keep house, cook food, serve meals, wash dishes, and care for babies. Girls, throughout the world, assumed these roles because of their awareness in the divisions of labor and the mother-child nexus.[10]

Toys or playthings are part of a child's life since they are material artifacts of a culture. Without money to purchase toys, young slaves fashioned their own toys from whatever was available, and they used their imaginations freely. The freedwoman Candis Goodwin explained that she and her friends gathered brown pine needles to build a play house and used the green needles for grass around their imaginary abode. Children molded marbles from clay and baked them in the sun, while rags and string were basic materials for making balls and dolls. Acorns became tiny cups and saucers. The South Carolinian Anderson Bates remembered children playing with cane whistles which they or someone else made. Children also crafted "horses" from branches and small tree limbs. The ex-slave George Briggs recalled playing "hoss" with his friend Chaney, whose brother was the "wagoner" while George was the mule. The smallest of the children, Henry, sometimes "rid our backs," he said.[11]

STOLEN CHILDHOOD

Emily Dixon of Simpson County, Mississippi, commented upon the uses of hickory trees when she grew up. First, she asked, "Did yo' eber take time ter think jist what a hickory-nut tree is to chillun?" Without waiting for a response, she answered:

> Deir's de shade ter play under, de tree ter climb, de big limbs ter hang swings from, de leaves ter pin tergether wid pine straw ter make dresses an' hats, de nuts ter eat . . . Den yo' can hid' hind de trunks in playin' hide an' seek, or hab hit fer de base.

She added, "I hab my fun under de ole hickory-nut tree."[12]

The experiences of James W. C. Pennington, who played with a by-product of the hickory tree, are less memorable. He found a stick which belonged to his overseer and immediately used it for a horse. The man was not amused. Pennington recalled how he pounced upon him and gave him a severe flogging with the hickory stick. Perhaps the overseer viewed the child's game as a mockery of his authority. Afterwards, Pennington "lived in constant dread of that man" and never repeated the innocent game.[13]

Enslaved children often had simple handmade toys while some white children enjoyed playthings of a different nature. The resources of Launcelot Minor Blackford serve as an example. In 1849 the youngster molded two-inch-long powder-filled cannons for his toy ship "Sea Bird." He also made colorful balloons and highly decorated kites of a "remarkably pretty shape." His supply of paper, paint, brushes, and pens for making toys seemed endless. Regardless of differences in resources and geographical locations, all children used ingenuity and creativity to fashion instruments for their enjoyment, and it is reasonable to assume that they were proud of their creations.[14]

Much of the play of enslaved children was not organized. Anderson Bates recalled that the children had a "good time" running around in the plum thickets and blackberry bushes and hunting wild strawberries. To be sure, they frolicked in the meadows, swam in streams, climbed trees, and rambled about their environs, although less than 20 percent of the male and fewer than 10 percent of the female WPA interviewees mentioned playing in nearby woods and streams. The meager number of responses probably means that work interfered with play or interviewers limited the specific number of questions about the subject.[15]

Other than unorganized play, there were amusements with rules, competition, individual or team goals, winners and losers. Popular pastimes included horseshoes, marbles, hopscotch, and ball and ring games. These activities were adaptable to plantation roads and city streets wherever children interacted with each other. Enslaved children devised games that tested their strength, skills, or endurance, such as jumping contests and foot races. Winners elevated themselves in the eyes of competitors.

PLAY AND LEISURE

Children playing "hide and seek" or "all hid" delighted in evading the seeker, who remained at the designated "base" with closed eyes while repeating a rhyme followed by counting. At the end of the count, the seeker called out, "Are all hid?" If players answered in the affirmative, the seeker looked for and tried to tag them before they returned to the base. If they avoided the seeker, they were free. Otherwise, another player became the seeker. The game tested skills in avoiding detection, and children learned to count in the process.[16]

Questions arise regarding the stages of childhood and whether they are shaped by biology, culture, or a combination of the two. To be sure, Africans recognized stages of human growth and development with their rites de passage as children advanced in age. Naming ceremonies and initiation rites marked occasions in their lives. The circumstances under which people of African descent lived disrupted cultural patterns that were not easily duplicated in the United States. Questions also arise about whether enslaved children experienced the storm and stress of life, when adolescents become "inwardly absorbed, perhaps egoistic, sometimes cruel?" Were they prone to tease, bully, or brag? Were they subjected to peer pressure? If slave autobiographers experienced the emotions, the inner turmoil, associated with adolescence, they did not write about them. This in itself does not mean that they did not feel the passion and behave as youth today. Interviewees did not talk about it probably because interviewers did not ask.[17]

Of the available nineteenth-century narratives, one includes a "bully" who consistently terrorized smaller children. The child intimidated Jacob Stroyer to the extent that his autobiography devoted a special section to "The Story of Gilbert." Initially, as Gilbert's favorite, Stroyer escaped a trouncing by agreeing not to tell about the mistreatment of the other boys. Stroyer claimed he was not afraid of Gilbert but was inclined to mind his "own business." Once Gilbert tired of the arrangement, he promised to whip the "fearless" Stroyer. Standing before his "merciless superior," the "trembling" Stroyer devised a plan to save himself. When begging for mercy did not absolve him from imminent punishment, Stroyer ran. The behavior does little to persuade readers that Stroyer was not afraid. Based upon his experiences, Stroyer knew he was no match for Gilbert.[18]

Enslaved children probably saw rough-and-tumble fighting in the backwoods among poor whites where eye gouging and other forms of maiming were common, and they may have seen adult slaves wrestling "primarily at the behest of and for the enjoyment of the whites," but slaves did not "seem to have encouraged their children to follow suit." Although they did not engage in social fighting, there are accounts of enslaved children fighting.[19]

Emily Dixon claimed that she and her "brudder would fight when de oder chillun meddled." She usually vented her anger when she found the children alone. Emily and her "brudder would fight 'em" again "if dey tole on us," she recalled. She admitted throwing hickory nuts, from her favorite tree no doubt, at the children, and they did the same if they wanted "ter fight." She described herself as "a spirited chap," but her testimony suggests that the slave community did not condone fighting.[20]

Perhaps more common than using fisticuffs to displace aggression was "playing the dozens," an oral counterpoint where torrents of aspersions received quick retorts of one-upmanship. Participants in the verbal duels sharpened their wits and reacted quickly with taunts as onlookers cheered them on. There are striking similarities between the game as played by Africans and African Americans. Girls as well as boys played the game, but girls were less likely to join in the dozens that touted sexual prowess. The nature of the game's insults about a player's parents or siblings sometimes resulted in fights.[21]

It is not unusual for children's games to include a certain amount of cruelty; however, neither Gilbert nor Emily were playing a game. Slave children played "Hide the Switch," which focused on locating a concealed switch and the finder having free reign to flog any player caught. Players thrashed some children more than others, especially those of less agility.

Thomas Webber, who studied life in the slave quarters, contends that "Hide the Switch" helped slaves cope with the fear of whippings. Bernard Mergen convincingly challenges this theory when he posits that white children in the United States and Europe, as well as Arawak Indians in Guiana, played whipping games including "Hide the Switch," "Rap Jacket," and "Daddy Wacker." The games reflect violence in society rather than in the slave society specifically. Only 5 percent of the WPA narratives mention "Hide the Switch," which is hardly a representative sample. Children probably played the games because of the excitement of anticipating a whipping and the challenge of successfully avoiding it. No doubt some children used the same tactics when faced with whippings by adults.[22]

Games often mirrored incidents in the larger society which made lasting impressions. In representative play, slave children became preachers, mothers, fathers, and auctioneers. Role play provided opportunities to face anxieties associated with slavery; however, play was not a solution to any psychological problems caused by slavery. Eugene D. Genovese claims slave children used games such as slave auctions to neutralize things they feared most. Mergen effectively argues that Genovese's interpretation has gone awry since the context of the auction was still slavery. He explains:

> A slave child may pretend to be a master, but he cannot pretend to be a slave, since one of the most important elements in fantasy play is what Catherine Garvey calls "negation of pretend" in which a child says, "I'm not a slave any more."

Representative play which did not take children from a real to an imaginary world was hardly worth playing.[23]

PLAY AND LEISURE

Representative play reflects a child's frame of reference and varies accordingly. The well-read Launcelot Minor Blackford was knowledgeable about local and national occurrences. He and his school chums devised a "court" game in 1848 based upon a local trial involving a merchant accused of selling "unwholesome provisions." Their game was complete with witnesses, lawyers, court officials, and a prisoner played by "little Willie Blackford." Although fascinated with court, publishing a newspaper held Blackford's interest longer. He set type daily and worked assiduously until the *Home Gazette* met his approval. The enterprise succeeded, in part because of external support and gifts of type from a local newspaper office. Supplies were available either as gifts or loans, after Blackford had offered to buy them. Moreover, his uncle warmly encouraged the venture with a five-dollar subscription for the *Home Gazette*.[24]

The representative play of Blackford may not be comparable to many nineteenth-century southern white children. It was not similar to that of enslaved children who did not have material resources at their disposal or the money to buy them. Neither did they have ready access to information nor the freedom to travel into town to observe trials. They never had the support from the white community that Blackford enjoyed. Furthermore, it was more difficult for them to learn to read and write after the 1831 Nat Turner rebellion; therefore, printing a newspaper was not a consideration for them.

Disparities in literacy were obvious, but similarities existed in how children, separately or together, slave or free, handled one aspect of life: death. This probably commanded their attention because of the high mortality rates at the time. Descriptions of mock funerals appear in the slave narratives and the writings of their white contemporaries. When Blackford's pet bantam rooster Jack died, the boy "paid him all the last respects in the way of a funeral."[25]

There are similarities between an actual funeral and the observance of social order in a service, for a chicken, staged by children on a Louisiana plantation in 1832.

> The boys made a wagon of fig branches, and [used] four of them as horses. We tied a bow of black ribbon around the chicken's neck, and covered him with a white rag, and then marched in a procession singing . . . negro hymns, all the white children next to the hearses, marching two by two, and the colored children following the same order.

After the procession, the children stood by the grave where a white girl in the fold preached the sermon, "We must all die." Long after slavery ended, Dinah Perry remembered that children "marched in a procession singing one of our folks funeral hymns" at a mock funeral in Arkansas. Nancy Perry "performed the ceremony" when the children stopped for the interment.[26]

There is no explanation as to why girls, one white and one black, assumed such an important role in the game. Did children attend enough funerals to know who delivered sermons? Following the 1831 Nat Turner rebellion, some southern states required white attendance at the religious gatherings of slaves. Perhaps the children were aware of this change, but it is more likely that they duplicated an ongoing practice. It was not unusual for older women to make remarks at funerals, which was true to life for slave children. Was it also realistic for white children? Certainly the death of a chicken is not a representative situation for duplication. It is of importance, however, to determine who made the decision regarding the sermons and how they did it. Children of both genders were present; therefore, other factors such as age and race were significant.[27]

Blackford did not describe the funeral; however, he mentions the epitaph "Jack, died Feb 29th 1848," which he placed on the tombstone. There is no discussion of grave markers in the other accounts. Slave children were more familiar with grave decorations such as the broken pottery used in the African tradition. Besides, the majority of slave children were incapable of writing inscriptions on tombstones. Race and class defined and circumscribed their play.[28]

Children, without regard for race or class, often played the same games and sang identical songs. William Wells Newell, the renowned collector of American games and songs, described "Haley-Over" as a nineteenth-century game requiring two groups of players to position themselves on different sides of a building. A player then tossed a ball over the roof. The objective was to catch the ball, proceed around the building, and hit an opponent. Players anticipated the strike and ran excitedly in all directions. Once hit, the player joined the opposing team. The game ended when all players were on one side of the building.[29]

Enslaved children played a game with rules closely akin to Newell's description. An ex-slave remembered:

> Dey played anti-over by a crowd gitting on each side of de house and throwing a ball from one side to de other. Whoever got de ball would run around on de other side and hit somebody wid it; den he was out of de game.

Newell did not mention children being "out." Wiggins maintains that slave children were sensitive to the feelings of peers and claims their games did not eliminate players. Perhaps anxieties associated with separations from families or friends prompted this act. Rather than ejecting a participant, they simply began anew. That is a plausible argument, but it obviously did not apply to all situations.[30]

Few black or white children mentioned games of chance because they probably associated them with unacceptable behavior. Betting was not openly accepted; therefore, interviewees did not admit participation in order to save themselves from condemnation. However, cards, dice, and backgammon games were fairly common among whites in antebellum America. Slaves had few material resources and little or no money to purchase such instruments of pleasure. One ex-slave did describe playing "smut" with grains of corn rather than cards. Other games including horseshoes, quoits, and marbles were conducive to betting, but there is almost no mention of it.[31]

Winning boosted self-esteem and was as good as rewards from peers. Leisure activities offered opportunities to feel good about one's self and develop esprit de corps. James Southall bragged about his victories in marble games, and there is no doubt that he was proud of his accomplishments when he said, "I got to be a professional. I could beat em all." He, no doubt, referred to all playmates without regard for color.[32]

Some slaveowners did not object to their children playing with bond servants, and they taught their children to behave charitably, in word and deed, toward them. An antebellum agricultural journal commented that southern children should "be taught that it is their duty to regard them with benevolence, to administer to their wants, and to protect them from injury" while cautioning them against "terms of familiarity." Minerva Cain Caldwell, whose husband Tod Robinson Caldwell, a Burke County, North Carolina, lawyer, served as the state's governor from 1871 to 1887, received words of wisdom from a relative regarding the treatment of others. The advice cautioned against offending relatives, friends, and servants employed for someone else's "comfort and gratification." The 1833 letter urged treatment "with much feeling" and giving "as little trouble as possible." The pithy reminder, "You will have to answer at the bar of God, for your conduct towards them," followed. Such humanitarian advice did not always overshadow childish willfulness.[33]

By contrast, there were white parents who objected to any interaction between their children and slaves because of the latter's "corrupting influence." For example, Mary Chaplin, the wife of a South Carolina cotton planter, complained that "the little Negroes are ruining the children" by teaching them "badness," which included "bad manners, crossing swollen creeks, eating green fruit." Slaves did not have a monopoly on bad behavior. Ester King Casey spent many of her youthful days around a "white lady" who did not abide rudeness. She whipped Ester for playing with white children who "told lies and talked bad." The woman's goal was to teach Ester to be "good and truthful."[34]

Tryphena Fox worried little about any negative influence the young "house pet" might have upon her daughter Fanny since she already knew that Adelaide was a good natured, tractable, "bright little negress." Whenever Fox did not feel up to entertaining her daughter, she called Adelaide in to dress doll-babies and play "set table" with Fanny. Although Adelaide played with Fanny, the child's mother complained, "there are no playmates here for her & she is sometimes very lonesome." What Fox really meant was there were no white children with whom Fanny could play. Without regard for her own contradictory remarks, she explained that Fanny "likes to go out into the back yard to play with the little negroes." Fox wrote about the "little girl & boy, one older [and] the other younger" with whom Fanny played. Fox referred to Adelaide's younger sister Margaret and brother Buddy. Fanny found the baby "very attractive" and begged "to go & see him two or three times a day." What the slave children thought about Fanny's visits remains unknown.[35]

Fanny Fox was not unique. Children of both races played together and learned from each other. African American children played ring and line games very much like those of Anglo-Saxon children. Similarities in the play of children of different cultures and national origins make it impossible to say definitively where an activity originated. Formal European games became part of the slave child's repertoire, but regional color and ethnic flavor added distinction. Children of African descent gave their songs unique sounds, with varied clapping rhythms, while adding dance steps and body motions that were unmistakably a part of their culture.[36]

Notice how the ring game "Little Sally Waters" differed according to its participants. White girls knelt in a circle and sang:

> Little Sally Waters,
> Sitting in the sun,
> Crying and weeping,
> For a young man.
>
> Rise, Sally, rise
> Fly to the East,
> Fly to the West,
> Fly to the one you love best.

As they sang the words "Rise, Sally, rise," the girl in the center stood and acknowledged one of the players who in turn sat in the circle.

Black children sang:

> Little Sally Walker
> Sittin' in a saucer
> Weepin' and cryin'
> for some young man.

A contextual analysis of the first verse suggests that if Sally, whose name changed from "Waters" to "Walker," represented a woman, she wept because of separation from her spouse or lover.[37]

The songs differed according to what children heard or thought they heard. In the oral tradition, slave children shared games and songs without knowledge of written directions or rules. Young bond servants sang:

> Can I git to Molly's bright?
> Three course and ten.
> Can I get there by candlelight?
> Yes, if your legs are long and light.

Their song was a derivation of "How Many Miles to Babylon?" from the British game "Barley Break" or the Americanized version "Marlow Bright," which white children played while singing:

> Marlow, marlow, marlow bright,
> How many miles to Babylon?
> Threescore and ten.
> Can I get there by candlelight?
> Yes, if your legs are long as light.

Slave children corrupted "Marlow Bright" into "Molly Bright" and "three course" became "threescore."[38]

As youngsters played together, they sometimes treated each other as equals. Frederick Douglass explained:

> When a boy in the street of Baltimore, we were never objected to by our white playmates on account of our color. When the hat was tossed up in for a choice of partners in the play, we were selected as readily as any other boy, and were esteemed as highly as any. No one ever objected to our complexion.

It is fallacious to assume that all white and black children enjoyed amicable relationships. There were mean-spirited adults and children of the same ilk. After an especially trying day in 1844, Anna Matilda King, who lived on Saint Simon's Island, Georgia, with scores of slaves, asserted that rearing boys under such conditions made them "tyrannical as well as lazy." She added, "girls too." Another observer said "slaveholders' children were encouraged to indulge their passions" thus allowing them to became slaves of their own fervor.[39]

Power relationships existed between children of different races just as they did between adults of different races. Thomas Jefferson argued that white children imitated the "whole commerce between master and slave" from observing their parents interact with bond servants. Afterwards, the white children put on the same airs with smaller slaves. The propensity toward "despotism" began at early ages when bonded children were obliged to obey the "young masters and mistresses." An ex-slave from Mississippi Magnus Brown remembered white children ordering him to do things that they were afraid to attempt. He suffered severe burns after throwing cartridges into a fire upon their direction. Based upon the research about selected slaveholding families in antebellum North Carolina, Jane Turner Censer agrees that Jefferson's view was "the guiding principle of such relations."[40]

Children learned or developed prejudices as they matured. When younger than three or four years of age, it was unlikely that they understood the social construction of race, but as they grew older they became more aware of distinctive factors and learned to discriminate. For example, Adelaide amused "Miss Fanny" when the latter was little more than a year old. The title denotes difference in their status. Fanny was not old enough to understand the distinctions; however, her mother initiated the process. Adelaide, who was six years old at the time, left no record of her reaction to the invitations, which insisted that she wash her face and hands, or to the title, but surely she noticed that they pointed out differences between the two girls. The age at which they understood racial differences varied according to their experiences.[41]

Slavery fostered unequal bonds between children, and there were numerous reminders of lopsided relationships. White girls sometimes owned porcelain dolls, while their enslaved playmates used rags or corn cobs to represent their babies. Enslaved girls did not own miniature china tea sets or play houses as did some of their white companions. Among the playthings owned by Fanny Fox was a doll with her own clothes along with a miniature farm house with animals, trees, and fences to complete the setting. Furthermore, a neighbor increased her cache with a box of toys in 1862. Enslaved children, Adelaide included, were painfully aware of differences in their playthings and levels of participation because of their race.[42]

Launcelot Blackford was very much aware of the status of enslaved persons and had contributed a small amount of money in 1849 to slaves whom his mother had liberated to Liberia, the West African republic founded under the auspices of the American Colonization Society in 1816 as a home for repatriated Africans. Yet, Blackford's treatment of the enslaved children who pulled the cart for Richard and Alice's ride appears callous. Moreover, he showed little sympathy when "one of the little black children fell down and hurt herself." He concluded that she "was of no loss as she was a hindrance to the rest as she could not keep up." There is no mention of rewarding her with a carriage ride for her efforts.[43]

In a similar situation, Sarah Alston, the widow of a great planter in antebellum North Carolina, described a new two-seat carriage built for her grandson. When telling the child about the toy, she wrote, "I reckon it will take all your little waiting men to pull it." She then offered an alternative, "unless you *hitch* the *old grey.*" In either case, the child could decide and there was no promise that the "little waiting men" would enjoy a ride.[44]

During the Civil War, J. G. Clinkscales decided to hitch Jack and Peter to a small wagon that he had received as a present. Clinkscales's "little sister did the riding," and he "did the driving." Although he used the "softest and prettiest" lines he had ever seen, Clinkscales cracked the whip "over the backs, and sometimes *on* the backs, of [his] two-legged horses." Acting out their parts, the enslaved boys delighted "the little queen who rode" and the driver when they "kicked and reared and snorted like real horses." Before long, Pete and Jack tired of the game and requested a change. Clinkscales replaced them with calves.[45]

Discrimination in children's games is often age related. Blackford's decisions about who pulled the cart and who played the prisoner in his court game all involved younger children. The older and more sophisticated children set parameters. Notice the intricacies of the Louisiana funeral. The children used ribbon and a shroud of appropriate colors, segregated the children by race, sang the proper songs, and transported the corpse with four horses. The details show degrees of maturity.

Differences in the roles played by the children indicate that they were indeed aware of differences in their race. A former slave described playing with white children whose attitudes of superiority were evident. "De whites was de soldiers an' me and de rest of de slave boys," he said, "was de Injuns." The "soldiers" who carried wooden guns, shot and scalped the Indians. The same group of children played another game during the Civil War, and the scenario hardly changed. Another group of children in Virginia played the game "Harpers Ferry" based upon their understanding of John Brown's raid. A white child portrayed Brown, and his supporters were black. This is a significant example of representative play, for it captures a class attitude and shows that the children were aware of national events. In another game, the white boys played the "'Federates," and the slaves played "Yankees." The Confederates always took the Union soldiers prisoner and threatened to slaughter them. When recalling the game, the former slave mused, "Guess dey got dat idea f'om dere fathers." On a more neutral note, another group of black and white children sat around a bonfire during the Civil War trying to "imitate the soldiers on picket."[46]

Games that required decisions about who filled a specific role were more open to race, gender, and age discrimination than games of chance or skill. Douglass recalled that black boys "could run as fast, jump as far, throw the ball as direct and true, and catch it with as much dexterity and skill as the white boys." Moreover, the young slaves prided themselves on their agility. Although Robert Ellett considered the "young masters" his pals, he did not allow them to win at any of their games. He believed that he had an unusual strength and spirit. Ellett claimed he "was the best of the young boys on the plantation" near West Point, Virginia.[47]

There are instances where such interactions furnished the bases for friendship between black and white children beyond the play activities. A former slaveowner recalled playing with his personal servant when they were nine or ten years old. The enslaved boy always asked, "Marse, will you give me a white man's chance?" The question gave pause to the potential for unsportsmanlike conduct based upon race. The boys had reached a moment of truth and recognized that racial and social differences existed between them. They continued playing together because the white boy agreed to give the black boy a fair chance and "always lived up to [the] contract, though sometimes the consequences were damaging." Their interaction had the potential for a lasting association.[48]

After slavery ended, Hilary Herbert, lawyer, author, and member of the house of representatives from 1877 to 1893, and secretary of the navy from 1893 to 1897, reminisced about playing with his constant companion, an enslaved boy, which attests to the fact that their play succeeded in bringing them into a cohesive unit and fostered camaraderie. Theirs was not the ordinary slaveowner-slave relationship; it was something more, for Herbert wrote, "We were friends."[49]

The Virginia-born Charles L. C. Minor, who also owned an enslaved companion, placed a different value upon their friendship. Having inherited

Ralph, a child who was only a few years older than himself in 1808 or 1809, Minor developed a fondness for his constant companion. In the opening lines of an 1832 letter informing Ralph that he had decided to free him, Minor wrote, "I am no longer your master, but I am still your friend, and as perhaps we shall never meet again, I have determined to give you this assurance of my esteem." Tracing the bonds through the years, Minor remembered his "playmate and nurse and the good will" which Ralph won during their childhood. It is "still warmly cherished," Minor added. Returning wages which Ralph had earned as an artisan, Minor liberated him and urged him to emigrate to Liberia and remove himself from the grasp of slave traders. Making it clear that the decision was ultimately Ralph's, Minor bade his former servant well. With the stroke of the pen he severed one relationship but wished to retain another. "No more your master," the former owner wrote, "but always your friend." Perhaps the friendship was mutual.[50]

Aside from interactions with their black and white peers, young slaves and their families enjoyed evenings, Sundays, holidays, and special days given for "making and laying by the crop." At night they gathered in their humble abodes for meals, discussions, and family fun. One former slave remembered that his family "sot by de fire in winter and popped corn, parched pinders [peanuts] and roasted corn ears." In addition to the entertainment, parents pondered daily events and taught their children how to avoid punishments. In the evenings, Jacob Stroyer's parents dealt with the thorny issue of his frequent whippings and concluded that they do nothing other than pray for a change.[51]

Former slaves did not include bedtime stories in their litany of leisure activities; however, storytelling at nightfall is one of the oldest forms of amusement. Former slaves recalled hearing their parents, grandparents, and others tell about their African childhoods or relate how slave traders stole Africans and transported them to America. Groves Scott remembered hearing of whites enticing Africans with trinkets, and capturing and holding them in pens before shoving off to the "big waters." Scott added that the captives left "the little children crying on the shore never to be seen no more."[52]

Traditional family celebrations, such as birthday parties, held little meaning for young slaves who rarely knew when their natal day occurred. Some witnessed birthday celebrations in their owners' households. When Fanny Fox was three years old, her mother invited the Stackhouse children, who lived nearby, to "take tea" with her in 1860. To celebrate the occasion, the woman made "ice cream and had some cakes, etc. for [Fanny's] supper table." To pass the time, they "looked at picture books and played with doll babies." Adelaide must have been aware of the party since she worked in the Fox household, and the arrival of guests would not have gone unnoticed. Perhaps she had helped prepare the food. If the eight-year-old Adelaide had not yet learned that as an enslaved child her "place" was in the kitchen and not among the invited guests,

Fanny's party would be such an instructive experience. Along with that lesson, Adelaide would understand that Fox called upon her to entertain "Miss Fanny" only if there were no white children present.[53]

Although the majority of slave children did not entertain themselves with parties, they sometimes enjoyed caring for pets which they found living in their natural environment. Susan Bradford Eppes claimed that Aunt Dinah encouraged the children in her plantation nursery to catch "'Mammy Doodles' and terrapins to be kept in the nursery as pets." Tryphena Fox mentioned a pet raccoon owned by one of the slaves. She also wrote at length about an unusual bird with "bright red on the back and breast with a circle of faun colored feathers around its neck" which the youngster Dan caught in a trap. The bird was likely to remain an object of interest while the "pet coon" would probably become an item for gastronomical pleasure.[54]

Some slave children spent time hunting, fishing, and collecting nuts or berries for themselves or their families. Hunting game was more than mere recreation. It supplemented the regular dietary fare with rabbits, squirrels, raccoons, opossums, and wild turkeys. Bond servants did not frown upon killing game for food as did certain classes of white hunters who looked down upon "pothunters." This attitude was clearly expressed by the Honorable William Elliot of Beaufort, South Carolina, who gave advice to his young sporting friends, claiming the worst use one could make of the game was to eat it. Persons who hunted for sport were to give their catch to those who needed it. Slaves were in no position to discriminate so lavishly. Simon Stokes remembered having a "big time possum huntin'" as only one part of the venture. Another was enjoying a meal of roast possum "wid sweet taters."[55]

Slaveholders sometimes orchestrated leisure activities for slaves and joined in for their own entertainment. Their motives for getting involved in such activities varied. Consider John Houston Bills, who gave a barbecue for his slaves on July 4, 1860. Bills accompanied his daughter and several of her friends to the slave quarters to watch. On another occasion, he commented about taking "13 children and negroes" to the "juvenile minstrels." He added, "They are all much delighted." He made no comments about their receptivity to an October 13, 1859, contest when twenty-two of the slaves paired off to pick cotton. The winners received a dime each. Bills created an activity and succeeded in getting the cotton picked in rapid time.[56]

Just as Bills organized a social event based upon the harvest, other slaveholders across geographical regions created similar entertainments. Corn shucking, a winter activity after the harvest of all crops, drew slaves together. The ultimate objective was to shell the corn quickly while singing and working. Corn songs are similar to spirituals or work songs wherein the soloist elicits a burst of energy from workers who respond with a chorus. The song "Come to Shuck That Corn To-night" told of their expectations:

> All dem puty gals will be dar
> Shuck dat corn before you eat,
> Dey will fix it fer us rare,
> Shuck dat corn before you eat.

They envisioned a "big" supper with "a fine roast pig." Other lyrics reveal further expectations:

> I hope dey'll have some whisky dar,
> Shuck dat corn before you eat.
> I think I'll fill my pockets full,
> Shuck dat corn before you eat.

Prizes occasionally went to participants who shelled the most corn. Intrinsic rewards included opportunities to socialize with slaves from other plantations who sometimes helped with the work.[57]

Martha Colquitt, who lived in Athens, Georgia, when interviewed, remembered the corn shuckings. But her mother only allowed the "chillen to watch 'em about a half hour . . . cause dey alway give de corn shuckin' folks some dram." Afterwards, the event "would get pretty lively and rough by the time de corn was shucked." Obviously, the mother feared the possibilities of some negative influence upon her children.[58]

Rice growers allowed festivities of a similar nature after their harvest ended. The slaves had a "big supper der fa aw dem wha' whip rice." One former slave remembered that to make their music, slaves "knock dem bones togedder en slap en pat dey hands" to make a "kind uv pretty tune." Slaves celebrated when they completed the 1856 sugar cane harvest in Plaquemines Parish, Louisiana. Their fetes signaled the end of one season and provided a reward to the slaves before the next season. Slaves labored as a unified force in this festive work and at other times as well. This was similar to communal work in Africa.[59]

Slaves received holidays at other times in the agricultural year. Such activities broke the monotony and offered respite at critical points. Workers could not keep up an accelerated pace indefinitely, nor would they want to. A short reprieve from arduous labor counteracted any growing restiveness with the job. John Nevitt, who lived near Natchez, Mississippi, rewarded his slaves with a "hollyday for the ballance of the day" on August 25, 1827, for their "good conduct during the making and laying by" of the crop. On November 8, 1857, R. R. Barrow granted his slaves a rest after arduous work for six weeks.[60]

In addition to participation in the celebrations, families spent time together during the lull before preparation for the next season. The respite gave slaves leisure to attend to their personal needs. Additionally, the corn shuckings and rice harvest days sometimes provided opportunities for visiting with friends and families who lived elsewhere.[61]

PLAY AND LEISURE

In a broader nonutilitarian context, of all special occasions for relaxation, Christmas drew the most attention. Henry Cathell, a northerner who traveled in the South in the 1850s, called the Christmas celebration "genuine Darkey Amusements in Excels of originality." Solomon Northup described it as "the carnival season with the children of bondage." It was not unusual for slaveholders to relax work schedules and award gifts. One planter forbade the whipping of all children during the Christmas season. Others gave tangible gifts of cash which allowed slaves to purchase desired items. Richard Jones remembered the excitement of his owner throwing coins among the slaves on Christmas day. "De chillum git dimes, nickels, quarters," he said. The children in another household received firecrackers and were having a "gay time" with them. On the White Hill plantation in Virginia, slaves gathered at the "big house" on Christmas morning to receive gifts of money, "lace collars, coffee mills and rattles" from their owner. An onlooker later noticed that "while distributions were going on, the young darkie turned summersaults on the grass or ran races around the circle, with an eye on the porch for the applause of the white person standing there." Beyond seeking attention, their antics carried no unusual significance.[62]

The holiday generally meant slaves received a special dinner and ate more than usual. Northup said whites gathered on the plantation to "witness the gastronomical enjoyment." In 1857 R. R. Barrow gave the slaves a barrel of flour and one beef cow. Children were more likely to remember celebrating with candy and popcorn.[63]

Aside from the gifts and extra food, Christmas was a special occasion since it ended the year for slaves who were hired out, and they rejoined their loved ones. Christmas was their apogee, and New Year's Day was the nadir since it signaled the hiring process anew. The first of January brought uncertainties as the slaves went to their new jobs. Slaves had no assurance that they would receive the same arrangement each year, nor was there any assurance that family and friends left behind would be there when they returned the following Christmas. Perhaps the pleasure of memories created by the Christmas celebrations warded off, as Frederick Douglass had predicted, the more dangerous thoughts and emotional anxiety created by the annual hiring process.[64]

It was customary for slaveowners to allow dances especially during the Christmas season. Dances were popular forms of entertainment among the old and young. Linkages between the African culture and that of African Americans exist in dances at Congo Square in New Orleans, where slaves gathered each week from the beginning of the nineteenth century until 1862. Whites often watched for their own entertainment.[65]

John Houston Bills carried his children into the slave quarters so they could "enjoy the Negro *dance.*" The music from two violins continued late into the night, and Bills noted, "All seem happy." Cathell observed slaves dancing and remarked cynically that "their love of dancing is great[.] the little niggers, from 4 years old to old grey beards, can't stand still when the fiddle begins." He was less pleased than Bills and his children. With or without whites present, slaves danced to the rhythm of musical instruments, the beat of drums, and rattle of gourds. In the absence of musical instruments, they made their own rhythm by "patting juba" or clapping their hands and patting their feet.[66]

Dances provided the "pleasure in prospect" and "pleasures of memory" that Frederick Douglass said kept down restiveness. Enslaved youngsters learned to play musical instruments from older slaves in the same manner as they learned to perform other chores from parents or older slaves. Moreover, musical talent boosted self-esteem and elevated the "musicianer" to a special place in the slave community. Beyond that, in time they would replace the older musicians.[67]

Apart from the music, there were a variety of dance steps that commanded attention. Fannie Berry, who spent her formative years in slavery, describes "Set de flo," a basic dance which slaves embellished with details:

> Dey come up an' bend over toward each other at de waist, an' de woman put her hands on her hips an' de man roll his eyes all roun' an' grim an' dey pat de flo' wid dey feet jus' like dey was puttin' it in place. Used to do dat bes' on dirt flo' so de feet could slap down hard against it.

As a variation, they sometimes set a glass of water atop their heads and made fancy steps. The fun of it all was dancing without spilling the water. This feat attracted attention and distinguished one from the crowd. The distinction would not go unchallenged by others, who tried to dance as well or better.[68]

Dances were occasions to seek and establish relationships with members of the opposite sex. Few slaves who experienced courtships during slavery did not speak of them in glowing terms. The parents sometimes made decisions about when youngsters, especially the girls, could entertain the opposite sex. Laura Bell met Thomas when she was twelve years old, but her parents objected because she was too young to "keep company." They defied her parents and met secretly for "seberal years." Dicy Windfield's parents allowed her to court when she "wuz 'bout eighteen years ole." Even so, she and her friend "wont allowed to go no whars together to 'mount to nothin'."[69]

After studying sexuality in the nineteenth-century slave community, Steven E. Brown asserts that young slaves, especially in Georgia, were "compelled to adhere to rigorous courtship strictures" including waiting until they reached the proper age. The WPA narratives suggest that the age constraint knew no geographical bounds among slave parents.[70]

Interest in courting catapulted youngsters, especially girls, toward a critical juncture in their lives. Harriet Jacobs reminded readers that the mothers of slaves lived "in daily expectation of trouble" once their children became teenagers. Parents were ever watchful because their ability to shield the children eroded more rapidly as they showed signs of physical maturity. The onset of childbearing in the late teens was a rite which signaled a female's passage from childhood to womanhood and reproduction. Moreover, the sale of "breeding" women was thought to occur less frequently than the sale of barren women. However, parents knew that chattel, with and without children, had no real protection from sales. Hesitancy on their part to allow their daughters to court at young ages reflected a desire to protect the girls as long as possible from owners who encouraged reproduction and from sexual abuse at the hands of lustful men.[71]

Nevertheless, when opportunities arose, the young slaves' courting manners were ritualistic and stylized. In keeping with "rules," girls used whatever skills of coquetry they possessed until they satisfied themselves that the suitor was a likely person. One former slave remembers that it was not "stylish fer young courting gals to let on like dey has any appetite to speak of." The girls "prettied" themselves with makeup created from dried chinaberries and sometimes added ribbon to their hair. Maggie Black remembered that "chillun'ud go in the woods en ge' wild grape vine en bend em round en put em under us skirt en make it stand out big lak." To add charm, according to Gus Feaster, the girls hid honeysuckle and rose petals "in dere bosom."[72]

Florid phrases and witty dialogue—"sweet talk"—was a vital part of courtship. In 1895 Fred D. Banks, a member of the Hampton Institute Folklore Society, described the influence of "Uncle Gilbert," an expert in "courtship's words and ways." "Slave lads" sought his advice about the "mighty ticklish bizness" of courting. Gilbert believed any young man who tried to "git a gal wuth havin, mus' know how to talk fur her." Whether they were sophisticated or clumsy, each young man tried to perfect his discourse.[73]

Young courting couples at parties played kissing games including "Walking the Lonesome Road," "Fruit in the Basket," "Fishing," "Peep, Squirrel," and "In the well." In the latter game a male called out:

> "I'm in the well!"
> question: "How many feet deep?"
> answer: The depth varied depending upon his choice.
> question: "Who will you have to pull you out?"
> answer: A name is given.

The person designated to rescue the victim pulls him out with the number of kisses equivalent to the depth of the well. Another game, "Peep, Squirrel," involved couples and entitled the player to a kiss if he caught the "squirrel."[74]

Former slave men tended to boast about winning affection. When together, young courting slaves engaged in playful banter to test wits, establish friendships, and win hearts. The feelings of pride and self-esteem were ever-present when favored by love. They wanted to appear in control of their lives and not subjected to that of the patrols, owners, or overseers. They suffered embarrassment and bruised egos if thwarted. Laura Bell was too young to remember slavery but recounted her father's bravery when the overseer intended to punish her mother. She said:

Pappy do' he ain't never make no love ter mammy comes up an' takes de whippin' fer her. Atter dat de cou't on Saddy an' Sunday an' at de sociables till dey gits married.[75]

Courting couples went to great lengths to see each other if they did not live in the same place. Regular church services, revivals, and camp meetings provided religious inspiration along with opportunities to visit with friends. In the absence of such gatherings, the infatuated found other ways. With or without permission, they visited their favorites. Many walked great distances and risked beatings by patrollers. When unable to visit, they sent messages or wrote letters. Jim Crawford apparently accompanied his owner to a campsite near New Market, Virginia, during the Civil War and decided to write a house servant on the Crawford plantation. Obviously Jim disclosed his true feelings for her but tried to make amends when he learned that she was serious about someone else. He explained:

Conflicting Emotions filled my heart when I heard that you who held my affections were about to become the bride of another nor was the pain which the News caused curred away until I heard that it was all a joke. . . .

Crawford begged for a quick response to relieve the "utmost anxiety" of waiting for a favorable reply.[76]

Additionally, some slaves gave gifts to their special friends. Some beaus presented gifts of a practical nature rather than trinkets. Omelia Thomas, who was too young to remember slavery, repeated an often told story about her parent's courtship. "He noticed that she was sewing with ravelings and he said, 'Lady, next time I come I'll bring you a spool of thread if you don't mind.'" Of course, she did not object and enjoyed his next visit as well as the gift.[77]

During the courtship between Henry and Melinda Bibb, he paid more attention to values of a higher nature. He insisted upon knowing her thoughts about religion and freedom because of his deep affinity for both. Bibb's spiritual and romantic love for Melinda did not dissuade him from wanting to run away. Neither did it fit the stereotypical formula which portrayed slave men as lascivious and women as promiscuous. Bibb never mentioned sexuality when writing about his affection for Melinda, nor did he repeat what her owner said when he gave the girl permission to marry. Bibb thought it was "too vulgar" to repeat.[78]

If courtships resulted in a desire to marry, slave parents probably offered advice. David Ross insisted that the parents of enamored couples play a role in such decisions, since he considered them the "best judges" in such matters. Otherwise, slaves sought permission to marry from owners. Those not owned by the same person made the request themselves or asked others to intercede on their behalf. The owner of one enamored slave sought permission for the couple. He wrote:

[My] negro boy James Informs me that he wished one of your negro girls to be his wife I can only say that I believe him to be as well disposed as common so fair [sic] as I know or believe.

If granted permission, marriages followed.[79]

In agricultural regions, especially where there were significant variations in work patterns, slave marriages followed a seasonal trend with the greatest number occurring between Christmas and New Year's Day. The lay-by season in July was another popular time for weddings. Few couples married during the plowing, planting, cultivating, or harvest seasons, which suggests that there was little time for leisure or festivities.[80]

Marriage by ministers and wedding celebrations depended upon the wishes of slaveowners. When Thomas Chaplain's wife fussed over preparations for a wedding for their slaves Eliza and Nelly, he grumbled, "I do not wish to be here to see the tomfoolery that was going on about it, as if they were ladies of quality." Chaplain went fishing, and the arrangements continued apace. In an atypical 1856 wedding ceremony in Mississippi, seven couples stood together in a circle, hand in hand, and were united in the presence of slaves and their owners in addition to several other whites. The person performing the ceremony asked each bride and groom individually, "Do you agree, before me & these witnesses to take [———] as your [———] & to solemnly pledge yourself to discharge toward [———] the duties of an affectionate & faithful [———]." He concluded the ceremony with "We have now gone through with every form necessary to authorize me to pronounce each of these several couples as man and wife." Each couple agreed to enter into married relations and took "a solemn vow of fidelity to the obligations of the married state." After repeating each set of names, the official pronounced the couples married and asked each groom to salute his bride according to "the good old custom of our fathers & mothers." In this wedding "of a novel and peculiar character," the familiar phrase "until death do us part" was missing. Slaves were not legally bound by the marriage, and wishes of owners took precedence over their desires.[81]

Most slaves married with less fanfare than the multiple wedding in Mississippi. At the opposite end of the spectrum was the December 22, 1860, marriage between two slaves at Green Mount, a Virginia plantation. The thirteen-year-old Benjamin Robert Fleet recorded a brief note about the wedding in his journal. "I married Phillis and Cousin John Fleet's Charles about 10 o'clock," he wrote. Fleet conducted the ceremony by reading "the Matrimony out of the Prayer Book." What the couple thought of a child playing such a significant role in their lives is unknown. But the child's role clearly reflects how seriously slaveowners viewed slave marriages.[82]

An often-repeated account about slave marriages suggests that couples united by simply jumping over a broom handle. This gesture, which was more symbolic than real, is comparable to throwing the bridal bouquet after modern weddings to determine who will be the next bride. In a similar vein, couples who leapt over a broom did so to determine who would "rule" their house. Consider the recollections of two former slaves. Columbus Williams, who was ninety-eight when interviewed, said, "I have heard of them stepping over a broom but I never saw it." And Penny Thompson who was twelve years younger, remembered that after a specially prepared dinner "dey puts de broom on de floor and de couple takes de hands and steps over de broom." The inflated importance of jumping over the broom comes from testimony of interviewees, children during slavery, who remembered the broom but not the actual ceremony.[83]

Following weddings there were occasional celebrations either at the slaveowners' homes or in the slaves' quarters. Thomas Chaplain missed the "grand supper" upon his family table set with his crockery, candlesticks, and "everything else they wanted," he surmised. The disgruntled owner later discovered and complained long afterwards that his wife had also used his "good" liquor in the bowl of punch. One slaveowner recalled that after the outdoor ceremony on July 5, 1856, which united Susan and Sam, the whites returned to their home and the slaves went to "big Lize's house and had toddy, cake & lemonade." After Dicy Windfield married in a double ceremony with her sister in the presence of "a big bunch o' people," they had "all kinds o' good stuff cooked up fer de weddin' feast."[84]

Without respect for the kinds of ceremonies and celebrations associated with uniting couples, it is fair to ask what slave couples expected in such marriages. The following ditty indicates that they were no different from others who wanted security and tranquillity:

> Harper's creek and roarin' ribber,
> Thar, my dear, we'll live forebber,
> Den we'll go to de Ingin nation,
> All I want in dis creation,
> Is pretty little wife and big plantation.

Living in the Indian nation meant residency in the unorganized territory, perhaps beyond the pale of slavery or other matters that could make slave marriages a farce.[85]

Without a doubt, some enslaved men and women never married the person of their choice because of interferences from owners. An estimated 10 percent of them were involved in "forced" marriages. They were understandably embittered. Although the circumstances differed, Harriet Jacobs loved a childhood friend with "all the ardor of a young girl's first love," but her owner James Norcom refused to give his permission for them to marry because of his own sexual desires for the girl. Rather than jeopardizing her beloved's life, Jacobs ended the relationship. "The dream of my girlhood," she wrote, "was over."[86]

The general thrust of Jacobs's association with a free man is similar to Harriet Smith's. Smith, a North Carolina-born slave, married a free man when

PLAY AND LEISURE

she was nineteen or twenty years old only to have her owner's sons break up the marriage. Sexual desires for Harriet motivated them. Smith, unlike Jacobs, did not write about the shattering of her dreams, but it is clear that neither of them enjoyed marriages with men of their choices while enslaved.[87]

The range of various forms of play and recreation from ring games to weddings provided "relief from the boredom and drudgery of labour." The adult Frederick Douglass was skeptical of slaveholders who created fetes for their slaves. He wrote:

> Holidays are conductors or safety valves to carry off the explosive elements inseparable from the human mind, when reduced to the condition of slavery. But for these, the rigors of bondage would have become too severe for endurance, and the slave would have been forced to a dangerous desperation.

Douglass saw holidays as gross frauds created not for the happiness of laborers but for the of owners of that labor.[88]

Certainly, some older slaves were suspicious of their owners' objectives, but it is unlikely that children and youth thought of the holidays and dances in the same manner. Until they reached the moment of truth regarding their owners' motives, they would enjoy the "pleasures in prospect" before the fete and the "pleasures of memory" afterwards. Otherwise, the child-centered activities which they initiated purely for their own amusement would continue to provide "all sorts of good times."[89]

4 "KNOWLEDGE UNFITS A CHILD TO BE A SLAVE"*

TEMPORAL AND SPIRITUAL EDUCATION

> The White folks feared for niggers
> to get any religion and education. . . .
>
> —W. L. Bost**

Slaves spent some of their leisure time in search of the fundamentals of education, both temporal and spiritual. Their primary concern with the secular was
literacy, while their interest in the sacred involved religion, especially Christianity. The extent to which they succeeded depended upon the owners' attitudes
about their intellectual and religious development. Owners were ever conscious
of the possibilities of undermining slavery with religion or education if it changed
the bond servants' worldview and made them restive. It was virtually impossible
to prevent slaves from exposure to knowledge, innocuous or pernicious, since
they learned at early ages to keep such information "under de covers." Differences in what slaveowners approved of slaves knowing and what the enslaved
people desired for themselves created tension.[1]

Being knowledgeable about how to resolve this tension was a vital part of an
enslaved child's education. This chapter examines how children gained literacy
and practiced their religious beliefs. Of equal importance, it examines the role
that parents and others played in teaching behavior that was appropriate for
children as well as for slaves.

Parental responsibilities were especially crucial in this matter because of
not only the limited time they spent with their offspring, but also the ever-
present possibility of slaveholders removing children from their protective
arms at will. Therefore, it was necessary to teach fundamental survival skills at
early ages. Despite their travails, many enslaved parents demonstrated an
unfailing love for their offspring and socialized them to endure slavery by

---

* Frederick Douglass, *Life and Times of Frederick Douglass: Written by Himself* (London: Collier, 1962), 79.

** George P. Rawick, ed., *The American Slave: A Composite Autobiography* (Westport: Greenwood, 1972), XIV: North Carolina Narr. (Series 2), Part 1:143.

STOLEN CHILDHOOD

paying deference to whites while maintaining self-respect. This embodied a major act of resistance and equipped children to defend themselves on the psychological battlefield.

Parents, whether together or alone, taught their youngsters how to tolerate inhumane acts and degradation while maintaining their humanity and keeping their spirit intact. An 1833 letter from the Tennessean Hobbs to his wife in Virginia is testimony to the difficulties of separation, especially from his daughter Elizabeth. Additionally, Hobbs expressed an abiding interest in the child's growth and development. Confidently he wrote of a singular dream: "I want Elizabeth to be a good girl." To be a "good girl" probably meant that she was to obey, help with chores, and do anything necessary to help mitigate the family's conditions.[2]

Two decades later, Prince Woodfin forwarded a similar message from a Jamestown, California, gold field to his wife back in North Carolina. The 1853 dispatch urged, "Rais your children up rite." The father added, "Learn them to be Smart and deadent and alow them to Sauce no person." This was pertinent advice for surviving slavery. Courteous children would not cause offense nor would they bring reprisals upon themselves or their parents. In this context "Smart" does not refer to intellectual development but to industrious behavior.[3]

Children learned the importance of performing chores satisfactorily at young ages. They observed such actions firsthand on large plantations as they worked in "trash gangs." In addition to serving as a "teaching-learning" experience, participation in the agricultural work units raised the consciousness of youngsters who imitated their elders. Much of the advice for maneuvering through the minefields of slavery came from parents, grandparents, and others who had grown up in bondage.[4]

Enslaved parents insisted upon respect from their children, who consequently learned to give deference to their elders. Prince Woodfin's edict "Alow them to Sauce no person" was not uniquely his own but a view held in common with many slaves. The northern-born teacher Charlotte Forten observed that among the children on South Carolina's Sea Islands it was "the rarest thing to hear a disrespectful word from a child to his parent." The Mississippi planter Everard Green Baker appeared unfamiliar with the custom when he wrote, "The young should be taught to be respectful & obedient to the older ones." He also insisted that enslaved adults be "kind and considerate to the younger ones."[5]

The suggestions show the limits of Baker's understanding of what slaves did in their own time and the character of their behavior within the slave community. Although good advice reinforces good practices, few slaves required such guidance from outsiders. An enslaved father impressed that lesson upon his son when he scolded, "You are my child and when I call you, you should come immediately, if you have to pass through fire and water." The simultaneous calls from the boy's father and owner precipitated the harsh-sounding order. The child had responded to the owner rather than his father.[6]

If faced with a recurring situation, a child would develop a strategy to pacify both the parent and owner. For example, a Cherokee freedwoman's mother addressed her as Sarah, and their owner called her Annie. Regardless of her response, the eight-year-old girl faced a whipping from one of the women. The tug-of-war, Sarah said, "made me hate both of them." She admits the scorn, but did not mention fearing her mother or owner. "I got the devil in me," she said, "and wouldn't come to either one." She found comfort in her grandmother, who watched the dynamics between the women from a nearby porch.[7]

Many slave parents demanded obedience from their children, but they were not sadistic. Their basic goal was to protect the children from harm at the hands of malicious whites. A comment made by Baby Suggs, a character in Toni Morrison's novel *Beloved* underscores the importance of being ever vigilant about her children facing dangerous situations. "It's my job to know what is," she said, "and to keep them away from what I know is terrible." Parents demanded obedience, respect, and unity from children to achieve that result. The lives of parents and children in bondage converged at so many points that the actions of one reverberated upon the other.[8]

Application of the axiom "Children are to be seen and not heard" served as a protective armor against children who talked too much. Parents could not tolerate "enemies" within their own families. Susan Snow, a youngster in Mississippi during the Civil War, learned the value of the saying after unwittingly singing:

> Jeff Davis, long and slim
> whipped old Abe with a hickory limb.
> Jeff Davis is a wise man, Lincoln is a fool
> Jeff Davis rides a gray and Lincoln rides a mule.

Although the first stanza was innocuous, other lyrics contained more poignant social commentary:

> Old Gen'd Pope had a shotgun,
> filled it full o' gum,
> killed 'em as dey come.
> Called a Union band,
> Make de Rebels understand
> To leave de land,
> Submit to Abraham.

This ditty gave pause to supporters of the Confederate States of America (CSA), since it predicted their defeat. Moreover, Snow sang about the president of the CSA, owner of a large plantation and scores of slaves in Warren County, Mississippi. This added another dimension of social criticism about the Magnolia State's slaveholders. Learning when to sing the song was more important than learning the song itself. Slaves sang it, but the child did not realize the tune was up "dey sleeves." She sang it within earshot of her owner and received a whipping.[9]

Slaveholders had clear ideas about the appropriate behavior for enslaved youngsters and made their expectations known through instructions to overseers and others. W. W. Gilmer commented specifically about the desirable conduct of children in an 1852 issue of the *Southern Planter*. He urged slaveholders to teach young servants not to run and hide from whites, but "to stand their ground, and speak when spoken to, in a polite manner. . . . Talk to them; take notice of them; it soon gives them confidence." It also "adds greatly to their value," he concluded. The children's self-esteem was less important than creating the impression that they were intelligent and malleable servants who recognized their place in the society. "Polite" slaves approached whites with bowed heads, downcast eyes, and hushed voices.[10]

The former slave Jacob Stroyer commented about his owner's interest in creating subservience through an exercise performed by the children. In anticipation of his arrival, the children bathed, groomed their hair, and dressed in their best clothes. Afterwards, Stroyer wrote:

> We were then drilled in the art of addressing our expected visitors. The boys were required to bend the body forward with head down, and rest the body on the left foot, and scrape the right foot backward on the ground, while uttering the words, "how dy Massie and Missie."

The girls curtsied and repeated the same words. This was acceptable demeanor for slaves.[11]

There were no special ceremonies to teach Adelaide deference rituals at Hygiene, yet Tryphena Fox set the machinery in motion to reinforce the social distance between her three-year-old daughter Fanny and Adelaide. The woman referred to her daughter as "Miss Fanny" when speaking of the child vis-à-vis the slaves, large or small, old or young. "Miss Fanny" gave "Old Reuben" a dime for Christmas in 1859. The title "Miss" denotes differences in their status and suggests that slaves, regardless of size or age, owed deference to the child. Adelaide's response to the situation is unknown. By contrast, a Juniper County, Mississippi, slave girl's reaction under similar conditions reveals the level of her understanding of the deference ritual. When introduced to her "young mistress," the eleven-year-old Lu looked at the infant in her mother's arms and said, "I don't see no young mistress, that's a baby."[12]

The examples above come from different quarters, yet the objective in each was to establish the "master-servant" relationship. In such situations slave children learned to pay deference to whites, adults or children. Tractable servants were not likely to run afoul of rules established by whites. Enslaved parents viewed compliance with the deference ritual as a way of avoiding slavery's punitive arm; however, they knew that it did not accurately represent their feelings. They juggled public behavior and private convictions without upsetting the routine established by whites. This behavior required a degree of sophistication which encroached upon their childhood since it compelled children to behave in a mature manner long before they became adults biologically.

Although children learned to behave as adults, it is doubtful if they understood paternalism, which defined the relations between superordinate and subordinate or master and slave wherein each party had responsibilities, duties, and rights. The "special sense of family shaped southern culture," writes Eugene Genovese, wherein blacks and whites melded "into one people with genuine elements of affection and intimacy." This was a difficult concept for children when owners and the slaves were not in agreement about its meaning. Owners saw themselves as benevolent patriarchs interested in the welfare of their families, white and black, while bond servants, in the privacy of their humble abodes, sometimes pointed to the differences between the rhetoric and reality of such relationships.[13]

Bond servants frequently adopted a demeanor to camouflage their understanding of those discrepancies. The ex-slave Henry Bibb's comment "The only weapon of self defence that I could use successfully was that of deception" illustrates the point. The mask, a protective device, became a part of their countenance. It functioned as protective covering for different inclinations as explained by the ex-slave who said, "Got one mind for the boss to see; got another for what I know is me." This was tantamount to keeping secrets from the enemy.[14]

Parents seized every opportunity to teach children how to forge a balance between social courtesies to whites and their own self-esteem. The urgency of the matter was ever-present, whether it was during the rigorous period between sunup and sundown or after dark in their quarters. Evenings served as special times to educate and entertain. Children learned adages that offered advice, reinforced truisms, and raised levels of consciousness. "What goes around comes around," "Beauty is only skin deep, but love is to the bone," and "The blacker the berry the sweeter the juice" are but a few of the maxims which cautioned them against capriciousness while instilling confidence about coloration in a society where pigmentation mattered.[15]

Children also learned about their culture from older Africans or their descendants, who passed on recollections in keeping with their oral tradition. After an 1832–1833 visit to South Carolina, the Congregationalist clergyman Samuel Cram Jackson from Andover, Massachusetts, commented about a slave who talked about the interior of Africa, which he reported had "cities & villages, proper education," and a class structure with scholars, farmers, and soldiers.[16]

The likelihood of enslaved youngsters knowing about Africa was very good since there were large numbers of African-born slaves in the United States in 1808 when the overseas trade ended. Furthermore, Africans were still coming into the United States through the illegal slave trade well into the 1850s. The WPA narratives contain many references to capturing, enslaving, and transporting Africans into America via the Atlantic slave trade legally or illegally. As a child in Henning, Tennessee, the writer Alex Haley listened to his grandmother recount such stories about an African foreparent called Kunta Kinte, who "lived across the ocean near what he called the *Kamby Bolongo*."[17]

Aside from the family lore, children heard tales that were directly related to their maturation process. In *The Uses of Enchantment*, Bruno Bettelheim argues that fairy tales serve a useful purpose whereby children gain wisdom through stories, "the purveyors of deep insights." Fairy tales fill the need for magic while instilling a belief that good will triumph over evil. It is possible that slave children working in homes among white children heard fairy tales since Jakob and Wilhelm Grimm published their famous collection of German folk tales including "Little Red Riding Hood" and "Snow White" well before slavery ended. Even so, fairy tales were not sufficiently widespread among bond servants to displace African folk tales, which served a similar purpose.[18]

The folk tales furnish behavioral models and satisfy the need for alternatives through dreams. Animal trickster tales, an integral part of the African oral tradition, teach lessons of survival and self-confidence. Irony and cynicism abound in the complex narratives of mythology and fantasy, which entertain and educate. Animals in the tales refer to each other as "brother" in the same manner that slaveholders referred to their chattel as "family." On one hand, they are indeed "brothers" and "family," for they belong to the same species. On the other hand, certain characteristics, such as race or class, circumvent true kinship. These lessons were not lost on the young.[19]

Animal tricksters have human properties; therefore, the powerful fox or wolf is an easy substitute for a slaveowner or any other oppressor, while a meek rabbit or terrapin symbolizes the oppressed person. Young slaves could readily identify with weak persecuted characters such as the helpless "Brer Rabbit," who faces danger yet endures. Brer Rabbit uses wit and guile to outmaneuver stronger and more vicious animals, but he is not content with survival alone and seeks to elevate his status in the eyes of others. At base, Brer Rabbit is as deceitful as Brer Fox, but the listener is encouraged to sympathize with Brer Rabbit, who carefully cloaks his callousness with an honest facade. Although inconsistent with religious teachings, Rabbit's behavior is overlooked inasmuch as the tales have no sacred or moral basis. Finally, the weak Brer Rabbit uses any means necessary to survive and overpower stronger animals. After an examination of African American trickster tales, John W. Roberts asserts that "the sadistic elements of the trickster tales more aptly reflect a modern sense of moral outrage over slavery."[20]

Aside from the animal trickster tales, slaves told stories about "John," who is analogous to Brer Rabbit in antebellum stories of human deception. Slaves exchanged these tales in the same fashion as the animal fables. The structure of human trickster tales is similar to the animal stories, yet it differs in that John does not always succeed. His triumphs are never as great as the animal trickster, who wins love, kills adversaries, and elevates his stature at every turn. John is not Brer Rabbit's equal, but his shrewdness serves a purpose. Lawrence W. Levine contends that the tales were "the vehicle through which slaves rehearsed their tactics, laughed at the foibles of their masters (and themselves), and taught their young the means they would have to adopt in order to survive." Survival was not so much a matter of being a trickster as it was of not being a trickster's victim.[21]

Parents also tried to prevent their children from falling prey to the more serious offense of sexual abuse. Many former slaves claimed that their parents did not provide any sex education. Anthropologist Melville J. Herskovits's study of Dahomey details the instructions given to boys and girls as they approach puberty. The simulation of sexual experiences constitutes much of the training for boys, who discuss and dramatize "love stories" in all male groups. Of those instructions, David Brion Davis writes, "Negro girls received from older women a well-planned sexual education, which included elaborate exercises and pro-longed stimulation of the appropriate organs." At the appropriate age, boys and girls engaged in stages of courting before consummating marriage. Dahomeans viewed this learning process as an essential part of their education.[22]

Considering the number of Africans coming into the New World from West Africa with such knowledge, it is also possible that they passed it on to their offspring just as they transferred other facets of their culture. Harriet Jacobs mentioned "the pure principles inculcated by my grandmother" when writing about her own sexuality. Perhaps WPA informants who denied receiving sex education while enslaved were uncomfortable with the subject and ended the discussions by claiming ignorance.[23]

Rather than open dialogue, it is possible that parents used indirect ways of sensitizing their children about sexuality and resisting exploitation. The avoidance of such discussions was a reflection of their time. Minnie Folkes remembered her mother saying, "Don't let nobody bother yo' principle; 'cause dat was all yo' had." The meaning of "principle" used by Folkes and Jacobs is left to interpretation. By contrast, Lucy McCullough's mother said nothing, but there is little doubt about her intentions. The former slave recounted her mother's reactions after seeing her "cummin' crost de yahd en she say mah dress too short." The woman ripped out the hem and wove "more cloff on hit, twel it long enuf, lak she want it." The added length was little protection against obvious signs of maturity, yet the mother believed it would shield her daughter a while longer.[24]

Because of differences in interpretations and the general reticence to discuss sexuality, it is difficult to know to what extent parents or others socialized boys and girls about their sexuality. To be sure, children were sensitized to the roles of expectant mothers and childcare for infants with working mothers through their contact with pregnant and lactating women in trash gangs. They must have overheard conversations between the women and their elders, who added a retrospective dimension, about childbearing and parenting. Furthermore, pre-dominantly female activities such as quilting or cooking, where women worked together in groups, may have served the same purposes. Trapping, hunting, animals, woodcutting, or other exercises thought to be predominantly male activities must have served as an agency for the sex-role socialization of boys.[25]

STOLEN CHILDHOOD

Plantation management rules and the division of labor in the slave quarters also served to socialize children. Examples abounded. One slaveowner declared that men were to provide firewood and the women were to cook, launder, and mend clothes for the family. Older girls were expected to help their mothers. Lina Hunter recalled that she was not at liberty to travel throughout the Georgia plantation where she grew up. "Master had a big old ginhouse on de plantation about 2 miles from de big house," she remembered, "but I never seed in it, 'cause dey didn't 'low 'omens and chilluns 'round it." More poignant examples include humiliation of recalcitrant men by making them dress in women's clothing or do "women's work." McDonald Furman's edict "No man must whip his wife without my permission" suggests male domination both on the plantation and in the quarters. Parents probably worked diligently to guide their children through a maze of practices that devalued humans according to gender and status.[26]

The advice that the children learned for maneuvering through the labyrinth of southern etiquette was not available to them through schools, child-rearing literature, or children's fiction. Parents and other adults provided examples of accepted behavior and passed survival tactics down to youngsters through oral lore.[27]

Although this is true, there were some boys and girls who learned to read and write while still in bondage. Their scanty educational opportunities contrasted sharply with those of white children like Launcelot Blackford. The opportunities for slaves also paled by comparison with those of free children of the time. Some slaveholders feared the usurpation of their power by educated slaves and deliberately kept them ignorant. Other slaveowners believed literacy was necessary to Christian salvation and permitted Bible literacy. In either case, slave children became literate in a haphazard manner, if at all. Of those who learned to read and write, the greater percentage were house and skilled servants. Because children often worked in the slaveholder's home before assuming jobs elsewhere, they had greater access to knowledge.[28]

Literacy made knowledge of pending events a real possibility. Besides, literacy elevated self-esteem in the bosoms of those who accomplished what some believed was beyond their mental capacities. "Comparing them [blacks] by their faculties of memory, reason, and imagination, it appears to me," wrote Thomas Jefferson, "that in memory they are equal to the whites; in reason much inferior." Remarking about the imagination of blacks, Jefferson believed they were "dull, tasteless, and anomalous." He noted that in comparing blacks and whites it would be "right to make great allowances for the differences of condition, of education, of conversation, of the sphere in which they move," yet he claimed to have never encountered a person of African descent who "had uttered a thought above the level of plain narration" or had painted or written anything worthy of the "dignity of criticism." Less learned slaveholders than Jefferson entertained such thoughts, and the debate questioning the mental capabilities of African Americans resurfaced with regularity.[29]

Despite adverse conditions, some enslaved children defied the odds against acquiring literacy. As a child, Booker T. Washington carried the books for his owner's daughter and caught glimpses of her schoolroom abuzz with learning. He developed a keen desire for knowledge and became one of the best-known American educators at the turn of the century. "The picture of several dozen boys and girls in a schoolroom engaged in study made a deep impression," he wrote. Washington thought going to school would be like "getting into paradise."[30]

There were a variety of ways that enslaved children entered "paradise." Anderson Whitted's father taught him to read, and Nat Turner's family taught him to read. The freedman James Thomas attended school in Nashville, Tennessee, while Jacob Stroyer did not disclose how he learned. Perhaps he taught himself. One of the WPA interviewees said that "some of de white folks" taught her to read and write and she passed the knowledge on to her daughter. The same was true of Stiles M. Scruggs.[31]

Thomas Pittus, a former slave, believed his owner taught him to read so he might "be half way able to use tolerably good language around his grand children." Another young driver carried his "Webster's blue back speller & history" along when he drove his owner to see patients. "I would study and masser would tell me how to pronounce hard words," he said. The boy's owner also pronounced the words in Latin. Another slaveholder taught his slave to read and write so he could copy the names and addresses of patients.[32]

Sometimes the teaching of slaves was an educational activity in which more than one member of a family participated. Such was the case with John Hartwell and Louisa Cocke. Her diary contains many references about the education of bond servants at their Virginia plantation. The pious John Cocke aimed to "increase the intelligence and improve the moral character" of his slaves. Cocke believed that the age of seven was an excellent one to begin teaching the children; besides, it removed them from the unfavorable influence of the slave quarters.[33]

The Cockes' earliest experiment with instructing enslaved children came in the late 1820s when Ellen Burrows, a northern teacher, worked along with Louisa Cocke. When this proved successful, Cocke decided to establish a permanent school and hired a teacher in early 1830. Louisa Cocke joyfully reported that the pupils "appeared to be the happiest creatures in the world" with their new situation. A week after the school began Louisa wrote:

> Good Miss Betsey has gone to work at her appointed vocation. . . . She seems much encouraged with the success which has attended her commencement, & seems to be quite as well pleased with her scholars as if their faces were of the finest white & red.[34]

When Miss Betsey left after a brief stay, Louisa Cocke continued teaching the children over the next five years with the help of her daughter, daughter-in-law, and slave women. Louisa Cocke staged a Christmas program and invited her husband to attend as an incentive for the children. Cocke's young scholars tried her patience in July 1831 when they were "dull & inattentive." A few weeks later she complained of "trying half an hour ineffectively to rouse them" and retreated from the classroom in distress. The continuous teaching and summer heat were probably responsible for their lethargy.[35]

Perhaps the brightest of the children was little Lucy Skipwith, who attended the school in 1834. Cocke soon believed the girl was "much above the ordinary cast" of pupils. Lucy was confident enough to visit the teacher's home to entertain her with "the recital of several hymns," besides asking "many questions." The visit was "pleasing proof that she had profitted much by her instruction in the Infant School," wrote the proud teacher.[36]

After moving to Alabama in 1840, Lucy Skipwith operated a school at Cocke's Hopewell, Alabama, plantation. The daily routine of the school troubled Skipwith, who believed she could not do much with the boys because the lesson did "not lay upon their mines as it ought to." The problem was irregular attendance caused by their work. Troubled by this situation, Skipwith pleaded with Cocke, "I hope that you will soon be here to help me in this cause for I needs your help very much." Rather than actual assistance, she wanted permission to allow the boys to miss work to attend school.[37]

In the midst of the cotton picking season, the children's attendance declined further; therefore, Skipwith opened a night school, but the children were too tired after work to study. She complained, "I cannot keep their eyes open." Her desire to teach superseded common sense and their ability to tolerate the extended day. Lucy Skipwith intended to impart knowledge to members of the slave community, and her efforts met Cocke's approval.[38]

Other slaveholders built schools and hired teachers. Motivated by the intrinsic value of education, a Kentucky slaveowner wrote:

> You colored boys and girls must learn to read and write, no matter what powers object . . . your parents and your grandparents were taught to read and write when they belonged to my forefathers and you young negroes have to learn as much.[39]

Literacy was useful and often necessary for slaves working in urban commercial operations or in maritime activities. Blacks in Elizabeth City County and Hampton, Virginia, availed themselves of educational opportunities before the Civil War since it was not unusual for slaveholders to teach their slaves to read and write. A small number of literate blacks lived in the area before the Civil War. Mary Peake, a free woman and local resident, operated the city's earliest school for blacks. Shortly after she moved to Hampton in 1847, she began teaching black children without regard for their status.[40]

In addition to schooling and individual instruction from adults, slaves learned to read through the tutelage of white children, who probably constituted a large percentage of the white teachers. The WPA narratives contain many such accounts. Robert Glenn of Raleigh, North Carolina, remembered his owner's son Crosby. The boy, he said

> . . . took a great liking to me. Once in an undertone he asked me how I would like to have an education. I was overjoyed at the suggestion and he at once began to teach me secretly. I studied hard and he soon had me so I could read and write well. I continued studying and he continued teaching me. He furnished me books and slipped all the papers he could get to me and I was the best educated Negro in the community without any one except the slaves knowing what was going on.

The sense of pride and elevated self-esteem are evident in the statement. Glenn's recollections indicate that the two children knew their act would not meet approval. Note the words "undertone" and "slipped." Black and white children and youth ignored prohibitions and transcended the hurdles to literacy.[41]

There are similarities in the way Susie King Taylor's white playmate Katie offered her lessons if she would not tell Mr. O'Connor, her father. "On my promise not to do so," writes Taylor, "she gave me lessons about four months." Their agreement remained a secret. Katie's mother was fully aware of the lessons, but she did not interfere. Again, the anecdote implies that the children knew their actions would not meet the approval of the white patriarch.[42]

In the above instances, white children approached both Glenn and Taylor, but when Frederick Douglass no longer received lessons from his owner's wife he devised a clever scheme to further his education. Whenever he met any boy who he knew could read and write, he claimed that he could read and write as well. "The next word would be, don't believe you. Let me see you try." Knowing only four letters of the alphabet, Douglass wrote them, then challenged the boys to "beat that." "In this way," he recalled, "I got a good many lessons in writing." The ploy shaped Douglass's early concept of barter. He used bread taken from his owner's kitchen to pay for the lessons, thereby establishing a trade relationship that benefited all parties.[43]

George Horton, who lived in Chapel Hill, North Carolina, provides an example of a slave passing on the benefit of his education to his white contemporaries. In this situation it is questionable as to who profited more from his knowledge. Born in Northampton County, North Carolina, in 1797, Horton taught himself to read and wrote his first poem while still a child. Beginning in 1815, he used his skill and talent to make himself very popular with students at the University of North Carolina with whom he enjoyed an amicable relationship. Besides, he earned extra money by writing poetry for pining students. "When the passion of the lady's admirer was not very intense, the price was twenty-five cents." On other occasions, "when the love-sick swain was in flames and consequently reckless of expense," Horton doubled his price. Horton sometimes accepted books or clothing as payment for his services when the students were short of funds. His poetry was so eloquent, it not only "touched but captured the fair hearts for which they pleaded."[44]

Horton used his ability to write creatively, while others used writing to circumvent slavery. "I often wrote passes for my grandmother," admitted Susie King Taylor long after slavery ended. Unlike some white adults who refrained from teaching slaves to write, the white children did not have the same reservations. They simply did not understand the gravity of slaves writing passes granting themselves permission to travel abroad. Mobility, temporary or permanent, could undermine slavery.[45]

The Virginian William Taylor Barry complained about slaves being kept in "a state of almost brutal ignorance," yet he believed to "enlighten them is to make them unhappy at their condition." More serious than the disenchantment, Barry feared the possibility of making them "more dangerous" if educated. Apparently many slaveholders feared the consequences of permitting their bond servants to gain literacy. Many slave narratives tell of amputations (or threats thereof) of the fingers and arms of determined scholars.[46]

Julia Frazier's owner did not threaten her with bodily harm, but she intimidated the child nonetheless. Julia discovered that "Ole Missus [sic] used to watch . . . mos' times to see dat I didn't open no books" when cleaning the library. Not satisfied with simply watching, the owner "would close up all de books an' put 'em on de shelf so's I couldn't see 'em," Frazier remembered. This solved nothing since the child continued gravitating toward the library whenever cleaning. Julia's owner appeared once while she was holding a book, but the woman said nothing. Intimidated and fearful of an instant beating, Julia refrained from touching books for a long time, but her desire to read was ever-present.[47]

Frederick Douglass, who had struggled to learn to read and write, longed to share his knowledge with his "brother-slaves." First, he lured two boys to his shade-tree school. Before long the young teacher had between twenty and thirty enthusiastic students. "It was surprising with what ease," Douglass commented, "they provided themselves with spelling-books." Although Douglass called it a "Sabbath school" and they met on Sunday, it was not a Sunday school in the sense that children received religious instructions.[48]

After the 1831 Nat Turner insurrection, it became more difficult for slaves to participate in sacred and secular activities because whites believed Turner's knowledge of education and religion contributed to the unrest. Some slave states enacted laws against their instruction, but the extensiveness of the laws has been exaggerated. Only four states consistently enacted prohibitions from the 1830s until slavery ended. Penalties for violations ranged from whippings to fines and imprisonments. Objections from slaveowners or state laws dissuaded some but intensified the desire in others. A former slave who attended college after the Civil War recalled the many obstacles to book learning and how he hated the law which "punished any attempt to teach us." He became disillusioned about any possibility of learning to read and write. He was "almost ready to give up in despair" but did not.[49]

Mary Peake had much to lose if prosecuted for violating the law of Virginia. She knowingly jeopardized her freedom and the safety of her family. John Cocke's Infant School continued to function in violation of the legislation, but Cocke and his wife decided to train slave women "sufficiently to impart all elementary knowledge" to the children rather than challenge the law directly. Cocke rationalized that the school would keep the children out of mischief and in a clean comfortable environment rather than living "as is usual to the filth and demoralizing misrule of our too much neglected Quarters."[50]

Unlike Peake and Cocke, Jane A. Crouch, another Virginian, was unwilling to violate the law. Born in 1835 in Alexandria, to a free mother and enslaved father who eventually purchased himself, Crouch entered school when only six years old and learned to read, write, and "cipher to some extent." As an adult in northern Virginia, she operated a school in a rented house with forty pupils. Crouch admitted that she "took care not to take in any slave children." Although her "will was good to do so," she feared an arrest, which would "make it doubly hard" to maintain the school; therefore, she chose "not to run the risk." As a child, Crouch attended a school that local police forced to close, and perhaps this influenced her decision.[51]

Daily obstacles to literacy frustrated the deep-seated desire for knowledge among slaves. If one examined Launcelot Blackford's academic experience, it is obvious that books and school activities stimulated his imagination and creativity. The school's debating society, with officers, a constitution, and regular meetings, provided excellent opportunities to debate current topics. Blackford used his financial acumen to purchase a vast array of supplies to support his interest, including chemicals for experiments, materials for political banners, and books to read. He learned to set type, established the "Minor, Blackford & Co.," and produced a newspaper. There is no comparison between his opportunities and those available to enslaved children, whose intellectual development was stifled by bondage.[52]

Determination and the willingness to endure punishments if caught resulted in literacy among an estimated 5 percent of the 1860 enslaved population. There is no way of knowing exactly how many slaves could read and write. Admissions of literacy might have been admissions of violating plantation rules or legal restrictions; therefore, some slaves pleaded ignorance. Among the 3,428 WPA interviewees were 179 former slaves who said they learned to read and write while still slaves.[53]

There were only a few females among the small number of literate slaves; consequently, there are fewer autobiographies by the women than the men. Of the well-known slave narratives, women are the subject of several, including Harriet Tubman, Harriet Jacobs, Elizabeth Keckley, and Sojourner Truth. Not all of these women were literate. Sojourner Truth's inability to read has been well publicized. The majority of the publications emphasize that fact without answering why this articulate, woman of note never learned to read. She lived in New

York, where the teaching of slaves was not illegal, and New York's gradual abolition law of 1810 required that slaves learn to read the Bible. As a youngster she worked in a household where newspapers, almanacs, and books were not unknown. Her owner John J. Dumont's two children were slightly younger and must have attempted to teach her. Author Carleton Mabee suggests that Truth probably had a learning disability. By her own account, "The letters all got mixed up and I couldn't straighten them out."[54]

Overwhelmingly, slavery rather than any learning disability inhibited the intellectual growth and development of the majority of bond servants. They sometimes turned to religion as a source of strength for adjusting to the oppressiveness of slavery. Ex-slaves, including Booker T. Washington, remembered a parent's fervent prayers for an end to slavery awakening them. Jacob Stroyer recalled his father praying for relief when he ran into trouble with the plantation horse trainer, who beat him with impunity. When Jacob's mother interceded on his behalf and received a beating, the boy realized his parents were powerless in such a situation and their only recourse was divine intervention. The elder Stroyer prayed, "Lord, hasten the time when these children shall be their own free men and women." Regardless of these supplications, their situation remained unchanged several years longer, but they did not give up hope.[55]

Enslaved youngsters were very much a part of family devotions and religious activities that made them believe in the possibility of deliverance from bondage. The 1833 letter from Hobbs attests to his belief in a supreme being and implies that Elizabeth was aware of it. With special reference to the child, he wrote, "Do not think that because I am bound so fare [far] that gods not abble to open the way." He encouraged her to believe God could and would ease their burdens. If earthly reunions were impossible, they believed heavenly rewards were possible.[56]

Ironically, a linkage existed between education and religion, which meant that youngsters who received Christian doctrine often gained literacy in the process. Scholars agree that Africans made no distinction between sacred and secular activities, which helps explain that the melding of the two was not an unusual activity for them.[57]

Some whites also recognized connections between literacy and religion and believed literacy was necessary for Christian salvation. A letter from a potential tutor at a southern plantation reveals her respect for religion and its importance in daily life. "To have the mind early imbraced with moral and religious truth, and trained to order decorum and good habits," she wrote on August 13, 1829, "must be the most efficient means of rendering a people happy and preparing them to act well their part in any sphere."[58]

Slaves used their faith to ease their suffering, explain mysteries, and ward off adversities for themselves and their children. The historian Norrece T. Jones cautions against overemphasizing the role of Christianity in the slave community, since many slaves retained their traditional religions long before slaveholders began systematic proselytizing. Prior to the American Revolution, slaveowners did little to convert their slaves to Christianity due to the lack of clarity regarding the relationship between baptism and emancipation. At the time of the Civil War only an estimated 15 percent of the adult slave population saw themselves as belonging to a Christian denomination.[59]

Those accepting Christianity often syncretized it with African traditional religions. They found facets of Christianity, especially as practiced by the evangelicals, compatible. Spirit possession and initiation, highly significant events for Africans, were not unknown in the evangelical church.[60]

To a great extent the slaves' religiosity depended upon slaveowners, who determined the extent and kind of religious knowledge they received along with how and where they practiced that belief. White ministers often sermonized about the slaveholders' duties of religious ministry to their chattel. And there were white southerners who sought to save souls and build Christian communities which included bond servants. "How much better it is for them," wrote a slaveholder, "to meet together and spend their evenings in singing and prayer, Than be running over the neighborhood." The controlling properties of the religion could make slaves more obedient and honest.[61]

There were many opportunities for them to attend formal religious services or receive approved religious instructions. Slaves sometimes accompanied their owners to church and attended evangelical meetings. Between 1830 and 1865, many southern plantations built established chapels and their owners used systematic efforts to convert slaves. In the absence of formal services, slaveholders taught the catechism at home and included slaves in family prayers.[62]

While traveling in central Alabama in the mid-nineteenth century, Reverend Francis Hanson observed slaves receiving religious instructions and commented about a Sabbath school run by a Mrs. Harrison, who devoted much time to the exhortation of her slaves. The children received instructions in the "catechism and the elementary principles of religion." They were familiar with the order of the Episcopal service, made the correct responses, and conducted themselves with "reverence and apparent devotion." "I understand," Hanson wrote, "that she assembles them every Sunday afternoon, reads prayers with them and gives them such instruction as she thinks they require." On another plantation, Hanson noted that an enslaved woman "had a prayer book and engaged in the service" while "nearly all" of the slaves, children included, "responded in the Creed, the Confession, and the Lord's Prayer."[63]

Anne Clay, a devout Presbyterian living near Savannah, Georgia, along with her brother established a ministry for their slaves on the family's Bryan County, Georgia, plantation. The enslaved children memorized scriptures, sang hymns, and received oral catechism lessons during the sabbath school's sixteen years of operation. Similarly, the wife of Charles Friend, owner of the White Hill Plantation, in Virginia, offered religious instructions to the bond children which differed little from the Sabbath schools run by Clay. "With her own children gathered close about her knees, she taught these dusky young ones Bible verses, hymns, Watt's Catechism, the Creed, the Lord's Prayer and the Ten Command-ments." Friend awarded prizes of sugar and molasses for quick mastery of lessons. The children's favorite rendition of the fourth commandment was "Thou shalt do no manner of work."[64]

There is little doubt about the sincerity of the teachers, but the quality of their instruction was superficial and governed by what they determined their bond servants should know. Teachers often asked questions and stated the answers to the catechumen, whose unison responses were identical to the teachers'. Included in their catechism was the "theology of slavery," which developed and grew throughout the nineteenth century. The theology, de-scribed as Christians thinking God and the Bible sanctioned slavery, embraced the belief that bond servants were inferior but could achieve salvation.[65]

It is erroneous to assume that bond servants accepted the doctrine without questioning it. To be sure, some slaves viewed it with nonchalance, and their children noted their indifference. Of more importance to slaves was the personal relationship with their God, which emanated from the spirit rather than theo-logical explanations or book learning. This is not to suggest that slaves dismissed the Bible, but they wanted to read and interpret it for themselves.[66]

Slaveowners who kept slaves illiterate deliberately either interpreted scrip-tures for them or hired ministers for the job. The Reverend Hanson, who traveled from one central Alabama plantation to another in the late 1850s and early 1860s, sometimes preached to mixed assemblages. At other times, he delivered sermons to white congregations in the mornings and to bond servants in the afternoon. To assure religious teachings, John Hartwell Cocke built a chapel and hired a minister to preach and to give oral instructions to the children.[67]

Slaves of all ages attended services at organized churches with their owners. Between 1844 and the end of the Civil War, there were nearly one hundred entries about African American parishioners in the records of Chapel of the Cross at Chapel Hill, North Carolina. More than forty of the entries refer to enslaved children. Annette, Emma, and Cornelia, children ranging in ages from six to ten, were among the worshipers. Their owner, Mary Ruffin Smith, daughter of the state legislator Francis Smith, saw to their regular attendance.[68]

The Smith children, like their contemporaries, probably listened to minis-ters who stressed subservience, fidelity, and obedience to owners. The general tenet of such sermons argued that disobedience was tantamount to "sinning against the Holy Ghost, *and . . . base ingratitude*" to owners who fed, clothed, and protected them. Lucretia Alexander recalled hearing sermons delivered by a white minister. "Same old thing all de time," she said. The ex-slave Cornelius Garner, who was nineteen years old when slavery ended, was more direct when he said, "We ain't keer'd a bit 'bout dat stuff he was telling us."[69]

Although many slaves were indifferent to sermons by white ministers, numerous church records contain references to their attendance and baptisms.

TEMPORAL AND SPIRITUAL EDUCATION

Reverend Hanson baptized fifteen children owned by Waller DuBose in 1858 at St. Andrew's Church in Prairieville, Alabama. In 1854 Mary Ruffin Smith stood as sponsor at the baptism of Lucy Battle Smith, a child owned by Mary Smith, and the property of Mary Smith. The Reverend Henry T. Lee, rector of Chapel of the Holy Cross from 1856 to 1858, baptized the less well-known Ann Elisa, Henry, Patsy Alice, and Rufus, the children of Lissy and Sam Morphis, on Easter Sunday, March 23, 1856. Their sponsors, Mrs. William Horn Battle and her invalid daughter Susan Catherine, also sponsored eight other children baptized on the same day. Reverend Lee baptized George, a youngster owned by the Chaves family. The records indicate that an enslaved woman was his sponsor.[70]

To be sure, there were many baptisms, but the theology of slavery, the strict decorum required by white churches, and their restraint against spontaneous expressions left many African American churchgoers empty emotionally. Furthermore, segregated seating and prohibitions against their participation in the operations of the church repelled many.

The dissatisfaction with facets of the white church caused some slaves to seek religious outlets by holding their own services, and they went to great lengths to keep them secret. Clandestine religious gatherings of the "invisible church" made it possible for slaves to bypass white scrutiny. They gathered in arbors and hollows called "hush harbors" to sing and pray. As a child in the plantation South, Charles Crawly recalled that "slaves met an' worshipped from house to house an' honey," he said, "we talked to God all us wanted." To worship undetected, they hung wet blankets across the room or placed an overturned iron pot on the floor to muffle sounds. The use of blankets or pots as acoustical barriers is not very convincing for modern readers, but they were part of their traditional beliefs. The number of secret gatherings probably intensified in response to stricter laws after Turner's rebellion and the slaves' continued desire for religious freedom.[71]

Anna Woods, a former slave, remembered that "grown folks used to have church . . . out behind an old shed. They'd shout and they'd sing." Singing was a major part of their worship. Whether catering to the beliefs of organized churches or traditional beliefs, slaves sang songs such as "Nobody Knows de Trouble I See, Nobody Knows but Jesus" and "Some Times I Feel Like a Motherless Child." Other spirituals told of the omnipotence of God, possibilities of divine intercession, and retribution. "Members Don't Git Weary," "Mos' done Toilin' Here," "Joshua Fit de Battle ob Jerico," and "Go Down Moses" embodied the hopes and dreams of an oppressed people. Their songs reflected the misery of bondage and anticipation of a final reward in heaven. Youngsters heard the spirituals at work and at worship. One writer has said that Negro spirituals were echoes of heartbeats, hence children learned about the grief, agony, and joy of their people.[72]

The Negro spirituals exemplified their anticipation of a brighter future. Spirituals such as "In That Great Getting-Up Morning" and "Run to Jesus" were as much a part of their repertoire as "A great Camp-Meeting in the Promised Land." Many slaves came to believe their distress would end, if not in their present life then certainly in the afterlife. The proverb "Trouble don' las' always" was also a reflection of their hope for a brighter future.[73]

Casual observers often commented about "happy" slaves after hearing them sing. Astute observers including Frederick Douglass pointed out that those "within the circle" did not see or hear what those "without" their circle noticed. Douglass insisted that many songs "told a tale of woe" and "breathed the prayer and complaint of boiling over with the bitterest anguish." Slaves sang about conditions that they could not talk about and tempered their songs accordingly. For safety's sake, they used metonymics whereby slaves likened slaveowners to Satan while benefactors became King Jesus. Slaves identified with the biblical Israelites and saw Canaan as their ultimate goal.[74]

Far from tunes of frivolity and joy, perceptive listeners heard in the songs promises of relief from physical and mental bondage. After slavery ended, Frederick Douglass presented the song "Run to Jesus" to the Fisk (University) Jubilee Singers and claimed it was the inspiration for his escape from slavery. As a youngster Douglass heard the slaves sing:

> Run to Jesus, shun the danger, I don't expect to stay much longer here. He will be our dearest friend, And will help us to the end, I don't expect to stay much longer here.

The last verse of the song promised "many mansions there" and reassured listeners that there will be "one for you and one for me." They saw a safe sanctuary in religion, if not on earth then in the other world. "When I get to heaven, gwin be at ease," another slave song promised.[75]

Anna Woods remembered singing and shouting as inseparable activities, and they should be studied within that context. The "saut" or "ring shout," a rhythmic walk which accompanied spirituals, was a part of the slaves' religious expression. The ring or circle was especially important to slaves, who saw it as a union between the living and the dead. After witnessing a "ring shout," an observer wrote:

> ...when the formal meeting is over, and old and young, men and women, sprucely-dressed young men, grotesquely half-clad fieldhands—the women generally with gay handkerchiefs twisted about their heads and with short skirts—boys with tattered shirts and men's trousers, young girls barefooted, all stand up in the middle of the floor, and when the "sperichil" is struck up, begin first walking and by-and-by shuffling round, one after the other, in a ring. The foot is hardly taken from the floor and the progression is mainly due to a jerking hitching motion, which agitates the entire shouter, and soon brings out streams of perspiration. Sometimes they dance silently, sometimes as they shuffle they sing the chorus of the spiritual, and sometimes the song itself is also sung by the dancers.

Just as outsiders thought singing slaves were happy slaves, casual observers saw the saut as a dance without understanding that the slaves' religion prevented secular dancing.[76]

Children began participating in ring shouts as toddlers and probably did not remember the first time they saw a saut or heard a spiritual, but they were likely to remember the time and special circumstances of a personal experience with God which led to their conversion. For example, the eighteen-year-old Josiah Henson was aware of the meaning of Christianity and professed religion when he heard a sermon containing the words:

> Jesus Christ, the Son of God, tasted death for every man; for the high, for the low, for the rich, for the poor, the bond, the free, the Negro in his chains, the man in gold and diamonds.

Hanson continued, "It touched my heart and I cried out, 'I wonder if Jesus Christ died for me?'"[77]

Of importance in the conversion experience were distressing incidents that caused feelings of depression or sinfulness. A youngster's age was an important link in the significance and attention given to such incidents. A former slave explained:

> God started on me when I was a little boy. I used to grieve a lot over my mother. She had been sold away from me and taken a long way off. One evening I was going through the woods to get the cows. I was walking along thinking about Mama and crying. Then a voice spoke to me and said, "Blessed art thou. An obedient child shall live out the fullness of his days." I got scared because I did not know who it was that spoke nor what he meant.

Full of anxiety about the meaning of the audition, he remembered thinking "more about God and my soul and . . . praying as best I knew how." The former slave reported hearing voices or seeing visions, which he believed was his "soul crying out for deliverance."[78]

The belief that a supreme being could remove this "melancholia religiosa" caused the likely candidate for conversion to search for deliverance. Following the intense incident a spiritual journey called seeking begins. In the low point of anguish or "the lonesome valley" of Negro spirituals the seeker spends time praying, meditating, and fasting. Afterwards the seeker hears voices, sees visions, or falls into a trance. Following this deeply spiritual and physical emotional episode, the seeker feels assured of salvation and lasting peace.[79]

Without this phenomenon the conversion was doubtful. This explains why the father of a twelve-year-old boy who wanted to join the church told the child not to come home unless he had a special experience with the supreme being. Obviously aware of the emotional experience required for conversion but unable to explain it, the father intimidated the child. "I was scared to go home, but just as I stepped out the door the heavens opened up, and I seed angels flying around," he recalled.[80]

Candidates for conversion told of seeing God, angels, or blinding streaks of light and hearing voices. The adherents viewed such experiences as signs of conversion. The age at which the conversion occurs is important for children to actually understand the meaning of a "sin-sick soul," the possible loss of salvation, and the relevance of being "born again."[81]

The personal experiences with God occurred in private settings, at church services, and during revivals or camp meetings. Beginning in 1800 the Presbyterians started camp meetings to bring western settlers into the church. Slaves attended these meetings, which lasted from several days to a week. The general openness of the gatherings made religious experiences more accessible to all. Lucy Skipwith felt a sense of achievement in 1859 when eleven slaves converted at the "prettyest revival" she had ever seen. "There is not a grown person among them," she wrote.[82]

Some slaveholders were truly concerned over the salvation of their slaves, while others objected to their slaves going to camp meetings and converting to Christianity if observation of religious holidays interfered with work. One such person went to great lengths by providing a great diversion during a camp meeting in his vicinity. Charles Arnold Hentz described an old-fashioned barbecue given by an "irreligious man" who "bribed" his slaves with a "feast of fat things gotten up on a grand scale." The fare included unlimited access to barrels of cider and "vast wooden trenches filled with barbecue pork," spread upon the grass along with "piles of bread and potatoes in the greatest profusion." The barbecue distracted the slaves of all ages. Hentz wrote, "Lots of little nigger 'picannies' here and there litterally in these trays; up to their knees and elbows in the savage pottage, cramming it down by the handfuls." Aside from food there was dancing accompanied by music created by young girls "singing through a paper & comb." Hentz's fascination was with the "jolly scene of purely animal enjoyment" rather than the reasons for the diversion.[83]

The extent to which slaves thwarted obstacles and inculcated religious teaching when they were children and youth is open to question. The historian John Blassingame writes, "The place of religion in slave life has been distorted, because most of the slave witnesses who recorded their stories of bondage were relatively old." A former slave accompanied his mother to a secret meeting, which he described:

> They would all get around a kettle on their hands and knees and sing and pray and shout and cry. My mother was a great prayer, and she always asked God to take care of her son—meaning me. I would look and listen; sometimes I would cry. I didn't know what I was crying for, but the meaning and singing was so stirring that I couldn't help it.

TEMPORAL AND SPIRITUAL EDUCATION

Children, sometimes too young to "know what it all meant," played church complete with the singing and shouting. "We just aped our elders," said one WPA informant. Another ex-slave reflecting upon his religious experiences as a child said, "Now, as I look back, I know that these things sunk deep in my heart."[84]

Charlotte Forten's telling description of shouting among Sea Islanders indicates the extent to which children accepted what their elders provided. Claiming not to know if shouts were "in connection with their religious meetings" or purely for her entertainment, Forten explained:

> In the evenings, the children frequently came in to sing and shout for us. These "shouts" are very strange,—in truth, almost indescribable. It is necessary to hear and see in order to have any clear idea of them. The children form a ring, and move around in a kind of shuffling dance, singing all the time. Four or five stand apart, and sing very energetically, clapping their hands, stamping their feet, and rocking their bodies to and fro.

The "little children, not more than three or four years old," amazed Forten when they entered "into the performance with all their might." Even more striking was "Prince . . . the principal shouter among the children," whose "performances were most amusing specimens of Ethiopian gymnastics."[85]

The children demonstrated their skill for mastering an African practice, and it indicates well the extent to which their parents and others influenced them. Moreover, it "tells us much about how culture is transmitted and received almost as an unconscious ornament of the child's inheritance." In "aping their elders," the children captured the physical aspect of the shout; however, Forten noted that "the shouting of the grown people is rather solemn and impressive than otherwise." The children, especially the youngest of the group, according to Forten, were "very comical" to watch. She apparently lacked an understanding of the cultural transferral from one generation to another. Moreover, she did not understand the blending of the temporal and spiritual. Adults shouted after the praise meeting, and the children shouted after school. Over time the children might relegate their "performances" to the religious setting since "church has always been the refuge of the old."[86]

A missionary observing an 1862 funeral procession in South Carolina commented about the blurring of the distinction between sacred and secular education when observing slave children attending a funeral:

> As we drew near to the grave we heard all the children singing their A, B, C, through and through again, as they stood waiting round the grave for the rest to assemble. . . . Each child has his school-book or picture book . . . in his hand,—another proof that they consider their lessons as in some sort religious exercise.[87]

Literacy was necessary to study the Bible, and many nineteenth-century teachers linked the two. Lucy Skipwith, for example, fortified the lack of distinction in sacred and secular education by using curricular materials in her teaching that reflected her religion. She rearranged the Ten Commandments for easier memorization. The first commandment read:

> Thou no god shalt have but me
> This Command I give to Thee
> love me then with all thy heart
> Never from my words depart.

The fourth commandment is equally impressive:

> Remember thou the Sabbath day
> Never work nor even play
> The god of Heaven will ever bless
> The man who keeps the day of rest.

Skipwith asked Cocke to print the verses "in a small tract" for distribution among the children. The children in the Sabbath school were the same children that Lucy had trouble keeping awake at the night school, and rather than giving up the school until after the harvest, she encouraged them to attend her Sabbath school regularly. It is doubtful if she redesigned the teaching materials to fit the new meeting day and time.[88]

The majority of slaves who practiced religion were protestants; however, there were some Catholic slaves, primarily in Maryland and Louisiana. The paucity of priests in rural areas, the hostile atmosphere within the slaveholding church, and lack of commitment by slaveowners account, in part, for the small number of black Catholics. Few baptized children knew their catechism or how to make the sign of the cross. Their ignorance reflected the owners' lack of commitment to their religious education and their parents' lack of enthusiasm for a faith that restrained them from praying, singing, and shouting as they wished. That mattered little to children who were more fascinated by having white dresses, glowing tapers, and flowing veils at first communion services.[89]

An estimated 16 to 22 percent of the total number of slaves brought from Africa were Muslims. Little has been written about them aside from Terry Alford's *Prince among Slaves,* the biography of Ibrahima, a Muslim prince who married a slave woman, on Christmas day, 1794, in a ceremony performed by their Presbyterian owner. Although Ibrahima remained steadfast in his faith, he attended Baptist services with his wife Isabella. The couple's children gravitated more toward the Baptist faith of their mother than that of their father.[90]

Samuel Jackson wrote about an enslaved Muslim owned by an acquaintance in South Carolina. Apparently the slave was something of a curiosity for the owner and visitors. Jackson commented that "after much urging" the man consented to repeating a prayer with his face to the east. Perhaps the slave objected to being a spectacle for viewers. Young slaves in his community probably raised questions about his religion. He was able to answer queries with certainty, for according to Jackson, the man could "read & write his native tongue."[91]

Dissatisfaction with Christianity caused some slaves to resort to hoodoo or voodoo. Voodoo, a functional religious system in West Africa, offered slaves strength and courage to meet daily challenges. The believers used voodoo to ward off harm, ensure good health, or assure success with desired companions. As an adolescent, Frederick Douglass accepted the advice of the fellow slave, Sandy, believed to have magical powers and knowledge of roots that would shield the boy from whippings by the slavebreaker on the plantation where Douglass worked. Douglass, a Christian, initially thought the talk of roots was "very absurd and ridiculous, if not positively sinful." Douglass took the roots not because he believed in their power, but out of respect for Sandy. Afterwards, Douglass engaged in a fight with Edward Covey which changed the direction of his life, yet, he does not attribute his unexplained strength, courage, or victory to the magic of the roots.[92]

When traditional courting measures failed, the lovesick sometimes consulted conjurers who reordered affections by casting spells and mixing love potions. Upon the advice of the conjurer, Henry Bibb scratched the girl of his choice with a bone from a dried bullfrog. Rather than winning her love, he incurred her wrath. Undaunted, Bibb attempted another way to win the object of his affection. This time he was to get a lock of her hair and wear it in his shoe. Finding no clever way to succeed, he yanked the hair from her head. Again he suffered the loss of all potential affection.[93]

Regardless of the denomination, formality of the services, or color of the minister, many slaves recognized the incongruence between rhetoric and reality in the slave society. Among the more poignant examples was the slaveholders' ability to terminate marriages by separations, temporary or permanent. In a July 1849 letter to her South Carolina owner, Lavina wrote, "I am tormented. My conscience is bruised, my feelings are vex." Lavina's agitated condition stemmed from her daughter's husband Jimmy being "givd to a base woman," Juddy, with the consent of their owners. She judged the woman to be "more worse than Mary Magdalene." The writer asked, "Do you thing it rite in the sight of God?" She beseeched the owner to weigh "Jimmy and his deeds with this Magdalene Juddy all on one side, and put justice, humanity and religion in the other."[94]

Lavina had accepted Christianity, was familiar with the teachings of the Bible, and was in a marriage of long duration. In her opinion the union between Jimmy and Juddy was "wretched business." Her major concern was the injustice done to her daughter Aggy. It is not clear if Aggy is a mature adult or a girl in upper adolescence. Regardless of her age, Lavina felt the need to intervene on her behalf. With astuteness, the mother urged her owner to "View this matter as you would if they were your children." She then asked, "Where is your con-science?" Having stated her case in terms of Christian morality, Lavina con-cluded: "Pray over it, Massa and you [Missis], if you can allow it [the marriage of Jimmy and Juddy]." Lavina's letter attests to her love for Aggy and her acceptance of Christianity and it points to the gulf between the practice and preaching on her plantation.[95]

Although neither the law nor the church recognized or protected their marriages, many bond servants regarded marriage as a serious matter and con-ducted themselves accordingly. Extramarital sex was a more serious violation of their code of morality than premarital sex. Data on bridal pregnancy among slaves show that couples tended to marry and develop long-lasting relationships. The young Tennessee couple, Willis and Martha, serve as one example. After only two months of marriage, they became the parents of a baby girl. The nonplused grandmother told their owner that her daughter "makes quick work of it."[96]

Taken literally the grandmother's comment suggests bewilderment, but it is unlikely that a mature woman would have so little understanding of the gestation process. Perhaps she was embarrassed at the very obvious fact that Martha was a pregnant bride. In either case, the woman's concern was about her daughter's sexuality in a community which had moral standards.[97]

The owner sensed her anxiety about the newly married couple's child and told her that "such things often happen with the first born, but never after-wards." Willis and Martha's first child, Creasy, was born September 30, 1854. Their other children arrived in 1856, 1858, 1860, and 1861. The slaveowner's words not only consoled the new grandmother, but confirmed that stable marriages and the birth of additional children at fairly regular intervals often followed bridal pregnancies.[98]

The births of children were occasions filled with bitter-sweet emotions, while funerals might have had a festive air. Slaves sometimes had death wishes for their children and were joyous if their offspring did not live to endure slavery. Those who survived and witnessed the hardships of bondage were sure to realize the importance of their parents' attempts to socialize them and protect them from harm. As the children matured, they probably resorted to religion to buffer abuses or cushion denials. They would learn to steel themselves against the gulf between the rhetoric of Christian slaveowners and the realities of slavery. In the process, they could reflect upon lessons learned from experienced teachers, their parents, grandparents, and others who had grown up in slavery in the United States.

5 "WHAT HAS EVER BECOME OF MY PRESUS LITTLE GIRL"*

THE TRAUMAS AND TRAGEDIES
OF SLAVE CHILDREN AND YOUTH

> Children have their sorrows as well as
> men and women; and it would be well to
> remember this in our dealings with them.
> SLAVE-children are children, and prove
> no exceptions to the general rule.
>
> —Frederick Douglass**

During the 1970s a number of historians elevated slavery from the dismal abyss of "bull whip days" through studies which showed bond servants working from sundown to sunup to forge communities that mitigated slavery's worst abuses. They provided a better understanding of how slaves faced tragedy and survived; nevertheless, there is no denying—despite extenuating circumstances—that slavery caused enough trauma to affect slaves of all ages. Forms of debasement including corporal punishment, sexual abuse, and separations were common. In the autobiographical *Incidents in the Life of a Slave Girl*, Harriet Jacobs wrote, "I have not exaggerated the wrongs inflicted by Slavery, on the contrary, my descriptions fall far short of the fact." The autobiographer Henry Bibb, a Shelby County, Kentucky, contemporary of Jacobs's who also spent the formative years in slavery, agreed. "No tongue," he wrote, "nor pen ever has or can express the horrors of American Slavery."[1]

Slavery fostered a continuous state of war wherein one of the combatants was bound but refused to surrender. In such a society slaveholders, overseers, drivers, and patrollers dispensed punishments freely to maintain slavery. Children and youth experienced the rancor of that war, and the ordeals made them old in experience rather than years. This chapter focuses upon the heinous nature of slavery and argues that children were not spared its bitterness. Moreover, it

---

* Lester to Miss Patsy, August 29, 1857, James Allred Papers, Perkins Library, Duke University, Durham, North Carolina.

** Frederick Douglass, *My Bondage and My Freedom* (New York: Dover, 1969), 1.

suggests that children were the most vulnerable members of the slave community because of their size and strength, which often made their physical resistance impotent. Parents used influence and shielded their offspring whenever possible, but their leverage was tenuous.[2]

In the patriarchal manner slaveholders referred to slaves as family, but the treatment meted out to slaves was not comparable to that received by their kindred. This resulted in a battle to subdue the bound party. Furthermore, the gulf between rhetoric and reality caused some owners to grapple with the character of slaves as persons or property. Paradoxically, the lack of a clear perception about slaves tempered circumstances. Slaveholders were sometimes reluctant to beat them unmercifully because it left visual testimony and raised questions regarding the behavior that warranted it. This could interfere with future sales or the slave's ability to work.[3]

Ambivalence about the slave's status and rights caused some owners to forge a balance between the two and treat them benevolently. Others ignored constraints and were brutal in every sense of the word. I. de Courcy Laffan understood more fully the delicate tension between the two after an 1841 visit to Brandon, a Virginia plantation where orderliness and kindness prevailed among well-clothed and adequately fed slaves. He saw "healthy & cheerful" looking children, yet he knew they were "consigned to eternal ignorance and forced to labour" without hope of a "profitable return for their daily toil." Notwithstanding their pleasant appearance, the possibilities of reversed circumstances were ever-present. This meant slaves of all ages could be "separated forever, or consigned to the hands of a ruthless Tyrant or unfeeling task master."[4]

Ruthless tyrants and unfeeling task masters, like warlords, used physical punishments, including whippings, with relish. They resorted to whippings for any reason and subjected any slave to a flogging. The mettle exhibited by some slaves was reason enough for a flogging if it annoyed owners or overseers. "My mamma's master whipped his slaves," said Sarah Graves, "for pastime." Another slaveowner beat a servant because he could not "recollec' ever whippin'" him.[5]

When describing the punishments, former slaves focus upon the hateful straps, excessive lashes, and bloody abrasions. The WPA narratives describe the "cross whips" when slaveowners stood on one side of a slave and covered the victim's back with stripes before moving to the opposite side to complete the job. Ex-slaves also described the "buck." It required the victim to stoop or squat with knees against the chest and hands tied in front of the shins. A stick placed behind the knees and in front of the elbows locked the person in a feeble position. Once the thrashing began "you couldn't do nothing," remembered an ex-slave, "but just squat there and take what he put on you." After beatings, owners sometimes rubbed salt into open wounds or used a brackish solution to "pickle" the slave from "haid to yo' foot jak you paint a house" to prolong the agony.[6]

TRAUMAS AND TRAGEDIES

Corporal punishment was so rife that young slaves suffered the indignities personally and vicariously. Seeing family or friends humiliated was painful, and it chipped away at their own self-esteem, thus leaving the way open for feelings of frustration and resentment. Slaves endured poor treatments, but to make matters worse, they had neither powerful voices of protest nor anyone to speak boldly on their behalf. This was especially true of youngsters. A British official traveling in the United States in 1807 discovered $500 missing from his hotel room. The local constable questioned an enslaved girl in addition to suspending her by the hands to the "joists of the garret." This did not solve the crime, but it made the official vividly aware of the child's harsh treatment. He commented privately in his diary, "I believe however they stretched their powers." His position prevented him from registering an official complaint, and his personal stake in the matter was not great. He neither spoke in her defense nor against the institution of slavery.[7]

There was no uniform opinion among whites regarding the treatment of slaves, but many believed that the absence of the power to punish would undermine slavery. The presence of arbitrary power rather than a mutually agreed upon social contract bound many slaves and slaveholders together. Certainly there were slaveowners who embraced the most threatening aspects of slavery, while others rejected them. Some owners limited punishments by their overseers and drivers and provided environments to mitigate some of slavery's evils. Thomas Affleck, agricultural writer and planter, frowned upon excessive whippings as "altogether unnecessary and inexcusable." The Alabamian William Henry Sims said slaves "should be corrected in a humane manner" when guilty and never "taunted" afterwards. Another cannon for managing slaves simply stated, "Avoid torture of body and mind."[8]

This cautious concern reflects an understanding of the physical and mental damage resulting from ruthlessness. McDonald Furman called for the observance of "A Fatherly care & conduct" toward his slaves. Another slaveowner said slaves were to be flogged as seldom as possible but when necessary. Willis P. Bocock required that his overseers and drivers never strike slaves when in a passion. The Lowndes County, Mississippi, slaveholder William Ethelbert Ervin provided that failure to adhere to plantation rules, "when proven," would result in correction by words first. Afterwards, if necessary, slaves were "corrected by the *whip*." The overseer could use his discretion; even so, Ervin specified that "under no circumstances shall the punishment exceed 15 lashes." Drivers at the Pierce Butler plantation in Georgia were not to exceed 12 lashes, but the overseer could inflict up to 50 lashes.[9]

The existence of the many prohibitions against brutality suggests that it was common but not accepted by all. The prescriptive orders make no distinction between bond servants based upon age or gender. Adults and children were whipped alike. So were males and females.

Antebellum legislatures in several of the southern states enacted laws against excessive punishment of slaves, yet impunity existed. Slaveholders were rarely, if ever, successfully prosecuted for brutalizing slaves. If whites corrected slaves owned by someone else, they faced different standards of responsibility. Owners did not arbitrarily punish whites for violations upon their slaves. They took strangers to court and fired employees.[10]

Despite possible legal consequences and written rules, many overseers brutalized slaves. James W. C. Pennington was convinced that they enjoyed torturing enslaved children. The traveler Frederick Law Olmsted witnessed "the severest corporeal punishment" in Mississippi when the overseer whipped a young girl for "shirking." Defending himself while justifying his cruelty, the overseer posited, "If I hadn't punished her so hard she would have done the same thing again to-morrow, and half the people on the plantation would have followed her example." It was not unusual to use a single infraction as an example for controlling the behavior of others. "They'd never do any work at all," he said, "if they were not afraid of being whipped."[11]

Such examples were more graphic when weak, helpless children were beaten severely. Pennington was not far from the mark, considering the effect that beating children could have upon their parents. Families were the greatest factors that slaves had to mitigate their conditions. The manipulation of families was also the slaveholders' greatest source of control over bond servants. Whipping a child also made parents tow the line. They, in turn, probably put additional pressure on their offspring to follow suit. Persons who dispensed punishments must have known of the added value of striking slaves in their most vulnerable spot.[12]

When faced with punishments, slaves made few distinctions between overseers and drivers since both wielded straps. An ex-slave interviewed during the 1930s said, "The worst thing I members [about slavery] was the colored overseer." Another freedperson who grew up in bondage said the driver was "de meanest man" who strutted "'round wid a leather strap on his shoulder and would whip de other slaves unmerciful."[13]

Nancy Williams maintained that the driver, her father, was a "mean man." Her complaint loses some of its venom upon learning that her charge stems, in part, from an unusual punishment when the father found her guilty of stealing. He enclosed the girl in a burlap bag, hung it on the wall, and left her there amidst the odor of burning tobacco. After the "smoking," she admitted that he whipped her "somepin awful." The elder Williams believed the crime warranted the punishment. Nancy's whipping served as forewarning of what he would do if anyone, relatives included, were guilty of theft. It is difficult to tell where his role as parent began and ended. His punishment was likely to end the thievish habit and save her from punishment at the hands of others.[14]

The brutal drivers as described by freedpersons were not as numerous or as depraved as the narratives suggest. The drivers' job placed them in awkward positions between slaveholders and slaves. Although it was difficult, Peter

Traumas and Tragedies

Randolph came to appreciate the precarious nature of his father's position. The boy thought "very hard" of him initially and believed he was a "very cruel man," but he later realized the man's choices were minimal. Demanding owners exacted much from their drivers; by contrast, a study of drivers owned by the North Carolinian William S. Pettigrew concluded that they had some latitude. Some drivers did temper punishments. Jacob Stroyer claims that both white and black men beat him, but the enslaved man's lashes were less painful.[15]

Among those who meted out punishment were slaveholding women and the wives of slaveholders. It is erroneous to assume that all white women objected to slavery and were secret abolitionists. Many white women had as much interest in maintaining slavery as did white men. The narratives contain accounts of punishments at the hands of women which do not differ substantially from those selected by men. Slaves were more likely to challenge slaveholding women than men; however, the fact remains that enslaved youngsters were punished by whites regardless of their gender or age.[16]

Solomon Northup described a boy of ten or twelve years of age who imitated his father, an overseer. Playing the role to perfection, the boy rode into the field with a whip in hand "greatly to his father's delight." The father commended his behavior as that of a "thorough-going boy." Using a rawhide whip, the would-be overseer urged the slaves on with "shouts, and occasional expressions of profanity." His indiscriminate use of the whip was striking. Northup commented:

> It is pitiable, sometimes, to see him chastising, for instance, the venerable Uncle Abram. He will call the old man to account, and if in his childish judgment it is necessary, sentence him to a certain number of lashes, which he proceeds to inflict with much gravity and deliberation.[17]

This behavior differed from what traditional customs required of enslaved children—deference to their elders. As they watched a respected member of their community humiliated, they must have experienced a sense of furor and helplessness. Perhaps they wondered who would protect them if the esteemed old man had no security from abuse.

Aside from punishments at the hands of slaveholders and others in their household, slaves who traveled abroad were subjected to punishments by patrollers. It is unlikely that children under ten or twelve years of age traveled more than a few miles away from their homes without adults. Whether they traveled alone or in groups, they were liable to encounter patrollers. Patrols, legally constituted armed watches linked to the state militia or court official, functioned primarily to monitor the movement of slaves and received monetary rewards for apprehending violators. Slaveholders often complained that patrols were not effective, but the testimony of ex-slaves differs. "Mos'a the slaves was afeared to go out" because of the patrols, remembered one ex-slave. Marrinda Jane Singleton, who was fifteen years old when slavery ended, agreed. John Finnely also remembered that he wanted to run away, but "den I thinks of de patterrolers,"

he said, and "what [would] happen if dey catches me off the place without a pas."
The thought of punishment dissuaded some but not others. Bond servants
expressed their perceptions about the patrollers in the song:

> Run nigger, run.
> De patteroll git you!
> Run nigger, run.
> De patteroll come!
> Watch nigger, watch.
> The patteroll trick you!
> Watch nigger, watch.
> He got a big gun!

Anxiety about armed men who planned to "git" or "trick" slaves is evident. A
longer and more sophisticated version of the song goes beyond a simple warning
when it cautions:

> Run, nigger, run patroler'll ketch yer,
> Hit yer thirty-nine [times] and sware 'e didn' tech yer.
>
> (Repeat several times.)
>
> Poor white out in de night
> Huntin' fer niggers wid all deir might
> Dey don' always ketch deir game
> D'way we fool um is er shame.
>
> I seed a patteroler hin' er tree
> Tryin to ketch po' little me.
> I ups wid my foots an' er way I run.
> Dar by spiling dat genterman's fun.[18]

Whites of means preferred not to serve the watch and often objected to
patrollers manhandling their property. Enslaved persons understood class differences among whites and scorned the poor white rowdies who made a sport of
abusing the slaves portrayed as "po' little me." This rendition implies that slaves
turned to a game of their own, "spiling dat genterman's fun."[19]

Youngsters might have heard this variation of the song, but because of their
age it is doubtful that they grasped its implications or engaged in the perilous
sport. The differing opinions about the patrols' effectiveness are age-related.
The majority of WPA informants were less than twenty years old when slavery
ended. They feared the patrols without ever having direct encounters with them
or opportunities to spoil their fun.

It is likely that their fear came from hearing how patrollers interfered with
travelers. Millie Barber spoke of the "confusion, mixup, and heartaches" when
her father fell prey to the patrollers, who sometimes beat him when he visited his
wife and children. The "cryin' and ahollerin'" by members of the family always
followed when the patrollers whipped her father.[20]

TRAUMAS AND TRAGEDIES

Hatred of the lash in the hands of whites did not dissuade some slave parents from whipping their children. They have been called stern disciplinarians insistent upon compliance. Their purposes went beyond simply correcting children for infractions. Casual observers misunderstood their intent to control their own children and earn their respect in return. For example, John Houston Bills disapproved of the "unmerciful thrashing" Angelina gave her son Wilson on August 31, 1864, and he forbade "her interference with him again." Angelina apparently interpreted his order to cease and desist as a usurpation of her parental rights. Her "boisterous & insulting" behavior "forced [Bills] to correct her for the first time."[21]

Bills's action goes beyond concern for the child and reflects responses to a woman who exceeded boundaries defined by the patriarchal system. Perhaps Wilson did not understand the nuances of such intricate interpersonal relations between a white slaveholding man and an enslaved woman, but he did not ask for an explanation. Early on, children learned not to question their parents as well as not to challenge their owners.[22]

Bills's use of the word "forced" implies that whipping Angelina was a difficult decision. In a similar vein, he expressed much regret after whipping Willis the first time, for reasons unknown, in 1860. If the incidents pained Bills, they probably did more to Angelina and Willis, who were troubled over the possible loss of self-esteem in front of their children. Of importance also is how the whippings affected the emotional well-being of Angelina's son and Willis's five children. They left no records describing the distress their children experienced while seeing their parents punished.

Unlike Angelina and Willis's children, James W. C. Pennington described the emotional impact of seeing his father punished. He called the fifteen or twenty stripes across Brazil Pennington's shoulders and back "the most savage cruelty." He asked, "how would you expect a *son* to feel at such a sight?" The incident created an "open rupture" in his family, and "each member felt the deep insult."[23]

On Bennett Barrow's Louisiana plantation corporal punishment was frequent and probably made bond children old well beyond their years. Sometimes Bennett whipped all hands in a "general whiping frollick" beginning with the driver. At other times, Barrow noted that he whipped "worse than I ever Whiped any one before." During these harrowing experiences children saw peers, parents, and others beaten indiscriminately. The atmosphere was akin to living in a war zone where the innocent suffered along with those believed to be responsible for infractions. A natural response was to flee from the hail of terror. Slaves on the Barrow plantation, like refugees from war, frequently fled to safety.[24]

Enslaved children often responded to the whippings of their parents in a more fundamental way. Unable to physically overpower persons administering whippings, children tried to distract them in other ways. Jacob Branch moved close enough to "take some dem licks" intended for his mother, while Jacob Stroyer ran back and forth between the overseer and his mother until the beating stopped. The boys received whippings along with their mothers. It was especially painful for Stroyer because he held himself responsible since his mother's whipping resulted from protests about his treatment.[25]

As a child in Virginia, Allen Wilson saw his mother tied to a tree and whipped. The punishment was terrible enough without the further degradation of seeing her stripped naked. As if paralyzed, Wilson remained at a distance and prayed to the "Lawd" with hopes "dat someday he'd open a way . . . to protect mother." At this point, Wilson behaved more like Jacob Stroyer's father than like his contemporary. The elder Stroyer had seen both his wife and son whipped but decided the best solution was to ask "the Lord to hasten the time" to end their despair. The child and the adult realized that a greater force than merely interfering with a whipping was necessary. Wilson's decision to abandon a childish response occurred long before he was an adult biologically.[26]

Whether they rebelled or retreated, children were indelibly scarred by seeing parents whipped. Perhaps the most chilling of all emotions came from knowing the extent of their parents' distress. An ex-slave in Nashville remembered tears streaming down her father's face after a beating while he sang:

> I'm troubled, I'm troubled, I'm troubled in mind,
> If Jesus don't help me I surely will die.
> O Jesus my Saviour, on thee I'll depend,
> When troubles are near me, you'll be my true friend.

The pitiful declaration resounded with helplessness and could frighten a child who did not understand its symbolism. Taken literally, a child might believe the troubled person had been abandoned and death was imminent.[27]

Baby Suggs, a character in Toni Morrison's *Beloved*, always feared the results of her offspring seeing her beaten by whites. "She said it made children crazy to see that," writes Morrison. If "crazy" in this context means that a parent was afraid the children would respond violently and bring more retribution upon the entire family, it is a reasonable assumption. Jacob Stroyer's response to his mother's punishment was commensurate with his age, but interference from older, stronger children was a different matter. In any case, parents steeled themselves against punishment to further protect children, which added another dimension to their duties. The emotional costs of these ordeals for families lasted far longer than the physical pain.[28]

The historian Robert L. Hall calls for a reevaluation of whippings in his "Lord Deliver Us from Cliometrics and from 70.56 Whippings per Year: Prolegomena to a Social History of Slave Whippings in the United States." In the aftermath of criticisms about Fogel and Engerman's *Time on the Cross*, Hall examined the Massachusetts-born abolitionist Jonathan Walker's 1844–1845 diary kept while awaiting trial in a Florida jail. It contains a detailed record of whippings administered mostly by the jailor's pregnant wife. The victim was the jailor's cook and the mother of an infant. The child was too young to understand why its mother received 42 whippings on 32 different occasions over a 214-day period, or a whipping every 5.1 days. Nor could the child fathom the infractions that merited four whippings in one day.[29]

The statistical evidence tells nothing about how the enslaved woman functioned as a mother, if the punishments interfered with her childcare responsibilities, or if childcare responsibilities interfered with her work. These whippings must have made the mother more aware of what the future held for her progeny destined to come of age in such an environment. When reflecting upon slavery an ex-slave who was fifteen years of age when slavery ended posited, "Some slaves have never recovered from some of dese severe whippin's." It is not clear if she meant emotional recovery or physical rehabilitation from maiming, but it is certain that she spoke from firsthand experience.[30]

"Ruthless tyrants," "unfeeling task masters," and ordinary slaveholders devised adroit forms of punishment which could be as devastating as the whippings. They locked slaves in stocks and shackled them in chains. Prisoners of war have reported similar treatment. Former slaves described "cat-hauling," an ingenious method of discipline which involved pulling a cat backwards by its tail across a slave's naked back. The natural resistance to such handling caused the animal's claws to sink deep into the victim's flesh.[31]

Failed efforts to make slaves tractable in combination with other factors prompted slaveowners to remove recalcitrant persons. Separations created physical voids and left deep emotional scars. By any standard, splitting families apart was one of the harshest aspects of bondage. The slaves' fear of separation gave owners their most powerful weapon of control. They sometimes used that mechanism directly. At other times it was indirect when changes in a slaveowner's family affected the lives of bond servants. In either case, the business of buying and selling slaves was devastating.[32]

Although the Atlantic slave trade ended in 1808, the sociologist W. E. B. Du Bois and others argued convincingly that an illegal trade continued well into the mid-nineteenth century. Estimates of the number of Africans imported into the United States after 1810 run into the tens of thousands. Opponents of the antislavery advocates charge them with exaggerating the size of the trade for political reasons. Because of its surreptitious nature, the exact number of Africans, regardless of their ages, brought into the United States illegally remains unknown.[33]

Accusations and denials aside, Charley Barber, who was born into slavery in South Carolina, maintained that his African-born parents traveled to North America along with hundreds of "others all together down under de first deck of de ship, where they was locked in." Obviously, his parents were aware of the ban and discussed it with their children. Barber, who related the account to WPA interviewers added, "It was 'ginst de law to bring them over here when they did." Barber's pithy question, "But what is de law now and what was de law then, when bright shiny money was in sight?" comments upon the act.[34]

3. Courtesy of Perkins Library, Duke University, Durham, North Carolina. Negro Collection—Slavery Division. 1858–1867.

Among the most widely publicized cases of smuggling after 1808 involved the Spanish ship *Amistad,* which carried fifty-three Africans including four children. The boy Kali, and three girls, Teme, Kague, and Margru, were between seven and twelve years of age. The Africans had boarded the ship in Havana and were destined for the sugar plantations in Puerto Principe, Cuba. A July 1, 1839, mutiny set the stage for an international drama. The Africans killed the captain and commandeered the *Amistad* with the intention to return to their home land. Unable to navigate the vessel, Joseph Cinqué, leader of the uprising, relied upon the maritime skills of José Ruiz and Pedro Montes. Rather than returning to Africa, they sailed along the North American coast for nearly two months and finally into the hands of the commander of the USS *Washington,* a revenue cutter, near Long Island.[35]

The surviving thirty-nine Africans including the children were arrested along with the other Africans. When unable to post the required $100 bond, they remained in the New Haven jail. The children's experiences differed from the ordinary crossing of the Atlantic because of the notoriety the mutiny caused, the extended time at sea following the uprising, and their

AUCTION SALES.

BY PULLIAM & SLADE, AUCTS.

TEN LIKELY NEGROES.
Will be sold on THURSDAY the 6th inst., at 10 o'clock, ten likely Negroes, 3 Men, 3 Women, 2 Boys and 2 Girls. These negroes are good farm hands, and sold for no fault.
Feb. 4   BENJAMIN DAVIS, Auct.

BY WELLINGTON GODDIN, AUCTIONEER.

COTTAGE RESIDENCE AND SIX BUILDING
LOTS ON CLAY STREET, BETWEEN 5TH AND 6TH STREETS.
WILL sell on TUESDAY AFTERNOON NEXT, the 4th day of February. at 4 o'clock, that beautiful Cottage reside ce, at the North East corner of Clay and Fifth streets; and at the same time six desirable building lots lying on the North side of Clay stre t, between the Cottage and Sixth street
The above sale will be made *without the least reserve.*
TERMS—One third cash, residue 3 and 6 months for negotiable notes, interest added, satisfactorily endorsed or title received.
Jan. 31—tds   W. GODDIN, Auct.

SALE OF VALUABLE SLAVES,
IN THE CITY OF WILLIAMSBURG. AND OF OTHER PRO-
PERTY, AND RENTING OF REAL ESTATE.
SHALL sell for cash, to the highest bid er. in the said city, before the Court House door, on MONDAY, the 10th day of February, 1851, (that being James City County Court day,) some thirty valuable Slaves, belonging to the estate of the late John M Maupin, consisting of Men, Women and Children. It is seldom purchasers can have so favorable an opportunity to be supplied with Slaves of such value as will then be sold. The sale will commence at 1 o'clock, and those at a distance, and others wishing to purchase, will do well to attend punctually.
I shall also sell, upon a suitable credit to the highest bidder, commencing the sale, as heretofore advertised, on the 29th day of January, 1851, the perishable estate of the deceased, consisting of a large and desirable variety of articles of husbandry; such as Horses, (among them an excellent pair of match Carriage Horses,) Mules, Oxen and other Cattle; Hogs, Wagons, Ox and Tumbrel Carts, and a great variety of Farming Implemer s, some of the most modern and improved construction and use ulness; such as a Wheat Threshing Machine, Wheat Fan, Wheat Drill, Corn Sheller and Grinder. &c., &c. Also, Corn, Oats, Fodder, Straw, Shucks, &c., &c. Also, will be then sold an excellent Carriage and Harness; also, the Household and Kitchen Furniture, of great variety and value. Many items of the Household Furniture are of the most costly and modern style. The Farms in the neighborhood, belonging to said estate, will be rented out, upon one of which is now growing a large and promising crop of wheat. Also, the lots of land and tenements in and adjoining the said city. The sale will take place upon the premises respectively, but the renting will be in Williamsburg, and the sales and renting will be continued, from day to day, until completed.
Jan. 17—cwtds   R. O. H. ARMISTEAD, Executor, &c.
☞ Whig requested to copy.

4. Advertisement for auction of slaves and other property in Virginia. Courtesy of the Virginia State Library, Richmond, Virginia.

arrest. Hunger, illness, or death aboard ocean-going ships were routine. Separation from families and friends along with the removal from one's place of birth were not unusual in the slave trading milieu. Slavers stole Kali and Teme from their parents while the other children Kague and Margru became slaves as a result of unpaid family debts. Many of the *Amistad* captives, including Cinqué, were parents. Although grieved by their own situations, they consoled the frightened and homesick children. Margru remembered Charlotte, "one of my fellow prisoners," she wrote, "who did comfort me when I was torn from my dear native land."[36]

STOLEN CHILDHOOD

Whether ripped away from homes in Africa or America the separations could be emotionally devastating. Large numbers of bond servants were part of the interstate slave trafficking which became more intense after the closing of the overseas trade. The greatest number of slaves sold in the upper South traffic were teenagers and young adults. In 1857 the New York-based Maury Brothers contacted Saint Mordecai, Esq., of Richmond, Virginia, about the increased number of slaves in the cotton states as a result of immigration from the non-cotton-producing states for the years between each decennial census. Having received information from "good authority," the writer questioned it. Some 60,000 slaves, according to the informant, passed through Memphis, and 30,000 through Montgomery in 1857. The numbers appeared too high; therefore, Maury Brothers contacted Mordecai for verification. Between 1850 and 1860, an estimated 269,287 slaves were exported from the selling to the buying states. Of that number, 111,136 were under nineteen years of age.[37]

The nineteenth-century domestic slave trade was age-specific. Children under ten were likely to be sold in family units, more specifically with the mothers. In 1820 the possibility of children living in the Upper South and the cumulative chances of being sold into the Lower South by 1860 was approaching 30 percent. Knowing that the chances of being sold increased as their children grew older placed families in a precarious position. A faux pas, like a land mine, could have disastrous results.[38]

Several of the southern states, including Alabama, prohibited separate sales of children before they reached ten years of age. In spite of these extenuating factors, separations occurred, and slaveholders sold children who were too small to manage on their own. On June 6, 1814, Benjamin Bealk and Rebecca Holt sold the seven-year-old Linder for $260 to Michael La Croese. Perhaps this only meant the change of households for Linder, since the buyer and one of the sellers lived in the same Louisiana parish. Beyond that, the bill of sale does not provide any information about Linder's family, the reason for the sale, or the seller's circumstances. Charles Ball opened his narrative with the claim of separation from his mother when less than five years of age. "My poor mother . . . saw me leaving her for the last time," he wrote, "and wept loudly and bitterly over me." For all of her trouble the mother incurred the wrath of the slave driver with a rawhide whip in hand. Although Ball was very young, the parting made an indelible impression. Ball and Linder's situations differed, but they were separated from their families nonetheless.[39]

Young children were also an integral part of the intrastate slave trade whether sold alone or in families. The 1846 *Charleston Mercury* contains numerous advertisements for the sale of children under varied circumstances. "Slave families" more often than not meant women and children. For example, on November 7, 1846, a notice for the sale of the thirty-two-year-old "Mary Ann," an "excellent Meat and Pastry Cook," appeared. The woman's four children, ranging in age from eleven months to eleven years old, were also for sale. Who would care for these children while their mother plied her skills? There was a mitigating factor. They remained together.[40]

Marriages, births, and deaths in slaveholding families also separated slave families. Slaves were presented as gifts to newly married couples and newborn babies. A slaveholder's death often resulted in estate settlements which scattered slaves to different locations. If sold at public auction but bought by members of the deceased's family, the possibilities of permanent separations were not as great. In other cases, heirs sold slaves and divided the proceeds. Yet another model existed for disposition of property. Executors might parcel out slaves equally among heirs, sell or hire out any remaining chattel, and then divide proceeds equally.[41]

Slaveowners with holdings scattered over a large geographical area often moved bond servants to disparate areas without legal transactions. The business of buying and selling slaves in the interstate or intrastate market differed from owner-controlled relocations, but slave families were still broken apart. A primary example of this kind of disruption occurred at Mount Airy, a Virginia plantation owned by John Taloe between 1799 and 1828. As slavery spread west, children migrated along with their families to the new locations. The same was true of John Hebron who moved some thirty slaves, nearly 50 percent of whom were under twenty, from Virginia to Mississippi in 1834. Furthermore, in 1840 John Hartwell Cocke relocated forty-nine slaves "of all sorts & sizes" from Virginia to Alabama. Cocke's motives were not entirely financial, he relocated the slaves as a measure of preparing them for emancipation. The results were the same for his bond servants as for the others. The involuntary moves separated them from relatives and friends.[42]

In view of the traumatic conditions that many bond servants faced, it is difficult to believe that they saw themselves as a part of an organic whole where honorable, selfless owners cared about their well-being. If hegemonic relations were built upon shared values and ideas rather than force, youngsters probably could not understand this paternalistic or parent-child relationship, which in actuality, was held together by force. Certainly there were slaveholders who did not resort to terror to control their chattel, but their benevolence does not overshadow the brutality. All too often, the slaveholders' sense of family differed from that of the enslaved men and women who sought desperately to protect their children from harm, especially from separations which encroached upon the integrity of their families. In a review of *Roll, Jordan, Roll*, which contains a lengthy discussion of paternalism, Eric Perkins asserts that enslaved children, "seldom felt paternalism's harsh and brutal side." On the contrary, each enslaved child—regardless of age—who was separated from a family member endured the harshest side of paternalism. The effects of the brutality lasted well beyond the end of slavery.[43]

If forewarned about separations, slave parents groped for ways to prepare their children for parting. Some told stories about taking long journeys, while others tried to disrupt imminent separations. Others ran away and hid their children in the woods or threatened to kill them. To minimize the tension, the slaveholder I. L. Twyman asked his brother-in-law, John Austin, not to tell the slaves about a pending sale which he declared would "set them to crying and howling."[44]

Perhaps a parent's most difficult job was to ease the despair of parting. They ignored personal pride and sought viable alternatives to prevent separations. Solomon Northup described Eliza's pitiable supplications to the trader at the Washington slave market. Her owner Elisha Berry offered the woman and her two children for sale in 1841. Berry was the father of Eliza's daughter Emily and had promised to liberate them. The mother's pleas for mercy were similar to Sukey and Ersey's 1842 pleas to keep their families together. The youngest of Ersey's six children was six weeks old while Sukey had an eight-month-old son. Their situations differed in that the two women remained with their children but wanted to stay with their husbands. Eliza had no husband and was losing her children. In 1859 Lucy Skipwith persuaded her owner not to sell Betsey, her daughter, by arguing that the girl was better off in her home. Lucy was again successful in 1863 when Cocke contemplated selling or hiring out another of her children. Lucy Skipwith succeeded in preventing the separations, but many enslaved mothers failed.[45]

The trauma of separation and the fear of never seeing each other again were pervasive. Northup admitted that he had "never seen such an exhibition of intense, unmeasured, and unbounded grief" as that displayed by Eliza. The distraught mother constantly talked "of them," Northup wrote, and "often to them as if they were actually present." Such conversations comforted her. Perhaps the children, Emily and Randall, kept the memories of their mother alive in a similar way.[46]

Eliza's distress was further complicated by knowing that mulatto and octoroon girls were sometimes sold as concubines for white men. Eliza became "absolutely frantic" when she heard the trader say he could earn as much as five thousand dollars for her daughter on the New Orleans market as a "fancy girl." The mother's tragic experiences reflected what the future might hold for her daughter.[47]

Slave children often ran and hid themselves from white strangers. Explaining this action simply as behavioral problems, slaveholders were advised to clothe the children well to help instill self-confidence. It was not unusual for children to wear shabby clothes, but they did not hide from other slaves and whites they knew. They feared that strangers were slave traders. Harriet Tubman's recollections of seeing whites reinforces the notion. The thought of speculators was a part of their consciousness expressed in their song:

> Johnny come down de hollow.
> Oh hollow!
> Johnny come down de hollow.

> Oh hollow!
> De nigger-trader got me.
> Oh hollow!

"Hollow" in this context is unclear. Perhaps it was urging slaves to slip away into the "bush harbor" to pray. One verse more clearly comments upon the business transaction:

> De speculator bought me.
> Oh hollow!
> I'm sold for silver dollars.
> Oh Hollow![48]

Another song marked the anxiety in anticipating a sale. With sorrowful chords a child asks what the future holds:

> Mammy, is Ole' Massa gwin'er sell us tomorrow?
> Yes, my chile.
> Whar he gwin'er sell us?
> Way down South in Georgia.

In another verse the child bids farewell and asks the mother to pray. The lyrics invoke a poignant plea: "Mother, don't grieve after me." In the same vein Randall begged, "Don't cry mama" while promising to be a "good boy." It goes without saying that his assurance along with the singer's request fell upon deaf ears because parents were always sorrowful at the sale of their children. These mournful partings were worse than death because parents did not know what lay ahead for their children. By contrast, death in its finality erased uncertainties and provided hope beyond the temporal world. Meanwhile, the children faced adjusting to circumstances without parents.[49]

If relocated to a new community, what kind of reception would they receive? Did they have new playmates or fictive kin to help with the transition? Frederick Douglass described the agony felt when separated from his grandmother. The women delivered her grandchildren to a distant plantation once they were old enough to work. It is difficult to tell which was more painful for the seven-year-old boy, the actual separation or the belief that she deceived him. The children, including Douglass's older sisters and a brother, understood his plight. They begged him to stop crying and offered peaches and pears to sooth him, but he flung the fruit away. He was indignant and felt betrayed. If he were so acutely distressed, his grandmother's pain must have been more intense since he was not the only grandchild she was forced to give up to a similar fate.[50]

Douglass felt abandoned and saw himself as a stranger in a strange land. Slavery had made his siblings alien to him. Eventually, their presence comforted him. His initial anger and hostility were not unlike the emotions of other children in similar situations.[51]

STOLEN CHILDHOOD

The hiring process, like sales, separated families and friends. The annual rental of slaves provided income for owners, relieved owners of the responsibility of supporting them, and made laborers available to persons who did not wish to purchase slaves. In the early nineteenth century, one out of every eight slave children in Elizabeth City County, Virginia, was hired out and working away from his or her parents. Hiring slaves out became quite profitable in Maryland before the Civil War. The annual rents were "often from one-fifth to one-fourth as much as the slave's local sales value."[52]

Ordinarily, the period of hire ended near Christmas, and the slaves returned to their families until the process began anew in January. The mitigating factor for those hired out was the reunion if matters remained constant, but that was not always the case. For example, in 1832 the Virginian Lewis Miller hired out an enslaved child whom his children had apparently inherited. Shortly afterwards, Miller, described as "somewhat drunk," retrieved the child, then had her "valued" by a trader and sold. In the meantime the child's mother sent her "a present of a little bundle" by I. L. Twyman. At this point, Twyman learned of her sale and initiated a protest, not because of an interest in her welfare, but because it was "unfortunate for Miller's poor children." Twyman claimed he could not "stand still & see orphan children wronged out of the[ir] rights." He asked Austin to "take steps to recover the girl." Twyman pitied the children, whose father usurped their financial stake by selling the enslaved girl. He showed no concern about further separating the slave child, nor was there any interest in reuniting her family. Twyman's sole interest in the child was the potential for the financial security of the white children.[53]

Like being displaced by war, it was virtually impossible for separated slaves to keep in touch with those left behind because of impediments to communication, illiteracy, lack of transportation, and ignorance of geography. The problems were even greater for children who were less experienced at forming supportive networks. Sometimes slaves never saw each other again after separations, but they did not forget, as indicated by the 1833 letter from Hobbs. Although distressed, he reassured Elizabeth of his love when he wrote, "Do not think that because I am bound so fare that gods not abble to open the way."[54]

The 1857 letter from a slave father in Georgia further underscores the pain of separation. "I wish to now," he wrote, "what has Ever become of my Presus little girl." He had "left her in goldsboro [North Carolina] with Mr. Walker" and had "not herd from her Since." Abraham Scriven, who was also separated from his family, wrote, "My pen cannot Express the griffe I feel to be parted from you all." Their letters are moving, but they do not convey their emotions as strongly as Northup's description of Eliza's "exhibition of intense, unmeasured, and unbounded grief" when separated from her children.[55]

The young victims of separations also remembered their parents. More than fifty years after Charles Ball and his mother were separated, he admitted to being so distraught at witnessing the cruelties inflicted upon his mother that he forgot his own sorrow. He remembered the "terrors of the scene return with painful vividness." Similar flashbacks haunted Caleb Craig. He often dreamed of his mother long after slavery ended.[56]

One could always argue that enslaved teenagers who were sold or hired out left home at an age comparable to that of white youth seeking jobs or apprentice-ships. Under normal conditions such discussions might have some merit; never-theless, enslavement and the sale of human beings, regardless of age, did not constitute normal circumstances. Besides, white youth who left home for ap-prenticeships were free to make such decisions either alone or with someone else who had their best interest in mind. Enslaved children and youth did not have the same considerations.[57]

The emotional cost of family separations was high regardless of the reasons and the ages of those involved. Long after slavery ended, the Missourian Mary Bell became melancholy when thinking of the hardships her parents faced because they belonged to different owners. Her father visited on Wednesday and Saturday, which was upsetting enough, but "so often he came home all bloody from beatings from his old nigger overseer would give him." Carefully and lovingly her mother bathed and applied salves to his open wounds. Bell said, "I so often think of de hard times my parents had in der slave days, more than I feel my own hard times."[58]

There are accounts of slaveowners reuniting slaves for a variety of reasons, but they offset only a minuscule number of the separations. John Houston Bills purchased Edney, a twenty-four-year-old woman, mother of two children, and pregnant with another child, in 1849, in order to reunite them with Tom, a slave he owned. In 1857 Farish Carter sought to purchase two slave boys because their mother was "very desirous [of the purchase] so that all of her family might be brought together." Bills and Carter acted on behalf of their slaves, but the incentive for Tryphena Fox was different.[59]

In November 1859 Fox wrote that Susan, "*the worst of all evils*," was returning to Louisiana after being hired out in Mississippi. The separation from her children began when Susan defied Tryphena's orders and received a whip-ping. She ran away for several days and probably intended to return when cooler tempers prevailed, but Dr. Fox refused. Following a five month absence, Try-phena Fox agreed to Susan's return. Tryphena Fox said Susan's children needed "a Mother's care these cold nights." Beneath the callousness that allowed the separation, Fox seemed interested in their well-being. She explained that Ann, a slave woman at Hygiene, had become "slack about taking care of them." She did not keep them covered at night, nor did she "dress them soon enough in the morning to prevent them from taking cold & having chills." Fox declared, "If it were not for her children she [Susan] would never come back." If the children sickened and died from exposure, it meant a financial loss for the owners.[60]

Tryphena noted a marked transformation in Susan once she returned. "I could not wish for a better servant," she wrote. One year later Tryphena observed, "Susan has turned over quite a new leaf." Fear of further separations from her children along with gratitude for her return prompted this change.[61]

William T. Barry's reason for repurchasing a slave family had nothing to do with monetary gains because it was a financial sacrifice to do so. Barry believed he could not afford to ignore the matter. The sale of the slaves had been "a source of infinite pain" to his wife. In the interest of his own domestic happiness, Barry succeeded in buying the family in August 1829. He claimed his wife was "more gratified" than he had seen her in many years at the reunion with the "faithful creatures." The slaves were also appreciative. Aside from the mutual satisfactions and returning harmony to the Barry household, this reunion had deeper implications. Perhaps it reunited Issac and Fanny with relatives and friends in the vicinity. Possibly, Issac's six-year-old son rejoined former play-mates. To be sure, Armistead Barry was "much pleased" with the boy's return. The slaves and slaveholders shared the benefits of the reunions.[62]

The great disparity in the numbers of separations overshadows the number of reunions before slavery ended by such a large margin that reunions receive almost no attention. If earthly reunions were impossible, bond servants had an abiding faith that heavenly rewards were possible. A northern teacher in South Carolina heard children sing:

> I wonder where my mudder gone,
> Sing oh graveyard!
> Graveyard ought to know me
> Sing Jerusalem!

Another line of their song, "Lay my body in the graveyard," completed the thoughts of an afterlife and reunion.[63]

Aside from the physical punishments and separations, slaves were vulnerable to sexual abuse including rape. As an instrument of terror, rape generally accompanies war. Susan Brownmiller, who has studied rape and war, writes, "Rape in war is a familiar act with a familiar excuse." Rape has been treated as an incidental atrocity of war used to destroy national pride and to solidify conquest. If slavery were indeed like war, then it follows that rape occurred. With or without the analogy, an untold number of enslaved females became pregnant through forced cohabitation and exploitation.[64]

Proslavery critics charged abolitionists with using stories about sexual exploitation to politicize their cause, but slaves passed them from one generation to another as true accounts. The evidence supports the allegations that white men used their status to exploit female slaves. Furthermore, there is testimony which implies that black men, especially drivers, also used their positions to exploit enslaved females.[65]

Testimony of this sort often raises more questions than it answers. The nature of the subject inhibited open discussion. What, for example, did WPA informant Ben Horry mean when he said, "if omen don't do all he [the driver] say, he lay task on 'em they aint able to do"? If the women did not finish "all" of the initial tasks why would the driver demand additional work from them? Horry added, "My mother won't do all he say." Was he conscious of word choices in the same context when he used both "don't" and "won't?" The task apparently was not impossible for his mother because she refused to complete it. There is no mention of the driver's relationship with the males. Perhaps he was a bully singling out the females because he could more easily wield power over them. It is also possible that assigning more work was his reaction to the rejection of sexual advances. In either instance, the potential for exploitation existed. Of more importance, the child was aware of the driver's tactics.[66]

Female slaves, regardless of age, were subjected to sexual abuse by men, black and white, slave and free. Much of the abuse heaped upon female slaves by whites emanated from the erroneous belief that the women were naturally promiscuous. The popularization of this notion served as a rationalization for the mistreatment of the women. Additionally, the more comely a slave girl the greater were possibilities of abuse and sale as fancy girls for illicit purposes. Eugene Genovese claims that married slaves "did not take white sexual aggression lightly and resisted effectively enough to hold it to a minimum." Many white men, he writes, avoided "resistant women and dangerous men" by directing their attention toward "single girls by using a combination of flattery, bribes and the ever-present threat of force." It is unlikely that these same "resistant women and dangerous men" would take sexual aggression lightly regardless of the perpetrator's race or the age of the women.[67]

Historians have paid little attention to how young single girls responded to sexual exploitation. They had no legal or social recourse. The apparent hopelessness of their situations does not mean that they acquiesced. For example, when Robert Newsom, a sixty-year-old widower bought the fourteen-year-old girl, Celia, at an 1850 auction in Audrain County, Missouri, and raped her while en route home from the sale, she had no one to turn to for help. Newsom's daughter appeared oblivious to the continued exploitation. Besides, Celia was Newsom's property without protection against sexual abuse.[68]

An 1859 case decided by a Mississippi court further illustrates the vulnerability of female slaves. George, a slave, was indicted for raping a child less than ten years old. The court quashed the charge because there was no legislation covering the "attempted or actual commission of a rape by a slave on a female slave." The social and legal responses to Celia and the young Mississippian diverged from attitudes about white females. William Shakespeare had made retribution for the rape of a "chaste woman" the theme of his sixteenth-century poem "Lucrece." Defending the honor of white women remained important in nineteenth-century America. This kind of thinking undergirded the stereotypical image of delicate, unsullied, white women beyond the reach of carnal desire. Unlike Lucrece, enslaved females had few if any to avenge their honor.[69]

STOLEN CHILDHOOD

The sordid treatment of enslaved females in the nineteenth-century South differed sharply from that awarded to white females. Furthermore, those who sought retribution for slaves were weak reeds against the social and legal institutions fortified by timeworn practices. Whites were upon the proverbial pedestal, while women of African descent served as objects of sexual pleasure. The historian Bertrand Wyatt-Brown explains:

> In the American South, as in England and France, sleeping with a woman was an informal rite of virilization. The obvious way was to pursue a black partner. If the initial effort were clumsy or brutal no one would object, in view of the woman's race and status. Moreover, black girls were infinitely more accessible and experienced than the white daughters of vigilant, wealthy families.

There is no hint of the girls' willingness to gain the sexual experience in the explanation. Nor is there any concern about the physical or psychological costs of gaining sexual precocity.[70]

The sexual exploitation of enslaved girls like Celia differed from the systematic and licentious use of slaves solely to reproduce children. That breeding occurred and the extent to which it happened remain subjects for debate. The lack of empirical evidence does not mean it did not occur. It is more likely that the immorality and inhumanity associated with the practice forced those responsible to hide evidence of their involvement. Regardless of the conditions surrounding a slave's birth, the infant was property and added value to a slave-owner's coffers.[71]

The subject of sexual exploitation needs additional research since its major focus is upon enslaved women and white men. Illicit activities between white women and enslaved men have not been investigated thoroughly nor have incestuous relations among slaves. The sexual exploitation of young male slaves also remains in need of study. Harriet Jacobs remembered the "despotic habits" of a slaveowner who frequently punished the young slave, Luke. Jacobs described the situation as the "strangest freaks" which she found "too filthy" to write about. Perhaps she referred to sexual abuse. Furthermore, contemporary discussions of sexuality among slaves often mention the sixteen-year-old Texan Rose Williams, whose owner forced her to marry without raising questions about its impact upon her spouse.[72]

Beyond those subjects, it is of interest to study the treatment of children resulting from forced marriages and other exploitative relationships to determine the response they received from their parents, owners, and peers. By 1860 there were 405,751 mulattoes in the United States. They constituted 12.55 percent of the African American population. More than half, or 7.70 percent, of them were in the South. The majority of the children were the offspring of involuntary relationships. Regardless of the circumstances of their birth, the children faced uncertain futures.[73]

In the traditional West African society, motherhood was the most important rite of passage for women. Furthermore, the mother-child nexus superseded the husband-wife relationship. Within this context, it is unlikely that Africans in the diaspora would deny love to children born under adverse circumstances. Care must be exercised in labeling unexplained deaths as infanticide. Recent investigations suggest that sudden infant death syndrome (SIDS) may have been the cause rather than any deliberate acts. There is a documented case of a mother killing her infant because it was "white," but there is no evidence to show that the majority of enslaved women including Rose Williams, Elizabeth Keckley, or Sally Thomas mistreated offspring resulting from involuntary relationships.[74]

The attention received by mulatto children from their fathers ranged from benevolent to abusive. It appears that the parents of Betty Brown, who grew up in Missouri, were mutually attracted when she said, "Our daddy; he was an Irishman . . . he had a white wife, an' five chillen at home, but mah mammy say he like huh an' she like him." Tryphena Fox disapproved of the living arrangements of Mr. Sarpy, an overseer on a nearby plantation. According to Fox, Sarpy purchased a house for his "'not negro *wife*,' but his negress, and his four mulatto children." Regardless of what neighbors thought, Sarpy provided for his children and their mother.[75]

A British soldier traveling in the South in the early nineteenth century observed the treatment of a mulatto girl whom he described as "quite a spoiled child." After her mother's death, "Col. H" and his wife "adopted" her and treated "her with as much care & attention or more than if she was their legitimate child." To the officer's amazement, the child slept with the parents and called them "father & mother." The terse comment, "So much for Va manners," ended the observer's notes.[76]

Inattention from white fathers was generally the order of the day. John Parker complained that his father, a Virginia aristocrat, did nothing for him. Annie L. Burton only saw her father from a distance and he consistently avoided any contact with her. Henry Bibb received no attention from his slaveholding father nor did William Wells Brown or Frederick Douglass.[77]

The relationships between mulatto children and their white siblings also varied, and it is clear that age was a factor in determining the quality of their associations. Joe Coney enjoyed an amicable relationship with his half-brother, who once saved him from drowning. Whether the child viewed this as lending a hand to someone in distress or helping his brother is not known. In either case, the boys shared a positive relationship unlike that of the offspring of the South Carolina lawyer Henry Grimké. At his death, Grimké left the pregnant Nancy Weston and her two mulatto children, Archibald Henry and Francis James, in the care of his son Montague. Nancy and her children, whom Henry Grimké fathered, were to be dealt with as family; however, Montague ignored the instructions and treated his half-brothers as slaves. Perhaps the legitimate children and relatives of the deceased resented the usurpation of their legacies.[78]

STOLEN CHILDHOOD

The relationship between Eliza Clitherall, a North Carolinian attending school in England, and two girls of "peculiar situations" was not bound by familial ties. Clitherall wrote about "Miss Berry, a light mulatto, from Jamaica" who told school mates of her family circumstances. Upon the death of her mother, a Jamaican woman, the child lived with her father, who subsequently married a British woman. When "Lady S" arrived at the Jamaican plantation, she would not allow the girl to "sit down in her presence," Clitherall explained. The new mistress and stepmother forbade her to "touch the piano . . . or open the bookcase." The girl now received daily tasks which required exact performance. The girl's mother "had always had entire charge of the house, and Sir T. [was] extremely fond of her & very kind to his two daughters before his marriage but they were not now permitted to see him or to occupy the room they had been accustomed to with their mother. Miss B was very amiable, but sad and unassuming she was grateful to those who were kind to her, or appear'd to feel for her." Clitherall continued, "I pitied her very much."[79]

The possible reasons for Clitherall's empathy abound. Did she pity all slave children with harsh mistresses? Was her attitude an indictment against the institution of slavery, or was there compassion because Berry was nearly white? Perhaps Clitherall's sentiments for Berry were typical for school girls of her time. The circumstances of Berry's life are not unlike the fabric used to construct the "tragic mulatto" character in American novels. Berry's circumstances elicited the kind of response from Clitherall that writers sought when creating nearly white characters whose conditions garnered sympathy and elevated moral indignation. Despite accusations that the layer of pity for the tragic circumstances of a mulatto's birth are too thin to cover racial prejudices, the genre succeeded as propaganda.[80]

Dora Franks, a mulatto without special privileges in the slave quarters, was not the object of compassion among her enslaved peers. "I knew dat dere was some difference," she said, "'tween me and de rest o' chillen." Franks explained that her parentage was the cause of her "sorrow many a time." The children chased and taunted her with shouts of "Old yellow nigger." She added, "Dey didn't treat me good neither."[81]

Although the circumstances surrounding Clitherall and Franks may not be representative peer responses, they emphasize the differences in the way children perceived them. The twentieth-century poem "Cross" by Langston Hughes reflects upon an individual's ethnicity:

> My old man's a white old man
> And my old mother's black.
> If ever I cursed my white old man
> I take my curses back.
>
> If ever I cursed my black old mother
> And wished she were in hell,

> I'm sorry for that evil wish
> And now I wish her well.
>
> My old man died in a fine big house.
> My ma died in a shack.
> I wonder where I'm gonna die,
> Being neither white nor black?[82]

Mulatto children born in bondage understood that skin color did not determine status. Their physical features sometimes attracted attention and raised the interest of casual observers. The correspondence of Silas E. Fales, a Union soldier from Massachusetts on duty near New Orleans, reflects his interest in the features and pigmentation of biracial children. He saw a large number of "nigros of al complexions." Perhaps the most striking was a little boy with "flaxen colored wool on his head and blue eyes." Another Union soldier commented that "one of the boys" seen near Washington, D.C., was "*white* as white . . . with straight black hair." Henry E. Simmons was certain that he "would not be taken for a black man anywhere."[83]

The extraordinary "attention" from others served notice that mulatto children were different. How they perceived themselves varied because color stratification within the slave community fostered ambiguities. Some children were embarrassed, humiliated, and angered at the thoughts of their fathers raping their mothers. Others were equally appalled at the thoughts of their mothers willingly consorting with white slaveholding men. Beyond the negative reactions, there were mulattoes who were proud of their heritage. Regardless of their emotions, the children were victimized by a system that neither penalized sex offenders nor legitimized paternity of enslaved children.[84]

The majority of the mulatto children lived among African Americans and were socialized to conform to the behavior expected of enslaved children. They were objects of sales, punishments, and other abuses the same as boys and girls of a darker hue. They were subjected to an added burden by slaveholding women who suspected their husbands of fathering the children. This was the source of trouble for the Cherokee freedwoman Sarah. After her mistress died, the girl's grandmother explained that the woman abused her because the child was a constant reminder of her husband's infidelity. At early ages, the children learned to deflect the comments about their physical features with finesse and to steer clear of the vindictive wives of slaveowners just as they learned to avoid punishment and other abuses.[85]

Far from being "childlike" throughout their lives, Africans in the diaspora who were subjected to enslavement confronted horror, injustice, and arbitrary power at early ages. They survived because of the protection from parents or others along with the mature use of their own skills. Kate Drumgoold remembered her mother's stern tenacity against the tragedies and traumas of slavery. Her recollections are telling comments about relationships between enslaved persons and those who claimed to master them. "My mother was one that the master could not do anything to make her feel like a slave," she recalled. "She would battle with them to the last that she would not recognize them as her lord and master." Drumgoold concluded, "She was right."[86]

6 "FREE AT LAST"

THE QUEST FOR FREEDOM

> I was earnestly considering
> and devising plans for gaining
> that freedom, which, when I was
> but a mere child, I had ascertained
> to be the natural and inborn right
> of every member of the human family.
>
> —Frederick Douglass*

John Parker recorded his hostility and described how he, when only eight years of age, vented his anger over separation from his family as he walked in shackles to a Richmond, Virginia, slave market. Parker admitted that his hatred of slavery "rankled and festered," thus making him resentful of freedom in the natural environment. The boy destroyed blossoms on shrubs in the countryside and threw stones at a bird while cursing and shaking his fist as it flew away. Of the bird he said, "I would have killed it and been glad of the deed." Several members of the coffle laughed at his hostility as they marched along.[1]

The concept of natural freedom also piqued Frederick Douglass's imagination. When contrasting his status with that of birds, Douglass believed they were "so happy" as he listened to their "sweet songs." "Their apparent joy," he wrote, "only deepened the shades of my sorrow." Their hatred of enslavement never subsided nor did punishment curb the boys' desire for freedom.[2]

It is erroneous to assume that enslaved youngsters were oblivious to their status. Many understood at early ages that they were bond servants and despised their condition along with those responsible for keeping them in bondage. Enslaved children experienced the tragedies and traumas of slavery personally and vicariously; therefore, a discussion of their responses is in order to determine if their behavior represented the storm and stress of adolescence or resistance to slavery. Once they reached a level of understanding, youngsters showed their dissatisfaction with slavery. They were the most vulnerable members of the slave

---

* *My Bondage and My Freedom* (New York: Dover, 1969), 273.

community, yet their reactions to bondage resembled those of experienced adults when they failed to obey orders or ran away. Finally, this chapter examines the ways enslaved children fought for and gained freedom.

One cannot discuss resistance without raising questions about the role of religion. Without a doubt it was significant, but the church was the refuge of the old, and the level of religious understanding among enslaved children remains unclear. The emphasis that parents or other influential persons placed on religion had much to do with whether it served to encourage or suppress resistance. Douglass raised serious doubts about the religiosity of slaveowners as he reflected upon his childhood in *My Bondage and My Freedom*. He was obviously disillusioned with their practices, but the moment of Douglass's disappointment is not certain. Freedpersons mentioned hearing their elders pray for emancipation, but they do not show linkages between resistance and religion. Religion influenced Jacob Stroyer's life, yet neither he nor Douglass was willing to wait for divine intercession to end their days of slavery.[3]

As a youngster, Stroyer's rebellious response to bondage stemmed from punishments at the hand of the horse trainer and the overseer. The overseer whipped him severely for ignoring orders to report to the cotton field rather than the carpenter's shop. Realizing his impotence and that of his parents, Stroyer worked in the fields several weeks before returning to the carpenter's shop. The overseer whipped him again, but the boy became more recalcitrant. Shortly afterward Stroyer and his cousin saw the hated whip attached to the overseer's saddle. "It ought to be put where he will never get it," one of the boys said, "to whip anybody . . . again."[4]

The comment was a catalyst for the boys to strike out at slavery. This was not a case of peer pressure since the boys acted in concert. Each boy understood the possible repercussion, certain punishment, for their conduct. After taking a vow of secrecy, they stole the whip, tied it to an iron rod, and threw it into the river. The overseer never recovered his instrument of torture. The boys' victory was more symbolic than real, but it gave them much satisfaction. It was a personal yet unselfish act with others in mind. Stroyer's cousin ran a greater risk since he had no quarrel with the overseer. With or without companions, youngsters resisted slavery in their own way.[5]

The age at which youngsters actively opposed slavery is significant since children had to be mature enough to understand their condition and the potential for change. For example, the ex-slave Sam Boykin reminisced about walking barefoot through the early morning frost to a cotton field, wrapping himself in a cotton sack, and hiding under some baskets. This behavior raises questions about whether Boykin behaved in this manner because he was enslaved or because he was cold and wanted to avoid work. To be sure, it was an impetuous, childish act which brought only momentary relief. The overseer found him quickly and did not consider hiding a serious enough offense to warrant punishment. Boykin did not persist in avoiding work.[6]

Jenny Proctor's response to a confrontation with her owner also raises questions about whether her behavior was indicative of a child her age or if it was an act of resistance. The incident began when the hungry girl took food without permission. The owner called Jenny a "low-down nigger" and promptly began beating her with a broom. "I guess I just clean lost my head 'cause I knowed better than to fight her if I knowed anything 't all," said Jenny. The response was not calculated to bring a permanent change in the amount of food received, nor was it to protest any other treatment. It was a spontaneous act more reflective of a person her age than an act of resistance to slavery. Jenny had already accepted the notion that she was not to "fight" her owner, and she did not persist.[7]

By contrast, Frederick Douglass assaulted slavery directly by objecting to regular whippings intended to make him submissive. The sixteen-year-old boy's owner found him "unsuitable"; therefore, he hired him out to Edward Covey, a tenant farmer known for breaking the wills of slaves. Covey's determination to make Douglass a slave matched the boy's tenacity for resisting. Douglass described the battle which ended the harassment:

> The brute was endeavoring skillfully to get a slip-knot on my legs. . . . As soon as I found what he was up to, I gave a sudden spring, and as I did so, he holding to my legs, I was brought sprawling to the stable floor. Mr. Covey seemed now to think he had me, and could do what he pleased; but at this moment—from whence came the spirit I don't know—I resolved to fight.

Reacting with heretofore unknown strength, Douglass flung Covey to the ground and drew blood. After a tug-of-war which lasted nearly two hours, each combatant recognized a winner and loser in his own way. Covey claimed that if Douglass had not resisted, he would not have beaten him. Douglass knew otherwise. Neither wished to push the matter further. The fight, a turning point in the young boy's life, "rekindled the few expiring embers of freedom." Exhilarated and full of renewed self-esteem over his physical and mental victory Douglass said, "I was nothing before; *I was a man now.*"[8]

Parallel testimony comes from Emma Gray of Morehouse Parish, Louisiana. After several whippings by an overseer, the sixteen-year-old girl responded with a frontal attack:

> Old Bumpus hit me with a bull whip—drawing blood. I grabbed it; he changed ends and hit me on the head. I then snatched the whip and struck him on the head. This drew blood, making both of us bleed. After fifteen minutes of hard tussling, he let me go. . . .

Gray's response to repeated abuse brought the desired results. This was a turning point in her life since the overseer made no further attempt to whip her.[9]

Douglass and Gray responded to repeated abuse and neither had reservations about the reactions which matched the strength of the adults they defied. They achieved success, whereas the eighteen-year-old Maria did not. After a lengthy absence when ordered to build a fire, the owner found Maria asleep before the roaring flames. She promptly punished Maria, but it did not stop the slave's belligerent behavior. "I disliked to say anything to her master," Tryphena Fox wrote, because "he whips her so severely." Concerned more with the degree than the kind of chastisement, Tryphena beat the girl again, but "not very severely." The extenuating circumstances mattered little; Maria ran away. Her flight was as much a protest as it was to avoid certain punishment once Dr. Fox learned of her behavior.[10]

Sleeping on the job as an act of defiance is debatable, but the connections between the punishment and flight are clear. Maria remained in hiding for nearly six months before Dr. Fox found and returned her to Hygiene. Of that home-coming, Tryphena wrote:

> [Maria] has been severely whipped, and has come back evidently resolved to do the best that she can; as to her being a run-away, we have forgiven and shall forget. As Dr. R says she is a negro and now that she has been punished, it is enough.

Maria fled because of a whipping and returned to the same. To make a perma-nent change in her condition she would have had to confront and defeat Dr. Fox and his wife just as Douglass and Gray triumphed over the slave breaker and overseer.[11]

The historical records are brimming with subtle and overt acts of resistance in the relentless war against slavery. They include feigning illnesses, mistreating livestock, and destroying property. Bond servants also fought against sexual abuse and ran away. Much of the defiance was not age- or gender-specific, but the runaways were primarily males, while protesters against sexual abuse were overwhelmingly females.[12]

Female slaves were not uniformly passive victims or willing participants in such sexual liaisons. Their patterns of behavior could be traced back to their early childhood when parents or other adults were likely to disapprove of sexual aggression.

The testimony of Rose Williams provides a firsthand account of her resis-tance to sexual exploitation. She told federal interviewers that her owner forced her to live with the slave Rufus "'gainst" her "wants." Describing herself as just an "igno'mus chile," she believed she was only to "tend de cabin for Rufus," who insisted upon sleeping with her. Rose literally kicked him from the nuptial bed. The following day, she begged their owner's wife for help in removing him permanently. The girl learned that it was "de Marster's wishes" for them to bring forth "portly chillen."[13]

Rose's situation was more complicated than Douglass's or Maria's. They acted in their own interest. By contrast, her fate was tied to her parents'. "I thinks 'bout massa buyin' me offen de block and savin' me," she said, "from bein' sep'rated from my folks." Rose then asked, "What am I's to do?" She hated the predicament, which forced her to become an adult quickly. Rose knew that if she remained belligerent to Rufus their owner would punish or sell her. The girl also understood that a fertile woman's chance of being sold was less than that of a barren woman's. Rose sacrificed her youth in order to remain near her parents and gave birth to two children while married to Rufus.[14]

Harriet Jacobs was much more adamant than Rose in her fight against sexual exploitation. The fifteen-year-old Jacobs did not find the advances of her owner's father, James Norcom, flattering when he "whisper[ed] foul words" in her ears. Although Norcom reminded Jacobs that she must yield to his will and continued the harassment with "unclean images such as only a vile monster could think of," she rejected his overtures and entered a willing relationship with an unmarried white man who fathered her two children. Jacobs's situation differed from Rose's in that her owner could not intimidate her by threatening to sell members of her family. In fact, the presence of Jacobs's grandmother, a freedwoman, acted as a protective shield for the girl.[15]

Ordinarily there was little protection for enslaved women and their daughters during slavery. The destiny of the Audrain County, Missouri, slave Celia shows the depth of their vulnerability. It also reflects the extent of Celia's resistance. On June 23, 1855, Celia ended Robert Newsom's sexual exploitation by ending his life. Charged with a capital crime, the nineteen-year-old Celia's fate was more certain than that of her toddlers and unborn child, probably fathered by Newsom. The deceased man's legitimate children would inherit them, but the quality of care in a household where their mother was responsible for their owner's death is debatable. Regardless of who cared for Celia's children, they would eventually learn of her indictment for murder, trial, and subsequent execution.[16]

The effect of traumatic experiences would follow enslaved children into adulthood and shape the socialization of their offspring. Slave parents devised ingenious ways to protect themselves and their children from the abuses of slavery. Many who succeeded before the Civil War did so by running away. Some fled into the woods temporarily, while others made conscious decisions to strike out for permanent changes in their conditions.

The average runaway was a young single man who fled alone. Of the newspaper advertisements in the Richmond, Virginia, *Enquirer* between 1804 and 1824, only 15.4 percent of the 1,250 runaways were females, and 2 percent were children. Of the 424 runaway advertisements in selected New Orleans newspapers in 1850, only 136 were females.[17]

Enslaved mothers, regardless of age or marital status, were less likely to run away than childless women because of an unwillingness to leave their offspring behind. The psychological impact of deserting them was too great. Additionally, there were community and family pressures to consider. "Nobody respects a mother who forsakes her children," said the ex-slave Molly Horniblow to her granddaughter, Harriet Jacobs, as the latter had reached maturity and considered running away alone. Jacobs believed if she ran away her owner would grow tired of her two children and sell them.[18]

STOLEN CHILDHOOD

"Stand by your own children," admonished the old woman and "suffer with them till death." Heeding the advice, Jacobs endured agonizing deprivation as she hid for seven years in an unheated and unventilated loft above a storeroom adjoining her grandmother's house. The deprivation that Jacobs suffered during the self-imposed exile may be compared to conditions of war when freedom lovers, such as the family of Anne Frank, sequester themselves to avoid death. From the inside of her drafty refuge, Jacobs watched her son and daughter as they suffered from her absence. The mother also suffered from seeing her children endure the loss of a mother's comfort and love, yet she could not expose herself. Never forsaking the dream of freeing them, Jacobs persevered. Fighting a psychological war with her owner, she manipulated him into thinking she had fled to the North.[19]

From her "prison cell" Jacobs orchestrated the sale of her children, arranged for her daughter to move to a free state, and finally succeeded in outwitting Norcum. At last, she gained freedom for herself and her children. Until this complicated scheme came to fruition, Horniblow also suffered emotionally. The burden of concealing her granddaughter, caring for her great-grandchildren, and leading a life of deception caused unusual anxiety for the aged woman, but she did it willingly. After all, Horniblow would never advise her granddaughter to do something that she herself would not live up to. Their anguish was a part of their intergenerational linkage.[20]

Enslaved parents who became fugitives faced extraordinary difficulties when accompanied by children. It was virtually impossible to carry enough food and water to sustain oneself let alone additional provisions for youngsters. Moreover, traveling over land, on foot, meant that the children walked or their parents carried them. In either case, it meant slow going. Besides, children crying from hunger or weariness drew attention and increased chances of detection. Despite the obstacles, some mothers dared to flee with their offspring. *Uncle Tom's Cabin* is a novel, yet Harriet Beecher Stowe modeled the character Eliza upon the actual flight of a woman with a child who crossed the icy Ohio River to freedom. A runaway woman, very much like Eliza, received assistance from abolitionists in Ripley, Ohio. This is only one example of a woman who fled from slavery with an infant. There were others.[21]

It was easier for slaves to escape alone; consequently, some parents encouraged their children to literally break the chains of slavery. The Missouri-born Lucy Delaney remembered that her mother "never spared an opportunity" to tell her children to seek their liberty "whenever the chance offered." By the time Lucy was twelve years old, she planned to run away and was "forever on the alert for a chance to escape." Lucy was not hesitant about leaving her mother, who had prepared her for running away. By contrast, William Wells Brown initially refused to escape alone. Knowing that his mother had carried him upon her back and received whippings for nursing him instead of working, Brown could not easily sever that tie. He insisted upon running away together. When their flight failed, his mother influenced him to flee alone and bade, "God be with you!"[22]

One cannot construe Brown's reluctance to escape alone as inadequate preparation for separation. In each instance the parents wanted a better life for their children and put their own well-being aside. The difference in the two children is in the degree and kind of socialization. A part of their education in the quarters was preparation for independence. The Delaney woman had taken a "solemn vow," at the sale of her husband, that her children would not remain slaves throughout their lives. Brown's mother encouraged him to leave without her. Brown appears to see himself as a man with a responsibility to protect his womenfolk. Perhaps slave children were socialized to think if men were present they were to take care of the family, whereas women alone taught their children to take care of themselves. In either case, the mothers believed their children were mature enough to flee and survive without them.[23]

Enslaved parents lived and succeeded only to the extent that their children did. They shared each others' triumphs and failures. Their firmly interlocked lives prevented them from behaving as individuals with singular purposes. Upon hearing that Nancy Delaney had succeeded in running away, her mother danced, sang, and clapped and waved her hands with ecstasy. The girl's success was also the mother's. In a similar situation, the runaway Mattie Jackson wrote, "I was overjoyed with my personal freedom but the joy at my mother's escape was greater than anything I had ever known." Theirs was a symbiotic relationship with everlasting qualities of love, trust, and honesty.[24]

Without the benefit of parental counsel, Frederick Douglass took inspiration for running away from the song:

> Run to Jesus, shun the danger,
> I don't expect to stay much longer here.
>
> He will be our dearest friend,
> And will help us to the end,
> I don't expect to stay much longer here.

The lyrics warned of obstacles, but they also promised, "Many mansions there will be, / One for you and one for me." More significant than the danger and mansions, the slaves "dearest friend" Jesus would be there "to the end."[25]

Douglass and several friends, all older than he, worked toward freedom. The plan, initiated by the nineteen-year-old Douglass, called for stealing a canoe and rowing away. Before taking any action, they were arrested upon suspicion of plotting to run away. The would-be fugitives conducted themselves as mature adults throughout the ordeal. They kept quiet, divulged no secrets, and were miraculously released without punitive actions. Perhaps the embarrassment of a nineteen-year-old successfully plotting an escape for himself and several other young males valued at thousands of dollars saved them from punishment. It is also possible that their actions were not taken seriously since they were not treated as adult runaways. To be sure, there was no evidence to show they planned to escape, but this did not always relieve slaves from punishment.[26]

Any slave who gained freedom as a fugitive was subject to seizure. The Fugitive Slave Act of 1850 was more stringent than the Fugitive Slave Act of 1793 because it created enforcement mechanisms that included the appointment of hundreds of U.S. commissioners to hear cases. Moreover, the 1850 law permitted officials to receive ten dollars for each ruling favorable to slaveowners and only five dollars for decisions against them. It was financially beneficial to officials to rule against "fugitives" regardless of their innocence.[27]

Since the law denied accused persons the right to a jury trial and the right to testify, the possibility of recapturing fugitives and returning them to slavery intensified. So did the possibility of capturing free African Americans and enslaving them. For these reasons "defiance of the Fugitive Slave Law," writes historian Benjamin Quarles, "became a new commandment to abolitionists throughout the North." The tug-of-war between abolitionists and slave catchers drew national attention when Anthony Burns, and William and Ellen Craft, fled from slavery.[28]

Margaret Garner's case was probably even more dramatic in that she was determined never to return to slavery when she, along with her husband, four children, and in-laws, escaped to Ohio in 1857. Margaret became alarmed when confronted by slave catchers. In an act of desperation, she slashed the throat of one child and attempted to kill the others and herself. The distraught woman was arrested but did not stand trial for murder in Ohio. Instead, the authorities sent her back to Gaines' Landing, Arkansas. An accident aboard the *Lewis* figured importantly in Margaret's plan to free herself and the children. Amidst the confusion, one witness claimed that Margaret's nine-month-old infant drowned. Another said Margaret threw the child into the river and leapt in afterward. Regardless of the conflicting reports, only the mother survived. She failed to free herself, but death freed her child.[29]

Freedom eluded many bond servants because they were too intimidated by stories of patrollers and fear of the unknown to ever strike out for freedom. One WPA informant said it did no good because the "nigger dogs" could track and find fugitives. Mom Ryer Emmanuel, aged seventy-eight when interviewed on December 16, 1937, described the effectiveness of tracking dogs. She claimed they went right to the "foot of dat tree en just stand up en howl at you. Dey would stand right dere en hold you up de tree till some of the white folks been get dere. . . . Chop de tree down en let you fall right in de dog's moth." Such stories were likely to deter would-be runaways.[30]

A child's frame of reference dictated his or her behavior when encountering runaways, and the sentiments ran the full gamut. The very mention of runaways scared Julia Brown. Her fear had nothing to do with the fugitives' quest for freedom, but with stories told by adults. "They made me hoe when I was a child and I'd keep right up with the others," she remembered, "'cause they tell me that if I got behind a runaway nigger would get me and split open my head and get the milk outen it." An unclear perception of runaways caused her trepidation, and the older workers capitalized upon her youthful vulnerability. Sis Shackelford was also fearful of runaways who found sanction within the boggy quagmire of the Dismal Swamp in Virginia. Once the fugitives befriended the children who lived nearby, they stole food to assist in their escape. Their anxiety arose from the portrayal of fugitives as potentially dangerous persons. If slaves assisted them, they placed themselves in danger as well.[31]

Shackelford's response to runaways was not unusual. Most children who encountered fugitives understood the gravity of the matter and assisted when possible. When the nine-year-old Mary, member of a family of runaways helped by the Pennsylvania underground railroad, met another fugitive—an older man who injured himself during the flight—she showed no fear, but remained at his bedside "manifesting almost womanly sympathy." Mary easily identified with the old man and knew the value of kindness toward fugitives.[32]

It was not unusual for owners to hunt, advertise for, and recapture runaways. Runaways were constantly on guard to avoid returning to slavery. The family of Henry Highland Garnet, who became an abolitionist, gained freedom through flight, and slave catchers nearly recaptured them when he was fifteen years old. With a recently purchased knife to bolster his courage, Garnet vowed to defend himself and pursue the slave catchers. Fortunately, the anticipated encounter never occurred.[33]

The most definitive way of undermining both production and reproduction was to free oneself and all offspring legally. Between 1790 and 1860 the free population increased from 59,466 to 487,970. The greatest period of growth in the nineteenth century was between 1800 and 1810, when the free population increased from 108,395 to 186,446, or by 72 percent. After 1810 the largest increase in the free black population was in 1830, when it reached 319,599, which was 36.87 percent larger than in 1820. By 1860 there were 240,921 free persons of African descent under twenty years of age in the United States.[34]

Private manumissions contributed to the growth of this population. The manumissions occurred when slaveowners such as George Washington, John Randolph, Robert Carter, and George W. P. Curtis freed hundreds of slaves and others like Thomas Jefferson liberated only a few. Less well-known slaveholders also emancipated slaves. For example, in 1839 Thomas Sewell, a medical doctor in Washington, D.C., purchased the forty-year-old Celia and three children ranging in age from nine to fourteen years for $1,400. He bought the family "with a view of procuring their freedom & to enable them to go to Massachusetts to join David a colored man the husband of Celia & the father of the three . . . named children." Sewell exacted conditions of liberation for the children. They were "subject to the parental care & authority of their father & mother, until they shall become of age according to the laws of Massachusetts." Possibilities for a reunion were boundless.[35]

Slaveholders initiated manumissions, formally and informally, through their willingness to reward servants with liberty. Formal procedures involved satisfying legal requirements, whereas informal manumissions ignored the law when severing connections. The latter method was as simple as turning slaves loose or not hunting for runaways. Such acts were fraught with complications since "freed" persons were still technically bound and at risk for reenslavement.

Private manumissions sometimes resulted from illicit relationships between white slaveowners and black paramours. Enslaved women rather than men were more likely to gain freedom for themselves and their children in this way. Antebellum legislation regarding property rights of women and the double standard of behavior help to explain this occurrence. Judith Schafer argues that this was not uncommon in Louisiana. She also notes that white heirs sometimes challenged such wills and overturned them. Complications arising from wills were not peculiar to Louisiana.[36]

Curiously the 1813 will of James McCray emancipated two biracial children, Kitty and Robert, along with their mother Franky, but it denied freedom to a third child in his Mississippi household. The child, born in 1810 or 1811, known as James Warner, William McCary, William Chubbee, William McChubby, and Okah Tubbee, was probably Franky's son but fathered by someone other than McCray. The will provided that the three-year-old Warner and his issue be "held as slaves during all and each of their lives," for the benefit of Kitty and Robert.[37]

Keenly aware of the differences in their status and his at an early age, Warner sought freedom and constructed a new life for himself by transcending both race and class. As an itinerant musician on the Mississippi River, he claimed that he was the son of an Indian chief as he traveled northward into free territory. Obviously, he did not believe that his siblings would eventually free him.

Promises of manumission occasionally went awry, as in the case of children belonging to Harriet Jacobs; Eliza, the woman Solomon Northup met in the slave trader's pen; and Betsey, the Georgia-born mother of two children, whose owner Patrick Gibson and the father of her children freed them only to learn in 1839 that he did not properly execute his wishes before he died. Betsey was more fortunate than Harriet or Eliza in that she and her children were living in the North at the time of Gibson's death and remained there where they enjoyed "freedom." Despite the differences in their situations, slaves recognized problems attendant to pledges of freedom when they quipped:

> My ole mistis promise me
> Dat when she died, she gwine set me free
> But she lived so long en got so po
> Dat she left me diggin wid er garden ho.

Another version of the song alludes to a long wait for fulfillment of the nebulous promise when the mistress "lived so long dat 'er head got bal." Of more importance, they claimed "she give out'n de notion a-dying at all."[38]

The ditty, far from a simple verse, reflects dissipation of the manumission fervor brought on by the American Revolution. Afterwards fewer and fewer slaves became free, as community pressures and political rhetoric galvanized against emancipations. Whites abhorred the unsettling idea of free blacks among slaves, which raised the latter's aspirations for freedom. "It was no accident," writes historian Ira Berlin, "that an articulate defense of slavery appeared with the emergence of the free Negro caste." Proslavery arguments became more systematic and widespread in the nineteenth century as slave-holders and their sympathizers saw slavery as a "positive good" or "a necessary evil."[39]

The percentage of manumissions declined steadily until the Civil War. After 1830 the growth rate among free blacks did not exceed 20.87 percent, and by 1860 it had fallen to 12.32 percent. This 12.32-percent increase between 1850 and 1860 was the smallest recorded growth in the nineteenth century. Many of the manumissions in this period were without encumbrances, while others only exacerbated the conditions of freedpeople. For example, an eighteen-year-old mother was to become free in eight years, while her four-month-old child was to remain enslaved until she reached twenty-eight years of age.[40]

Along with complications arising from contested wills, southern states passed laws that limited manumissions and the mobility of freedpersons. Louisiana's Black Code of 1807 stipulated that slaves be of "honest conduct" for four years prior to emancipation in addition to being at least thirty years of age. Ordinarily, children had no chance of acquiring freedom under this law. There were exceptions for slaves performing heroic deeds in the interest of a slaveholder or slaveholder's family. North Carolina allowed manumissions for meritorious acts upon court approval. After fulfilling rigid requirements for emancipation, slaves often faced other obstacles.[41]

In 1806 Virginia required newly emancipated persons to leave the state one year afterward or risk reenslavement. An 1852 Louisiana law was more stringent than Virginia's. It asked freedpersons to migrate to Liberia. In either case, newly freed persons faced separations from family and friends. The ages and numbers of freedpersons affected by these laws are unknown, but the number of persons emigrating to Liberia, from Louisiana or elsewhere in the United States, was miniscule. Between 1820 and 1856 the American Colonization Society and its associations assisted 9,502 blacks. Of that number only 3,676 were born free in the United States.[42]

The financial and emotional costs of disengagement played a role in the paucity of the numbers of freedpersons who moved to Liberia. In 1832 an observer recorded an astute comment about colonization in his diary when he wrote, "Poor creatures: leaving their friends & kindred to find a place where they may enjoy the rights Our god has given them." The alternatives to leaving family and friends weighed heavily in their decision. Besides, there were free blacks who believed America was their home, and they were entitled to live in the United States in peace.[43]

STOLEN CHILDHOOD

Enslaved persons did not wait for someone else to restore their natural rights; they fought for freedom through legal and illegal means. Possibilities of self-purchase were not entirely remote for many slaves, but the cost was often prohibitive for an entire family; therefore, parents sometimes worked to free children rather than themselves. Distinctions in craft workers by gender meant that women and girls had fewer opportunities for autonomy, to travel away from the plantation, or to hire their own time. Washerwomen, cooks, and seamstresses were not in high demand as were silversmiths, tinsmiths, and coopers. As a result, women were less likely than men to earn enough to purchase additional goods for their own comfort or freedom. Furthermore, young girls rarely honed housekeeping skills to the extent that they could replace adult washerwomen or cooks permanently.[44]

A study of a Nashville, Tennessee, family underscores the difficulties an enslaved mother faced in acquiring freedom for her three mulatto children. Between 1818 and 1826 Sally Thomas—a washerwoman—saved over $300 toward their purchase, but it was not enough to buy each child. Nevertheless, she succeeded in seeing the boys removed from bondage via three separate ways. Their owner emancipated one child, another escaped, and Sally purchased the third child. To avert the Tennessee law which required emancipated persons to leave the state, Sally arranged for a prominent white lawyer to hold the title to her six-year-old son. The boy remained technically enslaved. Henry, the son who ran away, eventually moved to Canada to free himself of anxiety about slave catchers. Sally Thomas's family predicament was that of other antebellum slave families in microcosm.[45]

The talented poet George Horton was unable to free himself with proceeds earned from his writing. The sales of his collection of poems, *The Hope of Liberty*, published in 1829, were not brisk enough for him to purchase his freedom and move to Liberia. Horton's *The Hope of Liberty* reappeared in 1837 and 1838 under different titles, yet it was not enough to purchase his liberty and that of his wife, son, and daughter.[46]

Thomas's and Horton's circumstances pale by comparison with those of the mulatto April Ellison, who was born in 1790. He became an apprentice and learned the skills of a machinist, carpenter, and blacksmith during fourteen years of training. In 1816 the apprenticeship ended, and April bought his freedom with money earned from extra work. As a skilled freedman, he changed his name to William, moved to Statesburg, South Carolina, and opened a business repairing and building cotton gins, for a largely white clientele, with the help of hired laborers and young enslaved apprentices. Over the years Ellison married, fathered three sons, acquired property, and became a prosperous gin maker, planter, and slaveowner. He passed his skill on to his sons and male slaves. It is unlikely that he considered allowing the slaves to purchase their freedom since he was profit oriented and interested in improving his status rather than that of his slaves.[47]

By 1840 Ellison owned over 300 acres of fertile land, a well-equipped shop, and thirty slaves. The enslaved women and children cultivated the fields, while men and older boys worked in his shop. There is a noticeable absence of adolescent girls and a disproportionate number of boys in that age group among his slaves. Ellison's biographers, James L. Roark and Michael P. Johnson, speculate that the freedman sustained an aggressive expansion program by turning human capital, girls, into cash to buy more land and adult males to work in the shop. Girls were valuable and had the potential for making Ellison wealthier through their progeny. Apparently, he did not care to wait until their offspring matured into skilled workers. Besides, there was no assurance that the girls would give birth to boys. Ellison's desire for a permanent labor force made it impossible for his artisans to work independently as he had done.[48]

Other than self-purchases, there were instances where slaves, without regard for their ages, gained freedom through the actions of abolitionist groups. One such case which resulted in the purchase of two children began April 15, 1848, when the Washington, D.C.-born Mary and Emily, children of the freedman Paul and slave woman Amelia Edmondson, fell into the hands of slave traders after their escape attempt failed. Coming from a large family where several of the fourteen children had gained their freedom, it was not unusual for the girls to follow their lead. Mary, who was fifteen years old at the time, and her thirteen-year-old sister Emily, along with four male siblings, joined seventy-one other slaves, including eleven children, aboard the schooner *Pearl*, which was destined for Philadelphia. Adverse winds and betrayal foiled their plans. After capture, the slaves returned to a Washington jail. In the meantime, the slaveowner sold Emily and Mary to Alexandria traders Bruin & Hill, who set an unusually high price on the "young and healthy girls who had those peculiar attractions of form, of feature, and complexion, which southern connoisseurs in sensualism so highly prize." In other words, he intended to sell them as "fancy girls" on the New Orleans slave market.[49]

The trader did not sell Emily and Mary because of the lateness of the season and the lofty asking price of $2,250. It was to their good fortune since the case drew national attention and allowed their father time to interest the New York Anti-Slavery Society in their fate. Working with the society, local churches, and Henry Ward Beecher, the Edmondson family raised enough money to free the girls. Furthermore, the abolitionists wanted them to join the circuit to solicit support for their cause.[50]

Antislavery groups helped to win freedom of slaves through legal measures as in the *Commonwealth v. Aves* and *Amistad* cases. Children figured importantly in each case, although the circumstances were quite different. The 1836 *Commonwealth v. Aves* case, tried in the Massachusetts Supreme Judicial Court, began when Mary Aves Slater traveled from New Orleans to Boston with the six-year-old girl, Med. The Boston Female Anti-Slavery Society claimed that Slater held Med against her will, and it interceded on the child's behalf. Chief Justice

Lemuel Shaw ruled that "slaves brought into Massachusetts with the consent of their owner became free the moment they arrived in the state." Med, unlike Dred Scott, an enslaved adult whose 1857 Supreme Court case based upon living in free territory, won a favorable ruling. Persons interested in winning their freedom focused more upon their presence in a free state or territory than upon the age of those involved.[51]

Through the efforts of abolitionists, the *Amistad* captives received their freedom, but not before the matter became a cause célèbre. The *Amistad* Committee, including Lewis Tappan, Joshua Leavitt, and Simeon Jocelyn, raised money for the legal defense of the captives and for publicizing the case. Roger S. Baldwin, known as a champion of the less fortunate, served as their chief defender, while additional attorneys Seth Staples, Theodore Sedgwick, and former President of the United States John Quincy Adams lent their expertise to freeing the captives.[52]

The initial round of the case occurred in the United States Circuit Court of Connecticut. The defense lawyers sought a writ of habeas corpus for the children, who remained in jail, along with the adults, without any criminal charges. This tactic served two purposes. First, it "would force the prosecution to bring formal charges against them, or see the court excuse them from appearing as witnesses." Second, the writ would serve as a basis for the debate about human rights versus property rights in the court. The status of the children, who spoke neither English, Portuguese, nor Spanish, was a key issue in the proceedings for the defendants. They were too young to have been slaves in Cuba before 1817, when England and Spain agreed to stop the African slave trade. Their ages suggested that the Spanish violated the law. The prosecution sought to shift the focus from the children to the criminal charges of murder and piracy against the adults. The court did not grant the writ because such an order would admit that the captives were human with rights to their freedom by any means.[53]

The case ended March 9, 1841, when Supreme Court Justice Joseph Story ruled that attorneys representing the defense did not prove their claim to the captives. After eighteen months, widespread publicity, and a bitter court fight, Kali, Teme, Kague, Margru, and the other *Amistad* captives were free. Following a custody dispute between the New Haven jailor Stanton Pendleton and the abolitionist Amos Townsend, Jr., for the three girls, they rejoined the others in Farmington, Connecticut.

On November 27, 1841, thirty-five *Amistad* survivors, including the three girls, boarded the barque *Gentleman* and began a fifty-two-day voyage back to Africa. Long before the trial ended Charlotte had pacified the children by telling them they would see Africa again.[54]

Few slaves became involved in protracted legal battles, widespread publicity, or international diplomacy in their quest for freedom. By comparison, more slaves liberated themselves illegally. A major distinction in this approach was the possibility of violence. Uprisings and insurrections, real or imagined, sent terror throughout slaveholding areas. There is no indication of the number of enslaved youngsters who felt tremors from the slave revolt which occurred in St. John, the Baptist Parish, thirty-six miles north of New Orleans, in 1811. Officials executed sixteen participants, decapitated them, and placed their heads on poles in a random fashion along the Mississippi River. These ghastly sights were visual reminders of what might await rebels regardless of their ages.[55]

Children and youth played no role in the insurrectionary plans of Gabriel Prosser, Denmark Vesey, Nat Turner, or Joseph Cinqué, yet they could not escape the panic resulting from their actions. In the wake of the Turner rebellion, numbers of slaves were killed as warnings against future conspirators increased. Others implicated in the plot received transportation outside of the state in lieu of the death penalty. Upon their return to the state, they subjected themselves to execution, if caught. In either case, the penalty was not to see their families and friends again. Young slaves must have noticed changes in their living conditions, daily activities, and parental behavior in the wake of rebellions, both real and imaginary.[56]

During slavery the lives of adults and children were so closely related that no one could escape the upheaval it caused. Like victims of war, they were affected by the pervasive terror regardless of what or who was responsible. The ever-present threat of punishments and separations along with physical and mental abuse kept acts of resistance to slavery alive. The relentless war against slavery would not end until slavery ended. Once the Civil War began in 1861, many bond servants experienced the effects of a declared war and took advantage of its tumult to free themselves.

Abolitionists argued that the Constitution of the United States no longer protected slavery in the Confederate States of America; therefore, enslaved persons were subjected to confiscation as enemy property or "contraband of war" under international law. Union General Benjamin Butler, commander of Fortress Monroe in Elizabeth City County, Virginia, applied the theory in May 1861 when Shepard Mallory, James Townsend, and Frank Baker, three runaway slaves belonging to Charles Mallory, a colonel in the Confederate army, sought refuge at the army fort.[57]

One of Butler's officers had warned that runaway slaves would "commence swarming" into Fortress Monroe within twenty-four hours. News circulated rapidly about the fate of the runaways. Before long hundreds of men, women, boys, and girls made their way to "Freedom Fort." The army immediately put able-bodied men to work constructing breastworks under the supervision of Private Edward L. Pierce. Some men earned eight dollars per month working as cooks, teamsters, stevedores, and carpenters. Women working as laundresses and cooks received four dollars per month. Children assisted their parents whenever possible along with performing other necessary chores.[58]

In the early stages of the war, General Butler recognized the gravity of similar conditions in Virginia and declared that it was manifestly wrong to accept men while leaving wives and children vulnerable to angry owners. Butler encouraged families to come into Fortress Monroe. Their numbers soon exceeded available space; consequently, officials diverted them to "Slabtown," a nearby shanty village of hastily built cabins of roughhewn planks and crates. Dwellings in Slabtown and other abandoned houses provided shelter for the ever-increasing black population. The August 1861 fires nearly destroyed the entire village and further exacerbated the housing shortages.[59]

Events at Fortress Monroe were not entirely unique. Slaves of all ages fled to U.S. military installations as soon as the hostilities began. As Union soldiers moved southward, slaves joined them. The South Carolinian Robert Smalls abducted the Confederate ship *Planter* on April 13, 1862, and sailed to freedom past five Confederate garrisons. Aboard the *Planter* were women and children including Smalls's wife and three young children. An estimated 15,000 slaves of all ages escaped from middle Georgia to the coast in the first nine months of Union occupation.[60]

Despite the fluid nature of events, the diarist Mary Chesnut, an astute observer of antebellum society, commented about the impervious expressions of the servants who appeared "profoundly indifferent" to circumstances around them. "Are they stolidly stupid," she asked, "or wiser than we are, silent and strong, biding their time." Slaves were not inane, but their ostensible detachment was so convincing that whites talked freely in their presence. A correspondent for the New York *World* claimed to have never met a slave in the Hampton Roads, Virginia, area who did not "perfectly understand the issues of the war." The slaves in Chesnut's household and elsewhere masked their feelings, and she was not wrong in thinking they were indeed waiting for the best moment to capitalize on the situation.[61]

As they worked, slave children learned about the war from discussions such as those in the Chesnut household. Other information came to them via the "'grape-vine' telegraph" which made its way into the quarters. Booker T. Washington remembered hearing many hushed discussions between his mother and others regarding Abraham Lincoln's election and the Civil War.[62]

Once the war began, slaves of all ages in Georgetown, South Carolina, sang:

> We'll fight for liberty
> Till de Lord shall call us home;
> We'll soon be free
> Till de Lord shall call us home.

The song caused some owners to whip their slaves, while other slaves were jailed. The punishments did not stop the widespread desire for liberty for oneself and one's children by fighting.[63]

Many slaveholders did whatever they could to halt the attack upon their way of life, which threatened them with personal and real losses. To maintain control, owners impressed upon the slaves that it was their "duty" to remain "faithful."

To further dissuade slaves from flocking to Union lines, slaveholders sometimes told tales of Union soldiers with horns devouring small children or living in houses made of snow and ice to frighten slaves into believing that "liberating armies" would harm rather than help them. Owners also moved the servants to areas of safety. When the Fox family left Plaquemines Parish immediately before the April 1862 fall of New Orleans, Adelaide, Margaret, and Buddy were taken along. The following year, a British traveler in Louisiana commented that the road was "alive with negroes, who are being 'run' into Texas out of General N. P. Banks's way."[64]

To be sure, some slaves remained loyal to their owners, but frightening stories and personal appeals did not stop others from seizing opportunities to make permanent changes in their lives. Basic necessities of life—food, clothing, and shelter—at the hands of slaveowners were not as attractive as liberty. When a seventeen-year-old slave in Tennessee prepared to run away and join the Union army, his owner chided him. She reminded him that she had nursed him back to health when he was a sickly child. "And now," she said, "you are fighting me!" The boy responded, "I ain't fighting you, I'm fighting to get free."[65]

Although the youngster was ready to fight for his freedom, the U.S. Army initially lacked a policy regarding the enlistment of African Americans. Some military commanders refused to accept runaways, while others allowed owners to come within their lines to recover them. On July 17, 1862, Congress made provisions to enroll African Americans. The secretary of war authorized the recruitment of 5,000 South Carolina freedmen on August 25, 1862. The following November, Thomas W. Higginson accepted command of the First Regiment of South Carolina Volunteers. Among the volunteers was a drummer-boy. The child was aware of the song "We'll Fight for Liberty" and understood its significance to both slaves and slaveholders. "Dey tink," he said, "'de Lord' meant for say de Yankees."[66]

The role of slave children and youth during the Civil War varied according to time and place. The job of the boy musician in South Carolina was probably no different from that of the Louisianian Drummer Jackson, a young musician who joined the army as a ragged, barefoot slave. Afterwards, he received a uniform and shoes, which probably raised his self-esteem and the aspirations of enslaved youngsters who saw him drumming out cadences as soldiers passed along their way (see figure 6).[67]

A former slave from Tennessee joined the U.S. Army when he was about fifteen years old. He and the other slaves "broke and ran" when they heard the "band playing" as the soldiers approached. Official duty at Fort Negley in Nashville "was the biggest thing that ever happened in my life," he said. With a gun and uniform, he "felt like a man."[68]

Contributions to the war effort made by females generally focused upon food and laundry services. The Georgia-born Susie King Taylor, who was fourteen years old when the war began, witnessed it from within a Union camp

STOLEN CHILDHOOD

5. Youngsters who "joined" Lieutenant John P. Shaw, Co. K, 2d Rhode Island Volunteer Infantry. Courtesy of the U.S. Army Military History Institute, Carlisle Barracks, Carlisle, Pennsylvania.

where she worked as a cook and laundress. She also helped bandage and nurse wounded soldiers. Moving beyond the traditional jobs for women, Taylor said that she "learned to handle a musket" well along with taking guns apart and reassembling them. The pressing needs of the war made it possible for her to perform such jobs.[69]

Youngsters who rendered service to the war effort on the Union side had their Confederate counterparts whose services also varied. For example, the twelve-year-old Georgia-born Thomas Green Bethune, a talented pianist, performed in a summer 1861 concert for the benefit of sick and wounded Confederate soldiers. Blind from birth, Bethune performed complicated compositions from classical musicians including Bach, Beethoven, and Mendelssohn after hearing arrangements. His extraordinary memory enabled him to memorize hundreds of compositions, and he composed arrangements of his own.[70]

Some youthful bond servants continued their agricultural work as usual, but this was not uniformly true. The teenagers belonging to Will Neblett, a Texan who joined the Confederacy in 1863, proved harder to manage than Neblett's wife, Lizzie, had imagined. During Neblett's absence, the slaves neglected their duties and gave the livestock improper attention. Lizzie believed the adolescents

6. Drummer Jackson. Courtesy of the Massachusetts Commandery Military
Order of the Loyal Legion and the U.S. Army Military History Institute.

Tom and Bill acted accordingly because of prompting from adult slaves. Lizzie
convinced herself that the "black wretches" were "trying all they can" to
aggravate her. To further exacerbate the problems, the crop yields dwindled and
the livestock either died in record numbers or fared poorly.[71]

Running the Grimes County farm with eleven slaves including five teenagers
was an exasperating experience for the Mississippi-born Lizzie, who admitted
that she had difficulty "trying to do a man's business." A great source of
consternation was the overseer's interaction with the slaves. He "bucked"—
whipped Tom, shot at Bill, and discussed "conquering" the slaves by killing
"some one of them" as an example. The boys had balked at his orders, resisted
whippings, and run away. The exasperated Lizzie did not object to the use of
dogs to track Tom. With reference to their behavior she wrote, "I expected such
things of Tom when he was grown, but am surprised at his early beginning." In
the same vein, she observed, "Bill seems very grown tonight, and walks across the
yard like any *100* year old." Bill and Tom reacted to Will Neblett's absence, their
forthcoming liberty, and hatred of the overseer's abusive tactics.[72]

As slaveowners left for the war, they sometimes carried bodyservants along.
Blanche K. Bruce, the first black American to serve in the U.S. Senate for a full
term, went to war and was his half-brother's bodyservant. Their relationship

STOLEN CHILDHOOD

7. Lieutenant James B. Washington along with child, probably a servant, at his surrender to Lieutenant George A. Custer. Courtesy of the U.S. Army Military History Institute, Carlisle Barracks, Carlisle, Pennsylvania.

ended during the Civil War when the valet ran away. Obviously, freedom was more important than the familial connection. By contrast, when Lieutenant James B. Washington surrendered to Lieutenant George A. Custer, a young bodyservant posed along with the officers for the photographer (see figure 7). Age differences were primary factors in the servants' behavior.[73]

Throughout the slaveholding areas, slaves took advantage of the turbulence and freed themselves as the war came within their environs. The northern teacher Elizabeth Botume remembered that a "half-grown boy had his blind daddy [upon his back] toting him along 'to freedom.'" The sight of a South Carolina woman striding along with her hominy pot, containing a live chicken, poised on her head, was more impressive. The woman carried one child on her back with its arms tightly clasped around her neck and its feet about her waist. The woman carried a smaller child under each arm. Undaunted by moving the children single-handedly, the woman headed toward the government steamer *John Adams* moored at a plantation. The woman exuded confidence and gave sanction to the image of a strong black woman, if not the stereotypical "matriarch." Her strength and power would erode quickly if the "meal" in the hominy pot

8. Servant child. Courtesy of the National Archives, Washington, D.C.

took to flight, the "dinner a la hoof" trotted away, a child misbehaved, or the dog strayed. Any one of the possibilities would upset the delicate balance she controlled. Despite her vulnerability, the woman and her children moved closer to freedom together.[74]

Another woman was not so fortunate; her owner fired upon her as she fled with a child. Although she made her way to the Union lines, her child died from a gunshot wound. She hastened on to bury her child "as she said, free." In a sense both women achieved the same goal, freedom of their children.[75]

Abraham Lincoln's January 1, 1863, Emancipation Proclamation heightened the expectations of freedom, although it liberated slaves only in designated areas of the Confederacy. Designed to undermine slavery without offending southern Unionists, the proclamation had no impact in slaveholding states which remained loyal to the Union. There were more than 700,000 slaves in these states. Of that number 225,828 were twenty years of age and younger. In 1860 there were only 1,150 slaves in that age group in Delaware, while 134,153 were among their cohorts in Kentucky. The number of young slaves in Maryland and Missouri reached 49,960 and 70,565 respectively. The number of young slaves in Union-occupied Tennessee, 163,968, was greater than in any of the border states. Additionally, there were thousands of slaves twenty years of age or less in other geographical areas under Union control.[76]

Although the proclamation ignored hundreds of thousands of slaves of all ages, it raised their hopes for imminent freedom. Thoughts of freedom were in the air on January 1, 1863, when South Carolina schoolchildren sang:

STOLEN CHILDHOOD

O, none in all the world before
Were ever so glad as we!
We're free on Carolina's shore,
We're all at home and free.

Charlotte Forten, granddaughter of the abolitionist James Forten, taught the children to sing the song, which the poet John Greenleaf Whittier wrote especially for them.[77]

Susie King Taylor heard the Emancipation Proclamation read and described January 1, 1863, as a "glorious day." The proclamation, along with orders such as General Orders No. 12, issued from the Department of the Gulf Headquarters on January 29, 1863, offered the possibility of freedom. The orders emphasized that military personnel could not encourage or assist slaves in leaving their owners nor could they "compel or authorize their [slaves'] return by force."[78]

The significance of Orders No. 12 did not escape thirteen St. James Parish, Louisiana, slaveholders, whose written response said without equivocation that the order, if enforced, was "equivalent to an actual and immediate emancipation of all slaves of the State of Louisiana." By early 1865 more than one million slaves had fled to Union lines within the Confederacy. The proclamation had a wider impact than the April 11, 1862, legislation, which abolished slavery in Washington, D.C., with its 1860 population of 1,691 slaves twenty years of age and younger.[79]

Two cases of young slaves exemplify the realities of the Emancipation Proclamation's effectiveness in Kentucky. Months after the issuance of the Emancipation Proclamation, a sixteen-year-old Tennessean ran away from his owner James Williams. Rather than gaining freedom, Henry found himself in a Madison County, Kentucky, jail. The court published a notice about his incarceration. When Williams did not reclaim the boy, the county court ordered him sold in September 1863. The highest bidder promised to pay the commonwealth $250 with interest over a twelve-month period for the youngster. Several months later on December 25, 1863, George, described as "about 14 or 15 years of age" met a similar fate when he ran away. The boy's owner John Anderson of Nashville, Tennessee, did not reclaim him. As a result, the Nelson County, Kentucky, court ordered the boy sold on March 14, 1864, at the courthouse in Bardstown. William Sisco, the highest bidder, agreed to pay the state $240 plus interest over twelve months for the "5 feet 2 or 3 inches high, dark copper color" youngster.[80]

Henry and George represented a modicum of the flow of slaves from Tennessee, Alabama, and Georgia going into Kentucky after Lincoln issued the Emancipation Proclamation. In order to stem the tide of runaways, Kentucky officials began arresting and holding fugitives for eight months before selling them. Severe crowding in public jails forced the legislature to change the law, thereby limiting confinement to one month. Many of the slaves sold at the sheriff's auction often escaped again within hours. It is not clear if Henry and

9. Permission to travel. Courtesy of Tulane University
Library, New Orleans, Louisiana.

George followed the lead of other fugitives or if they reconciled themselves to slavery and adjusted to their new owners. Whatever the case, Henry and George's newest tenure as slaves would not be long lasting.[81]

There was joy mixed with pain in fleeing to liberating armies. Women and children, considered encumbrances by the military units, were not welcome among their ranks. Those who remained after their husbands, fathers, and brothers joined the Union forces were more vulnerable to mistreatment than slaves who refrained from active support of the Union. Fears of what would happen to them became realities when slaveowners in Louisiana mistreated women and children "merely because they were families of black soldiers."[82]

Abuses included whippings, evictions, and sales. Furthermore, women and children lost whatever resources the absent males contributed to their welfare through the internal economy. The correspondence of the Union soldier Silas Everett Fales to his family in Massachusetts comments upon the impoverished circumstances of slave children where he served in Louisiana. Fales mentioned hungry children carrying bags and baskets around the soldiers' tents to beg for bread. The children were sometimes in a position to barter with eggs in exchange. One youngster "brot a puppy which he offered for a loaf of bread." There were no takers, but the boy did not leave empty-handed. Fales saw him "going home with the dog under one arm and a loaf under the other."[83]

Conditions for enslaved women and children were especially harsh in Kentucky as a result of more than 50 percent of the male slaves between fifteen and

STOLEN CHILDHOOD

forty-four joining the Union army between April 1864 and April 1865. Reports surfaced of slaveholders pulling cabins down upon women and children to dislodge them. Without places to stay, circumstances reduced them to begging.[84]

An affidavit of Joseph Miller, a Union soldier, describes the hardship his wife and four children, ranging in age from four to ten years of age, faced when army officials at Camp Nelson, Kentucky, expelled nearly four hundred black women and children. The poorly clad Miller woman and her ragged children had no place to go, but this did not prevent the soldier in charge from threatening to shoot them if they did not vacate the property. Miller was helpless in defending them from the abrasive treatment, but he learned where they had gone and walked the six mile distance to join them. When he arrived, he found that one of his children had died. "I know he was killed," wrote Miller, "by exposure to the inclement weather." Miller could not remain with his family overnight because of his military obligations. He walked back to the camp and returned the next day, dug a grave, and buried his son. His decision to join the army placed his wife and children in a threatening predicament whether they remained behind or followed him into the camp. Whatever they chose, they had little to lose. The Millers like many other enslaved people risked everything for freedom.[85]

Notwithstanding the manner in which bond servants achieved liberty, as the war progressed millions could sing:

> No more auction block for me, No more, no more,
> No more auction block for me, Many thousand gone.

Of equal importance were the succeeding lines:

> No more peck of corn for me,
> No more driver's lash for me,
> No more pint of salt for me,
> No more hundred lash for me,
> No more mistress' call for me.[86]

Toward the end of the war, former slaves faced the meaning of freedom. The differences in the expressions on the faces of blacks as they made their way into Vicksburg, Mississippi, on March 3, 1864, caught Issac Shoemaker's attention. He observed elderly blacks along with younger women and children making their way into town. They traveled on foot and in vehicles of all descriptions, in "plantation dress covered with dust and dirt, wayworn and tired." They appeared "sadly forlorn." "The older ones looked very sober and thoughtfull," he wrote, as if questioning "how they were to be dealt with; where to go or what was to be their future." By way of contrast, "the little ones looked pleased," according to Shoemaker, "wondering no doubt what it all meant . . . they stared in astonishment." The scene reminded the soldier of the biblical departure of the Israelites out of Egypt. In another part of the old South, a superannuated man watched the Thirty-Eighth Ohio Regiment drilling and knew it was simply a matter of time before all slaves would be free. Having grown old in bondage, he understood that the changes brought by the war would destroy slavery. He, like the sober-faced adults near Vicksburg, did not know how long it would take the dust to settle, nor did he know what freedom would bring, but the thoughts of its possibilities generated an emotional reaction. Shaking and trembling with the "spirit of freedom," he told a bystander, "I'se berry ol massa, but de little one— dey'l see it; dey'l see it yit."[87]

7 "THERE'S A BETTER DAY A-COMING"*

THE TRANSITION FROM SLAVERY TO FREEDOM

> It was commonly thought that the negroes, when freed would care very little for their children, and would let them die for want of attention, but experience has proved this surmise unfounded. On the contrary, I suppose they take as good care of them as do the same class of people anywhere.
>
> —David G. Barrow**

The turmoil caused by the Civil War and the attendant uncertainties of emancipation created a morass of problems for newly freed persons as they made the transition from slavery to freedom. This chapter examines the ways in which newly freed parents faced the challenge of reuniting families, earning livings, and establishing independence in the midst of numerous ex-slaveholders who resorted to vengeance rather than accept the new order. Children were frequently at the center of the struggle to reunite and maintain families. It is also clear that the parents' efforts to maintain the integrity of their families were often as strenuous as in days of slavery. Despite the reality of the matter, they never ceased trying to keep their children safe from hostile whites.

The Civil War ended in 1865 with the defeat of the Confederate States of America followed by the passage of the Thirteenth Amendment, which ended slavery. Ex-slaves now held total proprietorship in their person and could make all decisions about their children's welfare. Additionally, unfettered mobility was within their reach along with educational opportunities. These were dramatic

---

* Quoted from the spiritual "In That Great Getting-Up Morning," *Jubilee and Plantation Songs. Characteristic Favorites, As sung by the Hampton Students, Jubilee Singers, Fisk University Students, and Other Concert Companies* (Boston: Oliver Ditson, 1887), 68.

** Herbert G. Gutman, *The Black Family in Slavery and Freedom, 1750–1925* (New York: Vintage, 1977), 361.

STOLEN CHILDHOOD

events indeed, for they brought unprecedented change which affected the lives of nearly two million youngsters of African descent.

Scores of agencies, including the American Missionary Association (AMA), whose representative Lewis C. Lockwood arrived on the Virginia peninsula September 3, 1861, assisted blacks in their progression from bondage. Other AMA representatives followed Lockwood and interceded on behalf of the refugees to alleviate physical suffering. The Bureau of Refugees, Freedmen, and Abandoned Lands (Freedmen's Bureau), created by Congress in March 1865, assisted in settling displaced persons, negotiating labor contracts, and establishing schools, in addition to dispensing food and medicine. This agency and others worked toward the same end, assistance in the transition from enslavement to independence.[1]

Freedom gave pause to its recipients, and they greeted it in their own way. A northerner recalled seeing "an old negro surrounded by his whole family (two generations) bowing and blessing" the passing Union soldiers because they associated the men with their liberation. A more deeply ingrained memory was that of "a little boy about 4 years old, standing with an independence representing his former master, hands in his pockets as if he truly felt his freedom more firm when we passed along."[2]

Many newly freed persons revered their emancipation with celebrations that had antecedents in their traditional culture. Emancipation brought unparalleled jubilation among many African American men, women, and children. Some tempered celebrations with religious songs and prayers of thanksgiving. Regardless of the nature of their revelry, millions of African Americans experienced happiness like that of Mattie Johnson and Lucy Delaney when members of their families liberated themselves.[3]

Ex-slaveholders found little to celebrate in the dismantling of the social and economic system which had been an intricate facet of southern culture. Emancipation demanded the forfeiture of millions of dollars in chattel in addition to the loss of control over their labor. Knowledge of violence in Haiti and the British Caribbean following the emancipation of slaves may have exacerbated the ex-slaveholders' apprehension.[4]

Anxiety about the future moved one southerner to write, "No one can tell what we *shall* be *made* to suffer—it is worse than death." Another predicted the "beginning of the end." The diarist Edmund Ruffin, an ex-slaveholder, chronicled abhorrence of the "perfidious, malignant and vile Yankee race" for its part in the defeat of the Confederacy and the freeing of the slaves. Weary and sick at heart, Ruffin committed suicide June 17, 1865, rather than acquiesce to change. Many whites objected to the destruction of slavery but were less radical than Ruffin.[5]

A major reason for the anxiety was the issue of who would control labor. On the one hand, many whites viewed freedpeople as subordinates incapable of determining the best use of their own labor. On the other hand, newly freed people viewed themselves as capable of deciding how to use not only their own

TRANSITION FROM SLAVERY TO FREEDOM

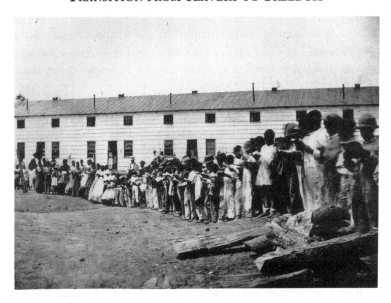

10. Freed children along with adults in Virginia. Courtesy of the National Archives, Washington, D.C.

labor, but that of their offspring as well. If freedpersons commanded their own labor and had land at their disposal, they could become truly independent. This was potentially revolutionary. It never occurred because the new society, like the old, allowed for the virtually unabated exploitation of young and old laborers alike.[6]

White objections to the possibilities of black economic independence combined with the strong desire to maintain white supremacy sparked the formation of extralegal organizations, including the Knights of the White Camelia, the Ku Klux Klan, and the White Brotherhood. They used violence and other measures of intimidation to frighten freedpersons into servility. A primary objective of the Klan was to keep newly enfranchised men from the polls; however, its terror spread far beyond the political arena in the postwar South.[7]

Aside from the organizations which used terrorism, southern lawmakers established rules that severely hampered the freedom of former slaves. During the summer of 1865, numerous state laws, Black Codes, which defined the rights of freedpersons went into operation and remained in place until the U.S. Congress took firm control of Reconstruction in 1867. The Black Codes focused heavily upon the regulation of black labor and punished vagrants, contract violators, and recalcitrant workers. The laws retained wording, such as "master" and "servant," that was reminiscent of slavery. Although some of the laws applied to both black and white workers, black workers were subjected to the severest penalties for violations.[8]

STOLEN CHILDHOOD

The actual combat between the North and South ended, but the war between ex-slaveholders and slaves was far from over. The venomous attitudes of individual ex-slaveholders spilled over to freedpersons, whom the ex-slaveholders regarded as benefiting from their losses. Kate Foster concluded that freedpersons were "an ungrateful set" when they claimed their liberty. Malevolent acts against them ranged from refusing to tell slaves of their freedom to endangering their personal safety. The more malicious acts were refusing to turn children over to parents and binding out minors until they reached biological maturity.[9]

During slavery owners had used the threat of family separation as a control measure to manipulate bond servants into malleability. Once slavery ended, some ex-owners reasoned that restraining freed children would again force the parents to yield to their continued control. It was an ill-founded notion driven by the potential of economic benefits to ex-owners. Parents refused to give in to emotional blackmail. Instead, they maneuvered around wrathful "masters without slaves" to face one of the most pressing issues of the time—reunification of their families. Ignorant of geography but fortified with hope, many freedpersons set out on foot to reclaim their kin. Ironically, they used newspaper advertisements to locate their relatives as antebellum slaveowners had used them to hunt runaways. "In their eyes the work of emancipation was incomplete until the families . . . dispersed by slavery were reunited," wrote an observer.[10]

Freedmen and women often asked for the help of the Freedmen's Bureau in the battle for their children. On February 6, 1866, Lucinda Jacoway complained that William Bryant was "restraining the freedom of her child Jane Ellen." He demanded fifty dollars for the four-year-old girl. John Vetter, a Freedmen's Bureau agent in Arkansas, directed a letter to Bryant on her behalf. "You are hereby instructed to surrender said child," he wrote "to the complainant." He added, "& that immediately." Ellen Halleck filed a similar complaint the same day. Rebecca Parsons also complained that her former owner wanted four hundred dollars for the release of her four children. Jackson Easley of Marietta, Georgia, asked the Freedmen's Bureau for help only after writing directly to the President of the United States regarding his children, who remained in the hands of their former owner. The final disposition of the complaints are unknown, but it is clear that the plaintiffs exercised parental rights and were not at all content with someone else holding their children.[11]

Other parents acted alone in searching for their children. The Virginian Kate Drumgoold remembered the many difficulties her mother encountered in locating her children, who were "all over in different places." Reports of their deaths did not dissuade the suspicious woman, who vowed to search for their remains. Drumgoold found her children—alive. Annie L. Burton's mother was no less adamant when their ex-owner refused to release Annie and her siblings. He "threatened to set the dogs" upon the mother. Unmoved by the warning, the woman sent a message to the children, by her oldest son, who eventually joined her with the others in tow. The ex-owner's son stopped them as they fled and demanded the return of the children. "My mother refused to give us up," recalled Annie; instead she insisted that they all go to "Yankee headquarters" to see if the children were indeed free.[12]

Accounts that end with little hope of reunion often overshadow the successful ones. The North Carolina freedwoman Milly Johnson had mixed results in finding her five children. She, with the help of the Freedmen's Bureau, located her daughter Anna and acquired information about two of the children, but she had no word about the others. John Allen of Austin, Texas, enlisted the aid of the bureau in finding his two children, whom he left in Batesville, Arkansas, in 1859. His daughter Rachel was nine years old at the time and his son Benjamin was seven. Although he had heard nothing from them since their separation, he was "anxious" to know if they were still alive and how they were "now situated." He wanted a reunion "so that they may be under his charge and protection." It is not clear if he succeeded, but it is obvious that he was unwilling to accept their separation as a permanent condition.[13]

The frustration of reuniting kin was boundless, especially when factors other than geography kept them apart. The Polly Ann Johnson case is an example of the bureaucratic structure undermining family integrity. The case first came to the attention of the Freedmen's Bureau in March 1867, when Gabriel Johnson and his wife Charity complained to a Freedmen's Bureau agent O. H. Howard in Albany, Georgia, that their ten-year-old daughter Polly Ann had left the state with Morgan L. Brown in December 1866. It seems that Brown sparked Polly's imagination with stories about money growing upon trees in Arkansas. The Johnsons asserted, and the agent agreed, that they were able financially to support her. Moreover, they wanted Polly home.[14]

The paper trail leading to Polly Ann Johnson wound its way from O. H. Howard in March 1867 to General O. O. Howard, head of the Freedmen's Bureau, by November 1867. O. H. Howard, who believed it was a "case of felonious and malicious kidnapping," forwarded the petition to C. C. Sibley, the assistant commissioner of the Georgia Freedmen's Bureau through Colonel F. A. H. Gaebel, in the sub-assistant commissioner's office. Gaebel then forwarded it to Capt. Eugene Pickett in Sibley's office.

At each level the petition received an endorsement and proceeded along the chain of command. It had advanced through the proper channels in Georgia by April 2, 1867, when Sibley routed it through Major General Ord, assistant commissioner of the Freedmen's Bureau in Little Rock to Major William D. Dawes, a bureau agent in Pine Bluff. After a futile search "all over" Pine Bluff for the child, Dawes concluded that neither she nor Brown were in the vicinity. Reaching an impasse, Dawes requested more information from Howard regarding Brown's whereabouts. This reversed the cycle and the process began anew to find Polly Ann.

By May 11 Pickett learned that Brown was indeed in Pine Bluff. He forwarded that information to Colonel E. H. Smith, assistant commissioner of the Freedmen's Bureau for Arkansas. The search for Polly Ann was again in motion, at the behest of Lieutenant S. Geisreiter in Pine Bluff.

On June 11 Geisreiter reported that Polly Ann lived with Brown and his wife about two miles southwest of Pine Bluff. Brown denied any malicious intent and said he took Polly Ann from Georgia as a charitable act. In a flood of tears, the child asserted that she left Georgia voluntarily since "she could not live with her parents" because they were "exceedingly cruel to her." Polly Ann was now "much attached to the [Brown] family." This raises questions about what constitutes child abuse, if Polly Ann were a credible witness, and if the Browns coerced her into making statements about her parents and themselves.

Howard, back in Georgia, had affidavits to dispute Polly Ann's charges against her mother and stepfather. There were also affidavits presented by William Calloway, James Calloway, and George McDonald on Brown's behalf to support his claim of benevolence. Amid the charges and countercharges, Howard remained convinced that Brown had no authority to take Polly Ann away. "The act was a gross outrage," he wrote on July 31, 1867. Howard also believed that the county judge would not apprentice the girl without parental consent. Polly Ann, in Howard's opinion, should be "restored to her parents" immediately. The bureau ordered transportation for her return to Georgia, but the case did not end here.

On November 13, 1867, Colonel Smith wrote to General Howard regarding the final disposition of the Polly Ann Johnson case. The child had refused the transportation back to Georgia, and agents could not coerce her into changing her mind. "She has a good home where she is," wrote Smith; therefore, he recommended that "she be allowed to decide whether she will return or not." General Eliphalet Whittlesey, in General O. O. Howard's office, endorsed Smith's letter and forwarded an official copy to General Sibley, who passed it on to O. H. Howard.

"It was not easy," Howard wrote on December 3, 1867, "to comprehend the justice of the written recommendation." Based upon the affidavits, he found no reason why the Johnsons could not have the girl back. He further predicted that the Lee County grand jury would find a true bill against Brown for kidnapping her. Howard recommended that Polly Ann be sent home, and the bureau had the authority to send her. The last piece of correspondence about Polly Ann Johnson, dated January 13, 1868, simply stated, "As the girl refuses to return, it is not deemed within the province of this Bureau to force her to do so. By order of Major General O. O. Howard." On January 18, 1868, correspondence regarding Polly Ann Johnson marked "respectfully returned to Lt. O. H. Howard" began its journey from Washington back to its point of origin in Albany, Georgia.

The case provides insight into the bureaucratic structure of the Freedmen's Bureau and reflects an unevenness in the official interest of its clients. It also raises questions about the agency's in loco parentis role. What motivated bureau agent Smith to accede to the tears and wishes of a gullible ten-year-old child? The empowerment of a black child was a different twist for white adults. As assistant commissioner of the North Carolina Freedmen's Bureau in 1865, Whittlesey had opposed apprenticeships. "The practice of binding out children is danger-ous," he wrote, "inasmuch as it fosters the old ideas of compulsory labor and dependence." Why did he change once in Howard's office? Perhaps he viewed Polly Ann Johnson's case as one of child custody rather than apprenticeship. Perhaps overburdened bureau officials chafed under the weight of the volume of work and wanted to bring closure on the matter.[15]

This case raises more questions about Gabriel and Charity Johnson than it answers. To be sure, the parents fell prey to a bureaucratic system that robbed them of the decision-making power about their daughter. What did they think of the bureau's procedures? Did they question the bureau for continuing parent-child separations rather than remedying them? Regardless of the kinds of ques-tions the Johnsons might have asked, their family remained incomplete without Polly Ann.

Laura Spicer's family also remained incomplete but for different reasons. Her owner separated the woman and her children from her husband and their father. He later assumed that Laura was dead and remarried. Once emancipated, Laura learned of his whereabouts and wanted a reunion, but Spicer would not desert his new wife and their two children. Enveloped in agony, he suggested that Laura remarry and make a new life for herself. There was no future for them together, but he wanted the best for his family. Aside from affection for Laura and their children, Spicer loved his present wife and children; therefore, he remained with them. His sense of marital fidelity and moral obligation were stronger than his heartache. "You know it never was our wishes to be separated from each other," Spicer reminded Laura, "and it never was our fault." Slavery was to blame, and his family, especially the older children, suffered as a result.[16]

The quandary they faced was little different from that of the Kentuckian Willie Ann Gray and her husband Philip. After an involuntary separation, the couple succeeded in finding each other in 1866, but a reunion was unlikely. She had remarried and given birth to three children, fathered by a man who became a Union soldier and died in the war. Philip wanted a new life with Willie Ann and their daughter, but he showed little interest in assuming responsibility for her fatherless children.[17]

A possible reconciliation did not bode well, since Philip talked of taking their daughter Maria away alone, and she was apprehensive about leaving her mother and siblings. Concerned about Maria's emotional well-being and unwilling to separate the children, Willie Ann wrote, "You will have to promise me that you will provide for them as well as if they were your own." Intent upon maintaining the integrity of her family and getting a commitment from Philip, she shifted the focus of her concern. "If you love me," she wrote, "you will love my children."[18]

Although Willie Ann and others exuded an unwavering love for their children, negative comments about their roles as parents were prevalent. One former slaveholder wrote, "It is a well founded fact that negro-mothers have but little maternal affection." Such comments emanated from disgruntled ex-slaveholders, ill-founded beliefs about overlaying, and misunderstanding parents who steeled themselves against high infant mortality rates. There were few differences in the reactions of many enslaved parents and puritan parents who prepared themselves emotionally to cope with the anticipated loss of their children in colonial America.[19]

Given the struggles that enslaved parents had faced to avoid separations during slavery, it is incongruent to think they would behave differently once freed. Even a cursory look at Freedmen's Bureau records does much to refute allegations about parental callousness toward their offspring. The parents exhausted all possibilities of finding their kin and did not give up easily. African American newspaper advertisements in search of dispersed relatives continued appearing for decades after emancipation. Some freedpersons failed to locate their children not because they did not try, but because the challenge was beyond their resources.[20]

Despite failures, the one remaining consolation for John Allen and others was the hope of a heavenly reunion. Otherwise, orphans remained with relatives, fictive kin, or friends until they were old enough to provide for themselves.

Interest in the welfare of orphaned children prompted African Americans to hold a fund-raising event in Mobile, Alabama. The 1866 fair, a decided success, netted more than $1,200 for the construction of a building for the children. An orphanage in Arkansas under the auspices of the Quakers served the needs of 130 children. Near Helena, Arkansas, black soldiers built an orphanage from contributions they and their officers made. After constructing "four substantial buildings," which they planned to dedicate on July 4, 1867, the soldiers cleared ground and planted crops for the benefit of the orphanage.[21]

To further support the facility, soldiers, earning money from private sources, agreed to contribute 20 percent of their wages for the facility. The energy exerted by the soldiers was not unlike that of other African Americans who helped the children until they were self-supporting.[22]

In cases where spouses and children reunited, the parents sought to protect their families by making their unions acceptable to the dominant population through legal marriages. They complied with laws such as the Florida statute which required ex-slaves living together as husband and wife to marry legally within nine months after the passage of the January 11, 1866, "Act to Establish and Enforce the Marriage Relation Between Persons of Color." The legislature later changed the law to recognize antebellum marriages if the couples had previously made them known publicly. Statutes in other southern states legalized pre-emancipation marriages, yet many freedpeople insisted upon exchanging vows.[23]

As a youngster Bongy Jackson attended his parents' wedding, which he recalled fondly. "After the Cibil War, soon's they got a little piece of money,"

Jackson said, "they got a preacher and had a real weddin'." Among the details, he recalled, "My ma dressed like a bride an' all." He pointed out that "she done already had nine children by my pa." Remembering the event, Jackson remarked, "We sure had a fine time." The occasion was filled with social, religious, and legal significance for the Jackson family.[24]

Just as freedom offered a chance to exchange nuptial vows and legalize marriages, it also provided the opportunity to terminate undesirable unions. Rose Williams ended her marriage immediately after freedom. The fact that she was pregnant had no bearing upon the separation. When the WPA interviewer asked if she ever remarried, Rose replied, "Never! No Sar! One 'sperience am 'nough fo' dis nigger." She severed the relationship with Rufus, but hatred of the person who forced her to become Rufus's wife remained a source of consternation. More than fifty years afterwards the psychological cost of the forced marriage remained. Rose said, "Dere am one thing Massa Hawking does to me what I can't shunt from my mind."[25]

There was no discussion of the fate of Rose's two minor children or the unborn fetus. But the issue of child custody surfaced among others. When Freedmen's Bureau agent F. E. Grossmann could not settle an 1866 child custody dispute between the Florida couple Madison Day and Maria Richard, he asked his superior to present the case to the state's assistant commissioner for a decision. It is also possible that Willie and Philip Gray had to seek outside counsel about which parent would have custody of Maria.[26]

With courage bolstered by freedom, ex-slave women demanded a shared responsibility for their children. The mothers sometimes asked the Freedmen's Bureau for assistance in acquiring financial support for children without regard for the fathers' race. Furthermore, their complaints received attention from agents who pursued the matters or asked plaintiffs to take their cases to civil courts. Julius Kraft, a white Kentuckian, appeared before the Freedmen's Bureau agent one week after Caroline Randolph filed a complaint. He denied paternity but paid the plaintiff twenty-five dollars nonetheless. Such complaints offer insight into the mettle of women fighting for what they perceived as their children's birthrights.[27]

Parents, together or alone, remained responsible for socializing their children. Lessons for surviving slavery were often appropriate for the postwar years when white hostility against freedpersons grew more threatening. In all probability, youngsters still received cues from parents or other adults which governed their interactions with whites. Charles Manigault claimed that all of his former slaves living on his Cooper River farm about six miles from Charleston were "Sulky." The children who "used to watch for my coming," he wrote, "Were *Now* taught *to shun me* & never to call me 'Master' again." The "Heddy Massa," an old greeting from the enslaved children, according to Manigault was now "Dead & gone." The change in their greeting was a reflection of the change in their status.[28]

STOLEN CHILDHOOD

Although they were legally free, parents did not tolerate disrespect from children toward black or white adults. Moreover, the deference rituals were useful in the hostile postwar environment. Freedpersons, regardless of age, who stepped out of their "place" could find themselves in physical danger. For example, Jim Allen who was a child when slavery ended talked about the Klan to a federal interviewer. "Dey skeered de breeches off of me," he recalled. Knowing when to speak or what to say was as important for youngsters in the postwar years as before.[29]

Although the fertility rate among African Americans declined once slavery ended, parents did not deviate from their naming practices intended to anchor their offspring firmly within the family. Freedpeople now used last names routinely and adopted the conventional use of patriarchal surnames. Jacob Stroyer's family reclaimed its surname and used it publicly. Some freedpeople retained the surnames of esteemed owners, while others jettisoned names, both first and last names, and selected new ones to reflect their changed status. The new names showed an understanding of roles played by liberators along with the meaning of emancipation. The names Lincoln, Grant, Armistice, Hope, Chance, and Deliverance freed them of slave appellations.[30]

Elizabeth Botume witnessed the naming and renaming process among children at the South Carolina school where she taught. The enrollment of children caused major confusion for Botume, who likened herself to the biblical Adam and wondered if he became puzzled when looking over the great variety of species. The teacher was unable to distinguish one child from another and the situation changed little when the children renamed themselves with rapidity. One youngster substituted the name Drayton for Middleton, explaining that the former was his "ole rebel master's title." He said, "him's nothing to me now. I don't belong to he no longer, an' I don's see no use on being called for him." The new name was good in "secesh times" when General Drayton "was a friend to we . . . fight on our side." In defense of his new name, one child promised to mash anyone's "mouf in" who insisted upon calling him Quash instead of Bryan. With less determination many freedpeople dropped remnants of slavery and became presidents and generals, in name only.[31]

With the new badge of liberty, many showed interest in knowing their ages. Frederick Douglass had complained about his inability to tell his own age, and he was no different from many other slaves who knew nothing about their dates of birth. Anthony Butler inquired about his age in the humble style of a slave. "Pleas Sir," he wrote to his former owner, "Send my age and what year I was born." He explained apologetically, "I learn my Self how to Right." The letter's tone suggests that Butler wished to avoid raising questions about faithfulness to his owner while enslaved. Long after emancipation the freedwoman Mary Evans, who probably never learned to read and write, asked her son to inquire about her age. She guessed that she was ten months older than the ex-owner's son.[32]

Transition from Slavery to Freedom

During their first days of freedom, the former slaves savored their liberty and spent time reconstructing families, but they did not ignore the responsibility of earning a living for themselves and their children. The redefinition of ownership of labor created tension between ex-slaves and owners. Economic historian Harold D. Woodman suggests that whites lacked the ability and necessary knowledge to negotiate with free laborers. When whites charged that blacks would not work, blacks countered with claims that whites would not pay. The unwillingness of whites to accept the implicit notion of equality between contracting parties in employer-employee relationships within a capitalistic society further exacerbated the impasse.[33]

Children were often at the center of this tug-of-war between ex-slaveholders and slaves. Of all protests about the control of labor immediately after emancipation, the most bitter complaints focused on apprenticeship laws involving minor children. The laws were particularly objectionable because they separated families and ultimately used the disadvantages of freedpeople against them. Poverty and the subsequent inability to provide for their children made freedpeople vulnerable to losing their offspring to a labor system that robbed them of wages along with their childhood.[34]

Many former Confederate states, especially North Carolina, Mississippi, and Georgia, allowed "responsible" employers to capitalize on the labor of minor children until they reached eighteen or twenty-one years of age depending upon the sex. Alabama, Mississippi, and Kentucky gave former owners preference in apprenticing freed minors. In exchange, children were to receive wholesome food, suitable clothing, and necessary medicine and medical care, along with training in industry, housekeeping, or husbandry. Within a paternalistic environment, as prescribed by law, apprentices were to learn to read, write, and cipher. The Georgia law required employers to use the same degree of force to compel the obedience of an apprentice as a father would exert upon his own minor children. If misunderstandings arose, the court heard complaints and rendered judgments.[35]

Wholesale violation of the laws ranged from apprenticing children without parental consent to falsifying their ages to retain the minors for a longer time. In the absence of parents, many former owners bound "orphans" to their services before parents could return to claim them. Without the protection of legal marriages, any child born in slavery could be considered an orphan and subjected to apprenticeships. The historian Barbara Fields reports that on the "very day of emancipation" ex-slaveholders in Maryland "began seizing freedmen's children and whisking them off to the county seats, sometimes by the wagonloads, to be bound as apprentices by the county orphan's court." More than 2,500 youngsters were apprenticed throughout the South within the first month of emancipation. Many of the persons binding apprentices did not keep them within their households, but hired them out elsewhere.[36]

Postwar apprenticeship laws allowed ex-slaveholders to salvage much of the old labor system. The value of the labor from children and youth could be as great in freedom as it was during slavery. A large percentage of the 990,000 slaves in the 1860 population between the ages of ten and nineteen were likely candidates for apprenticeships. Ostensibly, the laws protected children without regard for color; nevertheless, they invariably worked to the disadvantage of African Americans.[37]

Forced apprenticeships divested parents of labor, which was useful to a family's stride toward economic independence, while leaving the youngest nonproductive children in their care. This was the source of a complaint made by Enoch Braston, a freedman living in Grenada, Mississippi, in 1866. His former owner, John Heath, apprenticed five children ranging in age from ten to eighteen, but he did not care to bind the four youngest children. This suggests the need for labor rather than benevolence as a motivating factor.[38]

Many apprenticeships resulted in intense fights between parents or relatives and white employers. It was a contest over labor and the ownership thereof. The Freedmen's Bureau was a third party in the conflicts because of its responsibility to oversee contracts. Bureau records teem with accounts of parents asking for the nullification of contracts and the return of their children. While some bureau officials were reluctant to interfere with contracts, others tried to ferret out thinly disguised measures to reenslave children. An Alabama judge said that few black parents were "willing to bind their children whether they can support them or not." There were bureau agents who agreed. The weight of complaints from parents led Wager Swayne, assistant commissioner of the Alabama Freedmen's Bureau, to issue a general order in 1867 against needlessly apprenticing children to former owners.[39]

Many young apprentices responded to their duties in white households in ways that mirrored the behavior of enslaved youth. Records of complaints maintained by bureau agents serve as evidence of interactions between apprentices and employers. For example, Gloster, a twelve-year-old "colored boy" complained that his employer, Mrs. Moore, beat him about the head and arms with a fire shovel. Furthermore, she refused to pay him. One thirteen-year-old child who was "nearly barefoot and in rags" said his employer abused him because he would not lift a heavy log. Children sometimes responded to such treatment by running away.[40]

When parents or relatives learned of the children's conditions, they sought help from the Freedmen's Bureau in breaking contracts. At other times, parents simply refused to return the runaway children. In the absence of parents, relatives of orphans sometimes completed the legal process of binding the children and cited "duty" as their reason.[41]

Martin Lee, a former slave in Florence, Alabama, asked for assistance from the Freedmen's Bureau in getting custody of his nephew from his former owner Sebe Burson in Georgia. Penny Barksdale also appealed to the bureau for assistance in the return of her two grandchildren. According to the agent, the teenagers were

11. The Indenture of Susan. Courtesy of Special Collections Department, Manuscript Division, University of Virginia, Charlottesville, Virginia.

nearly old enough to support themselves and could help their aging grandmother. Agents in the subcommissioner's office agreed that Barksdale's grandchildren be returned not so much out of the injustice of an apprenticeship, but as social insurance against the grandmother becoming "an expense to the government." Their behavior, whether on the part of parents or grandparents, defied the popular notion that they cared little for their offspring.[42]

The number of relatives who attempted to dissolve apprenticeships, reasons notwithstanding, led James DeGray, a bureau agent in East Feliciana, Louisiana, to exasperation. The case which raised his ire involved a ten-year-old boy whose grandmother, Cyntha Nickols, complained that he was not bound to a "suitable" person. The agent admitted that the person in question was old and "addicted to ardent Spirits." On January 29, 1867, he wrote, "In every case where I have bound out children, thus far Some Grand Mother or fortieth cousin has come to have them released." The agent declared that the freedpersons viewed binding out as putting their children "back into slavery."[43]

Apprenticeships have received little attention by comparison with social, economic, and political issues of the time, yet they provide one of the best examples of ex-slaveowners' efforts to reinstate slavery and of African Americans resisting on behalf of their children. Such appeals to the Freedmen's Bureau resulted in assistance from agents who wavered "between a principled defense of black people's rights and deference to the interest of former slaveholders." Their reactions reflect the moral tension created by slavery when whites were ambiguous about the status of slaves as persons or property. Furthermore, racism continued to interfere with clear thinking about parental concerns and civil rights. The Polly Ann Johnson case which involved agents in Georgia and Arkansas provides a ready example.[44]

Although their options were limited, freedpersons preferred to avoid working directly for white employers. For example, some ex-slaves exercised customary rights and resorted to hunting, fishing, forging, and subsistence farming as a route to independence. They bartered off game which they could not use and sold excess produce for cash to buy necessities.

Before reconstruction ended in 1877, the South experienced a proliferation in game and stock laws which eroded customary rights. On the surface the legislation appeared concerned about keeping livestock from trampling over cultivated land, but the regulations did much to limit alternative employment. It became increasingly difficult for landless owners of livestock to peddle milk and butter if they had no place to graze their animals. They also found it impossible to pay fines when their animals damaged crops. Laws against trespassers had the same effect. Without the right to hunt or fish, youngsters had fewer opportunities to supplement their food supply. Moreover, they were now subject to arrest for trespassing. If jailed, they had no money to pay fines and could be leased out. At bottom, the laws made it virtually impossible to become economically independent.[45]

Without the resources to sustain themselves, many former slaves continued to work for whites. An observer remarked that they carried on the "tradition from the days of slavery, when pickaninies were brought to the master's house to be trained." The essential difference in the training was the parents' role in deciding if a child accompanied them. Work could still be a menacing thief to rob youngsters of their childhood, but parents who objected to working all of the time could now set some limitations on their work and that of their children.[46]

A ready example of children working in a white household with parents involves Tryphena Fox, who now managed her household with the help of hired servants and her twelve-year-old daughter Fanny. Rosella began work at Hygiene

12. Children with scuttle in Richmond, Virginia (late 1880s). Courtesy of the Cook Collection, Valentine Museum, Richmond, Virginia.

along with her parents Victor and Celestine in 1869. In return for help with the housekeeping and childcare, the girl received two dollars per month, and Fox, a former teacher, promised to devote one hour per day to tutoring her.[47]

Fox continued making differences between the children based upon race. When delegating responsibilities, it was clear that Fox's younger children, George and Frank, were under Rosella's "care" but in Fanny's "charge." Tryphena explained "you have no idea what a large girl [Fanny] is." The difference had little to do with the girl's size or age since Rosella was several months older than Fanny. The distinction was reminiscent of slavery and reflected the old social order which subjected black children to the will of whites, young and old. The association between Fanny and Rosella was that of a mistress and her maid in microcosm.[48]

In December 1869 Celestine "*left* suddenly taking Rosella," according to Tryphena without "*provocation from* or *notification to*" her employers. Celestine would not agree that reasons for their leaving were nonexistent. Dr. Fox had fired Victor. Obviously, Celestine decided that she and Rosella should leave Hygiene to avoid any further separation from her husband.[49]

Whether parents had domestic or agricultural jobs, they attempted to protect themselves and their children from abusive social and economic practices.

13. Boys hauling moss—used for pillows and mattresses (undated; probably late 1880s). Courtesy of the Cook Collection, Valentine Museum, Richmond, Virginia.

The strong desire to maintain the integrity of their families led to the withdrawal of women and children from agricultural work for whites. Among the reasons, women wanted to devote more time to their children. The men who headed such households agreed and prided themselves in being able to support their wives and children. The men were also concerned about protecting their wives and daughters from exposure to sexual exploitation in the work place.[50]

Before committing himself and his family to work for a former owner, Jourdon Anderson asked for clarification on such issues. Although Anderson never mentioned sexual abuse, his inferences are clear. "Please state," Anderson wrote, "if there would be any safety for my Milly and Jane." The girls, perhaps adolescents, were grown up and pretty according to their father. "You know how it was," he reminded the former slaveowner, "with poor Matilda and Catherine." Anderson preferred living in Ohio and starving to death, if necessary, to having his "girls brought to shame by the violence and wickedness of their young masters" if they returned to Tennessee. Protection against sexual exploitation was uppermost in his mind and reason enough for him not to return to the South without a favorable agreement regarding his family.[51]

Through trial and error former slaves negotiated with white employers until a new labor system evolved. They preferred tenancy to wage labor and favored kin-based "squads" of seven to twelve persons supervised by a family member

TRANSITION FROM SLAVERY TO FREEDOM

14. Cotton pickers accompanied by children. "Rose Mary Plantation Home Album," ca. 1890–1910. Carmack Papers. Courtesy of the Southern Historical Collection, University of North Carolina, Chapel Hill.

over gang labor. The squads were halfway between the gang system and family-oriented sharecropping.[52]

There are many examples of families working together in postwar labor units. The Wake County, North Carolina, planter Alonzo T. Mial, who produced a bountiful crop in 1859 with "mostly women and small boys and girls," entered a labor agreement with twenty-seven workers in 1866. Among those signing the contract were eleven males twenty-one years of age or younger. Three of the six females were eighteen years of age or younger. The workers received monthly wages and rations. For example, fifteen-year-old Steller received four dollars, twelve pounds of bacon, and one bushel of meal per month. The youngest worker in the group, nine-year-old John Miles, received two dollars, eleven pounds of bacon, and one bushel of meal per month. Punitive financial measures replaced corporal punishment for violation of contractual obligations. Labor contracts often list the names of children along with their signs, "x", which indicated that they were integral parts of the agreement.[53]

On December 30, 1865, George C. Hannah negotiated a labor contract for one hundred sixty dollars with the ex-slave Booker and his family. Hannah wrote, "That is to say. to Booker Eighty four Dollars [,] to Stephen Twenty four Dollars[,] to Sam Twelve Dollars & to Martha Jane Forty Dollars." The wage differential suggests age differences. Further south in Dougherty County, Georgia, immediately after freedom, 175 former slaves signed labor contracts with Benjamin C. Yancy as family units. Among the 42 families, 85 percent had one or more offspring within the household. The labor of children and youth was still important in labor intensive arrangements.[54]

A postwar observer in Oglethorpe, Georgia, described freed children helping haul water for use on a tenant farm of twenty-five to thirty acres. First, he wrote, "A little bit of a darky, not much taller than the vessel he is carrying, will surprise you by the amount of water he can tote on his head," which says much about the child's willingness to help. A second statement about the children was probably closer to the truth. The writer acknowledged that the amount of water diminished according to the child's size until the smallest in the family "would carry hardly more than two or three cupfuls." In either case, children were a part of the family's effort to succeed as freedpersons.[55]

Families working together as sharecroppers garnered some protection against economic and sexual abuses. Under the arrangement, workers agreed to cultivate land and share its yield with landowners in exchange for the right to use the land. The agreements covering the amount of the crop shared along with the use of tools, draft animals, and seeds varied with individuals. For example, in 1867 the freedman Dink and three minors agreed to work for D. T. Crosby in South Carolina's Fairfield District for "one-third of the corn peas and potatoes gathered and prepared for market, and one-third net proceeds of the ginned cotton or its market value."[56]

An Alabama planter offered a work arrangement to freedpersons whom he formerly owned. They received stock and tools to carry on production at the plantation. Additionally, they received hogs, cattle, and sheep for their own use. In return, the landowner asked that they maintain the stock and replenish it by its natural increase. There were no charges for rent "except the small grain crop." Afterwards, the laborers were to divide the remaining produce "according to services rendered and merit."[57]

The sharecropping arrangement allowed for some autonomy, but decisions regarding the choice of crops, ways of cultivation, and marketing the products rested with landowners. Laborers remained subject to their authority. A more ideal situation for the freedpersons remaining in southern agricultural pursuits was individual land ownership.[58]

Of the freedmen and women, those who had worked under the task system along the coast of Georgia and South Carolina were better off economically and more likely to purchase land. Also, some soldiers used their bounty money toward the purchase of land. The majority of freedpersons, regardless of the region, did not have enough money to purchase land to sustain their families. Even when they had the money, they could not always find persons willing to sell property to them. Many whites preferred to see blacks farm land owned by someone else. Ex-slaves in Davis Bend, Mississippi, Hale County, Alabama, and Richmond, Virginia, succeeded in purchasing property, as did others.[59]

15. Freedman and children. Courtesy of the U.S. Army Military History Institute, Carlisle Barracks, Carlisle, Pennsylvania.

A former slave paraphrased a Bible verse when he posited, "Every man should live under his own vine and fig tree." His reference was to economic independence and land ownership, which would do much to assure independence. The Texas-born Betty Powers, who was eight years old when the Civil War ended, remembered how her family worked to have their own property. After the war, her parents decided to remain on the plantation for several years working on shares until her father got a "foot-hold." Afterwards, Powers recalled:

> De Land father buys aint cleared, an' 'twarnt any buildin's on it, so weuns all pitches in an' fixed a cabin. Was weuns proud? Was weuns proud? Ise says weuns was w'en de cabins was done. Thar 'twas, our own home to do as weuns please after bein' slaves. Dat sho am a good feelin'.

Putting in a crop and watching it grow caused no less exuberance. Powers remembered, "Weuns watched it grow lak 'twas little chil's, 'cause it all b'longed to weuns. 'Twas ours." Similar echoes of pride and self-esteem must have rippled through other landowning freedpersons across the South. Landownership was a way of escaping poverty.[60]

Whether working land they owned or land owned by others, freedpeople reserved time for recreational diversions. Among the constants carried over from slavery were leisure activities. Stories at nightfall continued to amuse and educate. Passing the stories down from generation to generation, descendants of slaves chronicled their history and gave listeners a sense of person and place. Carter Godwin Woodson, born a decade after emancipation, learned about bondage from his parents, grandparents, and other relatives. Woodson, one of the first direct descendants of slaves to earn a doctorate degree in history, became known as the father of African American history. His "most fundamental perceptions of slavery were rooted in the oral traditions of his family." He used that personal history to "illuminate the larger slave experience."[61]

To authenticate the stories he had heard from his grandmother when he was a young boy in Tennessee, Alex Haley traveled across three continents and sifted through massive numbers of documents over a ten-year period. Haley traveled to Juffure, a Gambian village, where the sixteen-year-old Kunta Kinte had been abducted in 1767 and placed on the *Lord Ligonier,* a slaver bound for Maryland. Haley's genealogical and historical study of his family culminated in the publication of the novel *Roots: The Saga of an American Family.*[62]

Aside from the stories told at nightfall, postwar leisure activities included traditional games. There is no systematic study of the play of black children in the postwar years comparable to those of their antebellum play, yet the available evidence suggests that many games remained intact. At the turn of the century, ball games and marbles remained most popular among boys, while girls played dolls and ring games along with some ball games.[63]

Note the specific change in a postwar ring game. Little Sally still sat in the saucer and cried while players cheered her on with:

> Rise, Sally, rise,
> Wipe your weepin' eyes,
> Put your hands on your hips,
> Let your backbone slip.
>
> Shake it to the east.
> Shake it to the west,
> Shake it to the one
> you love the best.

Over time the words changed and the game took on a new meaning. Little Sally Walker became a game of choosing partners. Note how the central player rises and uses hip-swinging motions to choose another love. This not only suggests that older children, but boys, also played the ring game.[64]

The transition from bondage to freedom did not signal an end to free play or the creativity of the children. The newly freed John F. Van Hook used a pocketknife to shape two millstones from soapstone and built a "little mill that worked just fine." He operated the mill on a branch of the Sugar Fork River in Georgia. "We run pretty white sand through it," he said, "and called that our meal and flour." His mechanical ability and attention to details came from observing his father, a "good carpenter and mechanic" who "helped the Van

Hooks [the former slaveowners] to build mills." His environment and frame of reference enhanced his imagination and shaped his creativity.[65]

"My white folks," Van Hook said, referring to his former owners, "would come down to the branch and watch me run the little toy mill." Of equal importance was his recollection of "all sorts of *nice* playthings" he carved. The child's skill and ingenuity boosted his self-esteem and image among his peers and his "white folks" as well.[66]

The children of former slaveholders and slaves sometimes played together as in the past, and their interactions varied according to individuals. The ex-slave Homer was unable to continue his job as of May 6, 1866, due to an arm injury received while wrestling with James, his employer's son. There is no evidence of malice or unsportsmanlike conduct on James's part. Allen, another freed boy, replaced Homer. In all probability, Allen and James would play together if their interests and ages were compatible.[67]

As in times past when black and white children interacted, there were occasional disputes which required settling on a different playing field. A conflict between a white and a black youngster led to the severe beating of Samuel Geder, a Baker County, Georgia, freedman, at the hands of James Porter in 1868. Apparently Porter interceded and intended to punish the Geder child when the boys quarreled. When the elder Geder "tried to prevent" it by "trying to persuade him not to do so," Porter turned upon him with "a large white oak stick about as thick as a man's arm and afterwards stamped him so that he . . . spit blood several ways." The freed child watched helplessly while two white men held Samuel Geder "down on the ground by his head and feet." In exercising parental rights, Porter believed Geder usurped his authority. After examining Geder, the attending physician "considered his recovery doubtful." Samuel Geder's action was unlike that of Jacob Stroyer's mother only in that a whipping resulted from an incident between black and white children rather than between the child Jacob and the adult trainer. At bottom, parents, whether enslaved or free, showed interest in their children's welfare and considered themselves the proper authority to administer punishments if needed.[68]

As in days past, the descendants of Africans divided their leisure between recreational activities and those that focused on education and religion. Without prohibitions on literacy, they attended schools and learned to read and write for their own edification. They could now record history for the benefit of their progeny's education and entertainment. Although Woodson and Haley used different genres, their interests originated with stories told by slave ancestors during leisure moments. Pauli Murray acknowledged that *Proud Shoes*, a family history set in the antebellum South, germinated from the tales Murray heard from her grandmother when she was growing up in North Carolina.[69]

Throughout the Civil War the quest for freedom and education caused thousands of slaves to leave familiar surroundings to get closer to freedom and to take advantage of the long-denied privilege of literacy. With freedom secured, the pursuit of education continued. An AMA missionary, Reverend S. Jocelyn, assessed the freedmen's desire for education saying, "Their desire for learning and the aptitude of children and adults to learn are remarkable." Jocelyn also observed that "the religious knowledge, experience, character, unusual intelligence and gifts of numbers among them, have surprised the missionary teachers and visitors." Over time other white teachers admitted their amazement at the children's interest and abilities. Often taking the initiative, newly freed persons pledged money for the construction of schools. Those near Fortress Monroe, Virginia, subscribed seventy-five dollars while others without money pledged their labor. The children now sang:

> Oh happy is the child who learns to read
> When I get over
> To read that blessed book indeed.
> Chorus:
> When I get over, when I get over
> 'Twill take some time to study
> When I get over.[70]

The thirst for education was best summarized by a former slave who had equated going to school with getting into "paradise." Booker T. Washington wrote:

> Few people who were not right in the midst of the scenes can have any exact idea of the intense desire which the people of my race showed for education . . . it was a whole race trying to go to school. Few were too young, and none too old, to make the attempt to learn. As fast as any kind of teacher could be secured, not only were day-schools filled, but night-schools as well. The great ambition of the older people was to try to learn to read the Bible before they died. With this end in view, men and women who were fifty and seventy years old, would be found in the night schools. Sunday-school was formed soon after freedom, but the principal book studied in Sunday-school was always the speller. Day-school, night-school, and Sunday-school were always crowded, and often many had to be turned away for want of room.

Newly freed persons contributed their time and money to the building of schools in the same fashion as they built orphanages. Through their own efforts and with the help of the Freedmen's Bureau, hundreds of schools served tens of thousands of children across the South. This is not to suggest that all children went to school, but it is to say that education was now more readily accessible and would become even more so with the passing of time.[71]

There was excitement in learning for the young and old. In some cases it was a family matter, which helps to explain the reduction in the number of laborers available for agricultural work. Children and adults used spelling lessons as a pastime and attended classes together. A northern-born teacher remembered a

16. School children in Virginia in the 1860s. Girl, fourth from left in the second row, is the daughter of Mary Peake. Courtesy of the Hampton University Archives, Hampton, Virginia.

woman with a baby in her arms in school with her two boys. When her turn came, "They all stood up and read together." Elizabeth Botume noticed that children brought babies to school, but they prevented them from interfering with classes by taking turns keeping the children outside. As soon as one child recited, she would go outside to relieve the "baby sitter," who in turn filled the recently vacated seat inside the classroom. Whether caregiver or pupil, the child was always within earshot of class activities. Botume eventually engaged an older woman to attend to the babies to ensure that no one missed the lessons.[72]

A northern-born teacher wrote:

> I am rejoicing with the happy negro in his greed for letters. One word of instruction from a teacher brightens the face of the learner with shining content. Frock coat or shoes, he takes as his due; but every step of his creeping progress into the mysteries of letters elevates his spirit like faith in a brilliant promise.

The teacher's observation was not unlike one made by Louisa Cocke more than thirty years earlier. Cocke said the pupils at her Virginia plantation school "appeared to be the happiest creatures in the world" once the proud teacher, the "Good Miss Betsey," went to work at her appointed vocation.[73]

Whites did not uniformly share this zeal for the former slaves' education. Interferences by individuals and groups were not uncommon, nor was violence against teachers by the Ku Klux Klan and other white organizations. A witness testifying before the Joint Committee on Reconstruction, created by the Thirty-Ninth Congress, which met in December 1865, stated that blacks in Surry County, Virginia, were afraid to carry books although they were eager to learn to read and there was no school in the area. He claimed that "local whites would kill any one who would go down there and establish a colored school."[74]

When Tryphena Fox returned to her Louisiana home after the war ended, she found a "nigger school" in the old slave cabins. The school, established by the Freedmen's Bureau, was a ready reminder of the new social order. Although angered by its presence, Fox "determined to put up with the annoyance of the little darkey school." Too impoverished to do otherwise, she accepted the rent paid by the Freedmen's Bureau to refurnish her home and clothe her "half-naked children." The government paid eight dollars per month for use of the rooms, and "Miss Emma," the teacher who lived in the Fox home, paid twenty-five dollars per month for room and board.[75]

Negative reactions toward education for newly freed people stems from the desire for continued denial to equal rights and disdain for the curriculum that went beyond the three R's. Teachers sometimes used official documents such as the Emancipation Proclamation and speeches of radical Republicans in a partisan manner; therefore, the line between civic instruction and political indoctrination blurred. In his study of education during reconstruction, Robert C. Morris claims that southern reactions to the extent of political activities within the schools were based upon misconceptions about instructional materials, which was not at all radical. Lydia M. Child's *The Freedmen's Book* tempered the discussion of Toussaint L'Ouverture and Frederick Douglass along with William and Ellen Craft with "Advice From An Old Friend," which cautioned freed-people to "be respectful and polite toward your associates, and toward those who have been in the habit of considering you an inferior."[76]

Despite the opposition from whites, African Americans continued their quest for learning more about spiritual and temporal matters. Faith in a superior being continued to be a significant force in the lives of many African Americans. Freedom expanded religious opportunities for slaves who withdrew from white churches and either formed their own or joined the congregations in existing black churches.[77]

The churches served as a proving ground for public service and leadership roles which youngsters would assume as they matured. Religion was also a precursor for education. An 1867 comment by C. T. Watson, a Freedmen's Bureau agent in Georgia, serves as a reminder that education and religion remained intertwined even in freedom. Watson wrote to O. H. Howard regarding the cost of church repairs and noted that workers should complete them with a dual objective in mind. "It is necessary for school purposes," he wrote, "that the pews be constructed in such a way that they may be used as desks." He asked for a "shelf attached to back of pew[s] with hinges so that they can be let down out of the way when not required for School." It was cost efficient to have the building serve two purposes. The founding of colleges and universities in the postwar years by congregations of African descent further attests to the linkage between education and religion.[78]

With educational prowess, freedpersons sought to discard reminders of slavery. The poem, "De Linin' Ub De Hymns," comments upon changes in youngsters once they have opportunities for education and the tensions created between the old uneducated ex-slaves and themselves. The poem observed:

> De young folks say 'tain't stylish to lin' 'um out no mo';
> Dat dey's got edicashun, an' dey wants us all to know
> Dey likes to hav dar singin'-books a-holin' fore dar eyes,
> An' sing de hymns right straight along "to manshuns in de skies."

The poet noted that "de ol' folks will kumplain" because "slabry's chain don' kep' dem back frum larnin' how to read." Aware of how the young replaced the old, the poet surmised that the aged members in the congregation "mus' take a corner seat, an' let de young folks lead." The older generation accepted the inevitable, but the elders pleaded, "Jes' lebe a leetle place in church fur dem es kin not read."[79]

The generational tension did not affect adolescent boys and girls, who found that church services, revivals, and camp meetings still provided religious inspiration along with opportunities to woo and be wooed. Courtship changed little in style, especially with regard to the use of florid phrases. Anderson Bates, who remained on the plantation where he had been a slave for sixteen years claimed Carrie, his lady love, was as a "sugar lump of a gal" with seven other suitors "flyin' 'round." If courtships ended in marriages, church weddings and freedom from anxieties about the separation of spouses or children through sales or forced migration were realistic expectations for young lovers.[80]

Although many of the former slaves actively tried to eradicate memories of their enslavement, there were conscientious efforts to record their history for posterity. Hampton Normal and Agricultural Institute, founded in 1868 for freedmen and women, established a folklore club and began collecting data to document their lives. William Wells Newell visited the school and recorded the students singing plantation songs. The use of folklore by Hampton and other struggling schools and colleges encouraged potential donors to contribute money for operating expenses. When students objected to the use of the slave songs, one of the principals reassured them that it was fitting to "look backward a little" to measure their accomplishments since emancipation. He remarked, "We wish not only to preserve this folklore but to dignify it in your eyes and theirs," referring to their offspring. Many of the early students did not want any reminders of slavery.[81]

The song "Is Master Going to Sell Us Tomorrow?" became part of the repertoire used by Fisk University and other historically black colleges founded after the Civil War. A former Alabama slave said, "Dat was one of the saddest songs we sung en durin' slavery days." The ex-slave assured the WPA interviewer, "It always did make me cry." This song and others of a similar nature were the kinds of reminder that many ex-slaves sought to avoid.[82]

Freedpersons, without respect for age, realized that they could not completely avoid reminders of slavery any more than they could avoid the hostility of "masters without slaves." In the wider society there were daily reminders of white fear of a radical change in society when the bottom rail would be on top. Children either knew someone who suffered from the wrath of hostile whites, or they experienced it themselves. A twelve-year-old child accompanied a relative to a Republican rally in Camilla, Georgia, which ended in a riot. John Gaines, a white man, attacked her and "cut her severely with a knife over the back of the head and neck and on the arm." As a final insult for attending the meeting, Gaines "took her hand and split each finger from its end to the center of the hand." Gaines's behavior underscores the fact that hostile whites intentionally struck at the most vulnerable members of the society, defenseless children, to intimidate the youngsters and their elders into submitting to white control.[83]

Against the backdrop of this pervasive enmity one must ask, What did freedom mean and what was its cost to the former slaves? Nicey Pugh remembered the "secu'aty" of slavery and said, "Dem was de really happy days." When Pugh remarked, "Course we didn't hab de 'vantages dat we has now," it became clear that the WPA interviewer intimidated her or that she reflected upon slavery with a child's view in mind. In either case, the ambiguity of the testimony hearkens back to the past when slaves inculcated the adage "Got one mind for the boss to see; got another for what I know is me."[84]

Slaves who endured the tragedies and traumas of slavery did not overwhelmingly seek revenge. As an enslaved youngster Allen Wilson, who lived in Virginia, longed to grow older and stronger so that he could seek retribution after seeing an overseer beat his mother. He asked his brother to help him kill the overseer when he grew older. Another slave said that he intended to "pay his owner back" for the many whippings he received as a child. Years later he saw the ex-slaveholder moving about slowly as if to "drag" along and thought of his earlier desire for vengeance. He resisted the temptation. "I might as well be whippin' a year old child," he concluded.[85]

It is understandable that the freedman would be considerate. As a child, he had been socialized to respect the elderly. Furthermore, to think that whipping an elderly man would be like whipping a child bodes well for a person who had tolerated inhumane acts and degradation, either personally or vicariously, and emerged from slavery with his humanity and spirit intact.[86]

The absence of vengeful attacks upon whites by freedpersons does not mean that many were not angry about the physical and psychological tolls that slavery exacted from parents and children. When reflecting upon slavery's encroachment on the slave family, a freedwoman said, "White folks got a heap to answer for the way they've done colored folks! So much they wouldn't never *pray* it away." The woman's tone suggests that she was not contemplating forgiving her tormentors. It is unlikely that she was alone.[87]

Far from being "childlike" throughout their lives, persons subjected to American slavery learned to handle situations involving violence, injustice, and arbitrary power at early ages. As a result of parental guidance and child-rearing practices, enslaved children learned to resist slavery and maintain their integrity. When necessary, they donned the mask of compliance to hide their will to resist. As the children of slaves matured and became parents of free boys and girls, they would realize that their role was no different from that of their parents. It remained incumbent upon them to provide the salve, kindle hope, and maintain the love to assure that their children survived.

NOTES

Introduction

1. Philip D. Curtin, *The Atlantic Slave Trade: A Census* (Madison: University of Wisconsin Press, 1970), 73–75; *Compendium of the Seventh Census of the United States: 1850* (Washington: Government Printing Office, 1854), 34, 82–83; *Historical Statistics of the United States, Colonial Times to 1970*, bicentennial ed., Part I (Washington: Government Printing Office, 1975), 18.

There is no way of knowing how much the illegal traffic in slaves contributed to this increase.

2. Willie Lee Rose, *Slavery and Freedom*, ed. William W. Freehling (New York: Oxford University Press, 1982), 39.

3. Stanley M. Elkins, *Slavery: A Problem in American Institutional and Intellectual Life* (New York: Grosset and Dunlap, 1963), 82, 130; Tryphena Blanche Holder Fox (hereafter cited as TBHF) to Anna Rose Holder (hereafter cited as ARH), July 15, 1865, Tryphena Blanche Holder Fox Collection, MDAH; Harvey Wish, ed., *Antebellum Writings of George Fitzhugh* (New York: Capricorn, 1960), 89.

4. Melville J. Herskovits, *The Myth of the Negro Past* (Boston: Beacon, 1958), 1; Michael Wayne, *The Reshaping of Plantation Society: The Natchez District, 1860–1880* (Baton Rouge: Louisiana State University Press, 1983), 25.

5. N. Ray Hiner and Joseph M. Hawes, eds., *Growing Up in America: Children in Historical Perspective* (Urbana: University of Illinois Press, 1985), 169–70; Robert H. Bremner, ed., *Children and Youth in America: A Documentary History* (Cambridge: Harvard University Press, 1970), 316–39.

6. John W. Blassingame's *The Slave Community: Plantation Life in the Antebellum South*, rev. ed. (New York: Oxford University Press, 1979); Herbert G. Gutman's *The Black Family in Slavery and Freedom, 1750–1925* (New York: Vintage, 1977); Eugene D. Genovese's *Roll, Jordan, Roll: The World the Slaves Made* (New York: Vintage, 1976); Leslie Howard Owens, *This Species of Property* (New York: Oxford University Press, 1977); Thomas L. Webber, *Deep Like the Rivers: Education in the Slave Quarter Community, 1831–1865* (New York: Norton, 1978).

For a brief general discussion of slave children see Dorothy Burnham, "Children of the Slave Community in the United States," *Freedomways* 19 (Second Quarter 1979): 75–81; Patricia Romero Curtin, "Slave Children," in *Dictionary of Afro-American Slavery*, ed. Randall M. Miller and John David Smith (Westport: Greenwood, 1988), 99–102.

See David J. Rothman, "Documents in Search of a Historian: Toward a History of Childhood and Youth in America," JIH 2 (Autumn 1971): 367–77.

7. Rose, *Slavery and Freedom*, 39.

8. David J. Rothman, "Documents in Search of a Historian: Toward a History of Childhood and Youth in America," JIH 2 (August 1971): 367–68; Dom Cavallo, "Adolescent Peer Group Morality: Its Origins and Functions in the United States," PR 6 (Fall-Winter, 1977–1978): 88–90; Ross W. Beales, Jr., "In Search of the Historical Child: Miniature Adulthood and Youth in Colonial New England," AQ (1975): 379–98; John and Virginia Demos, "Adolescence in Historical Perspective," in *The American Family in Social-Historical Perspective*, ed. Michael Gordon (New York: St. Martin's, 1973): 209–17; Joseph F. Kett, "Adolescence and Youth in Nineteenth-Century America," in *The Family in History Interdisciplinary Essays*, ed. Theodore K. Rabb and

Robert I. Rotberg (New York: Harper, 1972), 95–110; Daniel Blake Smith, "The Study of the Family in Early America: Trends, Problems, and Prospects," WMQ 39 (January 1982): 3–28; Bruce Bellingham, "The History of Childhood since the 'Invention of Childhood': Some Issues in the Eighties," JFH 13 (1988): 347–58; Vivian C. Fox, "Is Adolescence a Phenomenon of Modern Times?" JPsy 5 (Fall 1977): 271–90.

9. Kett, "Adolescence and Youth in Nineteenth-Century America," 108.

10. G. B. Wallace to Andrew Grinnan, April 18, 1855, Wallace Family Papers (#2689), UVA; Elkins, *Slavery*, 130.

11. Booker T. Washington, *Up from Slavery: An Autobiography* (New York: Bantam, 1967), 1; George P. Rawick, ed., *The American Slave: A Composite Autobiography*, 19 vols. (Westport: Greenwood, 1972), II: South Carolina Narr., Part 1:181, 229–38.

12. Richard A. Wright, *African Philosophy: An Introduction*, 3d ed. (Lanham: University Press of America, 1984), 99; Frederick Douglass, *Narrative and Selected Writings*, ed. Michael Meyer (New York: Random House, 1984), 18.

13. See Karen Ellen Dawley, "Childhood in Eighteenth-Century Virginia" (M.A. thesis, University of Virginia, 1973).

14. Slaves in the "Maturity" category ranged in age from twenty up to fifty years of age. Afterwards slaves fell into the "Old Age" category, from fifty to ninety-nine years old. The "Extreme Old Age" category included those over one hundred years of age. The final group included those whose ages were unknown.

See *Compendium of the Seventh Census of the United States: 1850* (Washington: Government Printing Office, 1854), 91.

15. Olaudah Equiano, *The Life of Olaudah Equiano, or Gustavus Vassa the African* (London: Longman, 1988), 75.

16. Zlata Filipovic, *Zlata's Diary: A Child's Life in Sarajevo* (New York: Viking, 1994), 37, 65; Anne Frank, *The Diary of a Young Girl* (New York: Bantam, 1993).

17. Harriet Jacobs, *Incidents in the Life of a Slave Girl: Written by Herself*, ed. Jean Fagan Yellin (Cambridge: Harvard University Press, 1987), 77.

1. "You know I am one man that do love my children"

1. Frederick Douglass, *My Bondage and My Freedom* (New York: Dover, 1969), 56.

See Leonard Shengold, *Soul Murder: The Effects of Childhood Abuse and Deprivation* (New Haven: Yale University Press, 1989).

2. Robert Sunley, "Early Nineteenth-Century American Literature on Child Rearing," in *Childhood in Contemporary Cultures*, ed. Margaret Mead and Martha Wolfenstein (Chicago: University of Chicago Press, 1955), 150–67; Glenn Davis, *Childhood and History* (New York: Psychohistory Press, 1976), 49–56; Deborah Gray White, *Ar'n't I a Woman? Female Slaves in the Plantation South* (New York: Norton, 1985), 67–68, 107; Herbert S. Klein, "African Women in the Atlantic Slave Trade," in *Slavery in Africa: Historical and Anthropological Perspectives*, ed. Suzanne Miers and Igor Kopytoff (Madison: University of Wisconsin Press, 1977), 29–38; Nancy F. Cott, "Notes toward an Interpretation of Antebellum Childrearing," PR 6 (Spring 1978): 4; Harriette Pipes McAdoo and Rosalyn Terborg-Penn, "Historical Trends and Perspectives of Afro-American Families," TH 3 (Spring 1985): 97–111.

For discussions regarding childbirth and child-rearing practices in Africa, see G. M. Culwick, "New Ways for Old in the Treatment of Adolescent African Girls," *Africa* 12 (October 1939): 425–32; R. E. Ellison, "Marriage and Child-Birth among the Kanuri," *Africa* 9 (October 1936): 524–34; W. H. S. Curryer, "Mothercraft in Southern Nigeria," *United Empire* 18 (February 1927): 28–81; Charles T. Dooley, "Child-Training among the Wanguru," *Primitive Man* 8 (October 1935): 72–80.

3. Nancy Tanner, "Matrilocality in Indonesia and Africa and among Black Americans," in *Woman, Culture and Society,* ed. Michelle Zimbalist Rosaldo and Louise Lamphere (Stanford: Stanford University Press, 1974), 153; Herbert J. Foster, "African Patterns in the Afro-American Family," JBS 14 (December 1983): 201–32; John Thornton, "Sexual Demography: The Impact of the Slave Trade on Family Structure," in *Women and Slavery in Africa,* ed. Claire C. Robertson and Martin A. Kline (Madison: University of Wisconsin Press, 1983), 39–41; Barbara Jeanne Fields, *Slavery and Freedom on the Middle Ground: Maryland during the Nineteenth Century* (New Haven: Yale University Press, 1985), 24; Herbert G. Gutman, *The Black Family in Slavery and Freedom, 1750–1925* (New York: Vintage, 1977), 75–76; Mary Beth Norton, *Liberty's Daughters: The Revolutionary Experience of American Women, 1750–1800* (New York: Harper Collins, 1980), 73; Kenneth M. Stampp, *The Peculiar Institution: Slavery in the Ante-Bellum South* (New York: Knopf, 1967), 250; Eleanor Smith, "African American Women and the Extended Family: A Sociohistorical Review," WJBS 13 (Winter 1989): 179.

4. William Cohen, "Thomas Jefferson and the Problem of Slavery," JAH 56 (December 1969): 518; Gutman, *The Black Family,* 77–78.

5. Cornhill Plantation Book, May 11, 1838, McDonald Furman Papers, DU; Robert Ruffin Barrow Books, July 1857, SHC; Solomon Northup, "Twelve Years a Slave: Narrative of Solomon Northup," in *Puttin' On Ole Massa: The Slave Narratives of Henry Bibb, William Wells Brown, and Solomon Northup,* ed. Gilbert Osofsky (New York: Harper, 1969), 331; C. Peter Ripley, "The Black Family in Transition: Louisiana, 1860–1865," JSH 41 (August 1975): 369–71.

See family listings recorded in Edward Clifford Anderson Papers, SHC; John C. Cohoon Account Book (#8868), UVA; C. G. Holland, "The Slave Population on the Plantation of John C. Cohoon, Jr., Nansemond County, Virginia, 1810–1860," VMH 80 (April 1972): 333–40.

Philip D. Morgan's "The Ownership of Property by Slaves in the Mid-Nineteenth-Century Low Country," JSH 49 (August 1983): 399–420, shows that slaves in the low country of South Carolina and Georgia owned a significant amount of property by comparison with slaves in other areas. It should be noted that their property was a general accumulation by their own initiative over time rather than as gifts from slaveowners.

See also Appendix A.

6. William Ethelbert Ervin Book, January 1847, SHC; "Rules for Government of Plantation, *Negroes,*" Cornhill Plantation Book, 106, Furman Papers, DU; Randall Miller, ed., *"Dear Master": Letters of a Slave Family* (Ithaca: Cornell University Press, 1978), 150.

7. Cohoon Account Book (#8868), UVA; James O. Breeden, ed., *Advice among Masters: The Ideal in Slave Management in the Old South* (Westport: Greenwood, 1980), 51, 55, 58; Kenneth M. Stampp, *The Peculiar Institution: Slavery in the Ante-Bellum South* (New York: Knopf, 1967), 250.

8. Sukey and Ersey to Beverly Tucker, October 24, 1842, Tucker-Coleman Collection, EGS; Mrs. George P. (Mary Haldane Begg) Coleman, ed., *Virginia Silhouette: Contemporary Letters Concerning Negro Slaves in the State of Virginia* (Richmond: Dietz, 1934), 35–40; Donald M. Scott and Bernard Wishy, eds., *America's Families: A Documentary History* (New York: Harper and Row, 1982), 319; John W. Blassingame, *The Slave Community: Plantation Life in the Antebellum South,* rev. ed. (New York: Oxford University Press, 1979), 177.

9. Norton, *Liberty's Daughters,* 68; Fields, *Slavery and Freedom,* 24–25; Paul D. Escott, *Slavery Remembered: A Record of Twentieth-Century Slave Narratives* (Chapel Hill: University of North Carolina Press, 1979), 51–52; Edwin Morris Betts, ed.,

Thomas Jefferson's Farm Book, with Commentary and Relevant Extracts from Other Writings (Princeton: Princeton University Press, 1953), 7; Cohen, "Thomas Jefferson and the Problem of Slavery," 515, 517–18.

10. Cohoon Account Book (#8868), UVA.

See Appendix A.

11. Natalie Shainess, "The Structure of the Mothering Encounter," JNMD 136 (February 1963): 146–61; Natalie Shainess, "The Psychologic Experience of Labor," NYSJM 63 (October 15, 1963): 2923–32; White, *Ar'n't I a Woman?*, 67–69.

12. E. Franklin Frazier, *The Negro Family in the United States*, 2d ed. (Chicago: University of Chicago Press, 1967), 50–69.

See Richard H. Steckel, "Miscegenation and the American Slave Schedule," JIH 11 (Autumn 1980): 251–64.

13. John C. Gunn, *Domestic Medicine, or Poor Man's Medicine*, 2d ed. (Madisonvill, Tennessee: J. F. Grant, 1834), 337–79; Greenwood Plantation Record, June 25, 1861, LC; Michael P. Johnson, "Smothered Slave Infants: Were Slave Mothers at Fault?" JSH 47 (November 1981): 519; Willie Lee Rose, ed., *A Documentary History of Slavery in North America* (New York: Oxford University Press, 1976), 417–18; William Dosite Postell, "Birth and Mortality Rates among Slave Infants on Southern Plantations," *Pediatrics* 10 (November 1952): 538.

14. See John Campbell, "Work, Pregnancy, and Infant Mortality among Southern Slaves," JIH 14 (Spring 1984): 792–812; Frazier, *The Negro Family in the United States*, 36–37; George P. Rawick, ed., *The American Slave: A Composite Autobiography*, 19 vols. (Westport: Greenwood, 1972), II: South Carolina Narr. (Series 1), Part 1:20.

15. Charles B. Dew, "David Ross and the Oxford Iron Works: A Study of Industrial Slavery in the Early Nineteenth-Century South," WMQ 31 (April 1974): 212.

16. Jacqueline Jones, *Labor of Love, Labor of Sorrow: Black Women, Work and the Family, from Slavery to the Present* (New York: Vintage, 1986), 19; "Rules for the Overseer or Manager," Willis P. Bocock Paper, SHC; "Rules for Government of Plantation, *Negroes*," Cornhill Plantation Book, 106, Furman Papers, DU; Campbell,"Work, Pregnancy, and Infant Mortality," 809; White, *Ar'n't I a Woman?*, 94.

See Frances Anne Kemble, *Journal of a Residence on a Georgian Plantation in 1838–1839*, ed. John A. Scott (Athens: University of Georgia Press, 1984), 229–30; Campbell, "Work, Pregnancy, and Infant Mortality," 801–803.

17. Rose, *A Documentary History*, 418; Leslie Howard Owens, *This Species of Property: Slave Life and Culture in the Old South* (New York: Oxford University Press, 1977), 38–40.

18. Rawick, *The American Slave*, II: South Carolina Narr. (Series 1), Part 1:20; Kemble, *Journal of a Residence*, 229–31; Campbell, "Work Pregnancy, and Infant Mortality," 808–809.

19. Judith Walzer Leavitt, *Brought to Bed: Childbearing in America, 1750 to 1950* (New York: Oxford University Press, 1986), 125; Catherine M. Scholten, "'On the Importance of the Obstetrick Art': Changing Customs of Childbirth in America, 1760–1825," WMQ 34 (July 1977): 426–45; J. Jill Suitor, "Husbands' Participation in Childbirth: A Nineteenth-Century Phenomenon," JFH 6 (Fall 1981): 278–93; Catherine Clinton, *The Plantation Mistress: Woman's World in the Old South* (New York: Pantheon, 1982), 151–54; Todd L. Savitt, *Medicine and Slavery: The Diseases and Health Care of Blacks in Antebellum Virginia* (Urbana: University of Illinois Press, 1978), 117–18; John Houston Bills Diary, April 14, 1856, John Houston Bills Papers, SHC.

20. B. A. Botkin, ed., *Lay My Burden Down: A Folk History of Slavery* (Chicago: University of Chicago Press, 1965), 179–80.

See James Mellon, ed., *Bullwhip Days: The Slave Remember* (New York: Weidenfeld and Nicolson, 1988), 37; Norman R. Yetman, *Life Under the "Peculiar*

Institution": Selections from the Slave Narrative Collection (New York: Holt, Rinehart and Winston, 1970), 47; Rawick, *The American Slave*, III: Georgia Narr. (Supplement, Series 1), Part 1:95.

21. William Waller Hening, *The Statutes at Large; Being a Collection of All Laws of Virginia from the First Session of the Legislature in the Year 1619*, vol. II (Charlottesville: University Press of Virginia, 1969) 170.

22. See Ulla-Britt Lithell, "Breast-Feeding Habits and Their Relation to Infant Mortality and Marital Fertility," JFH 6 (Summer 1981): 182–94; Cheryll Ann Cody, "Slave Demography and Family Formation: A Community Study of the Ball Family Plantation, 1720–1896" (Ph. D. diss., University of Minnesota, 1982), 171–73.

See Appendix A.

23. Rawick, *The American Slave*, III: South Carolina Narr. (Series 1), Part 3:18; Colin M. Turnbull, *Tradition and Change in African Tribal Life* (Cleveland: World, 1966), 44–45; Foster, "African Patterns in the Afro-American Family," 217–219; Gutman, *The Black Family*, 188–90; Cheryll Ann Cody, "Naming, Kinship, and Estate Dispersal: Notes on Slave Family Life on a South Carolina Plantation, 1786–1833," WMQ 39 (January 1982): 203; Cheryll Ann Cody, "There Was No 'Absalom' on the Ball Plantations: Slave-Naming Practices in the South Carolina Low Country, 1720–1865," AHR 92 (June 1987): 573.

24. All references about Jacob and Fanny's children come from the John C. Cohoon Account Book (#8868), UVA.

See "Family and Kin Connections and Slave Ownership Involving Slaves Originally Owned by John C. Cohoon, Cedar Vale Plantation, Nansemond County, Virginia, 1863," in Gutman, *The Black Family*, 136.

See also Appendix A.

25. See Appendix A.

26. Cody, "There Was No 'Absalom,'" 588–91; See Appendix A.

27. Bills Diary, December 16, 1843, April 29, 1845, April 30, 1849, SHC; Thomas L. Webber, *Deep Like the Rivers: Education in the Slave Quarter Community, 1831–1865* (New York: Norton, 1978), 34; Cohen, "Thomas Jefferson and the Problem of Slavery," 519; Cody, "There was No 'Absalom,'" 573–75, 583; Blassingame, *The Slave Community*, 182.

28. Jacob Stroyer, *My Life in the South* (Salem: Salem Observer, 1889), 16.

29. Robert Moore Riddick, Inventory and Appraisement, 1819, Prentis Family Papers, EGS; "Inventory and valuation of the Property given off to Mary Davidson," December 1836, Davidson Family Papers, SHC; Rose, *A Documentary History*, 338–44; Bills Diary, January 1, 1860, SHC.

See notice from Betts and Gregory, Auctioneers, Richmond, Virginia, January 5, 1861, which lists children by sex and height rather than age with explanation "Girls of same height of boys about the same price." Negro Collection, Slavery Division, DU.

30. Kemble, *Journal of a Residence*, 95–96.

31. Stanley Feldstein, *Once a Slave: The Slave's View of Slavery*, (New York: Morrow, 1971), 56; Henry Bibb, "Narrative of the Life and Adventures of Henry Bibb," in *Puttin' On Ole Massa: The Slave Narratives of Henry Bibb, William Wells Brown, and Solomon Northup*, ed. Gilbert Osofsky (New York: Harper, 1969), 81.

32. Michael P. Johnson and James L. Roark, *Black Masters: A Free Family of Color in the Old South* (New York: Norton, 1984), 14–15, 101–106.

See Elizabeth Keckley, *Behind the Scenes: Thirty Years a Slave and Four Years in the White House* (New York: Arno and *New York Times*, 1968).

33. "Rules for Government of Plantation, *Negroes*," Cornhill Plantation Book, 106, Furman Papers, DU; Tryphena Blanche Holder Fox (hereafter cited as TBHF) to Anna Rose Holder (hereafter cited as ARH), December 27, 1857, MDAH.

34. Blassingame, *The Slave Community*, 181; Lithell,"Breast-Feeding Habits," 183; Kenneth L. Kiple and Virginia H. Kiple, "Slave Child Mortality: Some Nutritional Answers to a Perennial Puzzle," JSocH 10 (Spring 1977): 287–89.

35. Robert A. Margo and Richard H. Steckel, "The Heights of American Slaves: New Evidence on Slave Nutrition and Health," SSH 6 (Fall 1982): 516–38; Richard H. Steckel, "A Peculiar Population: The Nutrition, Health, and Mortality of American Slaves from Childhood to Maturity," JEH 46 (September 1986): 721–41.

36. Freeman Accounts Book, February 1861, Watson Family Papers (#530), UVA.

37. Franklin A. Hudson Diary, "Memoranda," July 3, 1852, July 30, 1852, SHC; Botkin, *Lay My Burden Down*, 111; Bayside Plantation Records, June 18, 1861, June 29, 1861, SHC; John Nevitt Diary, March 9, 1827, May 17, 1828, SHC; Lawton Diary (1810–1840), 1817, Alexander Robert Lawton Papers, SHC; Susanna to Master, June 3, 1862, Harding and Jackson Family Papers, SHC; Newstead Plantation Diaries, June 14, 1858, June 17–19, 1858, August 25, 1858, SHC; Greenwood Plantation Book, August 15, 1862, LC; Mary Ann Buie to Cousin, March 12, 1855, Mary Ann Buie Letters, DU; R. and B. to Jim, December 11, 1854, James S. Milling Papers, SHC; Bills Diary, May 14, 1864, June 23, 1864, SHC; Kiple, "Slave Child Mortality," 285; Nancy Schrom Dye and Daniel Blake Smith, "Mother Love and Infant Death, 1750–1920," JAH 73 (September 1986): 329–53; Richard H. Steckel, "A Dreadful Childhood: The Excess Mortality of American Slaves," SSH 10 (Winter 1986): 427–65; Cody, "Slave Demography and Family Formation," 215–38; Postell, "Birth and Mortality among Slave Infants," 540.

38. Rawick, *The American Slave*, X: Texas Narr. (Supplement, Series 2), Part 9:3916; Savitt, *Medicine and Slavery*, 149–64.

39. Everard Green Baker Diary, August 22, 1850, I:89, SHC; David Gavin Diary, December 1859, I:180, SHC.

40. A. C. (Nancy) Griffin to Mrs. Bethia Richardson, August 1848, Caffery Family Papers, SHC; Kiple, "Slave Child Mortality," 290–91.

For a discussion of health conditions among Africans see Gerald W. Hartwig and K. David Patterson, eds., *Disease in African History: An Introductory Survey and Case Studies* (Durham: Duke University Press, 1978).

41. Kiple, "Slave Child Mortality," 290–91; Steckel, "A Peculiar Population," 733–36.

42. Bills Diary, March 16, 1860, SHC; TBHF to ARH, February 1, 1860, March 17, 1860, MDAH; Baker Diary, August 22, 1850, I: 89, SHC; Elizabeth Fox-Genovese, *Within the Plantation Household: Black and White Women of the Old South* (Chapel Hill: University of North Carolina Press, 1988), 131.

43. Johnson, "Smothered Slave Infants," 499, 519–20; Freeman Account Book, June 1860, Watson Family Papers (#530), UVA.

44. Todd L. Savitt, "Smothering and Overlaying of Virginia Slave Children: A Suggested Explanation," *Bulletin of the History of Medicine* 49 (Fall 1975): 400–404; Savitt, *Medicine and Slavery*, 120–29, 137–38; Jones, *Labor of Love*, 19.

45. Kemble, *Journal of a Residence*, 222–23; Johnson, "Smothered Slave Infants," 493–520; Savitt, "Smothering and Overlaying," 400; Steckel, "A Dreadful Childhood," 450–53.

46. Baker Diary, April 29, 1849, August 22, 1850, SHC.

47. Johnson, "Smothered Slave Infants," 499; Yetman, *Life Under the "Peculiar Institution,"* 228; Margaret Washington Creel, "Gullah Attitudes toward Life and Death," in *Africanisms in American Culture*, ed. Joseph E. Holloway (Bloomington: Indiana University Press, 1990), 81–82.

48. Charles Ball, *Fifty Years in Chains: or The Life of an American Slave* (New York:

Dayton and Asher, 1859), 198; Blake Touchstone, "Planters and Slave Religion in the Deep South," in *Master and Slaves in the House of the Lord: Race and Religion in the American South, 1740–1870,* ed. John Boles (Lexington: University Press of Kentucky, 1988), 125.

49. James H. Ruffin Plantation Books, vol. 3, August-September 1843, August-October 1844, SHC; Webber, *Deep Like the Rivers,* 10.

See instructions to overseer requiring that "breeding and suckling" women work near the house in the William Henry Sims Papers, SHC. McDonald Furman specified that women "near being confined must be put only to light work & after delivery & able to go about must be put to light work for a time" in "Rules for Government of Plantation, *Negroes,*" Cornhill Plantation Book, 106, DU.

50. Harriet Jacobs, *Incidents in the Life of a Slave Girl Written by Herself,* ed. Jean Fagan Yellin (Cambridge: Harvard University Press, 1987), 87; Bibb, "Narrative of the Life and Adventures of Henry Bibb," 80–81.

51. Bobby Frank Jones, "A Cultural Middle Passage: Slave Marriage and Family in the Antebellum South" (Ph. D. diss., University of North Carolina, 1965), 108; White Hill Plantation Books, SHC; Gavin Diary, September 13, 1856, SHC; Webber, *Deep Like the Rivers,* 11; Bibb, "Narrative of the Life and Adventures of Henry Bibb," 80–81; Olive Gilbert, *Narrative of Sojourner Truth, A Bondswoman of Olden Time, Emancipated by the New York Legislature in the Early Part of the Present Century, with a History of Her Labors and Correspondence Drawn from her Book of Life* (Chicago: Johnson, 1970), 38–39.

52. White Hill Plantation Books, SHC; Jones, "A Cultural Middle Passage," 108; Gavin Diary, September 13, 1856, SHC; J. G. Clinkscales, *On the Old Plantation: Reminiscences of His Childhood* (New York: Negro Universities Press, 1969), 42–43.

53. Susan Bradford Eppes (Mrs. Nicholas Ware Eppes), *The Negro of the Old South: A Bit of Period History* (Macon: J. W. Burke, rev. copyright, 1941), 67–68.

54. George P. Rawick, *From Sundown to Sunup: The Making of the Black Community* (Westport: Greenwood, 1972), 93; Foster, "African Patterns in the African-American Family," 220–221; Douglass, *My Bondage,* 69; Smith, "African American Women and the Extended Family," 180–81; Jean E. Friedman, *The Enclosed Garden: Women and Community in the Evangelical South, 1830–1890* (Chapel Hill: University of North Carolina Press, 1985), 85–87.

55. Booker T. Washington, *Up from Slavery, An Autobiography* (New York: Bantam, 1967), 7–8; "Plantation Rules," William Henry Sims Papers, 1857–1865, SHC; December 1855, Furman Papers, DU; Douglass, *My Bondage,* 101; George L. Knox, *Slave and Freeman: The Autobiography of George L. Knox,* ed. William B. Gatewood (Lexington: University of Kentucky Press, 1979), 44–45.

56. Cornhill Plantation Book, March 27, 1854, April 14, 1856, DU; TBHF to ARH, January 1, 1860, MDAH.

57. W. W. Gilmer, "Management of Slaves," SP 12 (April 1852): 106; Kemble, *Journal of a Residence,* 68–69.

58. TBHF to ARH, January 1, 1860, MDAH; Winthrop D. Jordan, *White over Black: American Attitudes toward the Negro, 1550–1812* (New York: Norton, 1977), 159; Douglass, *My Bondage,* 161; Gilmer, "Management of Slaves," 106–107; Blassingame, *The Slave Community,* 292; Eugene D. Genovese, *Roll, Jordan, Roll: The World the Slaves Made* (New York: Vintage, 1976), 505.

59. Rawick, *The American Slave,* XI: Missouri Narr. (Series 2), 53.

See discussions on the internal economy among slaves in *Slavery and Abolition* 12 (May 1991).

60. Philip D. Morgan, "The Ownership of Property by Slaves in the Mid-Nineteenth Century Low Country," JSH 49 (August 1983): 399–407; Charles W. Joyner, *Down by the Riverside: A South Carolina Slave Community* (Urbana: University of Illinois Press, 1984), 51–57; Julia Floyd Smith, *Slavery and Rice Culture in Low Country Georgia, 1750–1860* (Knoxville: University of Tennessee Press, 1985), 58–59, 61.

See Philip D. Morgan, "Work and Culture: The Task System and the World of Lowcountry Blacks, 1700–1880," WMQ 39 (October 1982): 563–99.

61. Morgan, "Work and Culture," 566; Morgan, "The Ownership of Property by Slaves," 408–409.

62. Rawick, *American Slave,* II: South Carolina Narr. (Series 1), Part 1:39, 224–25; William Bonner to William B. Rodman, February 4, 1853, Rodman Papers, SHC.

63. Z. Haynes to Charles Manigault, October 25, 1847, Louis Manigault Papers, DU.

64. Washington, *Up from Slavery,* 8; Blassingame, *The Slave Community,* 181.

See Catherine M. Hanchett, "'What Sort of People & Families . . .': The Edmondson Sisters," AANY 6 (July 1982): 21–37.

65. Gutman, *The Black Family in Slavery and Freedom,* 6; Miller, *"Dear Master,"* 188–89.

66. Miller, *"Dear Master,"* 188–89.

67. Washington, *Up from Slavery,* 17; Douglass, *My Bondage,* 53; Frederick Douglass, *Narrative of the Life of Frederick Douglass: An American Slave, Written by Himself,* in *Frederick Douglass: The Narrative and Selected Writings,* ed. Michael Meyer (New York: Random House, 1984), 19; Waldo E. Martin, Jr., *The Mind of Frederick Douglass* (Chapel Hill: University of North Carolina Press, 1984), 4–5; Richard S. Dunn, "A Tale of Two Plantations: Slave Life at Mesopotamia in Jamaica and Mount Airy in Virginia, 1799–1828," WMQ 34 (January 1974): 54.

68. Lester of Georgia to Miss Patsy Padison of North Carolina, August 29, 1857, James Allred Papers, DU.

See Appendix C.1.

69. Brown, "Narrative of William Wells Brown," 209.

2. "Us ain't never idle"

1. Frederick Douglass, *My Bondage and My Freedom* (New York: Dover, 1969), 206.

2. Ibid.

3. James O. Breeden, ed., *Advice among Masters: The Ideal in Slave Management in the Old South* (Westport: Greenwood, 1980), 218.

4. Donald D. Wax, "The Demand for Slave Labor in Colonial Pennsylvania," PH 34 (October 1967): 337–39; Claudia Goldin and Kenneth Sokoloff, "Women, Children, and Industrialization in the Early Republic: Evidence from the Manufacturing Censuses," JEH 42 (December 1982): 741–74; Thomas E. Jordan, *Victorian Childhood: Themes and Variations* (Albany: State University of New York Press, 1987), 110; Edith Abbott, "A Study of the Early History of Child Labor in America," AJS 14 (July 1908): 15–37; Allen B. Sanderson, "Child-Labor Legislation and the Labor Force Participation of Children," JEH 34 (March 1974): 297–99.

See Viviana A. Zelizer, *Pricing the Priceless Child: The Changing Social Value of Children* (New York: Basic, 1985); see especially chapter 2, "From Useful to Useless: The Moral Conflict over Child Labor," 56–72.

5. Cornhill Plantation Book, McDonald Furman Papers, DU; Francis Terry Leak Books, vol. 4, June 4, 1856, SHC; Overseer Rules, William Henry Sims Papers, SHC.

6. Edwin Morris Betts, ed., *Thomas Jefferson's Farm Book, with Commentary and Relevant Extracts from Other Writings* (Princeton: Princeton University Press, 1953), 7.

Willie Lee Rose, ed., *A Documentary History of Slavery in North America* (New York: Oxford University Press, 1976), 337–44.
    See Wilson to A. D. Gage, May 8, 1847, Notley D. Tomlin Papers, DU.
    7. "A Proclamation," January 1, 1827, Jemison Papers, SHC.
    8. Norman R. Yetman, *Life Under the "Peculiar Institution": Selections from the Slave Narrative Collection* (New York: Holt, Rinehart and Winston, 1970), 40, 311; Paul D. Escott, *Slavery Remembered: A Record of Twentieth-Century Slave Narratives* (Chapel Hill: University of North Carolina Press, 1979), 31–33.
    9. Yetman, *Life Under the "Peculiar Institution,"* 232.
    10. Tryphena Blanche Holder Fox (hereafter cited as TBHF) to Anna Rose Holder (hereafter cited as ARH), November 15, 1858, July 12, 1860, MDAH.
    See J. G. Clinkscales, *On the Old Plantation: Reminiscences of His Childhood* (New York: Negro Universities Press, 1969), 39.
    11. TBHF to ARH, November 15, 1858, July 12, 1860, MDAH.
    12. See Tryphena Blanche Holder Fox Collection, MDAH.
    13. Sarah S. Hughes, "Slaves for Hire: The Allocation of Black Labor in Elizabeth City County, Virginia, 1782 to 1810," WMQ 37 (April 1978): 260; Clement Eaton, "Slave-Hiring in the Upper South: A Step toward Freedom," MVHR 46 (March 1960): 663; James William McGettigan, Jr., "Boone County Slaves: Sales, Estate Division and Families, 1820–1865," Part II. MHR 72 (1978): 271–78.
    See Robert S. Starobin, *Industrial Slavery in the Old South* (New York: Oxford University Press, 1970), 128–37; Richard C. Wade, *Slavery in the Cities: The South 1820–1860* (New York: Oxford University Press, 1964), 38–48.
    14. Charles L. Perdue, Jr., Thomas E. Barden, and Robert K. Phillips, eds., *Weevils in the Wheat: Interviews with Virginia Ex-Slaves* (Bloomington: Indiana University Press, 1980), 185. See Eugene D. Genovese, *Roll, Jordan, Roll: The World the Slaves Made* (New York: Vintage, 1976), 509.
    15. Yetman, *Life Under the "Peculiar Institution,"* 23, 71–72, 171; Charles Manigault to Mr. Louis, February 21, 1855, Louis Manigault Papers, DU; Frederick Douglass, "Narrative of the Life of Frederick Douglass an American Slave Written by Himself," in *Frederick Douglass: The Narrative and Selected Writings*, ed. Michael Meyer (New York: Random House, 1984), 40.
    16. J. H. Ingraham, *Not "A Fool's Errand." Life and Experience of a Northern Governess in the Sunny South; or the Southerner at Home* (New York: Carleton, 1880), 180; *Historical Statistics of the United States, Colonial Times to 1970*, Part 1 (Washington: U.S. Government Printing Office, 1975), 17–18.
    17. Yetman, *Life Under the "Peculiar Institution,"* 21–22; George P. Rawick, ed., *The American Slave: A Composite Autobiography*, 19 vols. (Westport: Greenwood, 1972), III: South Carolina Narr. (Series 1), Part 3:18.
    For discussions of slavery outside of the plantation South see Lorenzo Johnston Greene, *The Negro in Colonial New England* (New York: Atheneum, 1974), 101–23; Edgar J. McManus, *Black Bondage in the North* (Syracuse: Syracuse University Press, 1973); Hanford Dozier Stafford, "Slavery in a Border City: Louisville, 1790–1860," (Ph. D. diss., University of Kentucky, 1982).
    18. Rawick, *The American Slave*, II: South Carolina Narr. (Series 1), Part 1:85.
    19. Yetman, *Life Under the "Peculiar Institution,"* 12, 89, 96; Henry Bibb, "Narrative of the Life and Adventures of Henry Bibb: An American Slave Written by Himself," in *Puttin' On Ole Massa: The Slave Narratives of Henry Bibb, William Wells Brown, and Solomon Northup*, ed. Gilbert Osofsky (New York: Harper, 1969), 66; Carole Shammas, "Black Women's Work and the Evolution of Plantation Society in Virginia," LH 26 (Winter 1985): 10–11, 25.

20. Perdue et al., *Weevils in the Wheat*, 99.

See Genovese, *Roll, Jordan, Roll*, 3–5; Clarence E. Walker, "Massa's New Clothes: A Critique of Eugene D. Genovese on Southern Society, Master-Slave Relations, and Slave Behavior," UMOJA 4 (Summer 1980): 114–30; John W. Blassingame, "Using the Testimony of Ex-Slaves: Approaches and Problems," JSH 41 (November 1975): 473–92.

See also David Thomas Bailey, "A Divided Prism: Two Sources of Black Testimony on Slavery," JSH 46 (August 1980): 381–404; Donald M. Jacobs, "Twentieth-Century Slave Narratives as Source Materials: Slave labor as Agricultural Labor," AH 57 (April 1983): 223–27.

21. Yetman, *Life Under the "Peculiar Institution,"* 127; Perdue et al., *Weevils in the Wheat*, 288.

22. Genovese, *Roll, Jordan, Roll*, 505.

23. Rawick, *The American Slave*, XI: Missouri Narr. (Series 2), 1–2.

24. Perdue et al., *Weevils in the Wheat*, 97–98; John B. Cade, "Out of the Mouths of Ex-Slaves," JNH 20 (July 1935): 310; Catherine Clinton, *The Plantation Mistress: Woman's World in the Old South* (New York: Pantheon, 1982), 22–24.

25. Escott, *Slavery Remembered*, 16; Susan Strasser, *Never Done: A History of American Housework* (New York: Pantheon, 1982), 104–24; Martha Tabb Dyer Diary (#7776-D), November 11, 1823, UVA.

26. Ingraham, *Not "A Fool's Errand,"* 180; Shammas, "Black Women's Work," 16, 20–21; Clinton, *The Plantation Mistress*, 22–23.

27. For a detailed description of laundering clothes see "Blue Monday," in Strasser, *Never Done*, 104–24.

28. Ingraham, *Not "A Fool's Errand,"* 179–80; Strasser, *Never Done*, 108.

29. Lucy A. Delaney, "From The Darkness Cometh the Light or Struggles for Freedom," in *The Schomburg Library of Nineteenth-Century Black Women Writers: Six Women's Narratives*, ed. Henry Louis Gates, Jr. (New York: Oxford University Press, 1988), 25–27.

Rivers and streams must have served as sites for laundering clothes; however, there is no extensive discussion of it in the slave narratives. This is probably indicative of the majority of informants being too young to assume such responsibilities, therefore, lacking the experience to relate.

30. See TBHF to ARH, July 31, 1857, July 9, 1858, MDAH.

31. Tommy Lee Bogger, "The Slave and Free Black Community in Norfolk, 1775–1865" (Ph. D. diss., University of Virginia, 1976), 166; Cade, "Out of the Mouth of Ex-Slaves," 312; Frederick Douglass, *My Bondage and My Freedom* (New York: Dover, 1969), 105–12.

See John W. Blassingame, "Status and Social Structure in the Slave Community," in *Perspectives and Irony in American Slavery*, ed. Harry P. Owens (Jackson: University Press of Mississippi, 1976), 139.

32. Cade, "Out of the Mouths of Ex-Slaves," 311–12; Yetman, *Life Under the "Peculiar Institution,"* 133; Douglass, *The Narrative*, 39.

33. Yetman, *Life Under the "Peculiar Institution,"* 119, 188; Dyer Diary (#7776-D), November 11, 1823, UVA; TBHF to ARH, November 6, 1860, MDAH; Clinton, *The Plantation Mistress*, 24; Strasser, *Never Done*, 58–60.

34. Yetman, *Life Under the "Peculiar Institution,"* 163, 313; Clinton, *The Plantation Mistress*, 26–27; Elizabeth Fox-Genovese, *Within the Plantation Household: Black and White Women of the Old South* (Chapel Hill: University of North Carolina Press, 1988), 120–24, 128.

35. Yetman, *Life Under the "Peculiar Institution,"* 127, 312; Randall M. Miller, "The Fabric of Control: Slavery in Antebellum Southern Textile Mills," BHR 55 (Winter

1981): 473; Deborah Gray White, *Ar'n't I a Woman: Female Slaves in the Plantation South* (New York: Norton, 1985), 94–95, 123; Deborah Gray White, "The Lives of Slave Women: The Female Slave Network," SE 12 (November/December 1984): 34; Jacqueline Jones, *Labor of Love, Labor of Sorrow: Black Women, Work and the Family, from Slavery to the Present* (New York: Vintage, 1986), 16.

See December 8, 1836, letter from John Springs, Davidson Family Papers, SHC.

36. TBHF to ARH, January 4, 1857, MDAH; Yetman, *Life Under the "Peculiar Institution,"* 188.

37. See Blassingame, "Status and Social Structure in the Slave Community," 137–51; C. W. Harper, "Black Aristocrats: Domestic Servants on the Antebellum Plantation," *Phylon* 46 (June 1985): 123–35.

38. See Michael P. Johnson, "Work, Culture, and the Slave Community: Slave Occupations in the Cotton Belt in 1860," LH 27 (Summer 1986): 325–55; James Bonner, *A History of Georgia Agriculture, 1732–1860* (Athens: University of Georgia Press, 1964); John Hebron Moore, *Agriculture in Ante-Bellum Mississippi* (New York: Octagon, 1971).

39. Yetman, *Life Under the "Peculiar Institution,"* 48; William S. Pettigrew to Moses, June 12, 1857, Pettigrew Family Papers, SHC; Perdue et al., *Weevils in the Wheat*, 26; Rawick, *The American Slave*, XVI: Kansas Narr. (Series 2), 1.

40. Perdue et al., *Weevils in the Wheat*, 281, 322; Ronald Killion and Charles Waller, *Slavery Time When I Was Chillun Down on Marster's Plantation; Interviews with Georgia Slaves* (Savannah: Beehive, 1973), 138–39; John T. O'Brien, "Factory, Church, and Community: Blacks in Antebellum Richmond," JSH 44 (November 1978): 511.

See Paul W. Gates, *The Farmer's Age: Agriculture 1815–1860*, vol. 3: *The Economic History of the United States* (New York: Holt, Rinehart and Winston, 1960), 100–107; Lewis Cecil Gray, *History of Agriculture in the Southern United States to 1860*, vol. 1 (Gloucester: Peter Smith, 1958), 215–18.

41. See "Children at Tobacco Factory," February 5, 1853, Farish Carter Papers, SHC.

42. Perdue et al., *Weevils in the Wheat*, 39; Lawrence W. Levine, *Black Culture and Black Consciousness: Afro-American Folk Thought from Slavery to Freedom* (New York: Oxford University Press, 1977), 7; Gray, *History of Agriculture*, 216.

See Melvin G. Herndon, "The Significance of the Forest to the Tobacco Plantation Economy in Antebellum Virginia," PSA 1 (October 1981): 430–39.

43. Theodore Rosengarten, *Tombee: Portrait of a Cotton Planter* (New York: Morrow, 1986), 365, 368, 376.

44. See daily entries for October through November 1841 in the James H. Ruffin Ledger, 1841–1846, vol. 3, SHC.

45. See Ruffin Ledger, 1841–46, vol. 3, SHC.

46. Cade, "Out of the Mouth of Ex-Slaves," 320.

47. Alonzo T. Mial to Ruffin Horton, December 6, 1859, Alonzo T. Mial Papers, NCDAH.

See E. M. Landers, Jr., "Slave Labor in South Carolina Cotton Mills," JNH 38 (April 1953): 161–73; Miller, "The Fabric of Control," 471–90; Starobin, *Industrial Slavery*, 164–65.

48. Gates, *The Farmer's Age*, 128; Gray, *History of Agriculture*, I: 279–80, II:721–23; J. Carlyle Sitterson, *Sugar Country: The Cane Sugar Industry in the South, 1753–1950* (Lexington: University of Kentucky Press, 1953), 13–44; Walter Prichard, "Routine on a Louisiana Sugar Plantation Under the Slavery Regime," MVHR 14 (September 1927): 169–71.

49. Gates, *The Farmer's Age*, 119–20; Rawick, *The American Slave*, III: South Carolina Narr. (Series 1), Part 3:91–92.

For discussions regarding rice cultivation see Sam B. Hilliard, "The Tidewater Rice Plantation: An Ingenious Adaptation to Nature," GM 12 (June 20, 1975): 60; Sam B. Hilliard, "Antebellum Tidewater Rice Culture in South Carolina and Georgia," in *European Settlement and Development in North America: Essays on Geographical Change in Honour and Memory of Andrew Clark Hill*, ed. James R. Gibson (Toronto: University of Toronto Press, 1973), 91–115; Joyner, *Down by the Riverside*, 42; Gates, *The Farmer's Age*, 118–22; Gray, *History of Agriculture* 2: 726–29; Peter Wood, *Black Majority: Negroes in Colonial South Carolina from 1670 through the Stono Rebellion* (New York: Norton, 1974), 37, 59.

50. Rawick, *The American Slave*, III: South Carolina Narr. (Series 1), Part 3:91, 83–84; Rawick, *The American Slave*, II: South Carolina Narr. (Series 1), Part 1: 58–59; Smith, *Slavery and Rice Culture*, 46–55.

51. Gates, *The Farmer's Age*, 128; Robert Ruffin Barrow Books, November 8, 1857, SHC; Sitterson, *Sugar Country*, 11–16, 30; Sidney W. Mintz, *Sweetness and Power: The Place of Sugar in Modern History* (New York: Penguin, 1986), 21, 49–50; Prichard, "Routine on a Louisiana Sugar Plantation," 169–71.

52. Gates, *The Farmer's Age*, 123.

53. Rose, *A Documentary History*, 314–15; Mintz, *Sweetness and Power*, 21–22, 47–48.

54. Prichard, "Routine on a Louisiana Sugar Plantation," 172; Barrow Daybook, September 5, 1857, September 15, 1857, October 9, 1857, SHC; TBHF to ARH, October 4, 1856, MDAH.

55. Gates, *The Farmer's Age*, 128; Mintz, *Sweetness and Power*, 49–50.

56. Ulrich B. Phillips, *American Negro Slavery: A Survey of the Supply, Employment and Control of Negro Labor as Determined by the Plantation Regime* (Baton Rouge: Louisiana State University Press, 1966) 245; Michael Tadman, *Speculators and Slaves: Masters, Traders, and Slaves in the Old South* (Madison: University of Wisconsin Press, 1989), 65.

57. Perdue et al., *Weevils in the Wheat*, 26; Jones, *Labor of Love*, 16.

58. Perdue et al., *Weevils in the Wheat*, 115; John Edwin Fripp Diary, April 11, 1857, John Edwin Fripp Papers, SHC.

59. Mial to Ruffin Horton, December 6, 1859, Mial Papers, NCDAH.

60. John Hebron Moore, "John Hebron of LaGrange Plantation: Commercial Fruit Grower of the Old South," JMH 46 (November 1984): 281–303.

61. Clinton, *The Plantation Mistress*, 23–24.

See Harry Crews, *A Childhood: The Biography of a Place* (New York: Harper and Row, 1978), 109–13, for an account of the slaughtering and processing hogs. Thanks to Edward Ayers for bringing this book to my attention.

62. John Houston Bills Diary, December 16, 1858, December 21, 1858, December 22, 1858, December 31, 1858, January 1,1860, January 2, 1860, John Houston Bills Papers, SHC; Douglass, *The Narrative*, 40; Perdue et al., *Weevils in the Wheat*, 79; Rawick, *The American Slave*, XVI: Kansas Narr. (Series 2), 1.

63. Song quoted from Frederick Douglass, *Life and Times of Frederick Douglass: Written by Himself* (New York: Collier, 1962) 146–147; Thomas L. Webber, *Deep Like the Rivers: Education in the Slave Quarter Community, 1831–1865* (New York: Norton, 1978), 77.

See Phillips, *American Negro Slavery*, 310–13; Genovese, *Roll, Jordan, Roll*, 603–604; Robert William Fogel and Stanley L. Engerman, *Time on the Cross: The Economics of American Negro Slavery* (Boston: Little, Brown, 1974), 109–115; Herbert G. Gutman, "Time on the Cross: The Economics of American Slavery: The World Two Cliometricians Made," JNH 60 (January 1975): 64–65.

64. W. E. Burghardt Du Bois, ed., *The Negro Artisan: Report of a Social Study Made Under the Direction of Atlanta University; Together with the Proceedings of the Seventh Conference for the Study of the Negro Problems, Held at Atlanta University, on*

May 27th, 1902 (Atlanta: Atlanta University Press, 1902), 13–21; Ronald L. Lewis, "Slave Families at Early Chesapeake Ironworks," VMH 86 (April 1978): 172–73.

See Marcus W. Jernegan, "Slavery and the Beginnings of Industrialism in the American Colonies," AHR 25 (January 1920): 220–40.

65. Franklin A. Hudson Diary, 1854, 65, SHC; Herndon, "The Significance of the Forest," 435; Philip S. Foner and Ronald L. Lewis, eds., *The Black Worker: A Documentary History from Colonial Times to the Present*, vol. 1: *The Black Workers to 1869* (Philadelphia: Temple University Press, 1978), 11, 14, 16.

See John E. Stealey, III, "Slavery and the Western Virginia Salt Industry," JNH 59 (April 1974): 111–13; Percival Perry, "The Naval-Stores Industry in the Old South, 1790–1860," JSH 34 (November 1968): 509–26.

66. Douglass, *The Narrative*, 99–100; Starobin, *Industrial Slavery*, 29–30.

67. Johnson, "Work, Culture, and the Slave Community," 342–43; Dew, "David Ross and the Oxford Iron Works," 199; Charles B. Dew, "David Ross and the Oxford Iron Works: A Study of Industrial Slavery in the Early Nineteenth-Century South," WMQ 31 (April 1974): 199.

See Rayford W. Logan, ed., *Memoirs of a Monticello Slave: As Dictated to Charles Campbell in the 1840's by Isaac, one of Thomas Jefferson's Slaves* (Charlottesville: University of Virginia Press, 1951), 24–25, regarding Isaac, a fifteen-year-old boy, who in 1790 "larnt to cut out & sodder: make little pepper boxes & graters . . . out of scraps of tin." He made cups and delighted in showing them to Jefferson. The boy's skill won praise and improved greatly after four years with the master craftsman. Jefferson then sent Isaac back to Monticello "to car [carry] on the tin-business."

68. Dew, "David Ross and the Oxford Iron Works," 189–224.

See Ronald L. Lewis, *Coal, Iron, and Slaves: Industrial Slavery in Maryland and Virginia, 1715–1865* (Westport: Greenwood, 1979).

69. Dew, "David Ross and the Oxford Iron Works," 207–208.

70. Rawick, *The American Slave*, XVI: Kansas Narr. (Series 2), 9; George L. Knox, *Slave and Freeman: The Autobiography of George L. Knox*, ed. William B. Gatewood (Lexington: University Press of Kentucky, 1979), 44–45.

71. White, *Ar'n't I a Woman?*, 69; Jones, *Labor of Love, Labor of Sorrow*, 18; Shammas, Black Women's Work," 5–28; Leonard Stavisky, "The Origins of Negro Craftsmanship in Colonial America," JNH 32 (October 1947): 428; Newton, "Slave Artisans and Craftsmen," 35–42; Michael P. Johnson and James L. Roark, *Black Masters: A Free Family of Color in the Old South* (New York: Norton, 1984), 131–34.

72. White, "The Lives of Slave Women: The Female Slave Network," 32–39; Jones, *Labor of Love*, 18.

73. Landers, "Slave Labor in South Carolina Cotton Mills," 161–73; Starobin, *Industrial Slavery*, 12–14; Foner, *A Documentary History*, 16.

See Stephen J. Goldfarb, "A Note on Limits to the Growth of Cotton-Textile Industry in the Old South," JSH 48 (November 1982): Bess Beatty, "Textile Labor in the North Carolina Piedmont: Mill Owner Images and Mill Worker Response, 1830–1900," LH 25 (Fall 1984): 485–503.

74. Yetman, *Life Under the "Peculiar Institution,"* 73; Dew, "David Ross and the Oxford Iron Works," 207–208.

75. Dew, "David Ross and the Oxford Iron Works," 204, 208.

76. Perdue et al., *Weevils in the Wheat*, 88–89, 309.

77. TBHF to ARH, October 21, 1860, dated postscript to the October 14, 1860, letter, MDAH (emphasis in the original).

78. Stroyer, *My Life*, 19–25.

79. Yetman, *Life Under the "Peculiar Institution,"* 40 (emphases added).

3. "When day is done"

1. Launcelot Minor Blackford Diary, June 21, 1848, SHC.

2. George P. Rawick, ed., *The American Slave: A Composite Autobiography,* 19 vols. (Westport: Greenwood, 1972), II: South Carolina Narr. (Series 1), Part 1:85; "Rules for the Overseer or Manager," Willis P. Bocock Paper, SHC; Thomas L. Webber, *Deep Like the Rivers: Education in the Slave Quarter Community, 1831–1865* (New York: Norton, 1978), 234–35; J. Huizinga, *Homo Ludens: A Study of the Play Element in Culture* (Boston: Beacon, 1950), 2.

I wish to thank David Thomas Bailey for bringing Huizinga's work to my attention.

3. David K. Wiggins, "The Play of Slave Children in the Plantation Communities of the Old South, 1820–1860," JSpH 7 (Summer 1980): 22; Bernard Mergen, *Play and Playthings: A Reference Guide* (Westport: Greenwood, 1982), 3, 22, 39; Bernard Mergen, "The Discovery of Children's Play," AQ 27 (October 1975): 418; Keith A. P. Sandiford, "The Victorians at Play: Problems in Historiographical Methodology," JSocH 15 (Winter 1981): 272; Andrew W. Miracle, Jr., "Some Functions of Aymara Games and Play," in *Studies in the Anthropology of Play: Papers in Memory of B. Allan Tindall,* ed. Phillip Stevens, Jr. (Westpoint: Leisure, 1977), 103–105.

4. Huizinga, *Homo Ludens,* 9–10.

5. Rawick, *The American Slave,* II: South Carolina Narr. (Series 1), Part 2:98; III: South Carolina Narr. (Series 1), Part 3:56.

Regarding the interaction between black and white children in the plantation South, U. B. Phillips writes:

> The lives of the whites and the blacks were partly segregate, partly intertwined. If any special link were needed, the children supplied it. The white ones, hardly knowing their mothers from their mammies or their uncles by blood from their "uncles" by courtesy, had the freedom of the kitchen and the cabins, and the black ones were their playmates in the shaded sandy yard the livelong day. Together they were regaled with folklore in the quarters, with Bible and fairy stories in the "big house," with pastry in the kitchen, with grapes at the scuppernong arbor, with melons at the spring house and with peaches in the orchard.

Noting the end of play days, Phillips continues:

> Indeed, when the fork in the road of life was reached, the white youths found something to envy in the freedom of their fellows' feet from the cramping weight of shoes and the freedom of their minds from the restraints of school. With the approach of maturity came routine and responsibility for the whites, routine alone for the generality of the blacks.

See Ulrich B. Phillips, *American Negro Slavery: A Survey of the Supply, Employment and Control of Negro Labor as Determined by the Plantation Regime* (Baton Rouge: Louisiana State University Press, 1966), 313.

6. Norman R. Yetman, ed., *Life Under the "Peculiar Institution": Selections from the Slave Narrative Collection* (New York: Holt, Rinehart and Winston, 1970), 264; Wiggins, "The Play of Slave Children," 23; Rawick, *The American Slave,* II: South Carolina Narr. (Series 1), Part 1:42; Mergen, *Play and Playthings,* 39; Charles L. Perdue, Jr., Thomas E. Barden, and Robert K. Phillips, eds., *Weevils in the Wheat: Interviews*

with Virginia Ex-Slaves (Bloomington: Indiana University Press, 1980), 74–75.

7. Booker T. Washington, *Up from Slavery, An Autobiography* (New York: Bantam, 1967), 4.

8. Yetman, *Life Under the "Peculiar Institution,"* 40; Richard H. Steckel, "A Peculiar Population: The Nutrition, Health, and Mortality of American Slaves from Childhood to Maturity," JEH 46 (September 1986): 721–41.

9. Mergen, *Play and Playthings*, 39.

10. Wiggins, "The Play of Slave Children," 24.

11. Perdue et al., *Weevils in the Wheat*, 107; Rawick, *The American Slave*, II: South Carolina Narr. (Series 1), Part 1:42, 82; Mergen, *Play and Playthings*, 46; III: Georgia Narr. (Series 1), Part 1: 85–86; Susan Bradford Eppes, *The Negro of the Old South: A Bit of Period History* (Mason, Georgia: J. W. Burke, rev. copyright, 1941), 67–68; Tryphena Blanche Holder Fox (hereafter cited as TBHF) to Anna Rose Holder (hereafter cited as ARH), June 28, 1861, November 15, 1858, MDAH; Bernard Mergen, "Toys and American Culture Objects as Hypotheses," JAC 3 (Winter 1980): 743; Colin M. Turnbull, *Tradition and Change in African Tribal Life* (Cleveland: World, 1966), 50.

12. Rawick, *The American Slave*, VII: Mississippi Narr. (Supplement, Series 1), Part 2:621–22.

13. James W. C. Pennington, *The Fugitive Blacksmith or Events in the History of James W. C. Pennington Pastor of a Presbyterian Church New York, Formerly a Slave in the State of Maryland*, in *Great Slave Narratives*, ed. Arna Bontemps (Boston: Beacon, 1969), 208.

14. Mergen, *Play and Playthings*, 22, 46; Launcelot Minor Blackford Diary, April 12–20, 1848, March 13–14, 1849, June 7, 1849, SHC.

See D. D. Bruce, Jr. "Play, Work and Ethics in the Old South," SFQ 41 (1977): 37–38.

See also John R. Adams, *Edward Everett Hale* (Boston: Twayne, 1977), 6, for a discussion of the leisure activities of a northern child.

15. Mergen, *Play and Playthings*, 39; Rawick, *The American Slave*, II: South Carolina Narr. (Series 1), Part 1:42, 58; Wiggins, "The Play of Slave Children," 23; Eugene D. Genovese, *Roll, Jordan, Roll: The World the Slaves Made* (New York: Vintage, 1976), 505.

16. Bessie Jones and Bess Lomax Hawes, *Step It Down: Games, Plays, Songs and Stories from the Afro-American Heritage* (Athens: University of Georgia Press, 1987), 182.

17. Eric O. Ayisi, *An Introduction to the Study of African Culture*, 2d ed. (London: Heinemann, 1986), 46–48.

18. Jacob Stroyer, *My Life in the South* (Salem: Salem Observer, 1889), 11–14.

Unlike Gilbert, Emily Dixon and her brother seemed to fight when they perceived affronts; however, they bullied the children into not telling—the same as Gilbert. See below.

See Vivian C. Fox, "Is Adolescence a Phenomenon of Modern Times?" JPsy 5 (Fall 1977): 271–90.

19. Genovese, *Roll, Jordan, Roll*, 506; Yetman, *Life Under the "Peculiar Institution,"* 124–25; Rawick, *The American Slave*, VII: Mississippi Narr. (Supplement, Series 1), Part 2:622.

See Elliott J. Gorn, "'Gouge and Bite, Pull Hair and Scratch': The Social Significance of Fighting in the Southern Backcountry," AHR 90 (February 1985): 18–43.

20. Rawick, *The American Slave*, VII: Mississippi Narr. (Supplement, Series 1), Part 2:621–22.

21. Roger D. Abrahams, "Playing the Dozens," JAF 75 (July-September 1962): 209–220; Harry G. Lefever, "'Playing the Dozens': A Mechanism for Social Control," *Phylon* 42 (Spring 1981): 77–85; Donald C. Simmons, "Possible West African Source for the American Negro 'Dozens,'" JAF 76 (October-December 1973) 339–40; Amuzie Chimezie, "The Dozens: An African-Heritage Theory," JBS 6 (June 1976): 401–19.

22. Thomas Webber, *Deep Like the Rivers: Education on the Slave Quarter Community, 1831–1865* (New York: Norton, 1978), 184; Mergen, *Play and Playthings*, 43; Perdue et al., *Weevils in the Wheat*, 81; Genovese, *Roll, Jordan, Roll*, 506; Wiggins, "The Play of Slave Children," 26, 29–30; Rawick, *The American Slave*, II: South Carolina Narr. (Series 1), Part 1:167; Jones, *Step It Down*, 186.

23. Genovese, *Roll, Jordan, Roll*, 506; Mergen, *Play and Playthings*, 42; Huizinga, *Homo Ludens*, 8.

24. Blackford Diary, June 23, 1848, July 8, 1848, July 11, 1848, August 4, 1848, SHC; Mergen, *Play and Playthings*, 22.

See entries regarding typesetting in Blackford Diary, February–April, 1849, SHC.
See also Adams, *Edward Everett Hale*, 1, 6, for comparative purposes.

25. Blackford Diary, February 27, 1848, SHC.

26. Genovese, *Roll, Jordan, Roll*, 515; Wiggins, "The Play of Slave Children," 26; Rawick, *The American Slave*, V: Texas Narr. (Series 1), Part 3:24.

See David R. Roediger, "And Die in Dixie: Funerals, Deaths, and Heaven in the Slave Community 1700–1865." MR 22 (Spring 1981): 163–83.

27. Genovese, *Roll, Jordan, Roll*, 515.

28. Blackford Diary, February 27, 1848, SHC; Mechal Sobel, *The World They Made Together: Black and White Values in Eighteenth-Century Virginia* (Princeton: Princeton University Press, 1987), 219.

See Robert Farris Thompson, "Kongo Influences on African-American Artistic Culture," in *Africanisms in American Culture*, ed. Joseph E. Holloway (Bloomington: Indiana University Press, 1990), 167–72.

29. William Wells Newell, *Games and Songs of American Children* (New York: Dover, 1963), 181–82.

30. Rawick, *The American Slave*, II: South Carolina Narr. (Series 1), Part 1:55, 241; Wiggins, "The Play of Slave Children," 29.

31. Dickson J. Preston, *Young Frederick Douglass: The Maryland Years* (Baltimore: Johns Hopkins University Press, 1980), 92; Rawick, *The American Slave*, II: South Carolina Narr. (Series 1), Part 1:28.

See T. H. Breen, "'Horses and Gentlemen': The Cultural Significance of Gambling among the Gentry of Virginia," WMQ 34 (April 1977): 239–57; Bertram Wyatt-Brown, *Southern Honor: Ethics and Behavior in the Old South* (New York: Oxford University Press, 1982), 339–50; TBHF to ARH, July 14, 1856, and June 28, 1857, MDAH.

32. Rawick, *The American Slave*, VII: Oklahoma Narr. (Series 1), 306–11.

33. M. Cain to Minerva, April 14, 1833, Tod Robinson Caldwell Papers, SHC; Genovese, *Roll, Jordan, Roll*, 518; Jo Anne Sellers Huber, "Southern Women and the Institution of Slavery" (M.A. thesis, Lamar University, 1980), 41; Sudie Duncan Sides, "Southern Women and Slavery," part I, HT 20 (January 1970): 55; Frances Anne Kemble, *Journal of a Residence on a Georgian Plantation in 1838–1839*, ed. John A. Scott (Athens: University of Georgia Press, 1984), 93; Blackford Diary, June 21, 1848, SHC.

34. Theodore Rosengarten, *Tombee: Portrait of a Cotton Planter* (New York: Morrow, 1986), 172; Genovese, *Roll, Jordan, Roll*, 515; Deborah Gray White, *Ar'n't I a Woman? Female Slaves in the Plantation South* (New York: Norton, 1985), 54; James C. Bonner, ed., "Plantation Experiences of a New York Woman," NCHR 33 (October 1956): 411; TBHF to ARH, November 15, 1858, MDAH; Catherine Clinton, *The Plantation Mistress: Woman's World in the Old South* (New York: Pantheon, 1982), 91; Elizabeth Fox-Genovese, *Within the Plantation Household: Black and White Women of the Old South* (Chapel Hill: University of North Carolina Press, 1988), 147–48; Irving H. Bartlett and C. Glenn Cambor, "The History and Psychodynamics of Southern Womanhood," WS 2 (1974): 11–12.

35. TBHF to George Holder, May 20, 1861, MDAH; Genovese, *Roll, Jordan, Roll,* 515.

36. Mergen, *Play and Playthings,* 40; Harold Courlander, *Negro Folk Music, U.S.A.* (New York: Columbia University Press, 1963), 148.

37. Newell, *Games and Songs,* 70; Jones, *Step It Down,* 107; Courlander, *Negro Folk Music,* 157.

38. Rawick, *The American Slave,* III: South Carolina Narr. (Series 1), Part 3:56–57; II: South Carolina Narr. (Series 1) Part 1:167; Newell, *Games and Songs,* 153.

39. Preston, *Young Frederick Douglass,* 92; James Mellon, ed., *Bullwhip Days: The Slave Remember* (New York: Weidenfeld and Nicolson, 1988), 39; [Anna Matilda King] to Thomas Butler King, December 28, 1844, Thomas Butler King Papers, SHC; "Southern Women and Slavery," part 1, 55; Virginia Cary, *Letters on Female Character Addressed to a Young Lady on the Death of Her Mother,* 2d ed. (Richmond: Ariel, 1830), 203–207.

40. Thomas Jefferson, *Notes on the State of Virginia,* ed. William Peden (New York: Norton, 1982), 162; Jane Turner Censer, *North Carolina Planters and Their Children, 1800–1860* (Baton Rouge: Louisiana State University Press, 1984), 146–47; Cary, *Letters on Female Character,* 206; Mergen, *Play and Playthings,* 42.

41. TBHF to ARH, September 5, 1858, November 15, 1858, MDAH; Maxine Lorraine Clark, "Race Concepts and Self-Esteem in Black Children" (Ph. D. diss., University of Illinois, 1979), 17–22.

42. TBHF to ARH, August 8, 1861, June 13, 1859, September 4, 1860, January 4, 1862, MDAH; TBHF Diary Transcript, December 25, 1861, MDAH.

43. Blackford Diary, February 3, 1849, SHC.

44. Censer, *North Carolina Planters and their Children,* 147 (italics in the original).

45. J. G. Clinkscales, *On the Old Plantation: Reminiscences of His Boyhood* (New York: Negro Universities Press, 1969), 55–56 (italics in the original).

46. Perdue et al., *Weevils in the Wheat,* 109; Suzanne Lebsock, *The Free Women of Petersburg: Status and Culture in a Southern Town, 1784–1860* (New York: Norton, 1984), 11; Wiggins, "The Play of Slave Children," 31; Catherine Broun Diary, December 25, 1864, John Peter Broun Papers, SHC.

47. Preston, *Young Frederick Douglass,* 92; Perdue et al., *Weevils in the Wheat,* 84.

48. Hilary Abner Herbert, "Reminiscences" (unpublished manuscript) 19, Hilary Abner Herbert Papers, SHC; Leslie Howard Owens, *This Species of Property: Slave Life and Culture in the Old South* (New York: Oxford University Press, 1977), 204; Wiggins, "The Play of Slave Children," 30.

49. Herbert, "Reminiscences," SHC, 19.

50. L. Minor Blackford, *Mine Eyes Have Seen the Glory: The Story of A Virginia Lady Mary Berkeley Minor Blackford, 1802–1896 Who Taught Her Sons to Hate Slavery and to Love the Union* (Cambridge: Harvard University Press, 1954), 29–31.

51. Rawick, *The American Slave,* II: South Carolina Narr. (Series 1), Part 1:167; III: South Carolina Narr. (Part 3), 19; Stroyer, *My Life in the South,* 24.

52. Rawick, *The American Slave,* XII: Oklahoma Narr. (Supplement, Series 1), 268; II: South Carolina Narr. (Series 1), Part 1:30; III: South Carolina Narr. (Series 1), Part 3: 64; X: Mississippi Narr. (Supplement, Series 1), Part 5:2004; I: Alabama Narr. (Supplement, Series 1), 237.

53. TBHF to ARH, September 14, 1860, MDAH.

54. Susan Bradford Eppes (Mrs. Nicholas Ware Eppes), *The Negro of the Old South: A Bit of Period History* (Macon: Burke, 1941), 67–68; TBHF to ARH, March 9, 1854, September 8, 1856, December 29, 1856, April 26, 1857, MDAH; TBHF to Emma Holder, undated letter in correspondence from TBHF to ARH, August 12, 1856, MDAH; Preston, *Young Frederick Douglass,* 31–32.

55. Bruce, "Play, Work, and Ethics," 43–44; William Elliot, *Carolina Sports, by Land and Water: Including Incidents of Devil-Fishing* (Charleston: Burges and James, 1846), 107; Rawick, *The American Slave*, XIII: Georgia Narr. (Series 2), Part 4:76; Perdue et al., *Weevils in the Wheat*, 281.

56. John Houston Bills Diary, October 13, 1859, April 18, 1859, July 4, 1860, John Houston Bills Papers, SHC; Mergen, *Play and Playthings*, 41.

57. Perdue et al., *Weevils in the Wheat*, 279; John W. Blassingame, *The Slave Community: Plantation Life in the Antebellum South*, 2d ed. (New York: Oxford University Press, 1979), 117; "Negro Folk-songs," SW 24 (February 1895): 31; William Wells Brown, *My Southern Home: or, The South and Its People* (New York: Negro Universities Press, 1969), 92–93; Rawick, *The American Slave*, XIII: Georgia Narr. (Series 2), Part 4:81–82.

58. Yetman, *Life Under the "Peculiar Institution,"* 62.

59. Rawick, *The American Slave*, XII: Georgia Narr. (Series 2) Part 1:59; TBHF to ARH, December 29, 1856, SHC.

60. Robert Ruffin Barrow Plantation Records, November 8, 1857, SHC; John Nevitt Diary, August 25, 1827, SHC.

61. "Negro Folk-songs," SW 31; Yetman, *Life Under the "Peculiar Institution,"* 62.

Corn shucking was not solely a leisure activity of enslaved persons. Southern whites also had corn shuckings replete with competition, prizes, and singing, generally followed by a supper and dance. Songs inspired workers to shuck with vigor. The leader shouted, "Pull off the shucks boys, pull off the shucks," "The night's getting off boys, the night's getting off," or "Give me a dram, sir, give me a dram," while the participants responded with a chorus of "Round up the corn boys, round up the corn" after each call by the leader.

See Frank Owsley, *Plain Folk of the Old South* (Chicago: Quadrangle, 1965), 111–12.

62. Henry Cathell Diary, December 24, 1851, SHC; Solomon Northup, "Twelve Years a Slave: Narrative of Solomon Northup," in *Puttin' On Ole Massa: The Slave Narratives of Henry Bibb, William Wells Brown, and Solomon Northup*, ed. Gilbert Osofsky (New York: Harper, 1969) 213; Rawick, *The American Slave*, III: South Carolina Narr. (Series 1), Part 3:66; Isabella Ritchie to Carlotte Ritchie, [n. d.] folder 57, Ritchie-Harrison Papers, EGS; Genovese, *Roll, Jordan, Roll*, 234; John Peter Broun Papers, December 25, 1865, SHC; White Hill Plantation Books, 10, SHC.

63. Barrow Plantation Records, January 15, 1857, SHC; Northup, "Twelve Years a Slave," 215; Rawick, *The American Slave*, XVI: Kentucky Narr. (Series 2), Part 2:9.

64. Frederick Douglass, *My Bondage and My Freedom* (New York: Dover, 1969), 254.

65. Gary A. Donaldson, "A Window on Slave Culture: Dances at Congo Square in New Orleans, 1800–1862," JNH 69 (Spring 1984): 65–66.

66. Bills Diary, July 4, 1860, SHC (italics in the original); Henry L. Cathell Diary, December 24, 1851, SHC.

See "Negro Folk-songs," SW 24 (February 1895): 31; Jones, *Step It Down*, 36–37; Blassingame, *The Slave Community*, 125; Dena J. Epstein, *Sinful Tunes and Spirituals: Black Folk Music to the Civil War* (Urbana: University of Illinois Press, 1977), 132–35, 141–44.

67. Paul A. Cimbala, "Fortunate Bondsmen: Black 'Musicianers' and Their Role as an Antebellum Southern Plantation Slave Elite," SS 18 (Fall 1979): 298.

68. Nevitt Diary, August 25, 1827, SHC; Perdue et al., *Weevils in the Wheat*, 50.

69. Rawick, *The American Slave*, XIV: North Carolina Narr. (Series 2), Part 1:99–102; Rawick, *The American Slave*, X: Mississippi Narr. (Supplement, Series), Part 5:23–85.

70. Steven E. Brown, "Sexuality in the Slave Community," *Phylon* 42 (Spring 1981): 3.

71. Harriet Jacobs, *Incidents in the Life of a Slave Girl: Written by Herself*, ed. Jean Fagan Yellin (Cambridge: Harvard University Press, 1987), 56; Herbert G. Gutman, *The Black Family in Slavery and Freedom, 1750–1925* (New York: Vintage, 1977), 75–76; White, *Ar'n't I a Woman?*, 95–96.

72. Rawick, *The American Slave*, XIV: North Carolina Narr. (Series 2), Part 1:101; II: South Carolina Narr. (Series 1), Part 1:57–58, 61; II: South Carolina Narr. (Series 1), Part 2:52; Blassingame, *The Slave Community*, 157–60.

73. Frank D. Banks, "Old Time Courtship," SW 24 (January 1895): 15; Blassingame, *The Slave Community*, 158–59; Rawick, *The American Slave*, III: South Carolina Narr. (Series 1), Part 4:43.

74. Daniel Webster Davis, "Echoes from a Plantation Party," SW 28 (February 1899): 56–57.

See Jones, *Step It Down*, 214–16.

75. Rawick, *The American Slave*, XIV: North Carolina Narr. (Series 2), Part 1:101.

76. Jim Crawford to Fannie, October 8, 1864, Abel Crawford Papers, DU; Rawick, *The American Slave*, XII: Georgia Narr. (Series 2), Part 1:78.

77. Rawick, *The American Slave*, X: Arkansas Narr., Part 6:301; III: Georgia Narr. (Supplement 1), Part 1:41, 123, 169, 456, 630.

78. Bibb, "Narrative of the Life and Adventures," 74–79; Maria Diedrich, "'My Love Is Black As Yours Is Fair': Premarital Love and Sexuality in the Antebellum Slave Narrative," *Phylon* 47 (September 1986): 242.

79. William Ezell to Colonel E. Peete, July 24, 1825, William Ezell Papers, NCDAH; Ronald L. Lewis, "Slave Families at Early Chesapeake Ironworks," VMH 86 (April 1978): 177.

80. Richard H. Steckel, "Slave Marriage and the Family," JFH 5 (Winter 1980): 411–12.

81. Rosengarten, *Tombee*, 154.

For details of Alfred and Ermine, Issay and Rose, Allen and Harriet, Ben and Emma, Lewis and Peggy, and Horace and Bettly's wedding ceremony see Francis Terry Leak Diary, October 27, 1856, SHC. Leak probably delayed individual marriages until there was a lull of the harvest.

82. Betsy Fleet and John D. P. Fuller, eds., *Green Mount, A Virginia Plantation Family during the Civil War: Being the Journal of Benjamin Robert Fleet and Letters of His Family* (Lexington: University Press of Kentucky, 1962), 43.

83. Blassingame, *The Slave Community*, 166–67; Rawick, *The American Slave*, XI: Arkansas Narr. (Series 2), Part 7:157; V: Texas Narr. (Series 1), Part 5:105, 213.

84. Rosengarten, *Tombee*, 154; Mary E. Bateman Diary, July 5, 1856, SHC; Rawick, *The American Slave*, X: Mississippi Narr. (Supplement, Series 1), Part 5: 2385.

85. Northup, "Twelve Years a Slave," 346; Rawick, *The American Slave*, IV: Texas Narr. (Series 1), Part 1: 551; VII: Mississippi Narr. (Supplement, Series 1), Part 2: 624.

An antebellum diary describes a slave wedding where the bride wore a "white wedding dress with veil and orange blossoms. All went well until trouble came, the Groom's owner sold him to a planter in Alabama. 'The children wept and the older people looked grim but so far as I can remember it was a thing taken for granted.'"

See "Diary of Julia," 19:345, William Alexander Hoke Papers, SHC.

86. Jacobs, *Incidents in the Life of a Slave Girl*, Genovese, *Roll, Jordan, Roll*, 462; Brown, "Sexuality in the Slave Community," 9.

87. Jacobs, *Incidents in the Life of a Slave Girl*, 37–42; Pauli Murray, *Proud Shoes: The Story of an American Family* (New York: Harper and Row, 1984), 39–44.

See Catherine Clinton, "Caught in the Web of the Big House: Women and Slavery," in *The Web of Southern Social Relations: Women, Family and Education*, ed. Walter Fraser, Jr. (Athens: University of Georgia Press, 1985), 19–34.

88. Douglass, *My Bondage and My Freedom*, 254.

See Peter Kolchin, "Reevaluating the Antebellum Slave Community: A Comparative Perspective," JAH 70 (December 1983): 579–601.

89. Douglass, *My Bondage and My Freedom*, 254; Yetman, *Life Under the "Peculiar Institution,"* 265.

4. "Knowledge unfits a child to be a slave"

1. See Thomas L. Webber, *Deep Like the Rivers: Education in the Slave Quarter Community, 1831–1865* (New York: Norton, 1978).

2. Hobbs to wife, 1833, Before Freedom Came Exhibit, MC.

For a discussion of psychological abuse of children see Leonard Shengold, *Soul Murder: The Effects of Childhood Abuse and Deprivation* (New Haven: Yale University Press, 1989).

3. Prince Woodfin to Nickles Woodfin, April 25, 1853, Nicholas Washington Woodfin Papers, SHC.

4. Deborah Gray White, *Ar'n't I a Woman? Female Slaves in the Plantation South* (New York: Norton, 1985), 94–95, 123; Jacqueline Jones, *Labor of Love, Labor of Sorrow: Black Women, Work and the Family, from Slavery to the Present* (New York: Vintage, 1986), 16.

5. Woodfin to Woodfin, April 25, 1853, SHC; Charlotte Forten, "Life on the Sea Islands," AM Part I (May 1864): 592; Everard Green Baker Diary, "Projects of Life," II:195, SHC.

6. Harriet A. Jacobs, *Incidents in the Life of a Slave Girl: Written by Herself*, ed. Jean Fagan Yellin (Cambridge: Harvard University Press, 1987), 9.

7. Norman R. Yetman, ed., *Life Under the "Peculiar Institution": Selections from the Slave Narrative Collection* (New York: Holt, Rinehart and Winston, 1970), 327.

8. Toni Morrison, *Beloved* (New York: Plume, 1988), 165.

9. Yetman, *Life Under the "Peculiar Institution,"* 292.

10. W. W. Gilmer, "Management of Slaves," SP 12 (April 1852): 106–107; Webber, *Deep Like the Rivers*, 26; John W. Blassingame, *The Slave Community: Plantation Life in the Antebellum South*, 2d ed. (New York: Oxford University Press, 1979), 256–57.

11. Jacob Stroyer, *My Life in the South* (Salem: Salem Observer, 1889), 14–15.

12. Tryphena Blanche Holder Fox (hereafter cited as TBHF) to Anna Rose Holder (hereafter cited as ARH), September 5, 1858, November 15, 1858, MDAH; Ophelia Settle Egypt, J. Masuoke, and Charles S. Johnson, eds., *Unwritten History of Slavery: Autobiographical Account of Negro Ex-Slaves* (Nashville: Fisk University, 1954), 263; Jane Turner Censer, *North Carolina Planters and Their Children, 1800–1860* (Baton Rouge: Louisiana State University Press, 1984), 147; Maxine Lorraine Clark, "Race Concepts and Self-Esteem in Black Children" (Ph. D. diss., University of Illinois, 1979), 17–22.

13. Eugene D. Genovese, *Roll, Jordan, Roll: The World the Slaves Made* (New York: Vintage, 1976), 3–7, 74.

14. Henry Bibb, "Narrative of the Life and Adventures of Henry Bibb: An American Slave Written by Himself," in *Puttin' On Ole Massa: The Slave Narratives of Henry Bibb, William Wells Brown, and Solomon Northup*, ed. Gilbert Osofsky (New York: Harper, 1969), 66; Charshee Charlotte Lawrence-McIntyre, "The Double Meanings of The Spirituals," JBS 17 (June 1987): 390.

See Bertram Wyatt-Brown, "The Mask of Obedience: Male Slave Psychology in the Old South," AHR 93 (December 1988): 1228–1252; Adam Foster to Cynthia, January 9, 1847, Adam Foster Letter (#10103), UVA. Mary Boykin Chesnut, *A Diary from Dixie*, ed. Ben Ames Williams (Boston: Houghton Mifflin, 1950), 38.

15. See Jack L. Daniel, Geneva Smitherman-Donaldson, and Milford A. Jeremiah, "Makin' A Way Outa No Way: The Proverb Tradition in the Black Experience," JBS 17 (June 1987): 482–508.

16. Samuel Cram Jackson Diary, December 10, 1832, SHC; David Brion Davis, *The Problem of Slavery in Western Culture* (Ithaca: Cornell University Press, 1966), 465;

James Mellon, ed., *Bullwhip Days: The Slave Remember* (New York: Weidenfeld and Nicolson, 1988), 49.

17. See Alex Haley, *Roots: The Saga of an American Family* (Garden City: Doubleday, 1976); Rawick, *The American Slave*, VIII: Arkansas Narr. (Series 2), Part 2:157; III: South Carolina Narr. (Series 1), Part 3:64–65; XII: Oklahoma Narr. (Supplement 1), Part 1:268; I: Alabama Narr. (Supplement 1), Part 1:237.

See also J. C. Furnas, "Patrolling the Middle Passage," in *Readings in American History, 1607–1865*, ed. Robert M. Spector (New York: American Heritage, 1993), 155–62.

18. Bruno Bettelheim, *The Uses of Enchantment: The Meaning and Importance of Fairy Tales* (New York: Knopf, 1977), 26, 45–53.

See Ruth Michaelis-Jena, *The Brothers Grimm* (New York: Praeger, 1970).

19. Blassingame, *The Slave Community*, 127–28; Michaelis-Jena, *The Brothers Grimm*, 48.

See Paul D. Escott, *Slavery Remembered: A Record of Twentieth-Century Slave Narratives* (Chapel Hill: University of North Carolina Press, 1979), 18–35; Ariel Dorfman, *The Empire's Old Clothes: What the Lone Ranger, Babar, and Other Innocent Heroes Do to Our Minds* (New York: Pantheon, 1983), 3–64; Robert Bone, *Down Home: A History of Afro-American Short Fiction from Its Beginnings to the End of the Harlem Renaissance* (New York: Capricorn, 1975), 19–41.

20. Joel Chandler Harris, *Uncle Remus* (New York: Schocken, 1972), 78–79; John W. Roberts, "Strategy, Morality, and Worldview of the Afro-American Spirituals and Trickster Tales," WJBS 6 (Summer 1982): 102–103; Lawrence W. Levine, *Black Culture and Black Consciousness: Afro-American Folk Thought from Slavery to Freedom* (New York: Oxford University Press, 1977), 102–21; Ruth Polk Patterson, *The Seed of Sally Good'n: A Black Family of Arkansas 1833–1953* (Lexington: University Press of Kentucky, 1985), 95–97.

21. Levine, *Black Culture and Black Consciousness*, 121–33; Wyatt-Brown, "The Mask of Obedience," 1242; Bettelheim, *The Uses of Enchantment*, 58; Charles W. Joyner, "The Creolization of Slave Folklife," in *The Afro-American Slaves: Community or Chaos?* ed. Randall Miller (Malabar: Krieger, 1981), 131.

22. Melville J. Herskovits, *Dahomey: An Ancient West African Kingdom*, vol. I (Evanston: Northwestern University Press, 1967), 281–82; David Brion Davis, *The Problem of Slavery in Western Culture* (Ithaca: Cornell University Press, 1966), 469; White, *Ar'n't I a Woman?*, 96–97; Herbert G. Gutman, *The Black Family in Slavery and Freedom, 1750–1925* (New York: Vintage, 1977), 82–83; Charles L. Perdue, Jr., Thomas E. Barden, and Robert K. Phillips, eds., *Weevils in the Wheat: Interviews with Virginia Ex-Slaves* (Bloomington: Indiana University Press, 1980), 95–96.

See Herskovits, *Dahomey*, 278, for a description of the female exercises.

23. Jacobs, *Incidents in the Life of a Slave Girl*, 27.

24. Perdue et al., *Weevils in the Wheat*, 96; Rawick, *The American Slave*, XIII: Georgia Narr. (Series 2), Part 3:69.

See Thelma Jennings, "'Us Colored Women Had To Go Through a Plenty': Sexual Exploitation of African-American Slave Women," JWH 3 (Winter 1990): 46; Maria Diedrich, "'My Love Is Black As Yours Is Fair': Premarital Love and Sexuality in the Antebellum Slave Narrative," *Phylon* 47 (September 1986): 238–47; Catherine Clinton, *The Plantation Mistress: Woman's World in the Old South* (New York: Pantheon, 1982), 69–70, 207–208; Gutman, *The Black Family in Slavery and Freedom*, 82–83; Eric O. Ayisi, *An Introduction to the Study of African Culture*, 2d ed. (London: Heinemann, 1986), 6.

25. White, *Ar'n't I a Woman?*, 94–95.

26. Rawick, *The American Slave*, XII: Georgia Narr. (Series 2), Part 2:261; "Rules for Government of Plantation," Cornhill Plantation Book, 105–107, McDonald Furman Papers, DU; "Rules for Overseer," William Henry Sims Papers, SHC; William Ethelbert Ervin Book, January 1847, SHC; Kenneth M. Stampp, *The Peculiar Institution: Slavery in the Ante-Bellum South* (New York: Knopf, 1967), 172.

27. See Daniel T. Rogers, "Socializing Middle-Class Children: Institutions, Fables, and Work Values in Nineteenth-Century America," JSocH 13 (Spring 1980): 354–66, for a discussion of the socialization of middle-class white children in the nineteenth century.

28. Launcelot Minor Blackford Diary, February 24, 1848, March 30, 1848, April 12, 1848, July 16, 1848, September 4, 1848, November 12, 1848, December 15, 1848, December 27, 1848, February 2, 1849, SHC, for details of the boys' readings.

See John R. Adams, *Edward Everett Hale* (Boston: Twayne, 1977).

29. Thomas Jefferson, *Notes on the State of Virginia*, ed. William Peden (New York: Norton, 1982), 139–40; Rawick, *The American Slave*, XIII: Georgia Narr. (Series 2), Part 4:78.

30. Booker T. Washington, *Up from Slavery, An Autobiography* (New York: Bantam, 1967), 5.

31. Rawick, *The American Slave*, III: South Carolina Narr. (Series 1), Part 3:32; *The American Slave*, V: Texas Narr., 213; Janet Cornelius, "We Slipped and Learned to Read: Slave Accounts of the Literacy Process, 1830–1865," *Phylon* 44 (September 1983): 177; Loren Schweninger, "A Slave Family in the Ante Bellum South," JNH 60 (January 1975): 35; Anthony Butler to Franklin Benjamin Due, February 11, 1872, Thomas Roderick Dew Collection, EGS; Stroyer, *My Life in the South*, 33.

32. Thomas Pittus, First Summer School File, HUA; Cornelius, "We Slipped and Learned to Read," 179.

33. John Hartwell Cocke (hereafter cited as JHC) to Henry Smith, October 1, 1833, John Hartwell Cocke Papers (#640), UVA.

34. Ellen Burrows to JHC, August 10, 1829, August 13, 1829 (#640), UVA; Louisa Cocke to JHC, January 9, 1830 (#640), UVA; Martin Boyd Coyner, Jr., "John Hartwell Cocke of Bremo: Agriculture and Slavery in the Antebellum South," (Ph. D. diss., University of Virginia, 1961), 343–44.

35. Louisa Cocke to JHC, January 9, 1830 (#640), UVA; Louisa Cocke Diary, January 2, 1831, June 3, 1831, June 21, 1831, July 11, 1831, July 27, 1831, August 1, 1831, John Hartwell Cocke Papers (#640), UVA.

36. Cocke Diary (#640), January 12, 1834, UVA.

See Randall Miller, ed., *"Dear Master": Letters of a Slave Family* (Ithaca: Cornell University Press, 1978).

37. Miller, *"Dear Master,"* 196.

38. Ibid., 198, 201.

39. Cornelius, "We Slipped and Learned to Read," 178–79.

40. Marion L. Starkey, *The First Plantation: A History of Hampton and Elizabeth City County, Virginia, 1607–1887* (Hampton: Houston, 1936), 73; Robert F. Engs, *Freedom's First Generation: Black Hampton, Virginia, 1861–1890* (Philadelphia: University of Pennsylvania Press, 1979), 12–13.

41. Yetman, *Life Under the "Peculiar Institution,"* 137; Cornelius, "We Slipped and Learned to Read," 176; J. G. Clinkscales, *On the Old Plantation: Reminiscences of His Boyhood* (New York: Negro Universities Press, 1969), 44–46.

42. Gerda Lerner, ed., *Black Women in White America: A Documentary History* (New York: Vintage, 1973), 27.

43. Frederick Douglass, *The Narrative and Selected Writings*, ed. Michael Meyer (New York: Random House, 1984), 55–56.

44. "George Horton, The Slave Poet," *The University Magazine* 7 (May 1888): 229–30, North Caroliniana Collection, University of North Carolina, Chapel Hill, North Carolina; Richard Barksdale and Keneth Kinnamon, eds., *Black Writers of America: A Comprehensive Anthology* (New York: Macmillan, 1972), 219–22.

45. Lerner, *Black Women in White America*, 29.

46. William Taylor Barry Letterbook, May 11, 1833 (#2561), UVA.

47. Perdue et al., *Weevils in the Wheat*, 96–98.

48. Frederick Douglass, *Life and Times of Frederick Douglass: Written by Himself* (New York: Collier, 1962), 151.

49. June Purcell Guild, *Black Laws of Virginia: A Summary of the Legislative Acts of Virginia Concerning Negroes from Earliest Times to the Present* (Richmond: Whittet and Shepperson, 1936), 175–76; Pittus, Summer file, HUA; Janet Duitsman Cornelius, *When I Can Read My Title Clear: Literacy, Slavery, and Religion in the Antebellum South* (Columbia: University of South Carolina Press, 1991), 33; Albert J. Raboteau, *Slave Religion: The "Invisible Institution" in the Antebellum South* (New York: Oxford University Press, 1978), 239.
   Missouri passed a law prohibiting instruction of blacks in 1847.
   See R. I. Brigham, "Negro Education in Ante Bellum Missouri," JNH 30 (October 1945): 412–13.

50. JHC to Henry Smith, October 1, 1833 (#640), UVA.

51. Jane A. Crouch, First Summer School File, HUA.

52. Blackford Diary, February 12, 1849, March 6, 1849, March 19, 1849, April 12, 1849, SHC.

53. W. E. Burghardt Du Bois, *Black Reconstruction in America: An Essay toward a History of the Past Which Black Folk Played in the Attempt to Reconstruct Democracy in America, 1860–1880* (Cleveland/New York: World, 1965), 638; Genovese, *Roll, Jordan, Roll*, 563; James Page to Harriet Parkhill, November 18, 1868, John Parkhill Papers, SHC.

54. Carleton Mabee, "Sojourner Truth, Bold Prophet: Why Did She Never Learn to Read?" NYH 69 (January 1988): 55–77.
   See Henry Louis Gates, Jr., ed., *The Schomburg Library of Nineteenth-Century Black Women Writers: Six Women's Slave Narratives* (New York: Oxford University Press, 1988).

55. Washington, *Up from Slavery*, 5; Stroyer, *My Life in the South*, 24.

56. Hobbs to wife, 1833, Before Freedom Came Exhibit, MC.

57. Sterling Stuckey, *Slave Culture: Nationalist Theory and the Foundations of Black America* (New York: Oxford University Press, 1987), 24; George P. Rawick, *From Sundown to Sunup: The Making of the Black Community* (Westport: Greenwood, 1972), 32; Cornelius, *When I Can Read My Title Clear*, 3–4, 13.

58. Ellen Burrows to JHC, August 10, 1829, August 13, 1829 (#640), UVA.

59. Norrece T. Jones, Jr., *Born a Child of Freedom, Yet a Slave: Mechanisms of Control and Strategies of Resistance in Antebellum South Carolina* (Hanover: Wesleyan University Press, 1990), 129–61; Lester B. Scherer, "Slave Religion," in *Dictionary of Afro-American Slavery*, ed. Randall M. Miller and John David Smith (Westport: Greenwood, 1988), 631; Olli Alho, *The Religion of the Slaves: A Study of the Religious Tradition and Behavior of Plantation Slaves in the United States 1830–1865* (Helsinki: Academia Scientiarum Fennica, 1976), 58–59; Blassingame, *The Slave Community*, 134; Rawick, *From Sundown to Sunup*, 30–32.

60. See Jean E. Friedman, *The Enclosed Garden: Women and Community in the Evangelical South, 1830–1890* (Chapel Hill: University of North Carolina Press, 1985), 78; Mechal Sobel, *Trabelin' On: The Slave Journey to an Afro-Baptist Faith* (Westport: Greenwood, 1979).

61. Eugene D. Genovese and Elizabeth Fox-Genovese, "The Religious Ideals of Southern Slave Society," GHQ 70 (Spring 1986): 1–16; Hunter Brown Diary, vol. I, December 17, 1834, UVA; Alho, *The Religion of Slaves*, 61; Webber, *Deep Like the Rivers*, 44.

62. Webber, *Deep Like the Rivers*, 47.

63. Francis Hanson Diary, March 30, 1860, November 4, 1858, April 17, 1863, SHC; Bell Irvin Wiley, *Southern Negroes, 1861–1865* (New Haven: Yale University Press, 1965), 103.

See the James Hervey Greenlee Diary, especially 1848, SHC.

64. White Hill Plantation Books, 1:10, SHC. Page Putnam Miller, "Women in the Vanguard of the Sunday School Movement," JPH 58 (Winter 1980): 321–22; Webber, *Deep Like the Rivers*, 47; Julia Floyd Smith, *Slavery and Rice Culture in Low Country Georgia, 1750–1860* (Knoxville: University of Tennessee Press, 1985), 154.

65. Alho, *The Religion of Slaves*, 62–68.

66. Ibid., 136.

67. Hanson Diary, March 30, 1860, November 4, 1858, April 17, 1863, SHC; William Ethelbert Ervin Book, vol. 2, January 10, 1847, March 24, 1847, SHC; JHC to Henry Smith, October 1, 1833 (#640), UVA; Miller, *"Dear Master,"* 34.

68. Mary Arthur Stoudemire, "Black Parishioners of the Chapel of the Cross, 1844–1866," NCGSJ 9 (May 1983): 83–84; Catherine Clinton, "Caught in the Web of the Big House: Women and Slavery," in *The Web of Southern Social Relations: Women, Family, and Education*, ed. Walter Fraser (Athens: University of Georgia Press, 1985), 21; Pauli Murray, *Proud Shoes: The Story of an American Family* (New York: Harper and Row, 1984), 53.

69. Milton C. Sernett, ed., *Afro-American Religious History: A Documentary Witness* (Durham: Duke University Press, 1985), 64 (emphasis in the original); Webber, *Deep Like the Rivers*, 50–51; Perdue et al., *Weevils in the Wheat*, 100, 183; Yetman, *Life Under the "Peculiar Institution,"* 181–82.

70. Webber, *Deep Like the Rivers*, 55; Hanson Diary, March 30, 1860, November 4, 1858, April 17, 1863, SHC; Mary Arthur Stoudemire, "Black Parishioners of the Chapel of the Cross, 1844–1866," 78–84; Clinton, "Caught in the Web of the Big House," 21; Murray, *Proud Shoes*, 53.

71. Perdue et al., *Weevils in the Wheat*, 79; Raboteau, *Slave Religion*, 164–65, 215–16; Robert L. Hall, "Black and White Christians in Florida, 1822–1861," in *Masters and Slaves in the House of the Lord: Race and Religion in the American South, 1740–1870*, ed. John B. Boles (Lexington: University Press of Kentucky, 1988), 81; Charshee Charlotte Lawrence-McIntyre, "The Double Meanings of the Spirituals," JBS 17 (June 1987): 386.

72. Rawick, *The American Slave*, XI: Arkansas Narr. (Series 2), Part 7: 227; Benjamin E. Mays, *The Negro's God: As Reflected in His Literature* (New York: Atheneum, 1973), 19–30; Raboteau, *Slave Religion*, 264.

73. *Jubilee and Plantation Songs. Characteristic Favorites, As sung by the Hampton Students, Jubilee Singers, Fisk University Students, and Other Concert Companies* (Boston: Oliver Ditson, 1887), 8, 24, 57, 64–65, 68; Raboteau, *Slave Religion*, 218–19; George P. Rawick, ed., *The American Slave: A Composite Autobiography*, vol. 19: *God Struck Me Dead* (Westport: Greenwood, 1976), 41–45; Yetman, *Life Under the "Peculiar Institution,"* 227; Miller, *"Dear Master,"* 196–98, 224; Mary Ellison, "Resistance to Oppression: Black Women's Response to Slavery in the United States," SA 4 (May 1983): 59.

74. Douglass, *The Narrative*, 29; Douglass, *My Bondage and My Freedom* (New York: Dover, 1969), 99; Lawrence-McIntyre, "The Double Meanings of the Spirituals," 382, 389.

75. *Jubilee and Plantation Songs*, 76.

76. Sobel, *Trabelin' On*, 142; Charles W. Joyner, *Down by the Riverside: A South Carolina Community* (Urbana: University of Illinois Press, 1984), 160; Stuckey, *Slave Culture*, 11, 26, 87.

77. Stuckey, *Slave Culture*, 31; Raboteau, *Slave Religion*, 267.

See Robert Simpson, "The Shout and Shouting in Slave Religion of the United States," *Southern Quarterly* 23 (Spring 1985): 34–47.

78. Clifton H. Johnson, ed., *God Struck Me Dead: Religious Conversion Experiences and Autobiographies of Ex-Slaves* (Philadelphia: Pilgrim, 1969), 19–20; Friedman, *The Enclosed Garden*, 72.

79. Joyner, *Down by the Riverside*, 161; Alho, *The Religion of Slaves*, 182–83.

80. Johnson, *God Struck Me Dead*, 123.

81. Ibid., 122, 145, 164.

82. Miller, *"Dear Master,"* 224–25.

83. C. A. Hentz Diary, 1:40, Hentz Family Papers, SHC.

See Luther P. Jackson, "Religious Development of the Negro in Virginia from 1760 to 1860," *JNH* 16 (April 1931): 168–239; Perdue et al., *Weevils in the Wheat*, 150; James B. Lawrence, "Religious Education of the Negro in the Colony of Georgia," *GHQ* 14 (March 1930): 41–57, argues that provisions were made for the education of blacks less than three months after slavery was permitted in 1749 and those efforts continued down to the Revolutionary War.

84. John W. Blassingame, "Status and Social Structure in the Slave Community: Evidence from New Sources," in *Perspectives and Irony in American Slavery*, ed. Harry P. Owens (Jackson: University Press of Mississippi, 1976), 142; Johnson, *God Struck Me Dead*, 69; Rawick, *The American Slave*, XI: Arkansas Narr. (Series 1), Part 7:7, 227; Raboteau, *Slave Religion*, 267; Stroyer, *My Life in the South*, 23–24, 27.

85. Forten, "Life on the Sea Islands," 598–99.

86. Stuckey, *Slave Culture*, 88; Forten, "Life on the Sea Islands," 593; Blassingame, "Status and Social Structure," 142.

87. Raboteau, *Slave Religion*, 240.

88. Miller, *"Dear Master,"* 198, 201.

89. Randall Miller, "Slaves and Southern Catholicism," in *Masters and Slaves in the House of the Lord: Race and Religion in the American South, 1740–1870*, ed. John B. Boles (Lexington: University Press of Kentucky, 1988), 132–40.

90. Miller, "Slaves and Southern Catholicism," 127–52; Terry Alford, *Prince among Slaves: The True Story of an African Prince Sold into Slavery in the American South* (New York: Oxford University Press, 1986), 55, 57, 78–80; Raboteau, *Slave Religion*, 46–47; Michael A. Gomez, "Muslims in Early America," (unpublished paper presented at the Association for the Study of Afro-American Life and History Conference, October, 1990, Chicago, Illinois; in possession of the author), 16–17.

See Daniel B. Tho, "Chattel With A Soul: The Autobiography of a Moravian Slave," *PMHB* 112 (July 1988): 433–51.

91. Samuel Cram Jackson Diary, December 10, 1832, SHC.

92. Douglass, *My Bondage and My Freedom*, 238–49; Jessie Gaston Mulira, "The Case of Voodoo in New Orleans," in *Africanisms in American Culture*, ed. Joseph E. Holloway (Bloomington: Indiana University Press, 1990), 34–40; Raboteau, *Slave Religion*, 79–82; Joyner, *Down by the Riverside*, 144–45.

Voodoo is generally found in Haiti rather than in the southern United States.

93. Rawick, *The American Slave*, III: South Carolina Narr. (Series 1), Part 3:78; Rawick, *The American Slave*, XI: Arkansas Narr. (Series 2) Part 7:266; Bibb, "Narrative of the Life and Adventures," 73, 79.

94. Lavina to Dear Missis, July 1849, Lawton Family Papers, USC. Thanks to Stephanie McCurry for providing this reference.

See Blassingame, *The Slave Community*, 170–71; Genovese, *Roll, Jordan, Roll*, 481.

95. Lavina to Missis, July 1849, SC.

96. Willis and Martha's marriage of twelve years ended with his September 16, 1862, death. John Houston Bills Diary, September 30, 1854–September 16, 1862, John Houston Bills Papers, SHC.

See Appendix B.

97. See White, *Ar'n't I a Woman?*, 110.

98. John Houston Bills Diary, September 30, 1854–September 16, 1862, John Houston Bills Papers, SHC; White, *Ar'n't I a Woman?*, 98.

5. "What has Ever become of my Presus little girl"

1. Harriet Jacobs, *Incidents in the Life of a Slave Girl*, ed. Jean F. Yellin (Cambridge: Harvard University Press, 1987), 1; Henry Bibb, "Narrative of the Life and Adventures of Henry Bibb," in *Puttin' On Ole Massa: The Slave Narratives of Henry Bibb, William Wells Brown, and Solomon Northup*, ed. Gilbert Osofsky (New York: Harper, 1969), 65; Norrece T. Jones, Jr., *Born a Child of Freedom, Yet a Slave: Mechanisms of Control and Strategies of Resistance in Antebellum South Carolina* (Hanover: Wesleyan University Press, 1990), 3–10; Laurence Shore, "The Poverty of Tragedy in Historical Writing on Southern Slavery," SAQ 85 (Spring 1986): 147–162; Peter Kolchin, "Reevaluating the Antebellum Slave Community: A Comparative Perspective," JAH 70 (December 1983): 579–601.

2. Richard Hildreth, *Despotism in America: An Inquiry into the Nature, Results, and Legal Basis of the Slave-Holding System in the United States* (Boston: John P. Jewett, 1854), 36; Jones, *Born a Child of Freedom*, 10.

3. See J. Thomas Wren, "A 'Two-Fold Character': The Slave as Person and Property in Virginia Court Cases, 1800–1860," SS 54 (Winter 1985): 425–31.

4. I. de Courcy Laffan to Thomas Ritchie, May 27, 1841, Laffan Letter, EGS.

5. George P. Rawick, ed., *The American Slave: A Composite Autobiography*, 19 vols. (Westport: Greenwood, 1972), XI: Arkansas Narr. (Series 2), Part 7:15, 16, 23, 99, 145, 154, 159, 163, 191, 201–203; Rawick, *The American Slave*, XI: Missouri Narr. (Series 2), Part 7:131; George P. Rawick, *From Sundown to Sunup: The Making of the Black Community* (Westport: Greenwood, 1972), 56–61; Charles L. Perdue, Jr., Thomas E. Barden, and Robert K. Phillips, eds., *Weevils in the Wheat: Interviews with Virginia Ex-Slaves* (Bloomington: Indiana University Press, 1980), 299; Jane Turner Censer, *North Carolina Planters and Their Children, 1800–1860* (Baton Rouge: Louisiana State University Press, 1984), 145.

6. Rawick, *The American Slave*, XI: Arkansas Narr. (Series 2), Part 7:202; Bibb, "Narrative of the Life and Adventures," 115; Perdue et al., *Weevils in the Wheat*, 267.

See Dwight L. Dumond, *Anti-Slavery: The Crusade for Freedom in America* (Ann Arbor: University of Michigan Press, 1961), 115, 254.

7. Dick Journal (#4528), August 1807, UVA.

8. Kenneth M. Stampp, *The Peculiar Institution: Slavery in the Ante-Bellum South* (New York: Knopf, 1967), 178; Hildreth, *Despotism in America*, 38–39; "Instructions to overseer," William Henry Sims Papers, SHC; "Agreement between Willis P. Bocock and Louis O. Collins," July 15, 1860, Willis P. Bocock Paper, SHC.

See also James O. Breeden, ed., *Advice among Masters: The Ideal in Slave Management in the Old South* (Westport: Greenwood, 1980), 292–95.

9. William Ethelbert Ervin Book, January 1847, SHC (emphasis in the original); Cornhill Plantation Book, "Rules for Government of Plantation, *Overseer*," 103–104, McDonald Furman Papers, DU; Bocock Papers, "Rules for the Overseer or Manager," SHC; Frances Anne Kemble, *Journal of a Residence on a Georgian Plantation in 1838–1839*, ed. John A. Scott (Athens: University of Georgia, 1984), 79.

The Alabama slaveholder William Jemison's plantation rules contained a mixture of rewards and punishments. If found guilty of stealing, for the first offense slaves forfeited half of their wages. On the second offense, the wages were divided equally between the informant and the "honest." Along with the financial penalties were lashes.

See William Jemison, "Proclamation, 1827," Jemison Papers, SHC; William Kauffman Scarborough, *The Overseer: Plantation Management in the Old South* (Athens: University of Georgia Press, 1984), 67–109.

10. See Andrew Fede, "Legitimized Violent Slave Abuse in the American South, 1619–1865: A Case Study of Law and Social Change in Six Southern States," AJLH 29 (April 1985): 93–150, especially 133.

11. Frederick Law Olmsted, *A Journey in the Back Country* (New York: Schocken, 1970), 83–84, 87; James W. C. Pennington, "The Fugitive Blacksmith or Events in the History of James W. C. Pennington Pastor of a Presbyterian Church New York, Formerly a Slave in the State of Maryland," in *Great Slave Narratives*, ed. Arna Bontemps (Boston: Beacon, 1969), 208; Scarborough, *The Overseer*, 78–79.

12. Jones, *Born a Child of Freedom*, 61–63.

13. Rawick, *The American Slave*, III: South Carolina Narr. (Series 1) Part 3:49, 201; Rawick, *The American Slave*, II: South Carolina Narr. (Series 1), Part 2:310; Theodore Rosengarten, *Tombee: Portrait of a Cotton Planter* (New York: Morrow, 1986), 153.

14. Perdue et al., *Weevils in the Wheat*, 317.

William Wells Brown's owner hired him out to a man who used the "Virginia play," wherein the victim was tied, whipped, and kept in a smoke house while tobacco stems burned, as punishment. See William Wells Brown, "Narrative of William Wells Brown: A Fugitive Slave Written by Himself" in *Puttin' On Ole Massa: The Slave Narratives of Henry Bibb, William Wells Brown, and Solomon Northup*, ed. Gilbert Osofsky (New York: Harper, 1969), 183–84.

15. William L. Van De Burg, *The Slave Driver: Black Agricultural Supervision in the Antebellum South* (Westport: Greenwood, 1979), 19, 85; Eugene D. Genovese, *Roll, Jordan, Roll: The World the Slaves Made* (New York: Vintage, 1976), 377, 380; Jacob Stroyer, *My Life in the South* (Salem: Salem Observer, 1889), 25.

16. See Thomas Jefferson, *Notes on the State of Virginia*, ed. William Peden (New York: Norton, 1982), 162; Jane Turner Censer, *North Carolina Planters and Their Children, 1800–1860* (Baton Rouge: Louisiana State University Press, 1984), 146–47.

17. Solomon Northup, "Twelve Years a Slave: Narrative of Solomon Northup," in *Puttin' On Ole Massa: The Slave Narratives of Henry Bibb, William Wells Brown, and Solomon Northup*, ed. Gilbert Osofsky (New York: Harper and Row, 1969), 370.

18. David K. Wiggins, "The Play of Slave Children in the Plantation Communities of the Old South, 1820–1960," JSpH 7 (Summer 1980): 25; Norman R. Yetman, *Life Under the "Peculiar Institution": Selections from the Slave Narrative Collection* (New York: Holt, Rinehart and Winston), 125–26; "Negro Folk-Songs," SW 24 (February 1895): 31; Perdue et al., *Weevils in the Wheat*, 290, 294; Charshee Charlotte Lawrence-McIntyre, "The Double Meanings of the Spirituals," JBS 17 (June 1987): 386–87; Fede, "Legitimized Violent Slave Abuse," AJLH 29 (April 1985): 96–97, 105–106.

See Perdue et al., *Weevils in the Wheat*, 34, 267.

19. Michael Petersen, "Patrollers and Social Conflict in the Antebellum South" (seminar paper for History 601, The Antebellum South, Fall 1987, Indiana University of Pennsylvania, Indiana, Pennsylvania; in possession of the author), 12–15.

20. Rawick, *The American Slave,* II: South Carolina Narr. (Series 1), Part 1:38–41.

21. John Houston Bills Diary, August 31, 1864, SHC; John W. Blassingame, *The Slave Community: Plantation Life in the Antebellum South,* rev. ed. (New York: Oxford University Press, 1979), 178.

22. Brenda Stevenson, "Distress and Discord in Virginia Slave Families, 1830–1860," in *In Joy and in Sorrow: Family, and Marriage in the Victorian South, 1830–1900,* ed. Carol Bleser (New York: Oxford University Press, 1991), 110.

23. Pennington, *The Fugitive Blacksmith,* 211 (emphasis in the original).

24. Bennet H. Barrow, *Plantation Life in the Florida Parishes of Louisiana,* ed. Edwin Adams Davis (New York: AMS, 1967).

25. Yetman, *Life Under the "Peculiar Institution,"* 40; Stroyer, *My Life in the South,* 20; Douglass, *My Bondage and My Freedom,* 93.

26. Perdue et al., *Weevils in the Wheat,* 327; Stroyer, *My Life in the South,* 22–23.

27. *Jubilee and Plantation Songs. Characteristic Favorites, As sung by the Hampton Students, Jubilee Singers, Fisk University Students, and Other Concert Companies* (Boston: Oliver Ditson, 1887), 57.

28. Toni Morrison, *Beloved* (New York: Plume, 1988), 209.

29. See Robert L. Hall, "Lord Deliver Us from Cliometrics and from 70.56 Whippings per Year: Prolegomena to a Social History of Slave Whippings in the United States," (unpublished paper in possession of the author, n.d.), 1–8; Joe M. Richardson, ed., *The Trial and Imprisonment of Jonathan Walker at Pensacola, Florida for Aiding Slaves to Escape from Bondage* (Gainesville: University Press of Florida, 1974); Robert William Fogel and Stanley L. Engerman, *Time on the Cross: The Economics of American Negro Slavery* (Boston: Little, Brown, 1974), 144–47.

30. Perdue et al., *Weevils in the Wheat,* 267.

31. For an unusual way of chastising slaves, see Davis, *Plantation Life in the Florida Parishes of Louisiana* (New York: AMS, 1967), 183.

32. See Jones, *Born a Child of Freedom,* 37–63.

Michael Tadman cautions against the line of argument that slaveholders sold slaves because of the "need to discipline troublesome slaves," emergencies, or indebtedness. If these factors alone were indeed responsible for the massive scale of trading, the institution of slavery was in "chronic disorder." Tadman writes, "In reality, the great traffic in slaves stemmed, not from special emergencies, but instead from the fundamental racist insensitivity of masters, and from their receptiveness to the temptation of making extra profits through sales."

See also Michael Tadman, *Speculators and Slaves: Masters, Traders, and Slaves in the Old South* (Madison: University of Wisconsin Press, 1989), 111, 113, 117.

33. W. E. B. Du Bois, *Suppression of the African Slave Trade to the United States of America, 1638–1870* (New York: Dover, 1970), 109–30; Philip D. Curtin, *The Atlantic Slave Trade: A Census* (Madison: University of Wisconsin Press, 1970), 231–37; Tom W. Shick, *Behold the Promised Land: A History of Afro-American Settler Society in Nineteenth-Century Liberia* (Baltimore: Johns Hopkins University Press, 1980), 61, 63.

34. Rawick, *The American Slave,* II: South Carolina Narr. (Series 1), Part 1:30; III: South Carolina Narr. (Series 1), Part 3:64.

See J. C. Furnas, "Patrolling the Middle Passage," in *Readings in American History, 1607–1865,* ed. Robert M. Spector (New York: American Heritage, 1993), 155–62.

35. Ellen Nickenzie Lawson and Marlene D. Merrill, *The Three Sarahs: Documents of Antebellum Black College Women,* vol. 13 (New York: Edwin Mellen, 1984), 5; Ellen Nickenzie Lawson, "Children of the Amistad," *Instructor* 97 (February 1988): 44–48; Howard Jones, *Mutiny on the Amistad: The Saga of a Slave Revolt and Its*

Impact on American Abolition, Law, and Diplomacy (New York: Oxford University Press, 1987), 3–26.

36. Sarah Margru to George Whipple, September 18, 1847, American Missionary Association Papers, TU; John W. Barber, *A History of the Amistad Captives: Being a Circumstantial Account of the Capture of the Spanish Schooner Amistad, by the Africans on Board; Their Voyage, and Capture Near Long Island, New York; With Biographical Sketches of each of the Surviving Africans. Also, An Account of The Trials Had on their Case, Before the District and Circuit Courts of the United States, For the District of Connecticut* (New Haven: E. L. and J. W. Barber, 1840), 8–15; Jones, *Mutiny on the Amistad,* 29–30, 41.

37. Maury Brother to Jacob Mordecai, May 4, 1857, Mordecai Family Papers, SHC; Richard Sutch, "The Breeding of Slaves for Sale and the Westward Expansion of Slavery, 1850–1860," in *Race and Slavery in the Western Hemisphere: Quantitative Studies,* ed. Stanley L. Engerman and Eugene D. Genovese (Princeton: Princeton University Press, 1975), 173–210.

See Edmund L. Drago, ed., *Broke by the War: Letters of a Slave Trader* (Columbia: University of South Carolina Press, 1991), for relevant information regarding the domestic slave trade.

38. Tadman, *Speculators and Slaves,* 26, 45.

39. "Bill of Sale," June 6, 1814, Benjamin Bealk Papers, SHSW; Charles Ball, *Fifty Years in Chains: The Life of an American Slave* (New York: H. Dayton, 1859; republished by Negro History Press, Detroit, Michigan), 10–11.

40. See the *Charleston Mercury,* February 3, 1846; February 21, 1846; March 3, 1846; March 23, 1846; April 4, 1846; April 9, 1846; July 1, 1846; July 16, 1846; August 5, 1846; August 25, 1846; October 1, 1846; October 17, 1846; October 20, 1846; November 3, 1846; November 7, 1846; November 26, 1846, containing advertisements for the sale of children.

41. Tadman, *Speculators and Slaves,* 113–14; "Will," April 30, 1829, John Sterritt Papers, LC; "Deed," January 15, 1799, William Sabb Papers, SHSW; Yetman, *Life Under the "Peculiar Institution,"* 227; J. G. Clinkscales, *On the Old Plantation: Reminiscences of His Childhood* (New York: Negro Universities Press, 1969), 21; Frederick Douglass, "Narrative of the Life of Frederick Douglass an American Slave Written by Himself," in *Frederick Douglass: The Narrative and Selected Writings,* ed. Michael Meyer (New York: Random House, 1984), 57–59; Mary Ellison, "Resistance to Oppression: Black Women's Response to Slavery in the United States," SA 4 (May 1983): 59; Censer, *North Carolina Planters and Their Children,* 141.

See James William McGettigan, Jr., "Boone County Slaves: Sales, Estate Division and Families, 1820–1865," Parts I and II, MHR 72 (January, April 1978): 176–97, 271–95.

See Appendix D.

42. Herbert G. Gutman, "Time on the Cross: The Economics of American Slavery: The World Two Cliometricians Made," JNH 60 (January 1975): 62; Stampp, *The Peculiar Institution,* 245–51.

See Randall Miller, ed., *"Dear Master": Letters of a Slave Family* (Ithaca: Cornell University Press, 1978); Allen Kulikoff, "Uprooted Peoples: Black Migrants in the Age of the American Revolution, 1790–1820," in *Slavery and Freedom in the Age of the American Revolution,* ed. Ira Berlin and Ronald Hoffman (Charlottesville: University of Virginia Press, 1983), 143–71; John Hebron Moore, "John Hebron of LaGrange Plantation: Commercial Fruit Grower of the Old South," JMH 46 (November 1984): 281–303; Richard S. Dunn, "A Tale of Two Plantations: Slave Life at Mesopotamia in Jamaica and Mount Airy in Virginia, 1799 to 1828," WMQ 34 (January 1977): 32–65; William Calderhead, "How Extensive Was the Border State Slave Trade?: A New Look," CWH 18 (March 1972): 54.

43. Eric Perkins, "*Roll, Jordan, Roll*: A 'Marx' for the Master Class," RHR 3 (Fall 1976): 47–48; Jones, *Born a Child of Freedom*, 7.

See James D. Anderson, "Aunt Jemima in Dialectics: Genovese on Slave Culture," JNH 41 (January 1976): 99–114.

44. I. L. Twyman to John Austin, October 4, 1848, Austin-Twyman Collection, EGS; Leslie Howard Owens, *This Species of Property: Slave Life and Culture in the Old South* (New York: Oxford University Press, 1977), 184; Gerda Lerner, ed., *Black Women in White America: A Documentary History* (New York: Vintage, 1973), 38.

See Censer, *North Carolina Planters and Their Children*, 140, 148; "Will," April 30, 1829, Sterritt Papers, LC; Brown, "Narrative of William Wells Brown," 196.

See also Appendix A.

45. Sukey and Ersey to Beverley Tucker, October 24, 1842, Tucker Coleman Collection, EGS—see letter in *Slave Testimony: Two Centuries of Letters, Speeches, Dictations, and Autobiographies*, ed. John W. Blassingame (Baton Rouge: Louisiana State University Press, 1977), 13–14; Northup, "Twelve Years a Slave," 246–47; Miller, "*Dear Master*," 188–89.

46. Northup, "Twelve Years a Slave," 245–46, 267–69, 280; Tadman, *Speculators and Slaves*, 45.

47. Catherine M. Hanchett, "'What Sort of People & Families . . .': The Edmondson Sisters," AANY 6 (July 1982): 21–37; Northup, "Twelve Years a Slave," 267–68; Genovese, *Roll, Jordan, Roll*, 417.

See Willie Lee Rose, ed., *A Documentary History of Slavery in North America* (New York: Oxford University Press, 1976), 423–27.

48. W. W. Gilmer, "Management of Slaves," SP 12 (April 1852): 106–107; Owens, *This Species of Property*, 184; Levine, *Black Culture and Black Consciousness*, 15.

49. *Jubilee and Plantation Songs*, 51.

50. Douglass, *My Bondage and My Freedom*, 47–49; Waldo E. Martin, Jr., *The Mind of Frederick Douglass* (Chapel Hill: University of North Carolina Press, 1984), 5–6; Northup, "Twelve Years a Slave," 245.

See Dickson J. Preston, *Young Frederick Douglass: The Maryland Years* (Baltimore: Johns Hopkins University Press, 1980).

51. John Parker Manuscript, Rankin-Parker Papers, DU.

52. Sarah S. Hughes, "Slaves for Hire: The Allocation of Black Labor in Elizabeth City County, Virginia, 1782 to 1810," WMQ 35 (April 1978): 260–86.

See Frank Hawkins to William, January 4, 1849, Mary Ann Buie Papers, DU; *The Charleston Mercury*, January 18, 1846, October 26, 1846; Charles B. Dew, "David Ross and the Oxford Iron Works: A Study of Industrial Slavery in the Early Nineteenth-Century South," WMQ 31 (April 1974): 199; Lloyd A. Hunter, "Slavery in St. Louis, 1804–1860," MHSB (July 1974): 242–43; Philip S. Foner and Ronald L. Lewis, eds., *Black Workers: A Documentary History from Colonial Times to the Present* (Philadelphia: Temple University Press, 1989), 14, 27.

53. Twyman to Thomas Austin, April 21, 1832, EGS.

See John Woods to John Haywood, February 17, 1818, Ernest Haywood Collection, SCH, which discusses a Beaufort County, North Carolina, slaveholder's quandary involving a child. The enslaved boy Winston who was of "Sutch good qualities" that Woods "could not imbrace the thoughts of parting" with him under ordinary circumstances. It was no ordinary matter in 1818 when Winston wanted to end the separation from his parents and friends in Wake County. The boy's faithful service caused Woods to consider it his "Duty to let him go to his Parents." Woods declared:

I do pledge My Honour that he is a Boy of the best Prospectus that I ever had any thing to do With in my Life and no Consideration Could take him from me

if I did not think it Was my duty to part With him for the above nam. purpose.
. . .

Accolades aside, Woods would willingly fulfill his duty if John Haywood, owner of Winston's parents, "or any other person" would pay "a fair price" for the boy. Woods wanted "nothing But What is Just." His use of "just" and "duty" were inconsequential unless he found a buyer willing to purchase the boy and then allow him to remain in Beaufort several months—"in consequence of the Situation of My Crop," Woods explained. Woods's sense of duty was conditional, but he was certain about the needs for a faithful servant.

54. Hobbs to wife Virginia, 1833, Before Freedom Came Exhibit, MC.

55. Lester to Miss Patsy, August 29, 1857, James Allred Papers, DU; Abraham Scriven to Dinah, September 19, 1858, Special Collection, TU; Northup, "Twelve Years a Slave," 245–46, 267–68, 280.

56. Ball, *Fifty Years in Chains*, 11; Jones, *Born a Child of Freedom*, 43.

57. Frederick Bancroft, *Slave-Trading in the Old South* (New York: Unger, 1959), 206; Gutman, "Time on the Cross," 62.

See Barbara L. Bellows, "'My Children, Gentlemen, Are My Own': Poor Women, the Urban Elite, and the Bonds of Obligation in Antebellum Charleston," in *The Web of Southern Social Relations: Women, Family, and Education,* ed. Walter Fraser, Jr. (Athens: University of Georgia Press, 1985), 52–71; G. Melvin Herndon, "The Unemancipated Antebellum Youth," SS 23 (Summer 1984): 145–54; Durwood Dunn, "Apprenticeship and Indentured Servitude in Tennessee before the Civil War," WTHSP 36 (1982): 25–40.

58. Rawick, *The American Slave*, XI: Arkansas Narr. (Series 2), Part 7:27–28.

See Perdue et al., *Weevils in the Wheat*, 267.

59. Bills Diary, December 31, 1849, SHC; Farish Carter Papers, 1857, SHC.

60. TBHF to ARH, November 17, 1859, MDAH (emphasis in the original).

61. TBHF to ARH, February 20, 1860, May 22, 1860, June 24, 1860, July 12, 1860, October 14, 1860, MDAH.

62. William Taylor Barry Letterbook (#2569), April 11, 1828, August 7, 1829, August 16, 1832, UVA.

63. Charlotte L. Forten, *The Journal of Charlotte L. Forten: A Free Negro in the Slave Era*, ed. Ray Allen Billington (New York: Collier, 1967), 159.

64. Susan Brownmiller, *Against Our Will: Men, Women and Rape* (New York: Simon and Schuster, 1975), 32, 37–38.

65. Owens, *This Species of Property*, 125–26; De Burg, *The Slave Driver*, 82; Richard H. Steckel, "Miscegenation and the American Slave Schedule," JIH 11 (August 1980): 251–63; Rawick, *The American Slave*, III: Georgia Narr. (Supplement, Series 1), Part 1:94.

For further discussions of sexual abuse in the nineteenth century, see Thelma Jennings, "'Us Colored Women Had To Go Through a Plenty': Sexual Exploitation of African American Slave Women," JWH 1 (Winter 1991): 45–74; Peter Bardaglio, "'An Outrage upon Nature': Incest and the Law in the Nineteenth-Century South," in *In Joy and in Sorrow: Women, Family, and Marriage in the Victorian South, 1830–1900*, ed. Carol Bleser (New York: Oxford University Press, 1991), 32–51.

For contemporary research on the subject see George A. Awad, "Father-Son Incest: A Case Report," JNMD 162 (February 1976): 135–39; Norman S. Ellerstein and J. William Canavan, "Sexual Abuse of Boys," AJDC 134 (March 1980): 255–57; Katharine N. Dixon, Eugene Arnold, and Kenneth Calestro, "Father-Son Incest: Underreported Psychiatric Problem?" AJP 135 (July 1978): 835–38; Robert E. Freeman-Longo, "Brief Communication: The Impact of Sexual Victimization on Males," CAN 10 (1986): 411–14; Gail Elizabeth Wyatt, "The Aftermath of Child Sexual Abuse of African American and White American Women: The Victim's Experience," JFV 5 (1990): 61–81.

See also Missy Dehn Kubitschek, "Subjugated Knowledge: Toward a Feminist Exploration of Rape in Afro-American Fiction," in *Studies in Black American Literature,* vol. 3: *Black Feminist Criticism and Critical Theory,* ed. Joe Weixlmann and Houston A. Baker, Jr. (Greenwood, FL: Penkevill, 1988), 43–56. Kubitschek erroneously includes *Incidents in the Life of a Slave Girl* among the novels studied.

66. Rawick, *The American Slave,* II: South Carolina Narr. (Series 1), Part 2:310; Gutman, *The Black Family,* 83.

67. Genovese, *Roll, Jordan, Roll,* 423.

68. See Melton A. McLaurin, *Celia, a Slave* (Athens: University of Georgia Press, 1991); Brownmiller, *Against Our Wills,* 153–54; Deborah Gray White, *Ar'n't I a Woman? Female Slaves in the Plantation South* (New York: Norton, 1985), 152–53; Pauli Murray, *Proud Shoes: The Story of an American Family* (New York: Harper and Row, 1984), 41–44; Catherine Clinton, "Caught in the Web of the Big House: Women and Slavery," in *The Web of Southern Social Relations: Women, Family, and Education,* ed. Walter Fraser, Jr. (Athens: University of Georgia Press, 1985), 20–21.

69. See Helen Tunnicliff Catterall, ed., *Judicial Cases Concerning American Slavery and the Negro* (Washington: Carnegie Institution, 1929, reprinted by University Microfilms, Ann Arbor, 1969), 2:513; 2:520; 3:363.

Catterall, *Judicial Cases,* 3:363 notes that in the Session Acts of 1860, Mississippi made "the rape by a negro or mulatto on a female negro or mulatto, under twelve years of age" punishable with death or whipping. It is not clear if this statute applied to both free and enslaved persons alike.

See John Munro, ed., *The London Shakespeare: The Histories, the Poems* (New York: Simon and Schuster, 1958), 1321–84.

70. Bertram Wyatt-Brown, *Southern Honor: Ethics and Behavior in the Old South* (New York: Oxford University Press, 1982), 296; Catherine Clinton, *The Plantation Mistress: Woman's World in the Old South* (New York: Pantheon, 1982), 87–88.

See Gail Elizabeth Wyatt, "The Aftermath of Child Sexual Abuse of African American and White American Women: The Victim's Experience," JFV 5 (number 1, 1990): 61–81.

71. See Richard Sutch, "The Breeding of Slaves for Sale and the Westward Expansion of Slavery, 1850–1860," in *Race and Slavery in the Western Hemisphere: Quantitative Studies,* ed. Stanley L. Engerman and Eugene D. Genovese (Princeton: Princeton University Press, 1975), 173–210; Paul A. David, Herbert G. Gutman, Richard Sutch, Peter Temin, and Gavin Wright, *Reckoning with Slavery: A Critical Study in the Quantitative History of American Negro Slavery* (Oxford University Press, 1976), 154–61.

72. Jacobs, *Incidents in the Life of a Slave Girl,* 192; Rawick, *The American Slave,* X: Texas Narr. (Supplement, Series 2), Part 9:4121–23.

See Gutman, *The Black Family,* 84–85; Willie Lee Rose, ed., *A Documentary History of Slavery in North America* (New York: Oxford University Press, 1976), 434–37; Linda K. Kerber and Jane Sherron De Hart, eds., *Women's America: Refocusing the Past,* 3d ed. (New York: Oxford University Press, 1991), 102–104.

73. Jordan, *White over Black,* 137–44; James Hugo Johnston, *Race Relations in Virginia and Miscegenation in the South, 1776–1860* (Amherst: University of Massachusetts Press, 1970), 165–90; Carl N. Degler, *Neither Black nor White: Slavery and Race Relations in Brazil and the United States* (New York: Macmillan, 1971), 194–95; *Compendium of the Seventh Census of the United States: 1850* (Washington: Government Printing Office, 1854), 83; Joel Williamson, *New People: Miscegenation and Mulattoes in the United States* (New York: Free, 1980), 24.

See Gray B. Mills, *The Forgotten People: Cane River Creoles of Color* (Baton Rouge: Louisiana State University Press, 1977).

74. White, *Ar'n't I a Woman?*, 86–88, 106–108; Eugene D. Genovese, *Roll, Jordan, Roll: The World the Slaves Made* (New York: Vintage, 1976), 497.

See Elizabeth Keckley, *Behind the Scenes: Thirty Years a Slave and Four Years in the White House* (New York: Arno and *New York Times*, 1968); Loren Schweninger, "A Slave Family in the Antebellum South," JNH 40 (January 1975): 29–44; Rawick, *The American Slave*, X: Texas Narr. (Supplement, Series 2), Part 9:4121–23; Elizabeth Fox-Genovese, "Strategies and Forms of Resistance: Focus on Slave Women in the United States," in *Resistance: Studies in African, Caribbean, and Afro-American History*, ed. Gary Y. Okihiro (Amherst: University of Massachusetts Press, 1986), 157–58; Darlene C. Hine, "Female Slave Resistance: The Economics of Sex," WJBS 3 (1979): 123–27; Gutman, *The Black Family*, 80–82; Helen Tunnicliff Catterall, ed., *Judicial Cases Concerning American Slavery and the Negro* (Washington: Carnegie Institution of Washington, 1926, vol. I, reprinted by University Microfilms, Ann Arbor, MI, 1969), 2:59.

See also Michael P. Johnson, "Smothered Slave Infants: Were Slave Mothers at Fault?" JSH 47 (November 1981): 493–520; Todd L. Savitt, "Smothering and Over-laying of Virginia Slave Children: A Suggested Explanation," BHM 49 (Fall 1975): 400–404.

75. Rawick, *The American Slave*, XI: Arkansas Narr. (Series 2), Part 7:52; TBHF to ARH, January 4, 1857, MDAH (emphasis in the original).

See Earl F. Mulderink, III, "'The Whole Town is Ringing with It': Slave Kidnapping Charges against Nathan Johnson of New Bedford, Massachusetts, 1839," NEQ 61 (September 1988): 341–57.

76. Dick Journal (#4528), February 1808, UVA.

77. John W. Blassingame, ed., *Slave Testimony: Two Centuries of Letters, Speeches, Dictations, and Autobiographies* (Baton Rouge: Louisiana State University Press, 1977), 211–12; Douglass, *Narrative*, 20; Rankin-Parker, DU; Annie L. Burton, *Memories of Childhood's Slavery Days* (Boston: Ross, 1909), 7–8; Brown, "Narrative of William Wells Brown," 180; Preston, *Young Frederick Douglass*, 9, 23.

Allegations regarding Thomas Jefferson fathering children by the slave woman Sally Hemings generate much discussion without resolution.

See Fawn M. Brodie, *Thomas Jefferson, An Intimate History* (New York: Norton, 1974); Winthrop D. Jordan, *White over Black: American Attitudes toward the Negro, 1550–1812* (New York: Norton, 1968); Jerry Knudson, "Jefferson the Father of Slave Children? One View of the Book Reviewers," JH 3 (Summer 1976): 56–59.

78. Gerda Lerner, *The Grimke Sisters from South Carolina: Pioneers for Woman's Rights and Abolition* (New York: Schocken, 1971), 359–60.

79. Eliza Carolina Clitherall Autobiography, vol. 3, part 1, 4, SHC.

80. Jules Zanger, "'The Tragic Octoroon' in Pre–Civil War Fiction," AQ (Spring 1966): 63–70; Toplin, "Between Black and White," 190–91.

See the twentieth-century novel by Elizabeth Boatwright Coker, *Daughter of Strangers* (New York: Dutton, 1950).

81. Yetman, *Life Under the "Peculiar Institution,"* 127.

82. Richard Barksdale and Keneth Kinnamon, eds., *Black Writers of America: A Comprehensive Anthology* (New York: Macmillan, 1972), 519.

83. Silas E. Fales to Mary, February 18, 1863, Silas Everett Fales Book, SHC; M. W. Davidson to Brother, December 21, 1835, Davidson Family Papers, SHC; Henry E. Simmons to Anna, November 23, 1862, Henry E. Simmons Letters, SHC (emphasis in the original); Jordan, *White over Black*, 167–78.

See Jo Anne Sellers Huber, "Southern Women and the Institution of Slavery," (M.A. Thesis, Lamar University, 1980), 73; Toplin, "Between Black and White," 194–95.

84. See Brenda Stevenson, "Distress and Discord in Virginia Slave Families, 1830–1860," in *In Joy and in Sorrow: Women, Family, and Marriage in the Victorian South, 1830–1900,* ed. Carol Bleser (New York: Oxford University Press, 1991), 112–15.

See Pauli Murray, *Proud Shoes: The Story of an American Family* (New York: Harper and Row, 1987); Robert Brent Toplin, "Between Black and White: Attitudes toward Southern Mulattoes, 1830–1861," JSH 45 (May 1979): 189–92.

85. Yetman, *Life Under the "Peculiar Institution,"* 327; Northup, "Twelve Years a Slave," 247.

See Kemble, *Journal of a Residence,* 269, for comments regarding the treatment of the mothers of mulatto women by a slaveholding woman.

86. Kate Drumgoold, "A Slave Girl's Story: Being an Autobiography of Kate Drumgoold," in *The Schomburg Library of Nineteenth-Century Black Women Writers: Six Women's Slave Narratives,* ed. Henry Louis Gates, Jr. (New York: Oxford University Press, 1988), 32.

6. "Free at last"

1. Rankin-Parker Manuscript, Perkins Library, DU.

2. Frederick Douglass, *My Bondage and My Freedom* (New York: Dover, 1969), 133.

3. Douglass, *My Bondage and My Freedom,* 166–69, 190; Jacob Stroyer, *My Life in the South* (Salem: Salem Observer, 1889), 24, 27; Booker T. Washington, *Up from Slavery* (New York: Bantam, 1967), 5.

4. Stroyer, *My Life in the South,* 34–36.

5. Stroyer, *My Life in the South,* 34–36.

6. John B. Cade, "Out of the Mouth of Ex-Slaves," JNH 20 (July 1935): 313.

7. B. A. Botkin, ed., *Lay My Burden Down: A Folk History of Slavery* (Chicago: University of Chicago Press, 1945), 89–90.

8. Frederick Douglass, "Narrative of the Life of Frederick Douglass an American Slave Written by Himself," in *Frederick Douglass: The Narrative and Selected Writings,* ed. Michael Meyer (New York: Random House, 1984), 69–81 (emphasis in the original); Douglass, *My Bondage and My Freedom,* 242–46.

9. Cade, "Out of the Mouths of Ex-Slaves," 315.

10. Tryphena Blanche Holder Fox (hereafter cited as TBHF) to Anna Rose Holder (hereafter cited as ARH), March 29, 1861, MDAH.

See Marli Frances Weiner, "Plantation Mistresses and Female Slaves: Gender, Race, and South Carolina Women, 1830–1880," (Ph.D. diss., University of Rochester, 1985), 120–21; Elizabeth Fox-Genovese, *Within the Plantation Household: Black and White Women of the Old South* (Chapel Hill: University of North Carolina Press, 1988), 97.

11. Tryphena Blanche Holder Fox, "Civil War Diary Transcript," August 12, 1861, MDAH; TBHF to ARH, March 29, 1861; January 4, 1862, MDAH.

12. See Judith Kelleher Schafer, "New Orleans Slavery in 1850 as Seen in Advertisements," JSH 47 (February 1981): 33–56.

13. George P. Rawick, ed., *The American Slave: A Composite Autobiography,* 19 vols. (Westport: Greenwood, 1972), X: Texas Narr. (Supplement, Series 2), Part 9:4121–23; Thelma Jennings, "'Us Colored Women Had To Go Through a Plenty': Sexual Exploitation of African American Slave Women," JWH 1 (Winter 1991): 47–48.

14. See Rawick, *The American Slave,* X: Texas Narr. (Supplement, Series 2), Part 9:4116–21.

15. Harriet A. Jacobs, *Incidents in the Life of a Slave Girl: Written by Herself,* ed. Jean Fagan Yellin (Cambridge: Harvard University Press, 1987), 27, 55; Eugene D. Genovese, *Roll, Jordan, Roll: The World Slaves Made* (New York: Vintage, 1976), 415.

16. See Melton A. McLaurin, *Celia, a Slave* (Athens: University of Georgia Press, 1991).

17. Richard C. Wade, *Slavery in the Cities: The South, 1820–1860* (New York: Oxford University Press, 1964), 214–16; Barbara Jeanne Fields, *Slavery and Freedom on the Middle Ground: Maryland during the Nineteenth Century* (New Haven: Yale University Press, 1987), 52–53; Herbert G. Gutman, *The Black Family in Slavery and Freedom, 1750–1925* (New York: Vintage, 1977), 264; Michael P. Johnson, "Runaway Slaves and the Slave Communities in South Carolina, 1799 to 1830," WMQ 38 (July 1981): 418.

See Judith Kelleher Schafer, "New Orleans Slavery in 1850 as Seen in Advertisements," JSH 47 (February 1981): 33–56; Stanley W. Campbell, "Runaway Slaves," in *Dictionary of Afro-American Slavery*, ed. Randall M. Miller and John David Smith (New York: Greenwood, 1988), 650.

It is possible that fewer advertisements appeared in the papers for women because women traveling alone attracted more attention than men; therefore, it is possible that they were found before their owners advertised for them.

18. Jacobs, *Incidents in the Life of a Slave Girl*, 91.

19. Jacobs, *Incidents in the Life of a Slave Girl*, 91.

See Anne Frank, *The Diary of a Young Girl* (New York: Bantam, 1993).

20. Jacobs, *Incidents in the Life of a Slave Girl*, 91.

21. The Cincinnati journalist Frank Gregg wrote about the woman's flight after interviewing the sons of a local abolitionist, John Rankin, who guided her from their home to another underground railroad station as she made her way to freedom.

See Rankin-Parker Papers, DU; Harriet Beecher Stowe, *A Key to Uncle Tom's Cabin* (Cleveland: J. P. Jewett, 1854), 34; Jennie Arnold, "Lives of Teachers who attended Summer Institute, 1881," first summer school file, HUA; May 9, 1820, *Richmond Enquirer*.

For accounts of parents fleeing with children see William Still, *The Underground Rail Road. A record of facts, authentic narratives, letters, &c., narrating the hardships, hairbreadth escapes and death struggles of the slaves in their efforts for freedom, as related by themselves and others, or the largest stockholders, and most liberal aiders and advisers, of the road* (Philadelphia: Porter and Coats, 1872), 207–208, 228–29, 231, 302–303, 308–309, 326–28, 340–41, 387, 409, 440–41.

22. Lucy A. Delaney, "From the Darkness Cometh the Light or Struggles for Freedom," in *The Schomburg Library of Nineteenth-Century Black Women Writers: Six Women's Slave Narratives*, ed. Henry Louis Gates, Jr. (New York: Oxford University Press, 1988), 15–16; William Brown, "Narrative of William Wells Brown: A Fugitive Slave written by himself," in *Puttin' On Ole Massa: The Slave Narratives of Henry Bibb, William Wells Brown, and Solomon Northup*, ed. Gilbert Osofsky (New York: Harper, 1969), 187–88; Schweninger, "A Slave Family in the Ante Bellum South," 34.

For accounts of children escaping alone see Still, *The Underground Railroad*, 155, 232, 289, 332, 336, 381, 384, 385, 388–89, 392, 415, 435, 439, 440, 443, 451, 457, 459–60, 472, 475, 479, 483, 499, 503–504, 509, 515, 518, 524, 526.

23. Brown, "Narrative," 188.

24. Delaney, "From the Darkness," 19; Mattie Thompson, "The Story of Mattie Jackson," in *The Schomburg Library of Nineteenth-Century Black Women Writers: Six Women's Slave Narratives*, ed. Henry Louis Gates, Jr. (New York: Oxford University Press, 1988), 31–32.

25. *Jubilee and Plantation Songs. Characteristic Favorites, As Sung by the Hampton Students, Jubilee Singers, Fisk University Students, and Other Concert Companies* (Boston: Oliver Ditson, 1887), 78.

See Frederick Douglass, "Narrative of the Life of Frederick Douglass an American Slave Written by Himself," ed. Michael Meyer (New York: Random House, 1984), 19.

26. Douglass, *My Bondage and My Freedom*, 271–303.

27. Donald G. Neiman, *Promises to Keep: African-Americans and the Constitutional Order, 1776 to the Present* (New York: Oxford University Press, 1991), 30.

28. Benjamin Quarles, *Black Abolitionists* (New York: Oxford University Press, 1969), 204.

29. Gerda Lerner, ed., *Black Women in White America: A Documentary History* (New York: Vintage, 1973), 60–63.

30. Jane H. Pease and William S. Pease, *They Who Would Be Free: Blacks' Search for Freedom, 1830–1861* (New York: Atheneum, 1974), 238; Rawick, *The American Slave*, II: South Carolina Narr. (Series 1), Part 2:24; Brown, "Narrative," 206–208.

31. Yetman, *Life Under the "Peculiar Institution,"* 48; Charles L. Perdue, Jr., Thomas E. Barden, and Robert K. Phillips, eds., *Weevils in the Wheat: Interviews with Virginia Ex-Slaves* (Bloomington: Indiana University Press, 1980), 252.

32. Still, *The Underground Railroad*, 328–29.

33. Pease, *They Who Would Be Free*, 238; Rawick, *The American Slave*, II: South Carolina Narr. (Series 1), Part 2:24; Brown, *Narrative*, 206–208; *The Richmond Enquirer*, November 19, 1819, November 29, 1819, December 29, 1819, January 15, 1820, February 5, 1820; *Charleston Mercury*, February 15, 1820, January 2, 1846, April 10, 1846, April 22, 1846, May 18, 1846, June 5, 1846; Daniel F. Littlefield, Jr., ed., *The Life of Okah Tubbee* (Lincoln: University of Nebraska Press, 1988), xxxi–xxxii; Theodore Rosengarten, *Tombee: Diary of a Cotton Planter* (New York: Morrow, 1986), 159; Schafer, "New Orleans Slavery in 1850 as Seen in Advertisements," 43, 52.

34. Ira Berlin, *Slaves without Masters: The Free Negro in the Antebellum South* (New York: Oxford University Press, 1981), 90, 79–107; *Population of the United States in 1860: Compiled from Original Returns of the Eighth Census by Joseph C. G. Kennedy* (Washington: Government Printing Office, 1864), 2.

35. William Cohen, "Thomas Jefferson and the Problem of Slavery," JAH 56 (December 1960): 519; Manumission Document, March 11, 1839, Thomas Sewell Papers, LC; Ulrich B. Phillips, *American Negro Slavery: A Survey of the Supply, Employment and Control of Negro Labor As Determined by the Plantation Regime* (Baton Rouge: Louisiana State University Press, 1966), 426–27; Berlin, *Slaves without Masters*, 21, 29–31.

36. Judith K. Schafer, "'Open and Notorious Concubinage': The Emancipation of Slave Mistresses by Will and the Supreme Court in Antebellum Louisiana," LaH 28 (Spring 1987): 165–82. See Suzanne D. Lebsock, "Radical Reconstruction and Property Rights of Southern Women," JSH 43 (May 1977): 195–216.

37. See Daniel F. Littlefield, Jr., ed., *The Life of Okah Tubbee* (Lincoln: University of Nebraska Press, 1988).

38. Quoted from Lawrence W. Levine, *Black Culture and Black Consciousness: Afro-American Folk Thought from Slavery to Freedom* (New York: Oxford University Press, 1978), 13; Sterling Stuckey, "Through the Prism of Folklore: The Black Ethos in Slavery," in *The Underside of American History: Other Readings*, vol. 2, ed. Thomas R. Frazier (New York: Harcourt Brace Jovanovich, 1974), 268.

See Harriet A. Jacobs, *Incidents in the Life of a Slave Girl: Written by Herself*, ed. Jean Fagan Yellin (Cambridge: Harvard University Press, 1987); Solomon Northup, "Twelve Years a Slave: Narrative of Solomon Northup," in *Puttin' on Ole Massa: The Slave Narratives of Henry Bibb, William Wells Brown, and Solomon Northup*, ed. Gilbert Osofsky (New York: Harper, 1969), 246–48; Earl F. Mulderink, III, "'The Whole Town is Ringing with It': Slave Kidnapping Charges against Nathan Johnson of New Bedford, Massachusetts, 1839," NEQ 61 (September 1988): 341–57.

39. Berlin, *Slaves without Masters*, 90, 79–107.

40. *Population of the United States in 1860*, 2; Fields, *Slavery and Freedom on the Middle Ground*, 15, 30; Free papers, April 10, 1839, Enoch Tucker Papers, LC; Suzanne

Lebsock, "Free Black Women and the Question of Matriarchy: Petersburg, Virginia, 1784–1820," FS 2 (Summer 1983): 279; Berlin, *Slaves without Masters*, 102.

41. Schafer, "'Open and Notorious Concubinage,'" 166–67; Berlin, *Slaves without Masters*, 102; Nieman, *Promises to Keep*, 3.

42. *Population of the United States in 1860*, 2; Joseph E. Harris, *Africans and Their History* (New York: Mentor, 1986), 105; Mary Frances Berry and John W. Blassingame, *Long Memory: The Black Experience in America* (New York: Oxford University Press, 1982), 400; Berlin, *Slaves without Masters*, 102; Fields, *Slavery and Freedom on the Middle Ground*, 28.

43. Samuel Cram Jackson Diary, November 17, 1832, SHC.

For a detailed discussion regarding migration to Africa see Tom W. Shick, *Behold the Promised Land: A History of Afro-American Settler Society in Nineteenth-Century Liberia* (Baltimore: Johns Hopkins University Press, 1980).

44. Lebsock, "Free Black Women and the Question of Matriarchy," 275; Leonard Stavisky, "The Origins of Negro Craftsmanship in Colonial America," JNH 32 (October 1947): 417–29; Deborah Gray White, "The Lives of Slave Women," SE 12 (November/December 1984): 32–39; Jacqueline Jones, *Labor of Love, Labor of Sorrow: Black Women, Work and the Family, from Slavery to the Present* (New York: Vintage, 1986), 18; Elizabeth Fox-Genovese, "Strategies and Forms of Resistance," in *Resistance: Studies in African, Caribbean, and Afro-American History*, ed. Gary Y. Okihiro (Amherst: University of Massachusetts Press, 1986), 155; Loren Schweninger, "A Slave Family in the Ante Bellum South," JNH 60 (January 1975): 32.

45. Schweninger, "A Slave Family in the Ante Bellum South," 29–44.

Among the papers of slaveholder William Fitzhugh Gordon is a December 15, 1830, letter regarding the slave Nancy, age unknown, whose father Willie Davis paid Gordon $250 for her freedom with the intention of liberating her. The price of slaves had risen considerably by 1850. See Gordon Family Papers (#9553), UVA.

46. Richard Barksdale and Keneth Kinnamon, eds., *Black Writers of America: A Comprehensive Anthology* (New York: Macmillan, 1972), 219.

47. Michael P. Johnson and James L. Roark, *Black Masters: A Free Family of Color in the Old South* (New York: Norton, 1984), 3–29; Clement Eaton, "Slave-Hiring in the Upper South: A Step toward Freedom," MVHR 46 (March 1960): 663–78.

48. Johnson, *Black Masters*, 126, 131–33.

49. Catherine M. Hanchett, "'What Sort of People & Families . . .': The Edmondson Sisters," AANY 6 (July 1982): 22–27.

50. Hanchett, "'What Sort of People & Families,'" 22–27.

51. Paul Finkelman, *Slavery in the Courtroom: An Annotated Bibliography of American Cases* (Washington: Government Printing Office, 1985), 25–29.

52. Howard Jones, *Mutiny on the Amistad: The Saga of a Slave Revolt and Its Impact on American Abolition, Law, and Diplomacy*. New York: Oxford University Press, 1987), 39–40.

53. Jones, *Mutiny on the Amistad*, 63–78.

54. Jones, *Mutiny on the Amistad*, 190; Sarah Margru to George Whipple, September 18, 1847, Amistad Collection, TU.

For a discussion about the return of other Africans rescued from slavers see Shick, *Behold the Promised Land*, 66–72.

55. Richard Hofstadter and Michael Wallace, eds., *American Violence: A Documentary History* (New York: Knopf, 1970), 189–90.

56. Marion D. de B. Kilson, "Towards Freedom: An Analysis of Slave Revolts in the United States," in *The Making of Black America: Essays in Negro Life and History*, vol. I, ed. August Meier and Elliott Rudwick (New York: Atheneum, 1973): 165–78; Philip J. Schwarz, "The Transportation of Slaves from Virginia, 1801–1865," SA 7 (December 1986): 220–23.

57. Chester D. Bradley, "Controversial Ben Butler," the Casement Papers (Fortress Monroe, Virginia: n.p. n.d.), 1; "Highlights of Black History at Fort Monroe," the Casement Papers (Fort Monroe, Virginia, n.p. n.d.), 1–2; Robert F. Engs, *Freedom's First Generation: Black Hampton, Virginia, 1861–1890* (Philadelphia: University of Pennsylvania Press, 1979), xvi, 10.

58. Howard P. Nash, Jr., *Stormy Petrel: The Life and Times of General Benjamin F. Butler, 1818–1893* (Cranbury: Associated University Presses, 1969), 106; Edward L. Pierce, "The Contrabands at Fortress Monroe," AM 3 (November 1861): 626–40; Engs, *Freedom's First Generation*, 30–31.

59. Edward H. Bonekemper, "Negro Ownership of Read Property in Hampton and Elizabeth City County, Virginia, 1860–1870," JNH 55 (July 1970): 170–71; Marion L. Starkey, *The First Plantation: History of Hampton and Elizabeth City County, Virginia, 1607–1877* (Hampton: Houston, 1936), 81–82.

60. Benjamin Quarles, "The Abduction of the 'Planter,'" in *The Making of Black America: The Origins of Black Americans*, vol. I, ed. August Meier and Elliott Rudwick (New York: Atheneum, 1973), 341; Benjamin Quarles, *The Negro in the Civil War* (New York: Russel and Russel, 1968), 71–72.

61. Mary Boykin Chesnut, *A Diary from Dixie*, ed. Ben Ames Williams (Boston: Houghton Mifflin, 1950), 38; Quarles, *The Negro in the Civil War*, 52.

62. Washington, *Up from Slavery*, 5–6; Quarles, *The Negro in the Civil War*, 52–53.

63. Thomas Wentworth Higginson, *Army Life in a Black Regiment* (New York: Collier, 1962), 55; Quarles, *The Negro in the Civil War*, 51.

64. Emfield to Thomas Moore, June 6, 1863, Thomas Moore Papers, HNOC; C. Peter Ripley, "The Black Family in Transition: Louisiana, 1860–1865," JSH 41 (August 1975): 372; Litwack, *North of Slavery*, 111–16; Victor B. Howard, "The Civil War in Kentucky: The Slave Claims His Freedom," JNH 67 (Fall 1982): 245; TBHF, "Civil War Diary Transcript," March 10, 1862, December 14, 1862, MDAH; Daniel E. Sutherland, "Looking for a Home: Louisiana Emigrants during the Civil War and Reconstruction," LaH 4 (Fall 1980): 342, 344; Bell Irvin Wiley, *Southern Negroes, 1861–1865* (New Haven: Yale University Press, 1965), 5–6; Quarles, *The Negro in the Civil War*, 46–47.

During the war, the slaveholder Adel Petigru Allston urged the overseer to capture a runaway slave to quell the effect that his flight would have on others. Of more importance, she suggested that one slave couple be placed in jail and held hostage "for the conduct of their children," ages not given. The owner's manipulation of the family as a measure of control was evident in this action. "The older negroes should endeavor," Allston wrote, "to influence the younger ones to order and subordination while the war lasts." She held the parents responsible for the children's behavior and wanted to "make an example among the old people whose children have deserted."

See J. H. Easterby, ed., *The South Carolina Rice Plantation: As Revealed in the Papers of Robert F. W. Allston* (Chicago: University of Chicago, 1945), 292.

65. Clifton H. Johnson, ed., *God Struck Me Dead: Religious Conversion Experiences and Autobiographies of Ex-Slaves* (Philadelphia: Pilgrim, 1969), 102; Ophelia Settle Egypt, J. Masuoka, and Charles S. Johnson, eds., *Unwritten History of Slavery: Autobiographical Account of Negro Ex-Slaves* (Nashville: Fisk University, 1945), 253; Quarles, *The Negro in the Civil War*, 71.

66. James M. McPherson, *Ordeal by Fire: The Civil War and Reconstruction* (New York: Knopf, 1982), 350; Higginson, *Army Life in a Black Regiment*, 28, 55 (emphasis in the original).

67. U.S. Department of the Army, U.S. Army Military History Institute, Photographic Collection, Carlisle Barracks, Carlisle, Pennsylvania.

68. Johnson, *God Struck Me Dead*, 105.

69. Susie King Taylor, *Reminiscences of My Life in Camp* (New York: Arno and New

York Times, 1968), 26, 32–35; Edgar Allen Toppin, *A Biographical History of Blacks in America since 1528* (New York: David McKay, 1971), 259–60.

70. Eileen Southern, *The Music of Black Americans* (New York: Norton, 1971), 252–254.

71. Lizzie Neblett (hereafter cited as LN) to Will Neblett (hereafter cited as WN), March 7, 1864, March 18, 1864, Kenneth M. Stampp, ed., *Records of Ante-Bellum Southern Plantations from the Revolution through the Civil War*, Series G, Part I, Texas and Louisiana (Frederick, MD: University Publications of America, 1987).

See Drew Gilpin Faust, "'Trying to Do a Man's Business': Slavery, Violence and Gender in the American Civil War," GH 4 (Summer 1992): 197–214.

72. LN to WN, February 12, 1864, March 7, 1864, *Records of Ante-Bellum Southern Plantations* (emphasis in the original).

73. Photographic Collection, Carlisle Barracks, Carlisle, Pennsylvania.

74. Elizabeth Hyde Botume, *The First Days amongst the Contrabands* (New York: Arno and *New York Times*, 1968), 15.

75. Jones, *Labor of Love*, 50; Harriette Pipes McAdoo and Rosalyn Terborg-Penn, "Historical Trends and Perspectives of Afro-American Families," TH 3 (Spring 1985): 105–106; Leon F. Litwack, *Been in the Storm so Long: The Aftermath of Slavery* (New York: Vintage, 1980), 93–94; Eric Foner, *Reconstruction: America's Unfinished Revolution, 1863–1877* (New York: Harper and Row, 1988) 4, 10.

76. *Population of the United States in 1860*, 594.

77. Charlotte L. Forten, *The Journal of Charlotte L. Forten: A Free Negro in the Slave Era*, ed. Ray Allen Billington (New York: Collier, 1967), 167; L. Maria Child, *The Freedmen's Book* (Boston: Fields, Osgood, 1869), 252–53.

78. Taylor, *Reminiscences*, 18; Ira Berlin, Thavolia Glymph, Steven F. Miller, Joseph P. Reidy, Leslie S. Rowland, and Julie Saville, eds., *Freedom: A Documentary History of Emancipation 1861–1867*, Series I, vol. III: *The Wartime Genesis of Free Labor: The Lower South* (New York: Cambridge University Press, 1990), 414.

79. Berlin et al., *Freedom: A Documentary History*, 422–23; John Hope Franklin, *Emancipation Proclamation* (Garden City: Doubleday, 1963), 139–40; Foner, *Reconstruction*, 1–6, 10; Nieman, *Promises to Keep*, 54–55; *Population of the United States in 1860*, 594.

80. "Court Order," Madison County, Kentucky, September 15, 1863, "Court Order," Nelson County, Kentucky, March 14, 1864, Negro Collection, Division of Slavery, 1858–1867, DU.

The fate of a twelve-year-old runaway calling himself Dick was no different from that of the two runaways described herein. The Louisville slaveholders John Rizer and John S. Dixon failed to claim Dick after the court advertised his whereabouts. The highest bidder at the public sale promised to pay $265 with interest to the Commonwealth of Kentucky for the boy within one year of the sale.

See report by James Wood, January 11, 1864, Nelson County, Kentucky, Negro Collection, Division of Slavery, 1858–1867, DU.

81. Howard, "The Civil War in Kentucky," 250.

82. Ripley, "The Black Family in Transition," 375.

83. Silas Everett Fales, April 7, 1863, Silas Everett Fales Book, SHC.

84. Howard, "The Civil War in Kentucky," 251; Gutman, *The Black Family*, 368–69.

85. Gutman, *The Black Family*, 371–74; Berlin et al., "Family and Freedom," 4; C. Peter Ripley, "The Black Family in Transition: Louisiana, 1860–1865," JSH 41 (August 1975): 375; Howard, "The Civil War in Kentucky," 251.

86. *Jubilee and Plantation Songs*, 35.

87. Issac Shoemaker Diary, March 3, 1864, DU; Howard, "The Civil War in Kentucky," 247–48.

7. "There's a better day a-coming"

1. Eric Foner, *Reconstruction: America's Unfinished Revolution, 1863–1877* (New York: Harper and Row, 1988), 69; Henry L. Swint, *Dear Ones at Home: Letters from Contraband Camps* (Nashville: Vanderbilt University Press, 1966), 2; Robert C. Morris, *Reading, 'Riting, and Reconstruction: The Education of Freedmen in the South, 1861–1870* (Chicago: University of Chicago Press, 1981), 1–2; Richard Bryant Drake, "The American Missionary Association and the Southern Negro," (Ph. D. diss., Emory University, 1957), 1–2.

2. "Sevdegar Maria" to My Dear Friend, November 16, 1862, Federal Soldiers Letters (Miscellaneous), SHC.

3. William H. Wiggins, Jr., *O Freedom! Afro-American Emancipation Celebrations* (Knoxville: University of Tennessee Press, 1987), 25; James F. McGogy to Major O. D. Kinsman, July 10, 1866, Unregistered Letters Received, Greenville, Alabama, Series 9, Bureau of Refugees Freedmen and Abandoned Lands, Record Group 105, NA; Foner, *Reconstruction*, 72–73; Booker T. Washington, *Up from Slavery, An Autobiography* (New York: Bantam, 1967), 13; Robert L. Hall, "'Yonder Come Day': Religious Dimensions of the Transition from Slavery to Freedom in Florida," FHQ 65 (April 1987): 420–21; Gutman, *The Black Family in Slavery and Freedom*, 379–80.

4. Foner, *Reconstruction*, 133–34.

5. C. C. to Posey (Col. Powhatan R. Page), undated, Maxwell Troax Clarke Papers, SHC (emphasis in the original); Alice Pearson to Dear Aunt, March 17, 1864, Erastus Hoskins Papers (#7478), UVA; Mrs. J. E. White to Irene, February 20, 1865, Ada Bankhead Papers (#38–463), UVA; James L. Roark, *Masters without Slaves: Southern Planters in the Civil War and Reconstruction* (New York: Norton, 1977), 120–21; *Mary Chesnut's Civil War Diary*, ed. C. Vann Woodward (New Haven: Yale University Press, 1981), 800, 814; Virginia I. Burr, "A Woman Made to Suffer and Be Strong: Ella Gertrude Clanton Thomas, 1834–1907," in *In Joy and in Sorrow: Women, Family, and Marriage in the Victorian South, 1830–1900*, ed. Carol Bleser (New York: Oxford University Press, 1991), 222.

See Nancy T. Kondert, "The Romance and Reality of Defeat: Southern Women in 1865," JMH 35 (May 1973): 141–52.

6. Charles L. Flynn, Jr., *White Land, Black Labor: Caste and Class in Late Nineteenth-Century Georgia* (Baton Rouge: Louisiana State University Press, 1983), 10–12; Joseph Patrick Reidy, "Master and Slave Planters and Freedmen: The Transition from Slavery to Freedom in Central Georgia, 1820–1880," (Ph. D. diss., Northern Illinois University, 1982), 415; Kolchin.

See William Cohen, *At Freedom's Edge: Black Mobility and the Southern White Quest for Racial Control, 1861–1915* (Baton Rouge: Louisiana State University Press, 1991), 3–43.

7. Foner, *Reconstruction*, 425–34.

8. Ibid., 198–200.

9. Kate D. Foster Diary Transcript, July 16, 1863, July 28, 1863, DU; Foner, *Reconstruction*, 201; Robert H. Abzug, "The Black Family during Reconstruction," in *Key Issues in Afro American Experience*, vol. II, *Since 1865*, ed. Nathan I. Huggins, Martin Kilson, and Daniel M. Fox (New York: Harcourt Brace Jovanovich, 1971), 33; Reidy, "Master and Slave Planters and Freedmen," 166; Leon F. Litwack, *Been in the Storm so Long: The Aftermath of Slavery* (New York: Vintage, 1980), 232.

10. Foner, *Reconstruction*, 82.

See Ira Berlin, Steven F. Miller, and Leslie S. Rowland, "Afro-American Families in the Transition from Slavery to Freedom," RHR 42 (1988): 89–121.

11. John Vetter to William Bryant, February 6, 1866, John Vetter to Henry Kership, February 6, 1866, Register of Complaints, Arkansas, Record Group 105, BRFAL, NA; Register of Complaints, Kentucky, Series 1216–1219, vol. 152–53, BRFAL, NA; Mississippi Register of Complaints, Series 2128, vol. 144, BRFAL, NA; Jackson Easley to President Johnson September 24, 1866, Jackson Easley to General [Davis] Tilson, November 8, 1866, Unregistered Letters Received, Series 9 (A257), FSSP.

See Berlin et al., "Afro-American Families," 108–109; "Reports of Assistant Commissioners of the Freedmen's Bureau," *Senate Executive Documents*, vol. 2, 39th Cong., 1st. sess., 1865–1866, pp. 7–8.

12. Kate Drumgoold, "A Slave Girl's Story: Being an Autobiography of Kate Drumgoold," in *The Schomburg Library of Nineteenth-Century Black Women Writers: Six Women's Slave Narratives*, ed. Henry Louis Gates, Jr. (New York: Oxford University Press, 1988), 8; Annie L. Burton, *Memories of Childhood's Slavery Days* (Boston: Ross, 1909), 8, 11–12; Dorothy Sterling, ed., *The Trouble They Seen: Black People Tell the Story of Reconstruction* (Garden City: Doubleday, 1976), 68; Roark, *Masters without Slaves*, 80–85.

13. Berlin et al., "Afro-American Families," 103–104; May 11, 1867, Register of Complaints, Arkansas, vol. 286, BRFAL, NA.

For additional accounts relevant to the search for children by the Freedmen's Bureau see Kentucky Register of Complaints, August 14, 1866, September 8, 1866, September 22, 1866, April 16, 1866, April 24, 1866, April 25, 1866, May 24, 1866, June 8, 1866, June 18, 1866, June 19, 1866, July 10, 1866, Series 1216–1219, vol. 152, BRFAL, NA; Kentucky Register of Complaints, January 29, 1867, February 25, 1866, March 5, 1866, April 2, 1866, April 10, 1866, April 15, 1866, April 23, 1866, May 4, 1866, May 8, 1866, May 30, 1866, June 18, 1866, June 19, 1866, June 28, 1866, August 22, 1866, September 23, 1866, Series 1216–1219, vol. 153, BRFAL, NA; Mississippi Register of Complaints, March 17, 1868, May 13, 1868, Series 2128, vol. 144, BRFAL, NA.

14. For summarized details of the Polly Ann Johnson case see C. K. Smith to General O. O. Howard, November 5, 1867, Record Group 105, BRFAL, microcopy 798, Roll 17; Subassistant Commissioner, Albany, Georgia, register of letters received, Series 114, letters received, Series 693; Agent, Albany, Georgia, register of letters received, Series 115, Record Group 105, BRFAL, NA. These sources provided all references to the case.

15. See Rebecca Scott, "The Battle over the Child: Child Apprenticeship and the Freedmen's Bureau in North Carolina," *Prologue* 10 (Summer 1978): 102–104.

16. Swint, *Dear Ones at Home*, 243; Gutman, *The Black Family in Slavery and Freedom*, 6–7; Donald M. Scott and Bernard Wishy, eds., *America's Families: A Documentary History* (New York: Harper and Row, 1982), 325–26.

17. Berlin et al., "Afro-American Families," 100–101.

18. Ibid.

19. Tryphena Blanche Holder Fox (hereafter cited as TBHF) to Anna Rose Holder (hereafter cited as ARH), June 12, 1866, MDAH.

See Peter G. Slater, "'From the *Cradle* to the *Coffin*': Parental Bereavement and the Shadow of Infant Damnation in Puritan Society," in *Growing Up in America: Children in Historical Perspective*, ed. N. Ray Hiner and Joseph M. Hawes (Urbana: University of Illinois Press, 1985), 33–35.

20. Jacqueline Jones, *Labor of Love, Labor of Sorrow: Black Women, Work and the Family, from Slavery to the Present* (New York: Vintage, 1986), 52; Foner, *Reconstruction*, 84.

21. "Circulars and Circular Letters Received, June 11, 1866, Series 231 (A2250) FSSP; H. Sweeney to J. W. Sprague, August 15, 1855, Helena, Arkansas, Letters

Received, Series 231 (A2593), FSSP; George D. Robinson to C. Cadle, Jr., February 5, 1866, Reports of Operations from Subdistricts, Mobile, Alabama (1601), FSSP; S. I. Clark to Joseph Dickenson Clark, March 8, 1866, Letters Sent, 56th U.S. Colored Infantry, Regimental Books and Papers of the U.S. Colored Troops, Record Group 94, Adjutant General's Office (G258), FSSP; General Order No. 4, 56th U.S. Colored Infantry, March 8, 1866, Regimental Books and Papers of the U.S. Colored Troops, RG 94, Adjutant General's Office (G258), FSSP.

22. H. Sweeney to J. W. Sprague, August 15, 1855, Helena, Arkansas, Letters Received, Series 231 (A2593), FSSP.

23. Hall, "'Yonder Come Day,'" 425–26; Peter Kolchin, *First Freedom: The Responses of Alabama's Blacks to Emancipation and Reconstruction* (Westport: Greenwood, 1972), 60; Swint, *Dear Ones at Home*, 121; Berlin et al., "Afro-American Families," 93; Gutman, *The Black Family in Slavery and Freedom*, 11; Abzug, "The Black Family during Reconstruction," 31; Scott, *America's Families*, 324; Peter C. Ripley, "The Black Family in Transition: Louisiana, 1860–1865," JSH 41 (August 1975): 377–80; Michael Wayne, *The Reshaping of Plantation Society: The Natchez District, 1860–1880* (Baton Rouge: Louisiana State University Press, 1983), 133–34; Register of Marriage, Record Group 105, Entry 2073, No. 826, Roll 42, NA.

24. Albert J. Raboteau, *Slave Religion: The "Invisible Institution" in the Antebellum South* (New York: Oxford University Press, 1978), 229–30.

25. See George P. Rawick, ed., *The American Slave: A Composite Autobiography*, 10 vols. (Westport: Greenwood, 1979), X: Texas Narr. (Supplement, Series 2), Part 9: 4123; Sterling, *We Are Your Sisters*, 310.

26. Berlin et al., "Afro-American Families," 98.
After Maria Kiddoo and her husband ended their marriage voluntarily during slavery, both looked after the children.
See Complaints, June 24, 1867, vol. 238, Culbert, Georgia, Series 859 (A5558), FSSP.

27. Kentucky Register of Complaints, November 28, 1866, December 20, 1866, December 27, 1866, Series 1216–1219, vol. 152; J. C. Nain to James H. Rice, June 12, 1867, Jasamine County, Kentucky, Series 1198 (A4457), FSSP.

28. Memorial of Charles Manigault, Manigault Family Papers, SHC (emphases in the original). Thanks to Nell I. Painter for providing this citation.
See Gutman, *The Black Family in Slavery and Freedom*, 432–47.

29. Rawick, *The American Slave*, VI: Mississippi Narr. (Supplement, Series 1), Part 1:53.

30. Jacob Stroyer, *My Life in the South* (Salem: Salem Observer, 1889), 16; Reidy, "Master and Slave, Planters and Freedmen," 163–64.
See Herman Lantz and Lewellyn Hendrix, "Black Fertility and the Black Family in the Nineteenth Century: A Re-Examination of the Past," JFH 3 (Fall 1978): 251–61; Stanley L. Engerman, "Changes in Black Fertility, 1880–1940," in *Family and Population in the 19th Century*, ed. Tamara Hareven and Maris Vinovskis (Princeton: Princeton University Press, 1978), 126–53.

31. Elizabeth Hyde Botume, *The First Days amongst the Contrabands* (New York: Arno and *New York Times*, 1968), 45–49; Foner, *Reconstruction*, 79; Newbell N. Puckett, "American Negro Names," JNH 23 (January 1938): 38–40.

32. Anthony Butler to Franklin Benjamin Due [sic], February 11, 1872, Thomas Roderick Dew Collection, EGS; Henry Evans to Brian Pilpot, November 26, 1893, October 17, 1903, Evans Family Papers (#8485) UVA; Frederick Douglass, *Narrative and Selected Writings*, ed. Michael Meyer (New York: Random House, 1984), 18.

33. Harold D. Woodman, "Sequel to Slavery: The New History Views the Postbellum South," JSH 43 (November 1977): 550–51; Charles L. Flynn, Jr., *White Land, Black*

Labor: Caste and Class in Late Nineteenth-Century Georgia (Baton Rouge: Louisiana State University Press, 1983), 10–12; W. E. Burghardt Du Bois, *Black Reconstruction in America: An Essay toward a History of the Past Which Black Folk Played in the Attempt to Reconstruct Democracy in America, 1860–1880* (New York: Meridian, 1965), 167–71, 174–75; Reidy, "Coming from the Shadow of the Past," 415; Kolchin, *First Freedom*, 34; Foner, *Reconstruction*, 102–104.

    See William Cohen, *At Freedom's Edge: Black Mobility and the Southern White Quest for Racial Control, 1861–1915* (Baton Rouge: Louisiana State University Press, 1991), 3–43.

    34. Foner, *Reconstruction*, 201.

    35. "Laws in Relations to Freedmen compiled by Command of Major General O. O. Howard, Commander of the Bureau of Refugees, Freedmen, and Abandoned Lands," 39th Congress, 2nd Session, 1866–1867, Senate Ex. Doc. 6, pp. 172–74, 180–81, 190–91, 209–10; Reidy, "Master and Slave, Planters and Freedmen," 213–14; Du Bois, *Black Reconstruction*, 175.

    See District of Arkadelphia "Indenture of Apprenticeship," January 15, 1866, vol. 286, Box 1, BRFAL, NA.

    R. E. Reams and John Shackleford, a ten-year-old freed boy, executed a March 15, 1866, agreement whereby Shackleford would receive a suit of clothes and $150 upon reaching twenty-one years of age. "Indenture," March 15, 1866, vol. 286, Arkansas, Box 1, BRFAL, NA.

    36. Barbara Jeanne Fields, *Slavery and Freedom on the Middle Ground: Maryland during the Nineteenth Century* (New Haven: Yale University Press, 1985), 139; Reidy, "Master and Slave, Planters and Freedmen," 215; Scott, "The Battle over the Child," 102.

    37. *Historical Statistics of the United States, Colonial Times to 1970*, bicentennial edition, Part I (Washington: Government Printing Office, 1975), 18; Fields, *Slavery and Freedom on the Middle Ground*, 139.

    38. Berlin et al., "Afro-American Families," 110.

    39. Kolchin, *First Freedom*, 65–67; Berlin et al., "Afro-American Families," 102; Reidy, "Master and Slave, Planters and Freedmen," 216–17.

    40. Arkansas Register of Complaints, March 1866, vol. 89, 26, BRFAL, NA; Virginia Register of Complaints, March 15, 1867, Series 3839, vol. 143, BRFAL, NA; Kentucky Register of Complaints, May 4, 1866, December 31, 1866, Series 1216–1219, vol. 152, BRFAL, NA; South Carolina Register of Complaints, July 30, 1866, August 21, 1866, Series 3308–3309, vol. 254, BRFAL, NA; Scott, "Battle over the Child," 107; Fields, *Slavery and Freedom on the Middle Ground*, 139–40.

    See Kentucky Register of Complaints, August 1, 1866, Series 1216–1219, vol. 152, BRFAL, NA.

    41. Berlin et al., "Afro-American Families," 116–18.

    42. Berlin et al., "Afro-American Families," 102; C. C. Sibley to O. H. Howard, April 23, 1867 (Georgia), BRFAL, NA.

    43. Berlin et al., "Afro-American Families," 116.

    44. Scott, "Battle over the Child," 113.

    45. See Steven Hahn, "Hunting, Fishing, and Foraging: Common Rights and Class Relations in the Postbellum South," RHR 26 (1982): 37–64.

    46. Daniel E. Sutherland, "A Special Kind of Problem: The Response of Household Slaves and Their Masters to Freedom," SS 20 (Summer 1981): 164.

    47. TBHF to ARH, February 13, 1869, MDAH.

    48. TBHF to ARH, April 13, 1869, May 24, 1869, December 30, 1869, MDAH.

    49. TBHF to ARH, December 30, 1869, MDAH (emphasis in the original).

    50. Susan A. Mann, "Slavery, Sharecropping, and Sexual Inequality," *Signs* 14 (Summer 1989): 782; Ira Berlin, Thavolia Glymph, Steven F. Miller, Joseph P. Reidy, Leslie

S. Rowland, and Julie Seville, eds., *Freedom: A Documentary History of Emancipation, 1861–1867,* Series I, vol. III: *The Wartime Genesis of Free Labor* (Cambridge: Cambridge University Press, 1990), 469; Reidy, "Master and Slave, Planters and Freedmen," 196, 219–20; Flynn, *White Land, Black Labor,* 61–62; TBHF to ARH, October 2, 1868, MDAH.

See Susan Hamburger, "On the Land for Life: Black Tenant Farmers on Tall Timbers Plantation," FHQ 66 (October 1987): 153–59.

51. Child, *The Freedmen's Book,* 267; Reidy, "Master and Slave, Planters and Freedmen," 220–21.

52. Jones, *Labor of Love,* 60–61; Foner, *Reconstruction,* 103–104.

53. "Contract of January 29, 1866," Alonzo T. Mial Papers, NCDAH; Alonzo T. Mial to Ruffin Horton, December 6, 1859, Mial Papers, NCDAH; Flynn, *White Land, Black Labor,* 85–86.

54. "Freedman Work Agreement," December 30, 1865, George C. Hannah Papers (#2606), UVA; Cohen, *At Freedom's Edge,* 20–21; Flynn, *White Land, Black Labor,* 70–72.

See Joseph Reid, "Sharecropping as an Understandable Market Response: The Post Bellum South," JEH 33 (March 1973): 106–30.

55. "A Georgia Plantation," *Scribner's Monthly* 21 (April 1881): 832.

56. Jessie Melville Fraser, ed., "A Free Labor Contract, 1867," JSH 6 (November 1940): 548.

57. Jemison Proclamation 1865, Jemison Papers, SHC.

58. Jay R. Mandle, *Not Slave, Not Free: The African American Economic Experience since the Civil War* (Durham: Duke University Press, 1992), 13.

59. Abzug, "The Black Family during Reconstruction," 35–36; Berlin et al., *Freedom: A Documentary History,* 70–71; Sydney Nathans, "Fortress without Walls: A Black Community after Slavery," in *Holding on to the Land and the Lord: Kinship, Ritual, Land Tenure, and Social Polity in the Rural South,* ed. Robert L. Hall and Carol B. Stack (Athens: University of Georgia Press, 1982), 57–58; James M. McPherson, *Ordeal by Fire: The Civil War and Reconstruction* (New York: Knopf, 1982), 506; Verney, "Trespassers in the Land of Their Birth," 66–78.

See Philip D. Morgan, "Work and Culture: The Task System and the World of Lowcountry Blacks, 1700–1880," WMQ 39 (October 1982): 563–99; Thomas F. Armstrong, "From Task Labor to Free Labor: The Transition Along Georgia's Rice Coast, 1820–1880," GHQ 44 (Winter 1980): 432–47; Philip D. Morgan, "The Ownership of Property by Slaves in the Mid-Nineteenth Century Low Country," JSH 49 (August 1983): 399–420.

60. Rawick, *The American Slave,* VI: Mississippi Narr. (Supplement, Series 1), Part 1:64; VIII: Texas Narr. (Supplement, Series 2), Part 7:3140–41; Jones, *Labor of Love,* 64; Mandle, *Not Slave, Not Free,* 14.

61. Jacqueline Goggin, "Carter G. Woodson: Son of Slaves as Interpreter of Slavery" (paper in possession of the author), 2; Jacqueline Goggin, "Son of Slaves: The Contributions of Carter G. Woodson's Slave Background to the Historiography of Slavery," (paper presented at the Organization of American Historians Conference, Washington, D.C., March 24, 1990, in possession of the author), 1–2.

See Jacqueline Goggin, "Carter G. Woodson and the Collection of Source Materials for Afro-American History," AA 48 (Summer 1985): 261–71.

62. Alex Haley, "My Search for Roots: A Black American's Story," RD (May 1974): 73–78.

See Alex Haley, *Roots: The Saga of an American Family* (Garden City: Doubleday, 1976).

63. Bernard Mergen, "The Discovery of Children's Play," AQ 27 (October 1975): 410.

64. William Wells Newell, *Games and Songs of American Children* (New York: Dover, 1963), 70; Harold Courlander, *Negro Folk Music, U.S.A.* (New York: Columbia University Press, 1963), 157, presents a variation with differences in lines three and four:

> Li'l Sally Walker
> Sittin' in a saucer
> Cryin' for the old man
> To come for the dollar.

See Bessie Jones and Bess Lomax Hawes, *Step It Down: Games, Plays, Songs and Stories from the Afro-American Heritage* (Athens: University of Georgia Press, 1987), 107–109, for discussion of the game and song along with the score.

65. Rawick, *The American Slave*, XIII: Georgia Narr. (Series 2), Part 4:73, 85–86; Bernard Mergen, *Play and Playthings: A Research Guide* (Westport: Greenwood, 1982), 46.

66. Rawick, *The American Slave*, XIII: Georgia Narr. (Series 2), Part 4:85 (emphasis added).

67. Freemen Work Agreements, May 9, 1866, George Hannah Papers (#2602), UVA.
See "Freedmen Accounts, 1866," Watson Family Papers (#530), UVA.

68. Deposition enclosed in Christian Rausbenberg to M. Frank Gallagher, October 6, 1868, Governor's Incoming Correspondence, GDAH (Courtesy of Lee Formwalt); Flynn, *White Land, Black Labor*, 63; Reidy, "Master and Slave Planters and Freedmen," 165.

69. See Pauli Murray, *Proud Shoes: The Story of an American Family* (New York: Harper and Row, 1987).

70. Quoted from Swint, *Dear Ones at Home*, 125–26; Botume, *First Days amongst the Contrabands*, 93; Robert F. Engs, *Freedom's First Generation: Black Hampton, Virginia, 1861–1890* (Philadelphia: University of Pennsylvania Press, 1979), 20; Lewis C. Lockwood to the AMA, December 23, 1861, AMA; Jacqueline Jones, *Soldiers of Light and Love* (Chapel Hill: University of North Carolina Press, 1980), 117.

71. Booker T. Washington, *Up from Slavery* (New York: Bantam, 1967), 20–21; James D. Anderson, *The Education of Blacks in the South, 1860–1935* (Chapel Hill: University of North Carolina Press, 1988), 5–78.

See Elizabeth Hyde Botume, *The First Days amongst the Contrabands* (New York: Arno and *New York Times*, 1968); Charlotte L. Forten, *The Journal of Charlotte L. Forten: A Negro in the Slave Era*, ed. Ray Allen Billington (New York: Collier, 1967); Elizabeth Jacoway, *Yankee Missionaries in the South: The Penn School Experiment* (Baton Rouge: Louisiana State University Press, 1980).

72. Botume, *First Days amongst the Contrabands*, 93–95; Swint, *Dear Ones at Home*, 90, 126.

73. Swint, *Dear Ones at Home*, 41; Louisa Cocke to JHC, January 9, 1830 (#640), UVA.

74. Edgar A. Toppin, *A Biographical History of Blacks in America since 1528* (New York: David McKay, 1971), 121–22.

75. TBHF to ARH, July 15, 1865, MDAH.
See "Report of the First Superintendent State of Louisiana," BRFAL, NA.

76. Morris, *Reading, 'Riting, and Reconstruction*, 180–83; Paul David Phillips, "Education of Blacks in Tennessee during Reconstruction, 1865–1870," THQ 46 (Summer 1987): 107; Child, *The Freedmen's Book*, 269–76.

77. Hall, "Yonder Come Day," 413–14; Bell Irvin Wiley, *Southern Negroes, 1861–1865* (New Haven: Yale University Press, 1965), 98–102.

78. C. T. Watson to O. H. Howard, August 29, 1867, Albany, Georgia, Letters Received A 151, Record Group 105, BRFAL, NA.

79. Daniel Webster Davis, *'Weh Down Souf and other Poems* (Cleveland: Helman-Taylor, 1897), 54–56. Thanks to Elsa Barkley Brown for this citation.

80. See Rawick, *The American Slave*, II: South Carolina Narr. (Part 1), 43; X: Arkansas Narr. (Part 5), 2173.

81. Hollis B. Frissell, untitled, undated speech about "folk lore entertainment," 2, 5, Hollis B. Frissell Papers, HUA; "Folk-Lore and Ethnology," SW 24 (February 1895): 31.

82. *Jubilee and Plantation Songs*, 51; Rawick, *Slave Narratives*, VI: Alabama Narr., Series 1, 11.

83. Lee Formwalt, "Petitioning Congress for Protection: A Black View of Reconstruction at the Local Level," GHQ 73 (Summer 1989): 318.

84. Rawick, *The American Slave*, VI: Alabama and Indiana Narr. (Series 1), 323; Charshee Charlotte Lawrence-McIntyre, "The Double Meanings of the Spirituals," JBS 17 (June 1987): 390.

85. Perdue et al., *Weevils in the Wheat*, 327; Rawick, *The American Slave*, XI: Missouri Narr., 87.

86. See Terrence Des Pres, *The Survivors: An Anatomy of Life in the Death Camps* (New York: Oxford University Press, 1976).

87. Herbert G. Gutman, *The Black Family in Slavery and Freedom, 1750–1925* (New York: Vintage, 1977), 149 (emphasis in the original).

APPENDIX A

JOHN C. COHOON, ACCOUNT BOOK, SUFFOLK AND NANSEMOND COUNTY, VIRGINIA, 1810–1860

FANNY & JACOBS CHILDREN

1. Henry	October 2, 1811	Wed
2. Mary	August 4, 1816	
3. Charles	February 14, 1818	
4. Lucy	February 29, 1824	
5. Rachel	January 19, 1828	
6. Margaret	July 29, 1831	
7. Jefferson	February 2, 1833	
8. Matilda	February 9, 1835	

TOM & MARGARET OR PEGS CHILDREN

1. Tom	November 11, 1815	Sat
2. Lewis	October 17, 1817	Sun
3. Jack	August 3, 1819	Monday
4. Robert	March 8, 1821	Thursday
5. Lizzy	December 15, 1822	
6. Huddah	August 9, 1824	
7. Adaline	July 2, 1827	willed[*]
8. Bristol	May 23, 1831	d. unknown
9. Amy	January 24, 1833	sold
10. Sylvia	October 9, 1838	d.

CHLOE

1. David	October 1826	
2. Jackson	May 28, 1829	given to Wm Johnson
	Chloe died December 26, 1860	

EDMOND & NANCYS CHILDREN

1. Belsey	October (18)17 ?	Friday
2. Emaline	November 30, 1822	Saturday
3. Edmond	September 3, 1824	Friday
4. William	April 1, 1826	Saturday
5. Martha	December 28, 1829	Monday
6. Dinah	July 15, 1834	

APPENDIX A

BOB & JINNYS CHILDREN

1. Philip	November 27, 1823	
2. Hulda	November 27, 1825	
3. Edward	March 31, 1828	
4. Elijah	February 20, 1830	

BOB & MARYS CHILDREN

1. Fanny	February 27, 1836
2. Jacob	September 14, 1837

FARLEYS CHILDREN

1. William Augustus	November 25, 1836	
2. Sarah Elizabeth	June 8, 1840	2 o'clock
3. Emily (or Milly)	January 1844	d.
4. Virginia (Christina)		d.1846
5. Thomas		d.1848
6. Moses	February 2, 1850	

[In 1837 Cohoon gave Farley and her children to his son Willis.
Dick Pettis is mentioned as Farley's husband and the father of several of her children.]

BETSEYS CHILDREN

Adeline
Easter
William
Judith
Sam

CELIAS CHILDREN

1. Eliza	1829	
2. Ellick	July 29, 1831	
3. Issac	August 1835	sold bad conduct
4. Nancy	September 13, 1838	Thursday
5. Frank	July 8, 1840	
6. Cornelius	February 23, 1844	
7. Luke	September 6, 1845	
8. Jacob	February 5, 1849	
9. John	October 8, 1851	

HARRY & HARRIETS

1. Mariah	1837	
2. Washington	October 16, 1838	Tuesday am
3. Richard	February 11, 1840	

APPENDIX A

4. Jacob	December 4, 1841	
5. Lucy	March 26, 1843	5:30 am
6. James Henry	March 18, 1844	1/2 past 5 Monday
7. Fanny	May 11, 1845	4 am Monday
8. Indiana	November 26, 1846	5 am Wed
9. Easter	September 18, 1848	d. July 4, 1858†
10. Henry	November 19, 1849	d. July 9, 1858†
11. Wilson	May 14, 1852	d. July 1, 1858†
12. Josiah	September 11, 1854	
13. Missouri	January 17, 1857	
14. Jerusha	January 3, 1859	4 am Monday
15. Unnamed	June 30, 1861	11: o'clock

ISSAC HODGES & LIZZYS

1. Mirah	November 9, 1841	
2. Josephine	October 19, 1844	d. October 19,1844
3. Coharone [?]	April 1, 1846	d. April 1, 1846
4. Amey	May 4, 1849	
5. Washington	Unknown	d. November 1854
6. Mary Ann	August 24, 1853	
7. Unnamed	December 19, 1856	
8. Unnamed	October 18, 1858	
9. Unnamed	August 26, 1859	
10. Unnamed	1860	
11. Robert	December 15, 1862	Friday 3 o'clock

LITTLE BOB AND HULDAH JUNE

1. Miles	May 8, 1843	Mon 3 pm
2. Jenny	January 20, 1845	" 11 am
3. Samuel	March 29, 1847	
4. Edward	May 18, 1850	Sat 8 pm
5. Sarah Ann	April 13, 1853	died
6. Elijah	November 16, 1855	
7. Adeline	September 18, 1857	
8. Sylvia	December 23, 1859	d. July, 23, 1863
Little Bob died.	Unknown	

RACHEL‡CHILDREN & DAVID

1. Charles Edward	Friday 22nd Mar 1850
2. Mary Frances	Wed 4th May 1854
3. Alice Amelia	January 7, 1857
4. Josephine	March 11, 1859
5. Anna Mariah	May 28, 1860
6. Thomas (Aliscan)	December 23, 1862

APPENDIX A

HULDA AND LEWIS

1. Lucy Ann	November 29, 1846	
2. Lewis	January 14, 1850	d.unknown
3. Mary Va.	October 28, 1853	(recorded as no. 4)
4. Nathaniel	November 4, 1854	

MARGARET

1. Unknown	September 5, 1850	
2. Lucretia	October 15, 1854	d.unknown
3. Florence	December 9, 1855	
4. Margaret Louisa	May 20, 1857	
5. Georgiana	January 9, 1861	

MATILDA

1. Wash.	October 4, 1852	
2. Lucy Ann	January 5, 1854	
3. John Jefferson	November 14, 1862	5 o'clock am Friday

(Child of John Saunders and Matilda)

ELIZA

1. Octavia	(Torn)	
2. Henrietta	"	
3. Miles Washington	"	
4. Andrew Jackson	"	Henry Arthur is Andrew's father.
5. Samuel William	"	

Source: Alderman Library, University of Virginia, Charlottesville, Virginia.

Notes

* This child became the property of another person through a will.

† The cause of death is unknown. There is the possibility of a severe illness in Harry and Harriet's household. The absence of deaths among other children of comparable ages on the plantation suggests that the cause of death was not a widespread illness or disease.

Cohoon gave Jackson to his son, William. The date of the transfer is not recorded; therefore, there is no way of knowing Jackson's age or if this was before or after his mother died. Jackson is referred to as a "negro boy" in the original.

‡ Note that this is the only family listed where the woman's name appears before the man's. Rachel seems to have taken a husband on the Cohoon place after she gave birth to at least her first child.

APPENDIX B

WILLIS AND MARTHA

Creasy	September 30, 1854
Spencer	January 2, 1856
Wilson	June 24, 1858
Maria Jane	January 14, 1860
Unknown	August 29, 1861

Willis died September 16, 1862

Source: Bills Southern Historical Collection, University of North Carolina, Chapel Hill, North Carolina.

APPENDIX C

"RULES OF GOVERNMENT OF PLANTATION"

Negroes

1. To be kept in good order & at home & not to leave plantation without a ticket & that to express the place they are to go to & how long to be absent & not to be any greater distance than a few miles without my express orders, except to the nearest church. Tickets to be given alone by me, wife, or son.
2. They are not to be allowed to go to any village Store, shop, or Tavern without my express permission not to any place suspected of trading with negroes.
3. Not to have meetings on Plantation for Preaching, Funerals, or praying, dancing or other purposes or to go to any without my ——— order. But they are to be allowed & required to go to the nearest church one Sunday ——— twice on Saturdays. They are to be allowed to a ——— to getting to pray & sing on Sundays & Sunday evenings, but to disperse at bed time or nine o'clock at night.
4. No negro but those connected to my negroes & of good character to be allowed on Plantation & they must have a ticket for that permission from their owners & to be brought to me except them that have a wife or husband on the Plantation.
5. Allowance of Food must be given out every week on Monday morning in such quantities & of such articles as I may direct from time to time.
6. The little negro children must be taken care of.
7. Such women as may be near being confined must be put early to light work & after delivery & able to go about must be put to light work for a time.
8. They must plant a crop & tend it, but are not to be allowed to work on a Sunday. The women must take care of their familey & Clothing.
9. They must clean out their house, by Saturday night. Their yard & walks. get wood for Sunday wash their cloths ——— if not raining put out to air their bedding & woolen clothing.
10. They are not allowed to sell any articles without my permission nor to purchase any article.
11. They are not to raise for themselves any Hogs, Cows or horse, but may raise fowls & Ducks.
12. They must be kept from the use of *arduit* Spirits & discouraged from use of it & tobacco.
13. Their houses & chimnies must be kept in order & reparied when necessary. Their well must be kept clean.
14. All drunkeness, ——— lying, stealing or other ——— to be punished as I may direct For all violations of these rules they are to be corrected.
15. No man must whip his wife without my permission.
16. Reproof, rebuke, admonition & advice must be made use of in all instances of misconduct or neglect of duty or disobedience. A Fatherly care & conduct must be

APPENDIX C

observed towards them. & they taught "*To do to each other as they would that others should do to them.*"

17. For neglecting to ———— work, after the first time they must be corrected moderately.
18. In correcting a negro, no knife, stick or dangerous weapon must be used but a cowskin or whip.
19. All offences must be punished as I shall direct from time to time.
20. If a small negro runs away the meat of the family must be taken away or withholden until return.
    If a grown one the meat of all must be taken away or withholden.
21. Corn must be beat out every week.
22. On Saturdays must leave off *work or da male taker to be at home at least an hour before down.*

Source: "Rules for Government of Plantation," McDonald Furman Corn Hill Plantation Book, 105–107, Perkins Library, Duke University, Durham, North Carolina.

APPENDIX D

1. Abraham (58)...............sold to Richard Huston
   Mary (45) Susan (5 mos.)...sold to Alfred Keene
   George (16)................allotted to widow
   Malinda (10)..............sold to Andrew Spencer
   William (7)................sold to Samuel B. Spence
   Robert (5)................sold to Elias Redman

2. Harry (36)................sold to Samuel Dunham
   Nancy (36) George (3)......sold to Marcus Wills
   Mary (11).................sold to Exekial Kirtley
   Dinah (7).................sold to Jeremiah Hayden

3. Lucinda (37)..............allotted to the widow
   Allen (17)................allotted to the widow
   Frank (11)................sold to Peter Carter
   Betsy (9).................sold to Zachariah Ridgway
   Chaney (8)................sold to Fountain Toalson
   Fanny (5).................sold to James Coats
   Mary (3)..................sold to Joseph Fountain
   David (1).................sold to Absalom Fountain

Source: James William McGettigan, Jr., "Boone County Slaves: Sales, Estate Divisions and Families, 1820–1865," Part II, *Missouri Historical Review*, 72 (1978): 287–88.

BIBLIOGRAPHY

NEWSPAPERS

Charleston Mercury
Richmond Enquirer
Southern Workman

GOVERNMENT RECORDS

Compendium of the Seventh Census of the United States: 1850. Washington: Government Printing Office, 1854.

Historical Statistics of the United States, Colonial Times to 1970, bicentennial ed. Washington: Government Printing Office, 1975.

"Laws in Relations to Freedmen compiled by Command of Major General O. O. Howard, Commander of the Bureau of Refugees, Freedmen, and Abandoned Lands," 39th Cong., 2nd sess., 1866–1867, Senate Ex. Doc. 6.

Population of the United States in 1860, Compiled from Original Returns of the Eighth Census by Joseph C. G. Kennedy. (Washington: Government Printing Office, 1864).

Senate Executive Documents, vol. 2, 39th Cong., 1st sess., 1865–1866.

U.S. Department of the Army, U.S. Military History Institute, Photographic Collection, Carlisle Barracks, Carlisle, Pennsylvania.

U.S. Department of Census. *The Seventh Census of 1850.* Washington: Government Printing Office, 1854.

U.S. Department of Commerce, Bureau of Census. *Historical Statistics of the United States, Colonial Times to 1970,* bicentennial ed. 2 vols. Washington: Government Printing Office, 1975.

MANUSCRIPTS

Alderman Library, University of Virginia, Charlottesville, Virginia [UVA]
        William Taylor Barry Letterbook (#2569)
        Ada Bankhead Papers (#38-463)
        Hunter Brown Collection
        John Hartwell Cocke Papers (#640)
        John C. Cohoon Account Book (#8868)
        Dick Journal (#4528)
        Martha Tabb Dyer Diaries (#7776-D)
        Evans Family Papers (#8485)
        Adam Foster Letter (#10103)
        Freedman's Account Book
        Gordon Family Papers (#9553)
        George C. Hannah Papers (#1332)
        Erastus Hoskins Papers (#7478)
        Indenture (#6060)
        Wallace Family Papers (#2689)
        Watson Family Papers (#530)
Earl Gregg Swem Library, The College of William and Mary, Williamsburg, Virginia [EGS]

BIBLIOGRAPHY

        Austin-Twyman Collection
        Tucker-Coleman Collection
        Thomas Roderick Dew Papers
        I. de Courcy Laffan Letter
        John Marshall Papers
        Prentis Family Papers
        Ritchie-Harrison Papers
Fortress Monroe, Hampton, Virginia
        Casement Papers
Freedmen and Southern Society Project, University of Maryland [FSSP]
Georgia Department of Archives and History, Atlanta, Georgia [GDAH]
        Governor's Incoming Correspondence
Hampton University Archives, Hampton, Virginia [HUA]
        First Summer School Files
        Hollis B. Frissell Papers
Historic New Orleans Collection, New Orleans, Louisiana [HNOC]
        Thomas Moore Papers
Library of Congress, Washington, D.C. [LC]
        Greenwood Plantation Records
        Thomas Sewell Papers
        Sterritt Papers
        Enoch Tucker Papers
Mississippi Department of Archives and History, Jackson, Mississippi [MDAH]
        Tryphena Blanche Holder Fox Collection
Museum of the Confederacy, Richmond, Virginia [MC]
        Before Freedom Came Exhibit
National Archives, Washington, D.C. [NA]
        Southern Claims Commission
        Seventh United States Census
        Eighth United States Census
        Bureau of Refugees, Freedmen, and Abandoned Lands, Record Group 105
        [BRFAL]
North Carolina Department of Archives and History, Raleigh, North Carolina
        [NCDAH]
        Ezell Papers
        Alonzo T. Mail Papers
        Slave Collection 1748–1756
North Caroliniana Collection, University of North Carolina, Chapel Hill, North Carolina
        The University Magazine
South Caroliniana Library, University of South Carolina, Columbia, South Carolina
        [SC]
        Lawton Family Papers
Southern Historical Collection, University of North Carolina, Chapel Hill, North Caro-
        lina [SHC]
        Edward Clifford Andrews Papers
        Arnold and Screven Family Papers
        Everard Green Baker Diary
        Robert Ruffin Barrow Books
        Mary E. Bateman Diary
        Bayside Plantation Records
        John Houston Bills Papers

BIBLIOGRAPHY

Launcelot Minor Blackford Diaries
Willis P. Bocock Paper
John Peter Broun Papers
Caffery Family Papers
Carmichael Family Books
Tod Robinson Caldwell Papers
Farish Carter Papers
Henry L. Cathell Diary
Maxwell Troax Clarke Papers
Eliza Carolina Clitherall
Davidson Family Papers
Federal Soldiers Letters (Miscellaneous)
William Ethelbert Ervin Book
Silas Everett Fales Book
John Edwin Fripp Papers
David Gavin Diary
James Hervey Greenlee Diary
Francis Hanson Diary
Harding and Jackson Family Papers
Ernest Haywood Collection
Hentz Family Papers
Hilary Abner Herbert Papers
William Alexander Hoke Papers
William Henry Holcombe Books
Franklin A. Hudson Diary
Samuel Cram Jackson Diary
Jemison Papers
Manigault Family Papers
Thomas Butler King Papers
Alexander Robert Lawton Papers
Francis Terry Leak Diary
James S. Milling Papers
Mordecai Family Papers
John Nevitt Diary
Newstead Plantation Diaries
James Parkhill Papers
Pettigrew Family Papers
William Blount Rodman Papers
James H. Ruffin Plantation Books
Henry E. Simmons Letters
William Henry Sims Papers
White Hill Plantation Books
Nicholas Washington Woodfin Papers
State Historical Society of Wisconsin, Madison, Wisconsin [SHSW]
Benjamin Bealk Papers
William Sabb Papers
Tulane University, New Orleans, Louisiana [TU]
Amistad Collection
American Missionary Association Papers
Special Collection
Slave Manuscript Series

BIBLIOGRAPHY

Virginia State Library, Richmond, Virginia [VSL]
    Legislative Petitions
William R. Perkins Library, Duke University, Durham, North Carolina [DU]
    James Allred Papers
    Mary Ann Buie Papers
    Abel Crawford Papers
    Kate D. Foster Diary Transcript
    McDonald Furman Papers
    Louis Manigualt Papers
    Negro Collection, Slavery Division
    Rankin-Parker Papers
    Issac Shoemaker Diary
    Notley D. Tomlin Papers

MICROFILM

Stampp, Kenneth M., ed. *Records of Ante-Bellum Southern Plantations from the Revolution through the Civil War*, Series G, Part I, Texas and Louisiana. Frederick, MD: University Publications of America, 1987.

UNPUBLISHED PAPERS AND DISSERTATIONS

Bogger, Tommy Lee. "The Slave and Free Black Community in Norfolk, 1775–1865." Ph.D. diss., University of Virginia, 1976.

Clark, Maxine Lorraine. "Race Concepts and Self-Esteem in Black Children." Ph.D. diss., University of Illinois, 1979.

Cody, Cheryll Ann. "Slave Demography and Family Formation: A Community Study of the Ball Family Plantations, 1720–1896." Ph.D. diss., University of Minnesota, 1982.

Coyner, Martin Boyd, Jr. "John Hartwell Cocke of Bremo: Agriculture and Slavery in the Antebellum South." Ph.D. diss., University of Virginia, 1961.

Dawley, Karen Ellen. "Childhood in Eighteenth Century Virginia." M.A. thesis, University of Virginia, 1973.

Drake, Richard Bryant. "The American Missionary Association and the Southern Negro." Ph.D. diss., Emory University, 1957.

Goggin, Jacqueline. "Carter G. Woodson: Son of Slaves as Interpreter of Slavery." Unpublished paper in possession of the author, n.d.

———. "Son of Slaves: The Contributions of Carter G. Woodson's Slave Background to the Historiography of Slavery." Paper presented at the Organization of American Historians Conference, Washington, D.C., March 24, 1990.

Gomez, Michael A. "Muslims in Early America." Paper presented at the Association for the Study of Afro-American Life and History Conference, October, 1990, Chicago.

Hall, Robert L. "Lord Deliver Us from Cliometrics and from 70.56 Whippings per Year: Prolegomena to a Social History of Slave Whippings in the United States." Unpublished paper in the possession of the author, n.d.

Huber, Jo Anne Sellers. "Southern Women and the Institution of Slavery." M.A. thesis, Lamar University, 1980.

Jones, Bobby Frank. "A Cultural Middle Passage: Slave Marriage and Family in the Antebellum South." Ph.D. diss., University of North Carolina, 1965.

Petersen, Michael. "Patrollers and Social Conflict in the Antebellum South." History 601 Seminar Paper, Indiana University of Pennsylvania, Fall 1987.

BIBLIOGRAPHY

Reidy, Joseph Patrick. "Master and Slave Planters and Freedmen: The Transition from Slavery to Freedom in Central Georgia, 1820–1880." Ph.D. diss., Northern Illinois University, 1982.

Stafford, Hanford Dozier. "Slavery in a Border City: Louisville, 1790–1860." Ph.D. diss., University of Kentucky, 1982.

Weiner, Marli Frances. "Plantation Mistresses and Female Slaves: Gender, Race, and South Carolina Women, 1830–1880. Ph.D. diss., University of Rochester, 1985.

PUBLISHED SOURCES

Abzug, Robert H. "The Black Family during Reconstruction." In *Key Issues in Afro American Experience,* vol. II, *Since 1865,* ed. Nathan I. Huggins, Martin Kilson, and Daniel M. Fox, 26–43. New York: Harcourt Brace Jovanovich, 1971.

Adams, John R. *Edward Everett Hale.* Boston: Twayne, 1977.

Alford, Terry. *Prince among Slaves: The True Story of an African Prince Sold into Slavery in the American South.* New York: Oxford University Press, 1986.

Alho, Olli. *The Religion of the Slaves: A Study of the Religious Tradition and Behavior of Plantation Slaves in the United States 1830–1865.* Helsinki: Academia Scientiarum Fennica, 1976.

Anderson, James D. *The Education of Blacks in the South, 1860–1935.* Chapel Hill: University of North Carolina Press, 1988.

Ayisi, Eric O. *An Introduction to the Study of African Culture,* 2d ed. London: Heinemann, 1986.

Ball, Charles. *Fifty Years in Chains: or The Life of an American Slave.* New York: Dayton and Asher, 1859.

Bancroft, Frederick. *Slave-Trading in the Old South.* New York: Unger Press, 1959.

Barber, John W. *A History of the Amistad Captives: Being a Circumstantial Account of the Capture of the Spanish Schooner Amistad, by the Africans on Board; Their Voyage, and Capture Near Long Island, New York; With Biographical Sketches of each of the Surviving Africans. Also, An Account of The Trials Had on their Case, Before the District and Circuit Courts of the United States, For the District of Connecticut.* New Haven: E. L. and J. W. Barber, 1840.

Bardaglio, Peter. "'An Outrage upon Nature': Incest and the Law in the Nineteenth-Century South." In *In Joy and in Sorrow: Women, Family, and Marriage in the Victorian South, 1830–1900,* ed. Carol Bleser, 32–51. New York: Oxford University Press, 1991.

Barksdale, Richard, and Keneth Kinnamon, eds. *Black Writers of America: A Comprehensive Anthology.* New York: Macmillan, 1972.

Bellows, Barbara L. "'My Children, Gentlemen, Are My Own': Poor Women, the Urban Elite, and the Bonds of Obligation in Antebellum Charleston." In *The Web of Southern Social Relations: Women, Family, and Education,* ed. Walter Fraser, Jr., 52–71. Athens: University of Georgia Press, 1985.

Berlin, Ira. *Slaves without Masters: The Free Negro in the Antebellum South.* New York: Oxford University Press, 1981.

Berlin, Ira, Thavolia Glymph, Steven F. Miller, Joseph P. Reidy, Leslie S. Rowland, and Julie Seville, eds. *Freedom: A Documentary History of Emancipation, 1861–1867,* Series I, vol. III: *The Wartime Genesis of Free Labor.* Cambridge: Cambridge University Press, 1990.

Berry, Mary Frances, and John W. Blassingame. *Long Memory: The Black Experience in America.* New York: Oxford University Press, 1982.

BIBLIOGRAPHY

Bettelheim, Bruno. *The Uses of Enchantment: The Meaning and Importance of Fairy Tales.* New York: Knopf, 1977.

Betts, Edwin Morris, ed. *Thomas Jefferson's Farm Book, with Commentary and Relevant Extracts from Other Writings.* Princeton: Princeton University Press, 1953.

Bibb, Henry. "Narrative of the Life and Adventures of Henry Bibb: An American Slave Written by Himself." In *Puttin' On Ole Massa: The Slave Narratives of Henry Bibb, William Wells Brown, and Solomon Northup,* ed. Gilbert Osofsky, 51–171. New York: Harper, 1969.

Blackford, Launcelot Minor. *Mine Eyes Have Seen the Glory: The Story of A Virginia Lady Mary Berkeley Minor Blackford, 1802–1896 Who Taught Her Sons to Hate Slavery and to Love the Union.* Cambridge: Harvard University Press, 1954.

Blassingame, John W. *The Slave Community: Plantation Life in the Antebellum South,* rev. ed. New York: Oxford University Press, 1979.

———. "Status and Social Structure in the Slave Community: Evidence from New Sources." In *Perspectives and Irony in American Slavery,* ed. Harry P. Owens, 137–51. Jackson: University Press of Mississippi, 1976.

———, ed. *Slave Testimony: Two Centuries of Letters, Speeches, Dictations, and Autobiographies.* Baton Rouge: Louisiana State University Press, 1977.

Bone, Robert. *Down Home: A History of Afro-American Short Fiction from Its Beginnings to the End of the Harlem Renaissance.* New York: Capricorn, 1975.

Bonner, James. *A History of Georgia Agriculture, 1732–1860.* Athens: University of Georgia Press, 1964.

Botkin, B. A., ed. *Lay My Burden Down: A Folk History of Slavery.* Chicago: University of Chicago Press, 1965.

Botume, Elizabeth Hyde. *The First Days amongst the Contrabands.* New York: Arno and *New York Times,* 1968.

Breeden, James O., ed. *Advice among Masters: The Ideal in Slave Management in the Old South.* Westport: Greenwood, 1980.

Bremner, Robert H., ed. *Children and Youth in America: A Documentary History.* Cambridge: Harvard University Press, 1970.

Brodie, Fawn M. *Thomas Jefferson, An Intimate History.* New York: Norton, 1974.

Brown, William Wells. *My Southern Home: or, The South and Its People.* New York: Negro Universities Press, 1969.

———. "Narrative of William Wells Brown: A Fugitive Slave Written by Himself." In *Puttin' On Ole Massa: The Slave Narratives of Henry Bibb, William Wells Brown, and Solomon Northup,* ed. Gilbert Osofsky, 174–223. New York: Harper, 1969.

Brownmiller, Susan. *Against Our Will: Men, Women, and Rape.* New York: Simon and Schuster, 1975.

Burr, Virginia I. "A Woman Made to Suffer and Be Strong: Ella Gertrude Clanton Thomas, 1834–1907." In *In Joy and in Sorrow: Women, Family, and Marriage in the Victorian South, 1830–1900,* ed. Carol Bleser, 215–32. New York: Oxford University Press, 1991.

Burton, Annie L. *Memories of Childhood's Slavery Days.* Boston: Ross, 1909.

Campbell, Stanley W. "Runaway Slaves." In *Dictionary of Afro-American Slavery,* ed. Randall M. Miller and John David Smith, 649–52. Westport: Greenwood, 1988.

Cary, Virginia. *Letters on Female Character Addressed to a Young Lady on the Death of Her Mother,* 2d ed. Richmond: Ariel, 1830.

Catterall, Helen Tunnicliff, ed. *Judicial Cases Concerning American Slavery and the Negro.* Washington: Carnegie Institution of Washington, 1926, vol. I., reprinted 1969. University Microfilms, Ann Arbor, Michigan.

Censer, Jane Turner. *North Carolina Planters and Their Children, 1800–1860.* Baton Rouge: Louisiana State University Press, 1984.

BIBLIOGRAPHY

Chesnut, Mary Boykin. *A Diary from Dixie*. Ed. Ben Ames Williams. Boston: Houghton Mifflin, 1950.

———. *Mary Chesnut's Civil War Diary*. Ed. C. Vann Woodward. New Haven: Yale University Press, 1981.

Child, L. Maria. *The Freedmen's Book*. Boston: Fields, Osgood, 1869.

Clinkscales, J. G. *On the Old Plantation: Reminiscences of His Childhood*. New York: Negro Universities Press, 1969.

Clinton, Catherine. "Caught in the Web of the Big House: Women and Slavery." In *The Web of Southern Social Relations: Women, Family, and Education*, ed. Walter Fraser, Jr., 19–34. Athens: University of Georgia Press, 1985.

———. *The Plantation Mistress: Woman's World in the Old South*. New York: Pantheon, 1982.

Cohen, William. *At Freedom's Edge: Black Mobility and the Southern White Quest for Racial Control, 1861–1915*. Baton Rouge: Louisiana State University Press, 1991.

Coker, Elizabeth Boatwright. *Daughter of Strangers*. New York: Dutton, 1950.

Coleman, Mrs. George P. (Mary Haldane Begg Coleman). *Virginia Silhouette: Contemporary Letters Concerning Negro Slaves in the State of Virginia*. Richmond: Dietz, 1934.

Cornelius, Janet Duitsman. *When I Can Read My Title Clear: Literacy, Slavery, and Religion in the Antebellum South*. Columbia: University of South Carolina Press, 1991.

Courlander, Harold. *Negro Folk Music, U.S.A.* New York: Columbia University Press, 1963.

Creel, Margaret Washington. "Gullah Attitudes toward Life and Death." In *Africanisms in American Culture*, ed. Joseph E. Holloway, 69–97. Bloomington: Indiana University Press, 1990.

Crews, Harry. *A Childhood: The Biography of a Place*. New York: Harper and Row, 1978.

Curtin, Patricia Romero. "Slave Children." In *Dictionary of Afro-American Slavery*, ed. Randall M. Miller and John David Smith, 99–102. Westport: Greenwood, 1988.

Curtin, Philip D. *The Atlantic Slave Trade: A Census*. Madison: University of Wisconsin Press, 1970.

David, Paul A., Herbert G. Gutman, Richard Sutch, Peter Temin, and Gavin Wright, eds. *Reckoning with Slavery: A Critical Study in the Quantitative History of American Negro Slavery*. New York: Oxford University Press, 1976.

Davis, Daniel Webster. *'Weh Down Souf and other Poems*. Cleveland: Helman-Taylor, 1897.

Davis, David Brion. *The Problem of Slavery in Western Culture*. Ithaca: Cornell University Press, 1966.

Davis, Edwin Adams, ed. *Plantation Life in the Florida Parishes of Louisiana, 1836–1846: As reflected in the Diary of Bennett H. Barrow*. New York: AMS, 1967.

Davis, Glenn. *Childhood and History*. New York: Psychohistory Press, 1976.

De Burg, William L. Van. *The Slave Driver: Black Agricultural Supervision in the Antebellum South*. Westport: Greenwood, 1979.

Degler, Carl N. *Neither Black nor White: Slavery and Race Relations in Brazil and the United States*. New York: Macmillan, 1971.

Delaney, Lucy A. "From the Darkness Cometh the Light or Struggles for Freedom." In *The Schomburg Library of Nineteenth-Century Black Women Writers: Six Women's Slave Narratives*, ed. Henry Louis Gates, Jr. New York: Oxford University Press, 1988.

Demos, John, and Virginia Demos. "Adolescence in Historical Perspective." In *The American Family in Social-Historical Perspective*, ed. Michael Gordon, 209–17. New York: St. Martin's, 1973.

BIBLIOGRAPHY

Dorfman, Ariel. *The Empire's Old Clothes: What the Lone Ranger, Babar, and Other Innocent Heroes Do to Our Minds*. New York: Pantheon, 1983.

Douglass, Frederick. *Frederick Douglass: The Narrative and Selected Writings*. Ed. Michael Meyer. New York: Random House, 1984.

———. *Life and Times of Frederick Douglass: Written by Himself*. New York: Collier, 1962.

———. *My Bondage and My Freedom*. New York: Dover, 1969.

———. *Narrative of the Life of Frederick Douglass: An American Slave, Written by Himself*. Boston: Anti-Slavery Office, 1845.

Drago, Edmund L., ed. *Broke by the War: Letters of a Slave Trader*. Columbia: University of South Carolina Press, 1991.

Drumgoold, Kate. "A Slave Girl's Story: Being an Autobiography of Kate Drumgoold." In *The Schomburg Library of Nineteenth-Century Black Women Writers: Six Women's Slave Narratives*, ed. Henry Louis Gates, Jr. New York: Oxford University Press, 1988.

Du Bois, W. E. Burghardt. *Black Reconstruction in America: An Essay toward a History of the Past Which Black Folk Played in the Attempt to Reconstruct Democracy in America, 1860–1880*. New York: World, 1965.

———. *The Negro Artisan: Report of a Social Study Made under the Direction of Atlanta University; Together with the Proceedings of the Seventh Conference for the Study of the Negro Problems, Held at Atlanta University, on May 27th, 1902*. Atlanta: Atlanta University Press, 1902.

———. *Suppression of the African Slave Trade to the United States of America, 1638–1870*. New York: Dover, 1970.

Dumond, Dwight L. *Anti-Slavery: The Crusade for Freedom in America*. Ann Arbor: University of Michigan Press, 1961.

Easterby, J. H., ed. *The South Carolina Rice Plantation: As Revealed in the Papers of Robert F. W. Allston*. Chicago: University of Chicago, 1945.

Egypt, Ophelia Settle, J. Masuoka, and Charles S. Johnson, eds. *Unwritten History of Slavery: Autobiographical Account of Negro Ex-Slaves*. Nashville: Fisk University, 1945.

Elkins, Stanley M. *Slavery: A Problem in American Institutional and Intellectual Life*. New York: Grosset and Dunlap, 1963.

Elliot, William. *Carolina Sports, by Land and Water Including Incidents of Devil-Fishing*. Charleston: Burges and James, 1846.

Engerman, Stanley L. "Changes in Black Fertility, 1880–1940." In *Family and Population in the 19th Century*, ed. Tamara Hareven and Maris Vinovskis, 126–53. Princeton: Princeton University Press, 1978.

Engs, Robert F. *Freedom's First Generation: Black Hampton, Virginia, 1861–1890*. Philadelphia: University of Pennsylvania Press, 1979.

Eppes, Susan Bradford (Mrs. Nicholas Ware Eppes). *The Negro of the Old South: A Bit of Period History*. Macon: J. W. Burke, rev. copyright, 1941.

Epstein, Dena J. *Sinful Tunes and Spirituals: Black Folk Music to the Civil War*. Urbana: University of Illinois Press, 1977.

Equiano, Olaudah. *The Life of Olaudah Equiano, or Gustavus Vassa the African*. London: Longman, 1988.

Escott, Paul D. *Slavery Remembered: A Record of Twentieth-Century Slave Narratives*. Chapel Hill: University of North Carolina Press, 1979.

Feldstein, Stanley. *Once a Slave: The Slave's View of Slavery*. New York: Morrow, 1971.

Fields, Barbara Jeanne. *Slavery and Freedom on the Middle Ground: Maryland during the Nineteenth Century*. New Haven: Yale University Press, 1985.

Filipovic, Zlata. *Zlata's Diary: A Child's Life in Sarajevo*. New York: Viking, 1994.

BIBLIOGRAPHY

Finkelman, Paul. *Slavery in the Courtroom: An Annotated Bibliography of American Cases.* Washington: Government Printing Office, 1985.

Fleet, Betsy, and John D. P. Fuller, eds. *Green Mount, A Virginia Plantation Family during the Civil War: Being the Journal of Benjamin Robert Fleet and Letters of His Family.* Lexington: University Press of Kentucky, 1962.

Flynn, Charles L., Jr. *White Land, Black Labor: Caste and Class in Late Nineteenth-Century Georgia.* Baton Rouge: Louisiana State University Press, 1983.

Fogel, Robert William, and Stanley L. Engerman. *Time on the Cross: The Economics of American Negro Slavery.* Boston: Little, Brown, 1974.

Foner, Eric. *Reconstruction: America's Unfinished Revolution, 1863–1877.* New York: Harper and Row, 1988.

Foner, Philip S., and Ronald L. Lewis, eds. *The Black Worker: A Documentary History from Colonial Times to the Present,* 5 vols. Philadelphia: Temple University Press, 1989.

Forten, Charlotte L. *The Journal of Charlotte L. Forten: A Negro in the Slave Era.* Ed. Ray Allen Billington. New York: Collier, 1967.

Fox-Genovese, Elizabeth. "Strategies and Forms of Resistance: Focus on Slave Women in the United States." In *Resistance: Studies in African, Caribbean, and Afro-American History,* ed. Gary Y. Okihiro, 143–65. Amherst: University of Massachusetts Press, 1986.

———. *Within the Plantation Household: Black and White Women of the Old South.* Chapel Hill: University of North Carolina Press, 1988.

Frank, Anne. *The Diary of a Young Girl.* New York: Bantam, 1993.

Franklin, John Hope. *Emancipation Proclamation.* Garden City: Doubleday, 1963.

Frazier, Franklin. *The Negro Family in the United States,* 2d ed. Chicago: University of Chicago Press, 1967.

Friedman, Jean E. *The Enclosed Garden: Women and Community in the Evangelical South, 1830–1890.* Chapel Hill: University of North Carolina Press, 1985.

Furnas, J. C. "Patrolling the Middle Passage." In *Readings in American History, 1607–1865,* ed. Robert M. Spector, 155–62. New York: American Heritage, 1993.

Gates, Henry Louis, Jr., ed. *The Schomburg Library of Nineteenth-Century Black Women Writers: Six Women's Slave Narratives.* New York: Oxford University Press, 1988.

Gates, Paul W. *The Farmer's Age: Agriculture 1815–1860,* vol. 3: *The Economic History of the United States.* New York: Holt, Rinehart and Winston, 1960.

Gaven, Paul A. *Reckoning with Slavery: A Critical Study in the Quantitative History of American Negro Slavery.* New York: Oxford University Press, 1976.

Genovese, Eugene D. *Roll, Jordan, Roll: The World the Slaves Made.* New York: Vintage, 1976.

Gilbert, Olive. *Narrative of Sojourner Truth, A Bondswoman of Olden Time, Emancipated by the New York Legislature in the Early Part of the Present Century, with a History of Her Labors and Correspondence Drawn from Her Book of Life.* Chicago: Johnson, 1970.

Gordon, Michael, ed. *The American Family in Social-Historical Perspective.* New York: St. Martin's, 1973.

Gray, Lewis Cecil. *History of Agriculture in the Southern United States to 1860,* 2 vols. Gloucester: Peter Smith, 1958.

Greene, Lorenzo Johnston. *The Negro in Colonial New England.* New York: Atheneum, 1974.

Guild, June Purcell. *Black Laws of Virginia: A Summary of the Legislative Acts of Virginia Concerning Negroes from Earliest Times to the Present.* Richmond: Whittet and Shepperson, 1936.

BIBLIOGRAPHY

Gunn, John C. *Domestic Medicine or Poor Man's Medicine*, 2d ed. Madisonvill, Tennessee: J. F. Grant, 1834.

Gutman, Herbert G. *The Black Family in Slavery and Freedom, 1750–1925*. New York: Vintage, 1977.

Haley, Alex. *Roots: The Saga of an American Family*. Garden City: Doubleday, 1976.

Hall, Robert L. "Black and White Christians in Florida, 1822–1861." In *Masters and Slaves in the House of the Lord: Race and Religion in the American South, 1740–1870*, ed. John B. Boles, 81–98. Lexington: University Press of Kentucky, 1988.

Hall, Robert L., and Carol B. Stack, eds. *Holding on to the Land and the Lord: Kinship, Ritual, Land Tenure, and Social Policy in the Rural South*. Athens: University of Georgia Press, 1982.

Harlan, Louis R. *Separate and Unequal: Public School Campaigns and Racism in the Southern Seaboard States, 1901–1915*. Chapel Hill: University of North Carolina Press, 1958.

———, ed. *Booker T. Washington Papers*, 2 vols. Urbana: University of Illinois Press, 1972.

Harris, Joel Chandler. *Uncle Remus*. New York: Schocken, 1972.

Harris, Joseph E. *Africans and Their History*. New York: Mentor, 1986.

Hartwig, Gerald W., and K. David Patterson, eds. *Disease in African History: An Introductory Survey and Case Studies*. Durham: Duke University Press, 1978.

Hening, William Waller. *The Statutes at Large; Being a Collection of All Laws of Virginia from the First Session of the Legislature in the Year 1619*, vol. II. Charlottesville: University Press of Virginia, 1969.

Herskovits, Melville J. *Dahomey: An Ancient West African Kingdom*, vol. I. Evanston: Northwestern University Press, 1967.

———. *Myth of the Negro Past*. Boston: Beacon, 1958.

Higginson, Thomas Wentworth. *Army Life in a Black Regiment*. New York: Collier, 1962.

Hildreth, Richard. *Despotism in America: An Inquiry into the Nature, Results, and Legal Basis of the Slave-Holding System in the United States*. Boston: John P. Jewett, 1854.

Hilliard, Sam B. "Antebellum Tidewater in Rice Culture in South Carolina and Georgia." In *European Settlement and Development in North America: Essays on Geographical Change in Honour and Memory of Andrew Clark Hill*, ed. James R. Gibson, 91–115. Toronto: University of Toronto Press, 1973.

Hiner, N. Ray, and Joseph M. Hawes, eds. *Growing Up in America: Children in Historical Perspective*. Urbana: University of Illinois Press, 1985.

Hofstadter, Richard, and Michael Wallace, eds. *American Violence: A Documentary History*. New York: Knopf, 1970.

Huizinga, J. *Homo Ludens: A Study of the Play Element in Culture*. Boston: Beacon, 1950.

Ingraham, J. H. *Not "A Fool's Errand." Life and Experience of a Northern Governess in the Sunny South; or the Southerner at Home*. New York: Carleton, 1880.

Jacobs, Harriet. *Incidents in the Life of a Slave Girl: Written by Herself*. Ed. Jean Fagan Yellin. Cambridge: Harvard University Press, 1987.

Jacoway, Elizabeth. *Yankee Missionaries in the South: The Penn School Experiment*. Baton Rouge: Louisiana State University Press, 1980.

Jefferson, Thomas. *Notes on the State of Virginia*. Ed. William Peden. New York: Norton, 1982.

Johnson, Clifton H., ed. *God Struck Me Dead: Religious Conversion Experiences and Autobiographies of Ex-slaves*. Philadelphia: Pilgrim, 1969.

Johnson, Michael P., and James L. Roark. *Black Masters: A Free Family of Color in the Old South*. New York: Norton, 1984.

BIBLIOGRAPHY

Johnston, James Hugo. *Race Relations in Virginia and Miscegenation in the South, 1776–1860.* Amherst: University of Massachusetts Press, 1970.

Jones, Bessie, and Bess Lomax Hawes. *Step It Down: Games, Plays, Songs and Stories from the Afro-American Heritage.* Athens: University of Georgia Press, 1987.

Jones, Howard. *Mutiny on the Amistad: The Saga of a Slave Revolt and Its Impact on American Abolition, Law, and Diplomacy.* New York: Oxford University Press, 1987.

Jones, Jacqueline. *Labor of Love, Labor of Sorrow: Black Women, Work and the Family, from Slavery to the Present.* New York: Vintage, 1986.

———. *Soldiers of Light and Love.* Chapel Hill: University of North Carolina Press, 1980.

Jones, Norrece T., Jr. *Born a Child of Freedom, Yet a Slave: Mechanisms of Control and Strategies of Resistance in Antebellum South Carolina.* Hanover: Wesleyan University Press, 1990.

Jordan, Thomas E. *Victorian Childhood: Themes and Variations.* Albany: State University of New York Press, 1987.

Jordan, Winthrop D. *White over Black: American Attitudes toward the Negro, 1550–1812.* New York: Norton, 1977.

Joyner, Charles W. "The Creolization of Slave Folklife." In *The Afro-American Slaves: Community or Chaos?* ed. Randall Miller, 123–34. Malabar: Krieger, 1981.

———. *Down by the Riverside: A South Carolina Community.* Urbana: University of Illinois Press, 1984.

———. *Jubilee and Plantation Songs. Characteristic Favorites, As sung by the Hampton Students, Jubilee Singers, Fisk University Students, and Other Concert Companies.* Boston: Oliver Ditson, 1887.

Keckley, Elizabeth. *Behind the Scenes: Thirty Years a Slave and Four Years in the White House.* New York: Arno and *New York Times,* 1968.

Kemble, Frances Anne. *Journal of a Residence on a Georgian Plantation in 1838–1839.* Ed. John A. Scott. Athens: University of Georgia Press, 1984.

Kerber, Linda K., and Jane Sherron De Hart, eds. *Women's America: Refocusing on the Past,* 3d ed. New York: Oxford University Press, 1991.

Kett, Joseph F. "Adolescence and Youth in Nineteenth-Century America." In *The Family in History: Interdisciplinary Essays,* ed. Theodore K. Rabb and Robert I. Rotberg, 95–110. New York: Harper, 1972.

Killion, Ronald, and Charles Waller, eds. *Slavery Times When I Was Chillun Down on Marster's Plantation.* Savannah: Beehive, 1973.

Kilson, Marion D. De B. "Towards Freedom: An Analysis of Slave Revolts in the United States." In *The Making of Black Americans: Essays in Negro Life and History,* vol. I, ed. August Meier and Elliott Rudwick, 165–78. New York: Atheneum, 1973.

Klein, Herbert S. "African Women in the Atlantic Slave Trade." In *Slavery in Africa: Historical and Anthropological Perspectives,* ed. Suzanne Miers and Igor Kopytoff, 29–38. Madison: University of Wisconsin Press, 1977.

Knox, George L. *Slave and Freeman: The Autobiography of George L. Knox.* Ed. William B. Gatewood. Lexington: University Press of Kentucky, 1979.

Kolchin, Peter. *First Freedom: The Responses of Alabama's Blacks to Emancipation and Reconstruction.* Westport: Greenwood, 1972.

Kubitschek, Missy Dehn. "Subjugated Knowledge: Toward a Feminist Exploration of Rape in Afro-American Fiction." In *Studies in Black American Literature,* vol. III: *Black Feminist Criticism and Critical Theory,* ed. Joe Weixlmann and Houston A. Baker, Jr., 43–56. Greenwood, FL: Penkevill, 1988.

Kulikoff, Allan. "The Beginning of the Afro-American Family in Maryland." In *The American Family in Social Historical Perspectives,* ed. Michael Gordon, 444–66. New York: St. Martin's, 1978.

BIBLIOGRAPHY

———. *Tobacco and Slaves: The Development of Southern Cultures in the Chesapeake, 1680–1800.* Chapel Hill: University of North Carolina Press, 1986.

———. "Uprooted Peoples: Black Migrants in the Age of the American Revolution, 1790–1820." In *Slavery and Freedom in the Age of the American Revolution,* ed. Ira Berlin and Ronald Hoffman, 143–71. Charlottesville: University of Virginia Press, 1983.

Lane, Lunsford. "The Narrative of Lunsford Lane, formerly of Raleigh, N.C." In *Five Slave Narratives: A Compendium,* ed. William Loren Katz. New York: Arno and *New York Times,* 1968.

Lawson, Ellen Nickenzie, and Marlene D. Merrill. *The Three Sarahs: Documents of Antebellum Black College Women,* vol. 13. New York: Edwin Mellen, 1984.

Leavitt, Judith Walzer. *Brought to Bed: Childbearing in America, 1750 to 1950.* New York: Oxford University Press, 1986.

Lebsock, Suzanne. *The Free Women of Petersburg: Status and Culture in a Southern Town, 1784–1860.* New York: Norton, 1984.

Lerner, Gerda. *Black Women in White America: A Documentary History.* New York: Vintage, 1973.

———. *The Grimke Sisters from South Carolina: Pioneers for Woman's Rights and Abolition.* New York: Schocken, 1971.

Levine, Lawrence W. *Black Culture and Black Consciousness: Afro-American Folk Thought from Slavery to Freedom.* New York: Oxford University Press, 1977.

Lewis, Ronald L. *Coal, Iron, and Slaves: Industrial Slavery in Maryland and Virginia, 1715–1865.* Westport: Greenwood, 1979.

Littlefield, Daniel F., Jr., ed. *The Life of Okah Tubbee.* Lincoln: University of Nebraska Press, 1988.

Litwack, Leon F. *Been in the Storm so Long: The Aftermath of Slavery.* New York: Vintage, 1980.

Logan, Rayford W., ed. *Memoirs of a Monticello Slave: As Dictated to Charles Campbell in the 1840's by Isaac, one of Thomas Jefferson's Slaves.* Charlottesville: University of Virginia Press, 1951.

MacLeod, Anne Scott. *A Moral Tale: Children's Fiction and American Culture, 1820–1860.* Hamden, CT: Archon, 1975.

Mandle, Jay R. *Not Slave, Not Free: The African American Economic Experience since the Civil War.* Durham: Duke University Press, 1992.

Martin, Waldo E., Jr. *The Mind of Frederick Douglass.* Chapel Hill: University of North Carolina Press, 1984.

Mays, Benjamin E. *The Negro's God: As Reflected in His Literature.* New York: Atheneum, 1973.

McLaurin, Melton A. *Celia, a Slave.* Athens: University of Georgia Press, 1991.

McManus, Edgar J. *Black Bondage in the North.* Syracuse: Syracuse University Press, 1973.

McPherson, James M. *Ordeal by Fire: The Civil War and Reconstruction.* New York: Knopf, 1982.

Mellon, James, ed. *Bullwhip Days: The Slaves Remember.* New York: Weidenfeld and Nicolson, 1988.

Mergen, Bernard. *Play and Playthings: A Reference Guide.* Westport: Greenwood, 1982.

Michaelis-Jena, Ruth. *The Brothers Grimm.* New York: Praeger, 1970.

Miller, Randall M. "Slaves and Southern Catholicism." In *Masters and Slaves in the House of the Lord: Race and Religion in the American South, 1740–1870,* ed. John B. Boles, 127–52. Lexington: University Press of Kentucky, 1988.

———, ed. *"Dear Master": Letters of a Slave Family.* Ithaca: Cornell University Press, 1978.

BIBLIOGRAPHY

Mills, Gray B. *The Forgotten People: Cane River Creoles of Color.* Baton Rouge: Louisiana State University Press, 1977.

Mintz, Sidney W. *Sweetness and Power: The Place of Sugar in Modern History.* New York: Penguin, 1986.

Miracle, Andrew W., Jr. "Some Functions of Aymara Games and Play." In *Studies in the Anthropology of Play: Papers in Memory of B. Allan Tindall,* ed. Phillip Stevens, Jr., 98–115. Westpoint: Leisure, 1977.

Moore, John Hebron. *Agriculture in Ante-Bellum Mississippi.* New York: Octagon, 1971.

Morris, Robert C. *Reading, 'Riting, and Reconstruction: The Education of Freedmen in the South, 1861–1870.* Chicago: University of Chicago Press, 1981.

Morrison, Toni. *Beloved.* New York: Plume, 1988.

Mulira, Jessie Gaston. "The Case of Voodoo in New Orleans." In *Africanisms in American Culture,* ed. Joseph E. Holloway, 34–68. Bloomington: Indiana University Press, 1990.

Munro, John, ed. *The London Shakespeare: The Histories, the Poems,* vol. IV. New York: Simon and Schuster, 1958.

Murray, Pauli. *Proud Shoes: The Story of an American Family.* New York: Harper and Row, 1987.

Nash, Howard P., Jr. *Stormy Petrel: The Life and Times of General Benjamin F. Butler, 1818–1893.* Cranbury: Associated University Presses, 1969.

Nathans, Sydney. "Fortress without Walls: A Black Community after Slavery." In *Holding on to the Land and the Lord: Kinship, Ritual, Land Tenure, and Social Polity in the Rural South,* ed. Robert L. Hall and Carol B. Stack, 55–65. Athens: University of Georgia Press, 1982.

Newell, William Wells. *Games and Songs of American Children.* New York: Dover, 1963.

Nieman, Donald G. *Promises to Keep: African-Americans and the Constitutional Order, 1776 to the Present.* New York: Oxford University Press, 1991.

Northup, Solomon. "Twelve Years a Slave: Narrative of Solomon Northup." In *Puttin' On Ole Massa: The Slave Narratives of Henry Bibb, William Wells Brown, and Solomon Northup,* ed. Gilbert Osofsky. New York: Harper, 1969.

Norton, Mary Beth. *Liberty's Daughters: The Revolutionary Experiences of American Women, 1750–1800.* New York: Harper, 1980.

Olmsted, Frederick Law. *A Journey in the Back Country.* New York: Schocken, 1970.

Owens, Leslie Howard. *This Species of Property: Slave Life and Culture in the Old South.* New York: Oxford University Press, 1977.

Owsley, Frank. *Plain Folk of the Old South.* Chicago: Quadrangle, 1965.

Patterson, Ruth Polk. *The Seed of Sally Good'n: A Black Family of Arkansas 1833–1953.* Lexington: University Press of Kentucky, 1985.

Pease, Jane H., and William H. Pease. *They Who Would Be Free: Blacks Search for Freedom, 1830–1861.* New York: Atheneum, 1974.

Pennington, James W. C. "The Fugitive Blacksmith or Events in the History of James W. C. Pennington Pastor of a Presbyterian Church New York, Formerly a Slave in the State of Maryland," in *Great Slave Narratives,* ed. Arna Bontemps, 193–267. Boston: Beacon, 1969.

Perdue, Charles L., Jr., Thomas E. Barden, and Robert K. Phillips. *Weevils in the Wheat: Interviews with Virginia Ex-Slaves.* Bloomington: Indiana University Press, 1980.

Phillips, Ulrich B. *American Negro Slavery: A Survey of the Supply, Employment and Control of Negro Labor as Determined by the Plantation Regime.* Baton Rouge: Louisiana State University Press, 1966.

Pres, Terrence Des. *The Survivors: An Anatomy of Life in the Death Camps.* New York: Oxford University Press, 1976.

BIBLIOGRAPHY

Preston, Dickson J. *Young Frederick Douglass: The Maryland Years*. Baltimore: Johns Hopkins University Press, 1980.

Quarles, Benjamin. "The Abduction of the 'Planter.'" In *The Making of Black America: The Origins of Black America*, vol. 1, ed. August Meier and Elliott Rudwick, 339–44. New York: Atheneum, 1973.

———. *The Negro in the Civil War*. New York: Russel and Russel, 1968.

Raboteau, Albert J. *Slave Religion: The "Invisible Institution" in the Antebellum South*. New York: Oxford University Press, 1978.

Rawick, George P., ed. *The American Slave: A Composite Autobiography*, 19 vols. Westport: Greenwood, 1972.

———, ed. *The American Slave: A Composite Autobiography*, vol. 19: *God Struck Me Dead*. Westport: Greenwood, 1976.

———, ed. *The American Slave: A Composite Autobiography*, Supplement, Series 1, 12 vols. Westport: Greenwood, 1978.

———, ed. *The American Slave: A Composite Autobiography*, Supplement, Series 2, 10 vols. Westport: Greenwood, 1979.

———, ed. *From Sundown to Sunup: The Making of the Black Community*. Westport: Greenwood, 1972.

Richardson, Joe M., ed. *The Trial and Imprisonment of Jonathan Walker at Pensacola, Florida for Aiding Slaves to Escape from Bondage*. Gainesville: Univ. Press of Florida, 1974.

Roark, James L. *Masters without Slaves: Southern Planters in the Civil War and Reconstruction*. New York: Norton, 1977.

Rose, Willie Lee. *Slavery and Freedom*. Ed. William W. Freehling, expanded ed. Oxford University Press, 1982.

———, ed. *A Documentary History of Slavery in North America*. New York: Oxford University Press, 1976.

Rosengarten, Theodore. *All God's Dangers: The Life of Nate Shaw*. New York: Vintage, 1984.

———. *Tombee: Portrait of a Cotton Planter*. New York: Morrow, 1986.

Savitt, Todd L. *Medicine and Slavery: The Diseases and Health Care of Blacks in Antebellum Virginia*. Urbana: University of Illinois Press, 1978.

Scarborough, William Kauffman. *The Overseer: Plantation Management in the Old South*. Athens: University of Georgia Press, 1984.

Scherer, Lester B. "Religion, Slave." In *Dictionary of Afro-American Slavery*, ed. Randall M. Miller and John David Smith, 626–33. Westport: Greenwood, 1988.

Scott, Donald M., and Bernard Wishy, eds. *America's Families: A Documentary History*. New York: Harper and Row, 1982.

Sernett, Milton C., ed. *Afro-American Religious History: A Documentary Witness*. Durham: Duke University Press, 1985.

Shengold, Leonard. *Soul Murder: The Effects of Childhood Abuse and Deprivation*. New Haven: Yale University Press, 1989.

Shick, Tom W. *Behold the Promised Land: A History of the Afro-American Settler Society in Nineteenth-Century Liberia*. Baltimore: Johns Hopkins University Press, 1980.

Sitterson, J. Carlyle. *Sugar Country: The Cane Sugar Industry in the South, 1753–1950*. Lexington: University Press of Kentucky, 1953.

Slater, Peter G. "'From the *Cradle* to the *Coffin*': Parental Bereavement and the Shadow of Infant Damnation in Puritan Society." In *Growing Up in America: Children in Historical Perspective*, ed. N. Ray Hiner and Joseph M. Hawes, 27–43. Urbana: University of Illinois Press, 1985.

Smith, Julia Floyd. *Slavery and Rice Culture in Low Country Georgia, 1750–1860*. Knoxville: University of Tennessee Press, 1985.

Sobel, Mechal. *Trabelin' On: The Slave Journey to an Afro-Baptist Faith*. Westport: Greenwood, 1979.

BIBLIOGRAPHY

——. *The World They Made Together: Black and White Values in Eighteenth-Century Virginia*. Princeton: Princeton University Press, 1987.

Southern, Eileen. *The Music of Black Americans*. New York: Norton, 1971.

Stampp, Kenneth M. *The Peculiar Institution: Slavery in the Ante-Bellum South*. New York: Knopf, 1967.

——, ed. *Records of Ante-Bellum Southern Plantations from the Revolution through the Civil War*, Series G, Part I, Texas and Louisiana. Frederick, MD: University Publications of America, 1987.

Starkey, Marion L. *The First Plantation: A History of Hampton and Elizabeth City County, Virginia, 1607–1877*. Hampton: Houston, 1936.

Starobin, Robert S. *Industrial Slavery in the Old South*. New York: Oxford University Press, 1970.

Sterling, Dorothy, ed. *The Trouble They Seen: Black People Tell the Story of Reconstruction*. Garden City: Doubleday, 1976.

Stevenson, Brenda. "Distress and Discord in Virginia Slave Families, 1830–1860." In *In Joy and in Sorrow: Women, Family, and Marriage in the Victorian South, 1830–1900*, ed. Carol Bleser, 103–24. New York: Oxford University Press, 1991.

Still, William. *The Underground Rail Road. A record of facts, authentic narratives, letters, &c., narrating the hardships, hairbreadth escapes and death struggles of the slaves in their efforts for freedom, as related by themselves and others, or the largest stockholders, and most liberal aiders and advisers, of the road*. Philadelphia: Porter and Coats, 1872.

Stowe, Harriet Beecher. *A Key to Uncle Tom's Cabin*. Cleveland: J. P. Jewett, 1854.

Strasser, Susan. *Never Done: A History of American Housework*. New York: Pantheon, 1982.

Stroyer, Jacob. *My Life in the South*. Salem: Salem Observer, 1889.

Stuckey, Sterling. *Slave Culture: Nationalist Theory and the Foundations of Black America*. New York: Oxford University Press, 1987.

——. "Through the Prism of Folklore: The Black Ethos in Slavery." In *The Underside of American History: Other Readings*, vol. 1, ed. Thomas R. Frazier, 229–46. New York: Harcourt Brace Jovanovich, 1974.

Sunley, Robert. "Early Nineteenth-Century American Literature on Child Rearing." In *Childhood in Contemporary Culture*, ed. Margaret Mead and Martha Wolfenstein, 150–67. Chicago: University of Chicago Press, 1955.

Sutch, Richard. "The Breeding of Slaves for Sale and the Westward Expansion of Slavery, 1850–1860." In *Race and Slavery in the Western Hemisphere: Quantitative Studies*, ed. Stanley L. Engerman and Eugene D. Genovese, 173–210. Princeton: Princeton University Press, 1975.

Swint, Henry L. *Dear Ones at Home: Letters from Contraband Camps*. Nashville: Vanderbilt University Press, 1966.

Tadman, Michael. *Speculators and Slaves: Masters, Traders, and Slaves in the Old South*. Madison: University of Wisconsin Press, 1989.

Tanner, Nancy. "Matrilocality in Indonesia and Africa and among Black Americans." In *Woman, Culture and Society*, ed. Michelle Zimbalist Rosaldo and Louise Lamphere, 129–56. Stanford: Stanford University Press, 1974.

Taylor, Susie King. *Reminiscences of My Life in Camp*. New York: Arno and *New York Times*, 1968.

Thompson, Mattie. "The Story of Mattie Jackson." In *The Schomburg Library of Nineteenth-Century Black Women Writers: Six Women's Slave Narratives*, ed. Henry Louis Gates, Jr. New York: Oxford University Press, 1988.

Thompson, Robert Farris. "Kongo Influences on Afro-American Artistic Culture." In *Africanisms in American Culture*, ed. Joseph E. Holloway, 148–84. Bloomington: Indiana University Press, 1990.

Thornton, John. "Sexual Demography: The Impact of the Slave Trade on Family

BIBLIOGRAPHY

Structure." In *Women and Slavery in Africa,* ed. Claire C. Robertson and Martin A. Kline, 39–48. Madison: University of Wisconsin Press, 1983.

Toppin, Edgar Allen. *A Biographical History of Blacks in America since 1528.* New York: David McKay, 1971.

Touchstone, Blake. "Planters and Slave Religion in the Deep South." In *Masters and Slaves in the House of the Lord: Race and Religion in the American South, 1740–1870,* ed. John B. Boles, 99–126. Lexington: University Press of Kentucky, 1988.

Turnbull, Colin M. *Tradition and Change in African Tribal Life.* Cleveland: World, 1966.

Wade, Richard C. *Slavery in the Cities: The South 1820–1860.* New York: Oxford University Press, 1964.

Walker, Jonathan. *Trial and Imprisonment of Jonathan Walker, at Pensacola Florida, for Aiding Slaves to Escape from Bondage.* Ed. Joe M. Richardson. Gainesville: University Press of Florida, 1974.

Washington, Booker T. *Up from Slavery, An Autobiography.* New York: Bantam, 1967.

Wayne, Michael. *The Reshaping of Plantation Society: The Natchez District, 1860–1880.* Baton Rouge: Louisiana State University Press, 1983.

Webber, Thomas L. *Deep Like the Rivers: Education in the Slave Quarter Community, 1831–1865.* New York: Norton, 1978.

White, Deborah Gray. *Ar'n't I a Woman? Female Slaves in the Plantation South.* New York: Norton, 1985.

Wiggins, William H., Jr. *O Freedom! Afro-American Emancipation Celebrations.* Knoxville: University of Tennessee Press, 1987.

Wiley, Bell Irvin. *Southern Negroes, 1861–1865.* New Haven: Yale University Press, 1965.

Williamson, Joel. *New People: Miscegenation and Mulattoes in the United States.* New York: Free, 1980.

Wish, Harvey, ed. *Antebellum Writings of George Fitzhugh.* New York: Capricorn, 1960.

Wood, Peter. *Black Majority: Negroes in Colonial South Carolina from 1670 through the Stono Rebellion.* New York: Norton, 1974.

Woodward, C. Vann, ed. *Mary Chesnut's Civil War Diary.* New Haven: Yale University Press, 1981.

Wright, Richard A. *African Philosophy: An Introduction,* 3d ed. Lanham: University Press of America, 1984.

Wyatt-Brown, Bertram. "Black Schooling during Reconstruction." In *The Web of Southern Social Relations: Women, Family, and Education,* ed. Walter Fraser, Jr., 146–65. Athens: University of Georgia Press, 1985.

———. *Southern Honor: Ethics and Behavior in the Old South.* New York: Oxford University Press, 1982.

Yetman, Norman R., ed. *Life Under the "Peculiar Institution": Selections from the Slave Narrative Collection.* New York: Holt, Rinehart and Winston, 1970.

Zelizer, Viviana A. *Pricing the Priceless Child: The Changing Social Value of Children.* New York: Basic, 1985.

PERIODICALS

Abbott, Edith. "A Study of the Early History of Child Labor in America." *American Journal of Sociology* 14 (July 1908): 15–37.

Abrahams, Roger D. "Playing the Dozens." *Journal of American Folklore* 75 (July-September 1962): 209–220.

BIBLIOGRAPHY

Anderson, James D. "Aunt Jemima in Dialectics: Genovese on Slave Culture." *Journal of Negro History* 41 (January 1976): 99–114.

Armstrong, Thomas F. "From Task Labor to Free Labor: The Transition Along Georgia's Rice Coast, 1820–1880." *Georgia Historical Quarterly* 44 (Winter 1980): 432–47.

Awad, George A. "Father-Son Incest: A Case Report." *Journal of Nervous and Mental Disorders* 162 (February 1976): 135–39.

Bailey, David Thomas. "A Divided Prism: Two Sources of Black Testimony on Slavery." *Journal of Southern History* 46 (August 1980): 381–404.

Banks, Frank D. "Old Time Courtship." *Southern Workman* 24 (January 1895): 14–15.

Bartlett, Irving H., and C. Glenn Cambor. "The History and Psychodynamics of Southern Womanhood." *Women's Studies* 2 (1974): 9–24.

Bauer, Raymond A., and Alice H. Bauer. "Day-to-Day Resistance to Slavery." *Journal of Negro History* 27 (October 1942): 388–419.

Beales, Ross W., Jr. "In Search of the Historical Child: Miniature Adulthood and Youth in Colonial New England." *American Quarterly* 27 (1975): 379–98.

Beatty, Bess. "Textile Labor in the North Carolina Piedmont: Mill Owner Images and Mill Worker Response, 1830–1900." *Labor History* 25 (Fall 1984): 485–503.

Bellingham, Bruce. "The History of Childhood since the 'Invention of Childhood': Some Issues in the Eighties." *Journal of Family History* 13 (1988): 347–58.

Berlin, Ira, Francine C. Cary, Steven F. Miller, and Leslie S. Rowland. "Family and Freedom: Black Families in the American Civil War." *History Today* 37 (1987): 8–15.

Berlin, Ira, Steven F. Miller, and Leslie Rowland. "Afro-American Families in the Transition from Slavery to Freedom." *Radical History Review* 42 (1988): 89–121.

Blassingame, John W. "Using the Testimony of Ex-Slaves: Approaches and Problems." *Journal of Southern History* 41 (November 1975): 473–92.

Bonekemper, Edward H. "Negro Ownership of Real Property in Hampton and Elizabeth City County, Virginia, 1860–1870." *Journal of Negro History* 55 (July 1970): 165–81.

Bonner, James C., ed. "Plantation Experiences of a New York Woman." *North Carolina Historical Review* 33 (October 1956): 384–412, 529–46.

Breen, T. H. "Horses and Gentlemen: The Cultural Significance of Gambling among the Gentry of Virginia." *William and Mary Quarterly* 34 (April 1977): 239–57.

Bremner, Robert H. "Other People's Children." *Journal of Social History* 16 (Spring 1983): 83–103.

Brigham, R. I. "Negro Education in the Ante Bellum Missouri." *Journal of Negro History* 30 (October 1945): 405–20.

Brown, Steven E. "Sexuality and the Slave Community." *Phylon* 42 (Spring 1981): 1–10.

Bruce, D. D., Jr. "Play, Work, and Ethics in the Old South." *Southern Folklore Quarterly* 41 (1977): 33–51.

Burnham, Dorothy. "Children of the Slave Community in the United States." *Freedomways* 19 (Second Quarter 1979): 75–81.

Cade, John B. "Out of the Mouths of Ex-Slaves." *Journal of Negro History* 20 (July 1935): 294–337.

Calderhead, William. "How Extensive Was the Border State Slave Trade?: A New Look." *Civil War History* 18 (March 1972): 42–55.

Campbell, John. "Work, Pregnancy, and Infant Mortality among Southern Slaves." *Journal of Interdisciplinary History* 14 (Spring 1984): 792–812.

Cavallo, Dom. "Adolescent Peer Group Morality: Its Origins and Functions in the United States." *Psychohistory Review* 6 (Fall/Winter 1977–78): 88–90.

Chimezie, Amuzie. "The Dozens: An African-Heritage Theory." *Journal of Black Studies* 6 (June 1976): 401–19.

BIBLIOGRAPHY

Cimbala, Paul A. "Fortunate Bondsmen: Black 'Musicianers' and Their Role as an Antebellum Southern Plantation Slave Elite." *Southern Studies* 18 (Fall 1979): 291–303.

Clinton, Catherine. "Equally Their Due: The Education of the Planter Daughter in the Early Republic." *Journal of the Early Republic* 2 (April 1982): 39–60.

Cody, Cheryll Ann. "Naming, Kinship, and Estate Dispersal: Notes on Slave Family Life on a South Carolina Plantation, 1786 to 1833." *William and Mary Quarterly* 39 (January 1982): 192–211.

———. "There was no 'Absalom' on the Ball Plantations: Slave-Naming Practices in the South Carolina Low Country, 1720–1865." *American Historical Review* 92 (June 1987): 563–96.

Cohen, William. "Thomas Jefferson and the Problem of Slavery." *Journal of American History* 56 (December 1969): 503–26.

Cornelius, Janet. "We Slipped and Learned to Read: Slave Accounts of the Literacy Process, 1830–1865." *Phylon* 44 (September 1983): 171–85.

Cott, Nancy. "Notes toward an Interpretation of Antebellum Childrearing." *Psychohistory Review* 6 (Spring 1978): 4–20.

Culwick, G. M. "New Ways for Old in the Treatment of Adolescent African Girls." *Africa* 12 (October 1939): 425–32.

Curryer, W. H. S. "Mothercraft in Southern Nigeria." *United Empire* 18 (February 1927): 28–81.

Daniel, Jack L. Geneva Smitherman-Donaldson, and Milford A. Jeremiah. "Makin' A Way Outa No Way: The Proverb Tradition in the Black Experience." *Journal of Black Studies* 17 (June 1987): 482–508.

Davis, Daniel Webster. "Echoes from a Plantation Party." *Southern Worker* 28 (February 1899): 56–57.

Dew, Charles B. "David Ross and the Oxford Iron Works: A Study of Industrial Slavery in the Early Nineteenth-Century South." *William and Mary Quarterly* 31 (April 1974): 189–224.

Diedrich, Maria. "'My Love Is Black As Yours Is Fair': Premarital Love and Sexuality in the Antebellum Slave Narrative." *Phylon* 47 (September 1986): 238–47.

Dixon, Katharine N., Eugene Arnold, and Kenneth Calestro. "Father-Son Incest: Underreported Psychiatric Problem?" *American Journal of Psychiatry* 135 (July 1978): 835–38.

Donaldson, Gary A. "A Window on Slave Culture: Dances at Congo Square in New Orleans, 1800–1862." *Journal of Negro History* 69 (Spring 1984): 63–72.

Dooley, Charles T. "Child-Training among the Wanguru." *Primitive Man* 8 (October 1935): 73–80.

"Dr. [Booker T.] Washington on the Servant Problem." *Southern Workman* 34 (May 1905): 200–201.

Dunn, Durwood. "Apprenticeship and Indentured Servitude in Tennessee before the Civil War." *West Tennessee Historical Society Papers* 36 (1982): 25–40.

Dunn, Richard S. "A Tale of Two Plantations: Slave Life at Mesopotamia in Jamaica and Mount Airy in Virginia, 1799 to 1828." *William and Mary Quarterly* 34 (January 1977): 32–65.

Dye, Nancy Schrom, and Daniel Blake Smith. "Mother Love and Infant Death, 1750–1920." *Journal of American History* 73 (September 1986): 329–53.

Eaton, Clement. "Slave-Hiring in the Upper South: A Step toward Freedom." *Mississippi Valley Historical Review* 46 (March 1960): 663–78.

Ellerstein, Norman S., and J. William Canavan. "Sexual Abuse of Boys." *American Journal of Disease of Children* 134 (March 1980): 255–57.

241

BIBLIOGRAPHY

Ellison, Mary. "Resistance to Oppression: Black Women's Response to Slavery in the United States." *Slavery and Abolition: A Journal of Comparative Studies* 4 (May 1983): 56–63.

Ellison, R. E. "Marriage and Child-Birth among the Kanuri." *Africa* 9 (October 1936): 524–34.

Enck, Henry S. "Black Self-Help in the Progressive Era: The Northern Campaigns of Smaller Southern Black Industrial Schools, 1900–1915." *Journal of Negro History* 41 (January 1976): 73–87.

Faust, Drew Gilpin. "'Trying to Do a Man's Business': Slavery, Violence and Gender in the American Civil War." *Gender and History* 4 (Summer 1992): 197–214.

Fede, Andrew. "Legitimized Violent Slave Abuse in the American South, 1619–1865: A Case Study of Law and Social Change in Six Southern States." *The American Journal of Legal History* 29 (April 1985): 93–150.

———. "Folklore and Ethnology." *Southern Workman* 24 (February 1895): 31.

Formwalt, Lee. "Petitioning Congress for Protection: A Black View of Reconstruction at the Local Level." *Georgia Historical Quarterly* 73 (Summer 1989): 305–22.

Forten, Charlotte. "Life on the Sea Islands." *Atlantic Monthly,* Part I (May 1864): 587–96.

Foster, Herbert J. "African Patterns in the Afro-American Family." *Journal of Black Studies* 14 (December 1983): 201–32.

Fox, Vivian C. "Is Adolescence a Phenomenon of Modern Times?" *Journal of Psychohistory* 5 (Fall 1977): 271–90.

Fraser, Jessie Melville, ed. "A Free Labor Contract, 1867." *Journal of Southern History* 6 (November 1940): 546–48.

Freeman-Longo, Robert E. "Brief Communication: The Impact of Sexual Victimization on Males." *Child Abuse and Neglect* 10 (1986): 411–14.

Genovese, Eugene D., and Elizabeth Fox-Genovese. "The Religious Ideals of Southern Slave Society," *Georgia Historical Quarterly* 70 (Spring 1986): 1–16.

"George Horton, The Slave Poet." *The University Magazine* 7 (May 1888): 229–30.

"A Georgia Plantation." *Scribner's Monthly* 21 (April 1881): 830–36.

Gilmer, W. W. "Management of Slaves." *The Southern Planter* 12 (April 1852): 106–107.

Goggin, Jacqueline. "Carter G. Woodson and the Collection of Source Materials for Afro-American History." *American Archivist* 48 (Summer 1985): 261–71.

Goldfarb, Stephen J. "A Note on Limits to the Growth of the Cotton-Textile Industry in the Old South." *Journal of Southern History* 48 (November 1982): 545–58.

Goldin, Claudia, and Kenneth L. Sokoloff. "Women, Children, and Industrialization in the Early Republic: Evidence from the Manufacturing Censuses." *Journal of Economic History* 42 (December 1982): 741–74.

Gorn, Elliott J. "'Gouge and Bite, Pull Hair and Scratch': The Social Significance of Fighting in the Southern Backcountry." *American Historical Review* 90 (February 1985): 18–43.

Gutman, Herbert G. "Time on the Cross: The Economics of American Slavery: The World Two Cliometricians Made." *Journal of Negro History* 60 (January 1975): 53–227.

Hahn, Steven. "Hunting, Fishing, and Foraging: Common Rights and Class Relations in the Postbellum South." *Radical History Review* 26 (1982): 37–64.

Haley, Alex. "My Search for Roots: A Black American's Story." *Reader's Digest* (May 1974): 73–78.

Hall, Robert L. "'Yonder Come Day': Religious Dimensions of the Transition from Slavery to Freedom in Florida." *Florida Historical Quarterly* 65 (April 1987): 411–32.

BIBLIOGRAPHY

Hamburger, Susan. "On the Land for Life: Black Tenant Farmers on Tall Timbers Plantation." *Florida Historical Quarterly* 66 (October 1987): 153–59.

Hanchett, Catherine M. "'What Sort of People & Families . . .': The Edmondson Sisters." *Afro-Americans in New York Life and History* 6 (July 1982): 21–37.

Harper, C. W. "Black Aristocrats: Domestic Servants on the Antebellum Plantation." *Phylon* 46 (June 1985): 123–35.

Herndon, G. Melvin. "The Significance of the Forest to the Tobacco Plantation Economy in Antebellum Virginia." *Plantation Society in the Americas: An Interdisciplinary Journal of Tropical and Subtropical History and Culture* 1 (October 1981): 430–39.

———. "The Unemancipated Antebellum Youth." *Southern Studies* 23 (Summer 1984): 145–54.

Hilliard, Sam B. "The Tidewater Rice Plantation: An Ingenious Adaptation to Nature." *Geoscience and Man* 12 (June 20, 1975): 37–66.

Hine, Darlene C. "Female Slave Resistance: The Economics of Sex." *The Western Journal of Black Studies* 3 (Summer 1979): 123–27.

Holland, C. G. "The Slave Population on the Plantation of John C. Cohoon, Jr., Nasemond County, Virginia, 1810–1860." *Virginia Magazine of History* 80 (April 1972): 333-40.

Howard, Victor B. "The Civil War in Kentucky: The Slave Claims His Freedom." *Journal of Negro History* 67 (Fall 1982): 245–56.

Hughes, Sarah S. "Slaves for Hire: The Allocation of Black Labor in Elizabeth City County Virginia, 1782 to 1810." *William and Mary Quarterly* 37 (April 1978): 260–86.

Hunter, Lloyd A. "Slavery in St. Louis, 1804–1860," *Missouri Historical Society Bulletin* 30 (July 1974): 233–65.

Jackson, Luther P. "Religious Development of the Negro in Virginia from 1760 to 1860." *Journal of Negro History* 16 (April 1931): 168–239.

Jacobs, Donald M. "Twentieth-Century Slave Narratives as Source Materials: Slave Labor as Agricultural Labor." *Agricultural History* 57 (April 1983): 223–27.

Jennings, Thelma. "'Us Colored Women Had To Go Through a Plenty': Sexual Exploitation of African American Slave Women." *Journal of Women's History* 1 (Winter 1991): 45–74.

Jernegan, Marcus W. "Slavery and the Beginnings of Industrialism in the American Colonies." *American Historical Review* 25 (January 1920): 220–40.

Johnson, Michael P. "Runaway Slaves and the Slave Communities in South Carolina, 1799 to 1830." *William and Mary Quarterly* 38 (July 1981): 418–41.

———. "Smothered Slave Infants: Were Slave Mothers at Fault?" *Journal of Southern History* 47 (November 1981): 493–520.

———. "Work, Culture, and the Slave Community: Slave Occupations in the Cotton Belt in 1860." *Labor History* 27 (Summer 1986): 325–53.

Kiple, Kenneth L., and Virginia H. Kiple. "Slave Child Mortality: Some Nutritional Answers to a Perennial Puzzle." *Journal of Social History* 10 (Spring 1977): 284–309.

Knudson, Jerry. "Jefferson the Father of Slave Children? One View of the Book Reviewers." *Journalism History* 3 (Summer 1976): 56–59.

Kolchin, Peter. "Reevaluating the Antebellum Slave Community: A Comparative Perspective." *Journal of American History* 70 (December 1983): 579–601.

Kondert, Nancy T. "The Romance and Reality of Defeat: Southern Women in 1865." *Journal of Mississippi History* 35 (May 1973): 141–52.

Landers, E. M., Jr. "Slave Labor in South Carolina Cotton Mills." *Journal of Negro History* 38 (April 1953): 161–73.

BIBLIOGRAPHY

Lantz, Herman, and Lewellyn Hendrix. "Black Fertility and the Black Family in the Nineteenth Century: A Re-Examination of the Past." *Journal of Family History* 3 (Fall 1978): 251–61.

Lawrence, James B. "Religious Education of the Negro in the Colony of Georgia." *Georgia Historical Quarterly* 14 (March 1930): 41–57.

Lawrence-McIntyre, Charshee Charlotte. "The Double Meanings of the Spirituals." *Journal of Black Studies* 17 (June 1987): 379–401.

Lawson, Ellen Nickenzie. "Children of the Amistad." *The Instructor* 97 (February 1988): 44–48.

Lebsock, Suzanne D. "Free Black Women and the Question of Matriarchy: Petersburg, Virginia, 1784–1820." *Feminist Studies* 2 (Summer 1983): 195–216.

———. "Radical Reconstruction and Property Rights of Southern Women." *Journal of Southern History* 43 (May 1977): 195–216.

Lefever, Harry G. "'Playing the Dozens': A Mechanism for Social Control." *Phylon* 42 (Spring 1981): 73–85.

Lewis, Ronald L. "Slave Families at Early Chesapeake Ironworks." *Virginia Magazine of History* 86 (April 1978): 169–79.

Lithell, Ulla-Britt. "Breast-Feeding Habits and Their Relation to Infant Mortality and Marital Fertility." *Journal of Family History* 6 (Summer 1981): 182–94.

Mabee, Carleton. "Sojourner Truth, Bold Prophet: Why Did She Never Learn to Read?" *New York History* 69 (January 1988): 55–77.

Mann, Susan A. "Slavery, Sharecropping, and Sexual Inequality." *Signs* 14 (Summer 1989): 774–98.

Margo, Robert A., and Richard H. Steckel. "The Heights of American Slaves: New Evidence on Slave Nutrition and Health." *Social Science History* 6 (Fall 1982): 516–38.

McAdoo, Harriette Pipes, and Rosalyn Terborg-Penn. "Historical Trends and Perspectives of Afro-American Families." *Trends in History* 3 (Spring 1985): 97–111.

McGettigan, James William, Jr. "Boone County Slaves: Sales, Estate Division and Families, 1820–1865." Part I, *Missouri Historical Review* 72 (January 1978): 176–97.

———. "Boone County Slaves: Sales, Estate Division and Families, 1820–1865." Part II, *Missouri Historical Review* 72 (April 1978): 271–95.

Mergen, Bernard. "The Discovery of Children's Play." *American Quarterly* 27 (October 1975): 399–420.

———. "Toys and American Culture Objects as Hypotheses." *Journal of American Culture* 3 (Winter 1980): 743–51.

Miller, Page Putnam. "Women in the Vanguard of the Sunday School Movement." *Journal of Presbyterian History* 58 (Winter 1980): 311–23.

Miller, Randall M. "The Fabric of Control: Slavery in Antebellum Southern Textile Mills." *Business History Review* 55 (Winter 1981): 471–90.

Moore, John Hebron. "John Hebron of LaGrange Plantation: Commercial Fruit Grower of the Old South." *Journal of Mississippi History* 46 (November 1984): 281–303.

Morgan, Philip D. "The Ownership of Property by Slaves in the Mid-Nineteenth-Century Low Country." *Journal of Southern History* 49 (August 1983): 399–420.

———. "Work and Culture: The Task System and the World of Lowcountry Blacks, 1700–1880." *William and Mary Quarterly* 39 (October 1982): 563–99.

Mulderink, Earl F., III. "'The Whole Town is Ringing with It': Slave Kidnapping Charges against Nathan Johnson of New Bedford, Massachusetts, 1839." *New England Quarterly* 61 (September 1988): 341–57.

"Negro Folk-songs." *Southern Workman* 24 (February 1895): 31–32.

Newton, James E. "Slave Artisans and Craftsmen: The Roots of Afro-American Art." *Black Scholar* 9 (November 1977): 35–42.

O'Brien, John T. "Factory, Church, and Community: Blacks in Antebellum Richmond." *Journal of Southern History* 44 (November 1978): 509–36.

Perkins, Eric. "Roll, Jordan, Roll: A 'Marx' for the Master Class." *Radical History Review* 3 (Fall 1976): 41-59.

Perry, Percival. "The Naval-Stores Industry in the Old South, 1790–1860." *Journal of Southern History* 34 (November 1968): 509–26.

Phillips, Paul David. "Education of Blacks in Tennessee during Reconstruction, 1865–1870." *Tennessee Historical Quarterly* 46 (Summer 1987): 98–109.

Pierce, Edward L. "The Contrabands at Fortress Monroe." *Atlantic Monthly* 3 (November 1861): 626–40.

Postell, William Dosite. "Birth and Mortality Rates among Slave Infants on Southern Plantations." *Pediatrics* 10 (November 1952): 538–41.

Prichard, Walter. "Routine on a Louisiana Sugar Plantation Under the Slavery Regime." *Mississippi Valley Historical Review* 14 (September 1927): 168–78.

Puckett, Newbell N. "American Negro Names." *Journal of Negro History* 23 (January 1938): 35–48.

Reid, Joseph. "Sharecropping as an Understandable Market Response: The Post Bellum South." *Journal of Economic History* 33 (March 1973); 106–30.

Reidy, Joseph P. "'Coming from the Shadow of the Past': The Transition from Slavery to Freedom at Freedmen's Village, 1863–1900." *Virginia Magazine of History* 95 (October 1987): 403–28.

Ripley, C. Peter. "The Black Family in Transition: Louisiana, 1860–1865." *Journal of Southern History* 41 (August 1975): 369–80.

Roberts, John W. "Strategy, Morality and Worldview of the Afro-American Spirituals and Trickster Tales." *The Western Journal of Black Studies* 6 (Summer 1983): 101–107.

Roediger, David R. "And Die in Dixie: Funerals, Deaths, and Heaven in the Slave Community 1700–1865." *Massachusetts Review* 22 (Spring 1981): 163–83.

Rogers, Daniel T. "Socializing Middle-Class Children: Institutions, Fables, and Work Values in Nineteenth-Century America." *Journal of Social History* 13 (Spring 1980): 354–66.

Rothman, David J. "Documents in Search of a Historian: Toward a History of Childhood and Youth in America." *Journal of Interdisciplinary History* 2 (August 1971): 367–77.

Sanderson, Allen B. "Child-Labor Legislation and the Labor Force Participation of Children." *Journal of Economic History* 34 (March 1974): 297–99.

Sandiford, Keith A. P. "The Victorians at Play: Problems in Historiographical Methodology." *Journal of Social History* 15 (Winter 1981): 271–88.

Savitt, Todd L. "Smothering and Overlaying of Virginia Slave Children: A Suggested Explanation." *Bulletin of the History of Medicine* 49 (Fall 1975): 400–404.

Schafer, Judith Kelleher. "New Orleans Slavery in 1850 as Seen in Advertisements." *Journal of Southern History* 47 (February 1981): 33–56.

———. "'Open and Notorious Concubinage': The Emancipation of Slave Mistresses by Will and the Supreme Court in Antebellum Louisiana." *Louisiana History* 28 (Spring 1987): 165–82.

Scholten, Catherine M. "'On the Importance of the Obstetrick Art': Changing Customs of Childbirth in America, 1760–1825." *William and Mary Quarterly* 34 (July 1977): 426–45.

BIBLIOGRAPHY

Schwarz, Philip J. "The Transportation of Slaves from Virginia, 1801–1865." *Slavery and Abolition: A Journal of Comparative Studies* 7 (December 1986): 215–40.

Schweninger, Loren. "A Slave Family in the Ante Bellum South." *Journal of Negro History* 60 (January 1975): 29–44.

Scott, Rebecca. "The Battle over the Child: Child Apprenticeship and the Freedmen's Bureau in North Carolina." *Prologue* 10 (Summer 1978): 101–13.

Shainess, Natalie. "Abortion: Social, Psychiatric, and Psychoanalytic Perspectives." *New York State Journal of Medicine* 68 (December 1, 1968): 3070–73.

———. "The Psychologic Experience of Labor." *New York State Journal of Medicine* 63 (October 15, 1963): 2923–32.

———. "The Structure of the Mothering Encounter." *Journal of Nervous and Mental Disorders* 136 (February 1963): 146–61.

Shammas, Carole. "Black Women's Work and the Evolution of Plantation Society in Virginia." *Labor History* 26 (Winter 1985): 5–28.

Shore, Laurence. "The Poverty of Tragedy in Historical Writing on Southern Slavery." *South Atlantic Quarterly* 85 (Spring 1986): 147–162.

Sides, Sudie Duncan. "Southern Women and Slavery." Part I, *History Today* 20 (January 1970): 55–60.

———. "Southern Women and Slavery." Part II, *History Today* 20 (February 1970): 124–30.

Simmons, Donald C. "Possible West African Sources for the American Negro 'Dozens.'" *Journal of American Folklore* 76 (October-December 1963): 339–40.

Simpson, Robert. "The Shout and Shouting in Slave Religion of the United States." *Southern Quarterly* 23 (Spring 1985): 34–47.

Smith, Daniel Blake. "The Study of the Family in Early America: Trends, Problems, and Prospects." *William and Mary Quarterly* 39 (January 1982): 3–28.

Smith, Eleanor. "African American Women and the Extended Family: A Sociohistorical Review." *Western Journal of Black Studies* 13 (Winter 1989): 179–84.

Stavisky, Leonard. "The Origins of Negro Craftsmanship in Colonial America." *Journal of Negro History* 32 (October 1947): 417–29.

Stealey, John E., III. "Slavery and the Western Virginia Salt Industry." *Journal of Negro History* 59 (April 1974): 105–31.

Steckel, Richard H. "A Dreadful Childhood: The Excess Mortality of American Slaves." *Social Science History* 10 (Winter 1986): 427–65.

———. "Miscegenation and the American Slave Schedule." *Journal of Interdisciplinary History* 11 (Autumn 1980): 251–64.

———. "A Peculiar Population: The Nutrition, Health, and Mortality of American Slaves from Childhood to Maturity." *Journal of Economic History* 46 (September 1986): 721–41.

———. "Slave Marriage and the Family." *Journal of Family History* 5 (Winter 1980): 406–20.

Stoudemire, Mary Arthur. "Black Parishoners of the Chapel of the Cross, 1844–1866." *North Carolina Genealogical Society Journal* 9 (May 1983): 78–84.

Stowe, Steven M. "'The Thing Not Its Vision': A Woman's Courtship and Her Sphere in the Southern Planter Class." *Feminist Studies* 9 (Spring 1983): 113–30.

Suitor, J. Jill. "Husbands' Participation in Childbirth: A Nineteenth-Century Phenomenon." *Journal of Family History* 6 (Fall 1981): 278–93.

Sutherland, Daniel E. "Looking for a Home: Louisiana Emigrants during the Civil War and Reconstruction." *Louisiana History* 4 (Fall 1980): 341–59.

———. "A Special Kind of Problem: The Response of Household Slaves and Their Masters to Freedom." *Southern Studies* 20 (Summer 1981): 151–66.

BIBLIOGRAPHY

Tho, Daniel B. "Chattel With A Soul: The Autobiography of a Moravian Slave." *The Pennsylvania Magazine of History and Biography* 112 (July 1988): 433–51.

Toplin, Robert Brent. "Between Black and White: Attitudes toward Southern Mulattoes, 1830–1861." *Journal of Southern History* 45 (May 1979): 185–200.

Verney, Kreven J. "Trespassers in the Land of Their Birth: Black and Landownership in South Carolina and Mississippi during the Civil War and Reconstruction, 1861–1877." *Slavery and Abolition: A Journal of Comparative Studies* 4 (May 1983): 64–79.

Walker, Clarence E. "Massa's New Clothes: A Critique of Eugene D. Genovese on Southern Society, Master Slave Relations, and Slave Behavior." *UMOJA* 4 (Summer 1980): 114–36.

Wax, Donald D. "The Demand for Slave Labor in Colonial Pennsylvania." *Pennsylvania History* 34 (October 1967): 331–45.

———. "The Lives of Slave Women: The Female Slave Network." *Southern Exposure* 12 (November/December 1984): 32–39.

White, Deborah Gray. "The Lives of Slave Women: The Female Slave Network." *Southern Exposure* 12 (November/December 1984): 32–39.

Wiggins, David K. "The Play of Slave Children in the Plantation Communities of the Old South, 1820–1860." *Journal of Sport History* 7 (Summer 1980): 21–39.

Woodman, Harold D. "Sequel to Slavery: The New History Views the Postbellum South." *Journal of Southern History* 43 (November 1977): 523–54.

Wren, J. Thomas. "A 'Two-Fold Character': The Slave as Person and Property in Virginia Court Cases, 1800–1860." *Southern Studies* 54 (Winter 1985): 417–31.

Wyatt, Gail Elizabeth. "The Aftermath of Child Sexual Abuse of African American and White American Women: The Victim's Experience." *Journal of Family Violence* 5 (number 1, 1990): 61–81.

Wyatt-Brown, Bertram. "The Mask of Obedience: Male Slave Psychology in the Old South." *American Historical Review* 93 (December 1988): 1228–52.

Zanger, Jules. "The 'Tragic Octoroon' in Pre–Civil War Fiction." *American Quarterly* 18 (Spring 1966): 63–70.

INDEX

Abbot, James Monroe, 27
Abby, Tabby, 11, 12
Abolitionists, 4, 108, 136; assistance from, 120; respond to 1850 Fugitive Slave Act, 122; fight slavery in court, 127–28, 129
Adams, John Quincy, 128
Adolescence, xviii–xix, 47
Affleck, Thomas, 93
African customs, 2, 3–4, 73, 111
African Philosophy, xix
Age, importance of, xix, 150
Alexander, Lucretia, 26, 82
Alford, Terry, 88
Allen, Jim, 150
Allen, John, 145, 148
Alston, Sarah, 54
American Colonization Society, 54, 125
American Missionary Association (AMA), 142, 162
Amistad, 100; children aboard, 100, 101, 128; mutiny, 100; Committee, 128
Anderson, John, 136; slave of, George, 136
Anderson, Jourdan, 156
—children: Catherine, 156; Jane, 156; Matilda, 156; Milly, 156
Apprenticeships, 151–54; laws regarding, 151; responses to, 152
Archie, Chock, 29
Armstrong, Mary, 30
Austin, John, 104, 106
Bacchus, Josephine, 5
Baker, Everard Green, 10, 68
Baker, Frank, 129
Baldwin, Roger S., 128
Ball, Charles, 102, 106–107
Banks, Fred D., 61
Barber, Charley, 99
Barber, Millie, 96
Barksdale, Penny, 152, 153
Barrow, Bennett, 97
Barrow, R. R., 34, 35, 58, 59

Barry, Armistead, 108
Barry, William Taylor, 78, 108
—slaves of: Fanny, 108; Issac, 108
Bates, Anderson, 45, 46, 165
Battle, Susan Catherine, 83
Battle, William Horn (Mrs.), 83
Bealk, Benjamin, 102
Beecher, Henry Ward, 127
Bell, Frank, 25, 35
Bell, Laura, 60, 61
Bell, Mary, 25, 107
Berlin, Ira, 125
Berry, Elisha, 104
—slaves of: Emily, 104; Eliza, 105, 106; Randall, 104, 105
Berry, Fannie, 60
Bethune, Thomas Green, 132
Bettelheim, Bruno, 72
Bibb, Henry, 8, 26, 27, 62, 71, 89, 111
Bibb, Melinda, 62
Bills, John Houston, 7, 36, 59–60, 97, 107
—slaves of: Angelina, 97; Edney, 107; Lucinda, 7, 11, 97; Martha, 90; Tom, 107; Willis, 90, 97; Wilson, 97
Black Codes, 143; of Louisiana, 125
Black, Maggie, 34, 61
Blackford, Launcelot Minor: leisure activities of, 43, 46, 49, 50; awareness of slavery, 54; mentioned, 74; school activities, 79; Willie, 49
Blassingame, John, 9, 86
Bocock, Willis P., 44, 93
Boston Female Anti-Slavery Society, 127
Botume, Elizabeth, 134, 150, 163
Boykin, Sam, 116
Bradford, Lue, 29
Branch, Jacob, 23, 41, 45, 97
Braston, Enoch, 152
Breastfeeding, 6
Briggs, George, 25, 45
Brown, Betty, 111
Brown, Julia, 122
Brown, Mangus, 53

Brown, Morgan L., 145, 146
Brown, Steven E., 60
Brown, William Wells, 111, 120, 121
Brownmiller, Susan, 108
Bruce, Blanche K., 133
Bruce, James Coles, 8
Bryant, William, 144
Bureau of Refugees, Freedmen, and Abandoned Lands (Freedmen's Bureau), 142; assists in reuniting families, 144, 145–48; handles custody disputes, 149, 152, 154, 162; schools, 162, 164
Burns, Anthony, 122
Burrows, Ellen, 75
Burson, Sebe, 152
Burton, Annie L., 111, 144
Butler, Anthony, 150
Butler, Benjamin, 129, 130
Butler, Pierce Mease, 5, 93
Caldwell, Minerva Cain, 51
Caldwell, Tod Robinson, 51
Calloway, James, 146
Calloway, William, 146
Camilla, Georgia, riot, 166
Camp Nelson, Kentucky, 138
Cannon, Sylvia, xix
Carter, Farish, 31, 107
Carter, Robert, 123
Casey, Ester King, 51
Cathell, Henry, 59
Censer, Jane Turner, 53
Chaplin family:
—Thomas B., 32, 51, 64
—Mary, 51, 63
—slaves of: Eliza, 63; Nelly, 63
Charleston Mercury, 102
Cherokee freedwoman, 69, 113
Child, Lydia M., 164
Childbearing, 4, 5–6, 13, 90; decline in fertility rate, 150
Childcare, 9, 13, 14–15, 24
Christmas, 59
Cinqué, Joseph, 100, 129
Civil War, 129–39, 141; role of children in, 131–34; suffering during, 137–38
Clay, Anne, 81
Clinkscales, J. G., 54
Clitherall, Eliza, 112
Clothing, 15–16, 38

Cocke family:
—John Hartwell, 18; permits literacy, 75, 76, 79; builds chapel, 82, 103, 163
—Louisa, 75–76
—slaves of: Betsey Skipwith, 104; Lucy Skipwith, 18, 19, 76, 86, 88, 104
Cohoon, John C., 3
—slaves of: David, 3; Fanny, 6; Harriet, 6; Harry, 6; Jacob, 6; Mary, 7; Matilda, 7; Rachel, 3
Cole, Richard, 23
Collins, John, 17
Colquitt, Martha, 58
Commonwealth v. Aves, 127
Coney, Joe, 111
Confederate States of America, 69, 129, 141, 142
Congo Square, 59
Congress, U.S., 143
Contraband of war, 129
Courtship, 62
Covey, Edward, 89, 117
Craft, Ellen, 122, 164
Craft, William, 122, 164
Craig, Caleb, xix, 107
Crawford, Allen, 44
Crawford, Jim, 62
Crawly, Charles, 83
Crosby, D. T. (DTC), 158; sharecropper at DTC's, Dink, 158
Crouch, Jane A., 79
Cultivation of: corn, 35–36; cotton, 32, 33, 35; fruit, 36; indigo, 34; rice, 33–34, 35; slave gardens, 16, 36; sugar cane, 33, 34, 35; tobacco, 31, 32, 35; wheat, 35
Curtis, George W. P., 123
Custer, George A., 134
Davenport, Charles, 24, 39
Davis, Ada, 10
Davis, David Brion, 73
Davis, Jefferson, 69
Dawes, William D., 145
Day, Madison, 149
Deference: habits of, 95, 150; teaching of, 70
DeGray, James, 153
Delaney, Lucy, 28, 120, 142
Delaney, Nancy, 121
Dixon, Emily, 46, 47–48
Domestic Medicine or Poor Man's Medicine, 4

INDEX

Douglass, Frederick, xviii, xix; remembers his youth, 1, 19; on basic necessities, 16; comments about work, 21, 25, 29; plays with white boys, 53; comments about holidays, 59, 60, 65; gains literacy, 77, 78; inspiration from song, 84; seeks advice, 89; separated from grandmother, 105; hatred of slavery, 115, 116–18; runs away, 121, 150; mentioned, 111, 164

Drumgoold, Kate, 113–14, 144

Drummer, Jackson, 131

Du Bois, W. E. B., 37, 99

DuBose, Waller, 83

Dumont, John J., 80

Dyer, Martha Tabb, 29

Easley, Jackson, 144

Edmondson family (Amelia, Emily, Mary, Paul), 127

Education: literacy, 74–80, 161–65; prohibitions against, 78; sex, 73; for survival, 67–68, 71

Elliot, William, 57

Ellison, April (William), 8, 126–27; children of, 8; wife of, 8

Emancipation Proclamation, 135, 164; responses to, 136–37

Emmanuel, Mom Ryer, 122

Eppes, Susan Bradford, 14, 57

Ervin, William Ethelbert, 93

Evans, Mary, 150

Fales, Silas E., 113, 137

Fields, Barbara, 151

Finnely, John, 95

Fisk (University) Jubilee Singers, 84, 165

Folkes, Minnie, 73

Food: processing, 36; rationing, 36–37

Fort Negley, 131

Forten, Charlotte, 68, 87, 136

Fortress Monroe, 129, 130, 162

Foster, Kate, 144

Fox family:
—David Raymond (DRF), 107, 118, 131, 154
—Tryphena Blanche Holder, 16, 40, 51, 57, 70, 107–108, 111, 118, 154, 164
—children: Fanny, 51, 52, 54, 56, 70, 154; Frank, 155; George, 155
—servants of: Celestine, 154–55; Rosella, 154–55; Victor, 154–55
—slaves of: Adelaide, 16, 24, 40, 53, 54, 56–57, 70, 131; Buddy, 51, 131; Margaret, 16, 51, 131; Maria, 24, 117–18; Susan, 11, 107–108; Reuben, 70

Frank, Anne, xxi, 120

Franks, Dora, 26, 30, 112

Frazer, Julia, 27, 78

The Freedmen's Book, 164

Friend, Charles, 81

Fripp, John Edwin, 36

Fugitive Slave Act, 1850, 122

Furman, McDonald: presents gifts, 3; distributes cloth, 15, 16; increases food, 22; issues orders, 74; regarding punishment, 93

Gadsden, James, 13

Gaebel, A. H., 145

Gaines, John, 166

Galt, William, 37

Game and stock laws, 154

Garlic, Delia, 29

Garner, Cornelius, 26, 27, 82

Garner, Margaret, 122

Garnet, Henry Highland, 123

Gavin, David, 10

Geder, Samuel, 161

Geisreiter, S., 146

Genovese, Eugene D., 48, 71, 109

Gentleman, 128

Gilmer, W. W., 16, 70

Glenn, Robert, 77

Goodwin, Candis, 45

Grady, Charles, 36

Gray, Emma, 117

Gray, Maria, 147, 149

Gray, Philip, 147, 149

Gray, Willie Ann, 147–48, 149

Griffin, A. C., 10

Grimké, Archibald, 111

Grimké, Francis James, 111

Grimké, Henry, 111

Grimké, Montague, 111

Grimké, Nancy Weston, 111

Grimm, Jakob, 72

Grimm, Wilhelm, 72

Grossmann, F. E., 149

Haley, Alex, 71, 160, 161; publishes Roots, 160

Hall, Robert L., 98

Halleck, Ellen, 144

Hampton Normal and Agricultural Institute, 165; folklore society, 61

Hannah, George C., 157
—contract laborers of: Booker, 157; Martha Jane, 157; Sam, 157; Stephen, 157
Hanson, Francis, 81, 83, 85
Head of households, 3
Health: of pregnant women, 4–5; of children, 9–12
Heath, John, 152
Hebron, John, 36, 103
Hentz, Charles Arnold, 86
Herskovits, Melville J., xvii, 73
Higginson, Thomas W., 131
Hiring out, 59, 106
Holbert, Clayton, 31
Holt, Rebecca, 102
Horniblow, Molly, 119
Horry, Ben, 108–109
Horton, George, 77–78, 126; author of "The Hope of Liberty," 126
Horton, Ruffin, 33
Howard, O. H., 145, 146, 164
Howard, O. O., 145, 146
Hudson, Franklin, 10
Hughes, Langston, 112
Hughes, Sarah S., 24
Hunter, Lina, 74
Hutson, William, 25
Incidents in the Life of a Slave Girl, 91
Ingraham, Joseph H., 25, 28
Jackson, Bongy, 148–49
Jackson, Mattie, 121
Jackson, Samuel Cram, 71
Jacobs, Harriet: laments birth of daughter, xxi; comments about parenting, 60; suffers heartbreak, 64, 65; moral lessons of, 73; mentioned, xviii, 79; hatred of slavery, 91, 110; considers running away, 119–20
Jacoway, Jane Ellen, 144
Jacoway, Lucinda, 144
Jefferies, Isiah, 6
Jefferson, Thomas: comments about slave births, 2; encourages slave marriages, 3; mentioned, 7; orders work routine, 22; describes interactions with slaves, 53; discusses mental capacities, 74; freed slaves, 123
Jemison, William, 23
John Adams, 134
Johnson, Anna, 145

Johnson, Charity, 145, 147
Johnson, Gabriel, 145, 147
Johnson, Michael P., 127
Johnson, Millie, 145
Johnson, Polly Ann, 145–47, 154
Johnson, Prince, 30
Jones, Jacqueline, 39
Jones, Louise, 24
Jones, Norrece T., 80
Jones, Richard, 59
Jones, Thomas H., 8
Keckley, Elizabeth, 79, 111
Kelly, Martha, 33
Kemble, Frances Ann, 8, 12
King, Anna Matilda, 53
Kiple, Kenneth and Virginia, 10, 11
Knights of the White Camelia, 143
Knox, George, 39
Kraft, Julius, 149
Ku Klux Klan, 143, 150, 164
Labor contracts, 157–58
La Croese, Michael, 102
Laffan, I. de Courcy, 92
Lamar, John B., 5; slaves of, 5
Lance, Gabe, 33
Landownership, 158–59
Leak, Francis Terry, 22
Leavitt, Joshua, 128
Lee, Henry T., 83
Lee, Martin, 152
Leisure activities, 43, 44, 45; dances, 59–60; games, 45–50, 52–53, 160; of courting couples, 61; games of chance, 50; harvest festivities, 57–58; playing the dozens, 48; representative play, 48–49, 55, 160–61; social fighting, 47; storytelling, 72–73, 159–60; whipping games, 48; with white children, 49, 51, 53, 54, 55–56
Letters written by slaves: Hobbs, 68, 106; Lavina, 89–90; Prince Woodfin, 68
Levine, Lawrence W., 72
Liberia, 54, 56, 125, 126
Lincoln, Abraham, 130, 135, 136
L'Ouverture, Toussaint, 164
Mabee, Carleton, 80
Mallory, Charles, 129
Mallory, Shepard, 129
Manigault, Charles, 18, 25, 149; slaves of, 18
Manumissions, 123–25; by wills, 125;

INDEX

contested, 125; self-purchases, 126–27

Marriages, 2; "abroad," 6, 17; ideas of owners about, 2–3; rituals, 63–64; post-war, 148–49; dissolution of, 149

Massachusetts Supreme Judicial Court, 127

Mathews, John, 38

McCray, James, 124

—slaves of: Franky, 124; Kitty, 124; Robert, 124; James, or Okah Tubbee, 124

McCreight, William, 8

McCullough, Lucy, 73

McDonald, George, 146

Mergen, Bernard, 48

Mial, Alonzo T., 33, 157

—contract laborers of: John Miles, 157; Steller, 157

Miller, Joseph, 138

Miller, Lewis, 106

Minor, Charles L. C., 55–56; slave of, Ralph, 56

Miscarriages, 5

Montes, Pedro, 100

Moore, Eli, 31

Moore, Fannie, 12

Morris, Robert C., 164

Morrison, Toni, 69; character in *Beloved*, Baby Suggs, 69, 98

Mulattoes, 110; treatment of, 111–13

Murray, Pauli, 161; author of *Proud Shoes*, 161

Mutual cooperation, 40

My Bondage and My Freedom, 116

Myth of the Negro Past, xvii

Naming practices: African influence in, 6–7; day names, 7; owner intervention in, 7; post-war, 150

Neblett family:

—Lizzie, 132–33

—Will, 132

—slaves of: Bill, 133; Tom, 133

Nevitt, John, 58

Newell, William Wells, 50, 165

Newsom, Robert (RN), 109, 119

—slaves of: Celia, 109, 110, 119; George, 109

New York Anti-Slavery Society, 127

New York *World*, 130

Nickols, Cyntha, 154

Norcom, James, 64, 119

Northup, Solomon, xviii, 34, 59, 95, 104, 106

Not A Fool's Errand, 25

Olmsted, Frederick Law, 94

Orphanage for freed children, 148

Orphans, 148, 151

Overseers, 5, 22, 23, 29, 31, 32, 44, 46, 62, 70, 92, 93, 94, 111

Oxford Ironworks, 38

Parents, roles of, 1–2, 17–19, 67–68, 69, 80, 89–90, 113–14, 161

Parker, John, 111, 115

Parsons, Rebecca, 144

Paternalism, 71, 103

Patrollers, 62, 95–96, 122

Peake, Mary, 76, 79

Pearl, 127

Pennington, Brazil, 97

Pennington, James W. C., 46, 94, 97

Perkins, Eric, 103

Perry, Dinah, 49

Perry, Nancy, 49

Pettigrew, William S., 31, 95

Pickett, Eugene, 145

Pierce, Edward L., 129

Planter, 130

Playthings. *See* Toys

Porter, James, 161

Powers, Betty, 159

Prince among Slaves, 88

Proctor, Jenny, 117

Prosser, Gabriel, 129

Pugh, Nicey, 166

Punishments, 21, 40, 78, 91, 92, 93–94, 137; buck, 92, 133; "cat-hauling," 99; "smoking," 94; whipping, 92, 93, 97; by parents, 97; children, 95; by white women, 29, 98–99; fear of, 33, 40; responses to, 93, 94, 97–98

Randolph, Caroline, 149

Randolph, John, 123

Randolph, Peter, 94–95

Rape, 108–109

Reconstruction, 143

Religion, 80; African traditional, 81; Christianity, 80–88; Muslim, 88; voodoo, 89; as control mechanism, 82

Religious activities, 83–85; conversions, 85–86; revivals, 62, 86; ring shout (saut), 84–85, 87; secret, 83, 86

Resistance to slavery, 92, 115–19; by running away, 119–23, 130–31, 134–35; by insurrection, 128–29

Reunification of families: before the war, 107; after the war, 144–48; belief in afterlife, 108, 148

Richmond (Virginia) *Enquirer,* 119

Riddick, Robert Moore, 8

Roark, James L., 127

Roberts, John W., 72

Roll, Jordan, Roll, 103

Rose, Willie Lee, xvii

Ross, David, 5, 38, 40, 62

—slaves of: Edmund, 38; Jenny, 4

Ruffin, Edmund, 142

Ruffin, James H., 32

—slaves of: Amy, 32, 33; Emaline, 32, 33; Fanny, 32, 33

Ruiz, Jose, 100

Runaway slaves, 97, 118, 119–22, 129, 131

Savitt, Todd, 11

Schafer, Judith, 124

Schools, 74, 75–76, 79, 162–65; sabbath, 78

Scott, Groves, 56

Scriven, Abraham, 106

Scruggs, Stiles M., 75

Sedgwick, Theodore, 128

Separation: of freedpersons, 149; of mothers and babies, 13; of families, 102–105, 106–107; fear of, 104; threat of, 3, 104, 144

Sewell, Thomas, 123

Sexual abuse, 108–10, 118–19; protection against, 156, 158

Shackelford, Sis, 123

Shainess, Natalie, 4

Shakespeare, William, 109

Shaw, Lemuel, 128

Shepherd, Robert, 44

Shoemaker, Issac, 138

Sibley, C. C., 145, 146

Sickle-cell anemia, 10

Simmons, Henry E., 113

Sims, William Henry, 22, 93

Singleton, Marrinda Jane, 95

Sisco, William, 136

Slater, Mary Aves, 127

Slave drivers, 29, 94–95, 107

Slave revolts, 129

Slave trade, 102; in "fancy girls," 104,
109, 127; illegal, 99–100; interstate, 102–103; intrastate, 102–103

Slave traders, 102, 127

Slaves: status of, 6, 92; valuation of, 8, 22

Smalls, Robert, 130

Smith, E. H., 145, 146, 147

Smith, Francis, 82

Smith, Mary Ruffin, 82, 83

—slaves of: Cornelia, 83; Harriet, 64–65; Lucy Battle, 83

Snow, Susan, 69

Socialization of children, 70–71, 72, 73, 97, 113, 149, 150, 166

Southall, James, 51

Southern Planter, 2, 16

Spicer, Laura, 147

Spirituals, 83–84

Stackhouse, Blanche, 56

Stackhouse, Herbert, 56

Steckel, Richard, 9, 45

Stokes, Simon, 31, 57

Story, Joseph, 128

Stowe, Harriet Beecher, 120

Stroyer, Jacob: family name of, 7–8; difficulties at work, 40–41; child intimidates, 47; family discussions, 56; describes deference ritual, 70; literacy of, 75; hears prayers, 80; reaction to punishment, 97; rebelliousness of, 116; reclaims name, 150

Sudden Infant Death Syndrome (SIDS), 11–12, 111

Swayne, Wager, 152

Tales: African folk, 72; animal trickster, 72; fairy, 72; human trickster, 72

Taylor, Susie King, 77, 78, 131, 132, 136

Terry, Annie, 27

Theology of slavery, 82

Thirteenth Amendment, 141; responses of ex-slaveholders, 142; responses of ex-slaves, 142; tensions resulting from, 142–43, 166

Thirty-Eighth Ohio Regiment, 139

Thirty-Ninth Congress of the U.S., 143, 164

Thomas, James, 75

Thomas, Omelia, 62

Thomas, Pittus, 75, 78

Thomas, Sally, 111, 126

Townsend, Amos, Jr., 128

Townsend, James, 129

INDEX

Toys, 45–46

Truth, Sojourner, 79

Tubman, Harriet, 79, 104

Turner, Nat, 49, 75, 78, 129

Turner, West, 26

Twyman, I. L., 104, 106

Union soldiers, 131, 137, 138

The Uses of Enchantment, 72

USS *Washington,* 100

Van Hook, John F., 160–61

Vesey, Denmark, 129

Vetter, John, 144

Virginia Assembly, 6

Washington, Booker T.: comments about clothing, 15; remembers kindnesses, 18; describes early childhood, 18–19; lacks recreation, 45; interest in literacy, 75; hears prayers, 80; overhears conversations, 130; describes post-war schools, 162

Washington, George, 123

Washington, James B., 134

Washington, John (brother of Booker T.), 18

Watson, C. T., 164

Webber, Thomas, 48

Weddings: presents, 3; ceremonies, 63, 64, 148–49; "receptions," 64

White Brotherhood, 143

White, Deborah Gray, 39

White Hill Plantation, 13, 59, 81

White, Mingo, 23, 30

Whitted, Anderson, 75

Whittlesey, Eliphalet, 146, 147

Wiggins, David K., 44, 50

Williams, James: slave of, Henry, 136

Williams, Nancy, 31, 40, 94

Williams, Rose: forced to marry, 110, 118–19; mentioned, 111; ends marriage, 149

Williams, Rufus, 110, 149

Wilson, Allen, 98, 166

Windfield, Dicy, 60, 64

Woodman, Harold D., 151

Woods, Anna, 83

Woodson, Carter Godwin, 160, 161

Work: agricultural, 23, 26, 31; craft, 25, 126; domestic, 25, 26, 27–28, 31; housewifery, 29, 30, 38, 39; rewards for, 39; sharecropping, 23, 157, 158; skilled, 30, 37–38; squads, 156; task system, 17, 23, 158; trash gang, 30, 68, 73; wage labor, 156; withdrawal of women from, 156; attitudes about, 26, 31

Wright, Richard A., xix

Yancy, Benjamin C., 158

WILMA KING, Professor of History at Michigan State University, is the editor of *A Northern Woman in the Plantation South: Letters of Tryphena Blanche Holder Fox, 1856–1876,* co-editor of *"We Specialize in the Wholly Impossible" : A Reader in Black Women's History* with Darlene Clark Hine and Linda Reed, and author of *Toward the Promised Land: From **Uncle Tom's Cabin** to the Onset of the Civil War (1851–1861).*